C000138313

Capitalist Discipline

Capitalist Discipline

On the Orchestration of Corporate Games

Arthur Wassenberg

First published 2013 by
PALGRAVE MACMILLAN

Palgrave Macmillan in the UK is an imprint of Macmillan Publishers Limited,
registered in England, company number 785998, of Houndmills,
Basingstoke, Hampshire RG21 6XS.

Palgrave Macmillan in the US is a division of St Martin's Press LLC,
175 Fifth Avenue, New York, NY 10010.

Palgrave Macmillan is the global academic imprint of the above companies
and has companies and representatives throughout the world.

Palgrave® and Macmillan® are registered trademarks in the United States,
the United Kingdom, Europe and other countries

ISBN 978–1–137–33983–6

This book is printed on paper suitable for recycling and made from fully
managed and sustained forest sources. Logging, pulping and manufacturing
processes are expected to conform to the environmental regulations of the
country of origin.

A catalogue record for this book is available from the British Library.

A catalog record for this book is available from the Library of Congress.

To the lasting memory of D., who had to wait too long to witness the return from my search for Excalibur

Contents

List of Tables, Figures and Boxes

Tables

Figures

Boxes

Acknowledgments

Retracing the roots of my inspiration and tracking the route that finally led to the synthesis of my earlier peregrinations on "games organizations play" is virtually impossible. To paraphrase Konstandinos Kafàvis's *Poems*: "As you set out for Ythaca ... Arriving there is what you are destined for, But don't hurry the journey at all ... So you are old when you reach the island. Wealthy with all you have gained on the way." I acknowledge mainly the decisive influence on the final framing of my story that evolved from the conversations and criticisms by the incisive spirits of, most particularly, Professors Kees Schuyt (Amsterdam) and John Groenewegen (Delft). More remote but no less pertinent is my awareness of the imprints of such eminent scholars as Professors Henk de Jong, Gerd Junne, Bart Nooteboom, Alexander Rinnooy Kan, Arie van der Zwan, Hans Schenk and, in another life, Jacques van Doorn (Rotterdam), Fritz Scharpf (Berlin), Eli Cohen, Erhard Friedberg and Michel Crozier (*tous* Paris). The only beloved one, however, who can truly testify to my appreciation of all these "animating" spirits, and how I tried their patience, is no more. To her at the end of this journey I owe this work.

ARTHUR WASSENBERG

Preface

From time to time, in wavelike movements, societies become unsettled by economic crises. This book is focused on the sort of derailment that follows from endogenous coordination failures that emanate from within the political economy itself. The more radical disruptions arise whenever virtual innovations by the financial superstructure do not correspond, in a supportive or triggering way, with real interdependences in the economic substructure. Separating the two structures is not a simple enterprise. The same holds for the separation of private vs public "parts" of the financial and real economy. The interpenetration is too deep.

Not "too big", but rather "too connected to fail", seems to cause the trouble. Yet, theoretically speaking, it remains a first order priority to distinguish what practically speaking operates as a non-decomposable entity, if we aim to get to grips with the cyclical causes of economic order and disorder.

"Capitalist discipline" stands for the capacity to create, and replicate, credible commitments. That capacity must be studied at distinct levels of appearance, to wit: first, at the level of *individual* organizations, including the internal politics of strategy-formation (micro); second, at the level of *coalitions* of organizations (meso); and finally, at the level of the institutional *web*s of interorganizational alliances comprising the political economy as a whole (macro). This kind of multilevel theatre – suggesting the need for a "nested games" perspective (games-within-games) – helps to clarify how higher order "disciplinary" arrangements *pre*condition lower level strategic search-and-selection behaviors and how, inversely, lower level behaviors *re*condition higher level institutional arrangements.

For the explanation of the resulting social order and disorder the principle of "bounded rationality" turns out to be as important as the principle of "bounded hands". But "bounded *accountability*" plays a role as well (the latter remains conspicuously missing, for reasons to be explored in my study, in the mainstream of strategic management literature). As my study sets out to document, organizations differ in a non-trivial way in the extent to which they effectively may be held accountable for the boundedly "rational" uses of their "creative destruction", respectively "creative obstruction" powers when coping with their dilemmas of strategic choice. Creative destruction refers, in the usual sense, to new combinations of resources, relations and markets; creative obstruction, on the other hand, refers to the capacity to frustrate this sort of new combination. The powers to construct and obstruct are the key components in my conceptualization of bargaining power. For a proper understanding of the dynamics of order and disorder we must know how *asymmetric* the social distribution of negotiating power eventually turns out to be, and what, more specifically, might explain the asymmetry of that distribution and its periodicity over time.

In this book I propose that such an understanding asks for a political-economic game theory. "Political", because the anatomy of power and authority constitutes the basis of the analysis. "Economic", because the circulation of tangible and intangible resources – cash, competence and connections – play a decisive role in the evolution and retainment of disciplinary arrangements. It is a theory of "games" because strategic search and selection tactics under conditions of bounded rationality combined with bounded accountability are based upon what actors expect that others will do or refrain from. The triangle of key parameters in such a "nested games" theory are the arena, agenda and timing: players who are – for reasons explored in this book – in a position to orchestrate the *arena*, have a decisive say in the framing (the "mobilization of bias") of the *agenda* (the "stakes and rules of the game"), and thereby decide to a large extent the *timing* and therefore the (dis)continuity of the games organizations play.

ARTHUR WASSENBERG

1
The Quest for Discipline

When prophesies of coordination fail

In 2002, in the slipstream of a series of major corporate scandals (Enron, Tyco, Worldcom) the US House of Representatives and Senate passed an Act. This bill came to be known as Sarbanes–Oxley, after the chairmen of the Senate Banking Committee and the House Financial Services Committee. When, after fierce partisan opposition from within and obstruction from outside the House and Senate, the bill managed to reach the White House for signature, it was seen to be aimed at:

- Strengthening the regulatory system by rebuilding the objectivity and reliability of accountants and credit rating agencies.
- Creating a public accounting oversight board for developing and enforcing strict accounting standards.
- Making the system less dependent on self-monitoring by the industry;
- Establishing codes of ethics to make chief financial officers responsible for full and timely disclosure and chief executive officers to certify personally financial statements with criminal penalties for failure to do so;
- Tightening insider trading rules.
- Empowering the Securities and Exchange Commission (SEC) to adopt rules addressing conflicts of interest for securities analysts and other "reputational intermediaries" that keep the financial system running.
  (Gourevitch and Shinn, 2007: 256–8)

Two years later, on April 28, 2004, a lobby of five leading US investment banks, including Goldman Sachs, headed by Henry Paulson Jr., who later became the 2007 US Treasury Secretary, persuaded the SEC to exempt these banks from the Sarbanes–Oxley regulation that limited the amount of debt the banks were allowed to take on – which allowed them to release billions of dollars in cash, securities, credit derivations and other exotic vehicles (*International Herald Tribune*, October 4, 2008). Barely three years later, on June 26, 2007, at the eve of the implosion of the international credit bubble, Treasury Secretary Henry Paulson Jr. attended a dinner with some of Wall Street's most powerful bankers. In his memoir, *On the Brink*, Paulson remembers: "All were concerned with excessive risk taking in the markets and appalled by the erosion of underwriting standards". James Pressley, editor in chief for the Bloomberg Press, recounts Paulson's story: "[The bankers] felt forced by competitive pressures to make loans they didn't like…'Isn't there something you [Paulson] can do to *order us not to take all these risks*', was the gist of a question posed by [one of the bankers]". That quote, says Pressley, encapsulates the "bizarre tango that enveloped Paulson as he struggled along with Bernanke [the Federal Reserve chairman] and Geithner [the then New York Fed chief] *to save the free-market system from itself*. Banks, hedge funds and other financial institutions were playing a game of chicken, the economic equivalent of the Cuban Missile Crisis. *Paulson's mission was to prevent mutually assured economic destruction*" (Bloomberg, "Books", February 1, 2010).

Another example of coordination failure is the case of Iceland. According to a 2,300 page report by an independent "truth commission", set up by the Parliament of Iceland, the implosion of the country's financial system – until March 2008 still granted a triple-A rating – has to be seen as the result of "a complacency that spread from the bank headquarters to the regulators, central bank, government and, ultimately, the Icelandic public, *most of whom were happy to share in the spoils of the financial boom*" (*Financial Times*, April 13, 2010).

Both examples show the "domino" features of the collapse of financial institutions and its aftermath in the real economy worldwide. They illustrate how micro-rationales – "sharing the spoils" – may entail macro-irrationalities that threaten the survival of the system as a whole. The request addressed to Paulson, to intervene in order to prevent systemic failure, raises the question of coordination and the causes of its eventual failure.

The issue of coordination is related to strategic dilemmas the actors in socio-economic systems face. They find their origin in the split between individual rationales and systemic rationality.

Strategy traps

Rival states and rival firms face a double-bind. First there are the shadows of the past. In order to survive, firms and nations specialize. However, yesterday's advantage from specialization may become today's hindrance and result in a competitive disadvantage for the day after tomorrow. Whether a distinctive competence turns into a distinctive disadvantage depends on what others do. This contingency is the *competence trap*. It refers to the switching of costs by early movers who see their advantages being snatched away by new entrants. Past investments may stand in the way of a flexible response to new challenges. Yesterday's decisions bind: financially, institutionally and in terms of "sunk" beliefs.

Looking ahead, one then sees the shadows of the future. When nations and firms invest in new ventures they must make sure that there will arise a critical mass of suppliers and customers. Competing for tomorrow means mobilizing an infrastructure of supporters and sponsors. Even if nations and firms imitate others when investing in new activities, they typically will try to prevent others from imitating them. Suppliers and clients, however, prefer as many alternative providers as possible. Given these opposing preferences, imitators or innovators will always be uncertain about the sustainable exclusivity of their investments. In other words, whether a new activity pays depends, again, on what others do. The latter contingency may be called the *competition trap*. This refers to the costs of anticipating what rivals and supporters will decide to do. The future is binding too.

The double-bind may be summarized as the *strategy trap*. Countering this strategy trap implies the development of distinctive competences without being entrapped in past choices and minimizing the imitability of future choices. Both varieties are manifestations of the same phenomenon: the split between individual and shared rationality. As will be argued extensively below, the split applies both to rival firms and rival states, although they differ in the means and modes of coping with it.

Two generic types of this split between individual rationales and collective rationality can be distinguished. One is the dilemma known as "the tragedy of the commons". In Hardin's (1968) original, somewhat apocalyptic, wording: "Ruin is the destination toward which all men rush, each pursuing his own best interest in a society that believes in the freedom of the common. Freedom in a common brings ruin to all". In Hardin's parable the fear of overgrazing the collectively held village grounds – the "commons" – can induce pre-emptive grazing by the neighbors. The "tragedy" is that the mere *threat* of a "pre-emptor" will trigger the self-fulfilling prophecy the commoners are afraid of: "The common will be overgrazed and destroyed as a public resource because each citizen will pre-emptively graze his/her sheep rather than risk being a victim of the free riders" (Best, 1990: 239).

The concept has been applied, convincingly, to a variety of "common pool" resources problems, ranging from over-fishing and the insufficiency of quota "solutions" (Dubbink and van Vliet, 1996) to the politics of pollution and natural resources management (Ostrom, 1990; Schelling, 1993; Weissing and Ostrom, 1993). The idea looms up in the economics of a *non-fixed*-resources world as well: "the awareness that a rival can respond to unsold goods in the market by expanding supply and dropping prices, may be enough to engender a pre-emptive price drop and lead to a price war. For the follower will be at a double disadvantage: the early bird will enjoy economies from increased market share, and the follower will suffer diseconomies with reduced sales" (Best, 1990: 75).

Being the opposite of the first, the second archetype of the gap between individual and encompassing rationality may be called the "tragedy of the fallows". Three sub-types can be distinguished. One refers to the problem of "under-" or "non-exploited" resources originating from the propensity to refrain from investments as long as there is no certainty that others will follow in a complementary or confirmative fashion. In the alternative case, large, established firms try to smother the breakthrough of smaller, innovative players by annexing or allying with the new entrants in order to protect their sunk investments and market position. A third manifestation of under- or non-exploited opportunities is the case in which commitments are postponed or dissolved because each expects that his or her counterparts, sooner or later, will give in and accept the burden of taking the lead in bringing about some form of comprehensive rationality. Under each of these conditions, corrective arrangements are required to offset the bounds of narrow-minded "local" rationality (Nelson, 1995). The politics of standardization serve as an example. New processes and products will only be a commercial success if they are applied at a sufficiently large scale. Large scale application requires compatibility with related products and practices or interchangeability combined with low switching costs for the users of existing products and production processes. As a rule, each firm wants to see its own innovations become the patented standard for the sector as a whole. However, as long as rival firms are reluctant to be *the first* to sacrifice the potential profits of their exclusive innovation by conceding to a common norm, each of them will be worse off. The trade-off between rational "chauvinism" and some form of shared rationality ascertains that a collective optimum will remain out of reach.

Whatever the type of split between rational individualism and other-directedness, the remedy against overgrazing and/or undergrazing turns out to be some form of shared anticipation, followed by a critical minimum of coordination. Box 1.1 offers a case in point.

Box 1.1 "Rational" utilities

The large scale production and distribution of electricity illustrate the puzzles of anticipation and coordination when "myopic" or chauvinist rationality clashes with "non-myopic" or comprehensive rationality.

Two developments, one of a political and the other of a technological nature, eroded around the turn of the last century the monopolistic position of the six regional electricity producers in the Netherlands. Liberalization of the energy market opened possibilities of importing electricity from abroad and the introduction of smaller, less-polluting, heat-power facilities resulted in a larger and less-centralized supply of electricity. The new technology could thrive because of a close harmony of interests between electricity distributors and energy-intensive users, such as the chemical industry, and the producers of artificial fertilizers and salt. The heat (steam) that this type of firm needs for its own production generates an electricity surplus that is channeled back into the public net of distributors. The eclipse of the regional producers' monopoly and the rise of a technologically and environmentally superior substitute radically enhanced the bargaining position of both distributing firms and big end-users. The individual rationales of the producers (looking for economies of scale and the prolongation of their privileged position) *and* the individual rationales of distributing firms and clients (looking for reduction of their dependence on monopolistic suppliers and high tariffs) resulted – however contrary their strategic *intents* – in a collective outcome of structural excess capacity for the sector as a whole. Even worse, the surplus was generally expected to grow – partly by the path-dependent nature of past investments (the *competence trap*) and partly through the adversarial and imitative nature of current and future investments (the *competition trap*) – at least until 2004. Excess capacity follows the logic of *overgrazing*, as explained in the parable of the commons, that is, it results from individually rational moves (intended to break a monopoly) *and* the absence of a non-myopic (sector-encompassing) rationality, thus fulfilling the prophecy that each of the players fear. (The tragedy-of-the-commons eventually mutated into a tragedy-of-the-fallows as persistent excess capacity discouraged the breakthrough of alternative, possibly superior, technological-institutional substitutes.)

When rationalities clash

In my research I aim at unraveling the forces that govern the swings of political and economic order. How can the disorder in the financial system that "started" in 2006 be understood? The lack of strictness of financial regulation per se does not offer an adequate explanation. Initially no wave of financial scandals of corresponding proportions broke out in Europe, and the scandals that *did* occur appear to have had American roots (Vivendi, Ahold, Adecco): "Given the higher level of public and private enforcement in the United States for securities fraud, this contrast seems perplexing" (Coffee, 2005). Neither is it merely size or "bigness" that explains the "tango" of regulatory permissiveness and the subsequent bailout of the major players – as some "too big to fail" narratives like to suggest (Sorkin, 2010). The downfall of Lehman Brothers on the one hand, a big financial player, and the collapse of Iceland and Greece, relatively minor players in the international financial system, on the other, suggest where we might look for a more convincing explanation. The "sharing-the-spoils" mechanics of the Icelandic scenario may serve as an instructive first cut.

Sharing the spoils is not the outcome of a deliberately coordinated public or private consensus nor a specimen of the epidemics of herd behavior (cf. Keynes' infamous "animal spirits" (Keynes, 1936: 161–2); more about them in chapter 9). It has to do, instead, with a train of implicit understandings: a tacitly shared sequence of *sous-entendues* (tacit understandings) that sets the deceptive domino into motion. The mechanism entails, apart from auxiliary conditions that will be explored later, the willing suspension, if not outright suppression, of the spread of *corrective skepticism*. As we will show later, the *how* of the suppression of disbelief and the delay of timely corrections originate *inside* organizations: the *culture of ignoring* applies not only in firm-to-firm, firm-to-state and firm-to-regulatory agency relationships – the "functional" conspiracy of blindness is a *structural* property in executive versus non-executive relations and further down the ranks inside firms and public agencies as well.

Box 1.2 Conspiracies of blindness

As Jérôme Kerviel, the man who inflicted billions of euros in losses at the French bank Société Générale, as a result of his enormous, unauthorized bets, maintained that his bosses "deliberately turned a blind eye" and tacitly endorsed his activities "*as long as they were earning profits*". Echoing the moral of the "Icelandic scenario", in his testimony Kerviel's former direct supervisor, Eric Cordelle, could not clearly answer the judge's question as to where the line should be drawn between negligence and tacit endorsement: "If you are not looking for something, you don't find anything" ("A Société Générale Trader Remains a Mystery as His Criminal Trial Ends", *The New York Times*, June 25, 2010).

Due to the absence of *organized* dissent the rationales and mores of the most adjacent *links* in the chain-of-decisions take precedence over and "rationalize" the irrationality (and amorality) of the systemic *domino*. So the question reappears: how to explain the origin and the momentum of the domino?

A second cut may be to distinguish between insiders and outsiders. Listen for instance to the former CEO of one of the troubled banks, Washington Mutual Inc., testifying before the Senate Homeland Security and Governmental Affairs Committee after his bank was seized and sold to J.P. Morgan Chase: "For those that were part of the inner circle and were 'too clubby to fail', the benefits were obvious... For those outside the club, the penalty was severe" (*The Wall Street Journal*, April 14, 2010). Yet how to become, and remain, a member of the "club"? Many are invited to take part in the rallies of value-creation but fewer are entitled to appropriate the returns. What determines the divide? Much or most, so we will see, has to do with bargaining power. This study sets out to unravel the determinants of bargaining power and to spell out the nature of the negotiated order resulting from these basics.

"Clubbiness" smacks too much of a wronged feeling of having been excluded from the old boys and their turfs. And "bigness" appears not to be decisive, maybe even not necessary, once we take into account the loss of internal oversight and self-control and the external hazards that come with an "imperial" overstretch (Lehman Brothers was clearly a member of the "club"). What seems to count is *nodality* in a sequence of interconnected, partly competitive, partly complementary games that happen at different levels of interest aggregation and intermediation. "Nodal" players are the ones that serve as *catalysts* in a texture of systemic interdependencies. Next comes *acumen*, involving, as Schelling (1969:15) put it, "the fact that each participant's 'best' choice of action' depends on what he expects the other to do, and that 'strategic behavior' is concerned with influencing another's choice by working on his expectation of how one's own behavior is related to his."

Concepts like nodality and acumen (in the context of the *uses*-of-nodality) appear to be helpful for uncovering the origins and the workings of the *suppression of the forces of organized skepticism*. Bankers operating "on the brink", including former bankers who cross the private–public fence from time to time, *and* the players in the "real" economy that partake in the "sharing of spoils", clearly qualify for Schelling's notion of "strategic behavior".

A multilevel theatre: the inquiry

At the micro-level of political-economic constellations there is a variety of actors. Actors make decisions and moves driven by financial and other strategic motives in order to make themselves less dependent on the expectationss and moves of other players in the system. They are influenced and motivated by the behavioral rules and routines of the institutional setting in which they operate. Out of their micro-decisions and moves arise disciplinary arrangements (laws and regulations) and collaborative structures, such as vertically integrated firms, alliances and public–private partnerships at the meso-level. At the top of the pyramid, at the macro-regime level, consequences eventually occur that may ruin the constellation as a whole, such as is illustrated by Paulson's backhanded plea to "save the free-market system from itself".

The central question addressed in this inquiry is about the determinants of micro-moves and meso-movements that result in routines and regularities that produce intended and non-intended consequences at the macro-level. An inquiry into the sources of compliance and control at different levels of interest aggregation and intermediation is obviously a complex enterprise, encompassing several disciplines. First, both private and public actors are involved, each with their own incentives, objectives and competences. Second, different constellations are involved such as market and technology structures, but also social, political and cultural conditions that constrain the room for maneuvering. At the same time actors try to make use of these very structures or to change them in such a way that their objectives are better served when they are in a position that enables them to do so. Third, there are clashes-of-rationality between levels of interest aggregation that we described earlier. As a consequence "strategic behavior" – in the sense of "imposing upon the enemy the place and time and conditions for fighting preferred by oneself" – turns out to be a complex affair. Since "fighting" in situations of interdependence between rival firms and rival states is a matter of constraining, binding or outguessing and by-passing rivals – in short a question of (implicit or explicit) bargaining rather than open and unconditional confrontation – I will use the terms "diplomacy" for the games organizations play and "negotiated order" for the (formal and informal) outcomes of these games at the regime level. That order may be orderly or disorderly, but in whatever shape it is a *self-made order,* as the illustrations at the beginning of this chapter have shown. To summarize: uncovering the micro-origins and meso-mechanics of the orchestration of corporate games and tracing the intended and non-intended macro-impact on the discipline of undisciplined interests is the leading question addressed in this inquiry.

Organizing questions

My analysis starts by distinguishing among the urge, room and capacity for discipline. The *urge* for discipline originates from the cumulative, not necessarily intended, macro-consequences of micro-rational moves and countermoves by the individual players, as for instance illustrated by the "jump" from the links to the domino in the "Icelandic scenario". It is the story of the clash between individual and collective rationalities and the divide between processes of collective value creation and individual value appropriation.

The *room*-for-discipline refers to the enabling and constraining structures of competitive and symbiotic interdependences – among states, firms and their intermediaries. It is the story of partner switches, and informs us about nodal versus peripheral players. "Nodal" players derive their bargaining leverage or veto power from, among other things, the room they have for maneuvering, whilst facing relatively less or negligible *costs to themselves when imposing a loss of maneuverability upon others* – for instance "late entrants" or "last resort" players compared to those who trigger the chain of down- and upstream dependences. Here we operate at the meso-level of analysis, which informs us of the composition and the entry and exit conditions of the arena. Those who are in a position to change the composition of the arena are in a position to reframe the agenda; those who have a decisive say in agenda-framing are in a position to affect the time horizon of disciplinary arrangements and, ultimately, to affect the duration of the negotiated order erected upon these arrangements.

The *capacity*-for-discipline, finally, is a micro- or actor-specific attribute: it refers to the Schellingian acumen in the mobilization of critical combinations of partners and the Schumpeterian notion of the mobilization of critical combinations of resources. It is the story of an organization's sense-of-direction, and informs about the degree of internal cohesion and the strengths and weaknesses of the disciplining role of the dominant coalitions *inside* organizations – for public and private players alike as well as for a range of intermediary players in-between.

The centerpiece of my inquiry is the exploration of the interplay of internal and external discipline, that is, the interplay between the dynamics of horizontal coalition-formation (micro), vertical alliance-formation (meso) and how this interplay affects the pulse of the negotiated order at the regime level (macro). This multilevel signature clarifies why we think a *nested* games perspective – "games-within-games" – is needed to arrive at a more adequate understanding of the orchestration of corporate games and the swings of capitalist discipline.

Most of the social-scientific approaches that we will come across later (see Chapter 3) fail to join their insights into an integrative framework that grasps the intricacies of the cumulative interplay between the three distinct manifestations of the logics of interest aggregation and intermediation, to wit: the micro-logic of the formation and dismantling of coalitions, the meso-logic of the formation and demise of alliances and the systemic or macro-logic of the rise and fall of disciplinary regimes. The ambition of my study is to demonstrate that a "nested" games perspective is better able to accomplish what other approaches, however instructive for parts of the puzzle, fail to accomplish in a comprehensive way: explaining the macro-swings of institutional order and disorder from the micro-dynamics of rival coalitions and the meso-dynamics of rival alliances. Figure 1.1 illustrates the logic of the "shuttle" between horizontal moves and vertical movements, and the resulting momentum at the regime-level.

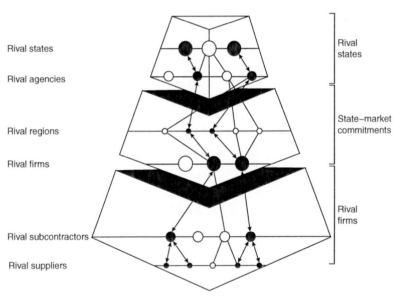

	Horizontal lines——	Linking Pins ●	Arrows ↓↑
Level of analysis	Micro: actors	Meso: arrangements	Macro: regimes
Type of dependence	Competitive	Complementary	Recursive
Structure	interdependences	interdependences	interdependences
Process	Rival coalitions	Rival alliances	Rival mixed clusters
Objective	Moves	Movements	Momentum
	Dividing and combining horizontal rivals	Partitioning and encapsulating upward and downward dependences	Orchestrating the negotiated order within and between markets and states by rotating coalitions and alliances

Figure 1.1 The shuttle logic of capitalist games: horizontal rivals looking for vertical allies, and vertical allies looking for horizontal divides

Box 1.3   On method

A thorny problem of interpretation with regime change is the difficulty to maintain a clear distinction between the architects of change and the changing architecture of the disciplinary "pyramid". My objective is the construction of a micro-perspective for demonstrating the cumulative impact of private and public actor moves and movements on macro-regime transformations. At the same time, however, the "reverse" objective is to demonstrate how macro-transformations feedback on lower-level moves and movements.

With "demonstrating" I mean less than offering a conclusive validation. As will be stressed in the chapters that follow the empirical data and the methods of assembling the associated pieces of evidence are meant to corroborate the *heuristic* potential of the approach, not to deliver a definitive proof of scientific truth. My observations and case studies are intended to test the plausibility and reach of a specific way of looking at social reality. The quality mark of the study is, in other words, its realism and, so I hope, the epistemic persuasiveness of the underlying analytical framework. That framework collects its primary inspiration from the apparent *steadiness* of intriguing, while virtually contradictory, occurrences (like the "Paulson" cycle or "Icelandic" scenario reported above). Once we have arrived at what seems to be the beginning of an understanding of the "rationale of irrationality" or the "logic of inconsistency", we can then move back to a broader spectrum of phenomena, over a longer span of time, so as to test and improve the concision and reach of our analytical construct. So, the *inspiration* for our study stems from "surprising" events reported by the qualified press, monographs, personal memoirs by insiders and other chroniclers from the corner of Wall Street or the City. Call this the reality check.

The *rationality* check stems from the academic premises that are devoted to the study of the organization of economic life, negotiation dynamics and the world of political and corporate stratagems. My analytical prism is a *bricolage* of insights from several disciplines, especially from the zones where their prospects fail to make the best of the credits of their academic neighbors. Compared to the "storytelling" evidence (Ward, 1972) provided by insiders and chroniclers of Wall Street society, academics sometimes produce remakes of reality that seem to belong more in a Madame Tussauds exhibition, that is, a cabinet of irrelevant imputations of rationality and regularity. Our streetwise reporters do not compete with academics for the "truth". Where they compete, instead, is for pertinence: they are indispensable for inserting a measure of streetwiseness into the elements that figure in many an academic exercise. Academics, however, remain indispensable for distilling the behavioral *logic* behind the "surprises" of the orchestration of corporate games and capitalist discipline. The sort of insight we expect from the teaming-up of the streetwise chroniclers and academic scholars looking for "system" in the virtual disorder resounds perfectly in the observation by a private iquity-trader annex IT-lobbyist, seasoned in the "wiring" of Silicon Valley economics to Washington politics: "If you go to a rave it looks like chaos from the balcony. But on the floor it's clear what's happening, and what appears to be chaos is structured. The old companies are going, 'this is messy, this is overvalued, it doesn't make sense. Well, yeah. From the *balcony* it doesn't make sense" (quoted in Miles, 2001: 240).

In an "Addendum" included in his memorable *The New Industrial State*, Galbraith (1968: 408) "solves" the (never-ending) disputes among "specialists" and "generalists" on the merits of quantitative versus qualitative analysis (respectively, inductive versus deductive epistemology) by invoking the judgment of a third "disputant": the dedicated *reader*. Scholars, says Galbraith, that probe deeply into specific parts of a subject will mistrust as superficial those who range more widely; conversely, specialists are considered to lack vision or reach. On the other hand, those "who are mathematically inclined see others as in retreat from rigor… The statisticians believe those who prove points deductively to be dangerously intuitive", and so on. Reminding us that "specialisation is a scientific convenience, not a scientific virtue", the author proposes to settle the dispute on "exposition" versus "analysis" by asserting that "justice requires, no doubt, that much be left to the reader. Writing is hard enough work without having to make it comprehensible, and scholarship endorses a division of labor between those who write and those who read" (ibid.: 410).

Given the "nature of social argument" the ultimate task of social scientific inquiry is *not* to establish the "truth" but to tighten the net around the questions that we still do not know the definitive answers to.

For answering the lead question about regime dynamics we have to examine three sub-questions in greater depth. First, what triggers the *urge*-for-discipline? Second, what conditions the *options* for responding to the urge? Third, what determines the *search-and-selection* of disciplinary responses, given the specifics of the range of available options?

Discipline builds upon credible commitments, i.e. credible threats and promises. The last question triggers a series of supplementary questions: what constitutes the *credibility* of threats and promises? As will be elucidated later, credibility has to do with *bargaining power*, pushing the last question further to its "origins": what are the *bases* of bargaining power? For answering that question and tracing its implications the idea of a strategic "triangle" – arena, agenda and timing – proves to be useful as an explanatory vehicle: the stability and composition of the *arena* frames the bargaining *agenda* and the latter frames the *timing* and *duration* of commitments, and thus the time horizon of the disciplinary arrangements built upon them.

The answers we find to these organizing questions provide the causal links of a "nested" games perspective: How do the conditions of internal and external dependence and the mechanisms of inclusion versus exclusion of critical resources and players affect the codification of commitments? How do disciplinary codes, *including what is left non-codified*, affect the substance and stability of commitments? And how do these commitments affect the reproduction of the initial conditions of interdependence that triggered this circular sequence of causation? Accepting that there appears to exist something like a strategic *cycle* of conditions, codes and commitments will be helpful, so we expect, in understanding the final consequences, to wit: the *drift* of capitalist discipline.

Figure 1.2 encapsulates the argument. It shows the phenomenon we want to explain: the dualism of capitalist discipline, that is, the causal loops between on the one hand corporate and state behaviors ("diplomacy") and capitalist order ("discipline") on the other. In our grammar "diplomacy" represents the behavioral dimension and "discipline" the variable outcome. The structuring concepts are conditions, codes and commitments. *Conditions* refer to the (a)symmetry of interdependences; *codes* to the rules of rivalry and cooperation; and *commitments* inform us about coordination and compliance, that is, specific disciplinary arrangements for coping with the dilemmas that relate to the problems of interdependent choice. The hypotheses to

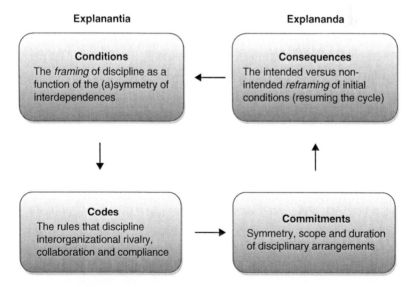

Figure 1.2 The framing of discipline: a double-loop causation

be tested deal with the orchestration of nested games, as a function of the covariance of conditions, codes and commitments. The prefix "nested" stands for the multilevel architecture of interdependences and "orchestration" for the process dimension, that is, the modus operandi of nested games. Behavior, architecture and process are supposed to explain the interrelated twists of the logic of corporate games and capitalist discipline.

In spite of the clear complexities of the subject, the bottom line turns out to be simple: conditions explain codes, codes explain commitments, and commitments lead to consequences – be they intended or non-intended. As will be demonstrated in the following pages, this bottom line must suffice to expose the cumulative logic of the "laws" that link micro-moves, meso-movements and macro-motion.

Recapitulation and preview

The ambition of this study is to devise a micro-foundation for explaining the macro-swings of capitalist discipline. That ambition implies a deconstruction of so-called systemic "imperatives" and "compulsions" into testable propositions about the logic of the moves and counter-moves of the players who have a decisive role in the constitution of the negotiated order of modern capitalist "pyramids". So, the lead question in this expedition is *how* disciplinary arrangements arise and spread into regimes and dissipate again. Understanding the forces of the emergence, dissemination and dissipation of disciplinary arrangements is a precondition for understanding the capacity of modern capitalism to discipline *itself*.

This lead question can be dissected into three main issues: the urge, the room and the capacity for discipline – where each of them is to be situated at distinct but interlocking levels of accumulation. One of our upcoming tasks is to find out how the interlocking works precisely between these three, equally real, manifestations of social reality. The *urge* for discipline refers to the forces that "push" the quest-for-discipline: as argued earlier it is primarily the clash between selfish/local versus systemic/comprehensive rationality that produces the sort of strategy traps that, sooner or later, force actors to look for realignments of their partially complementary, partially competing, interests. The *room* for discipline refers to forces that "pull" interdependent actors into specific directions when looking for disciplinary solutions that provide immunization against the undesired, respectively counter-productive consequences of unfettered selfishness. The room for discipline identifies the objective entry and exit conditions of the arena that *enable* specific responses to the urge-for-discipline. *How* interdependent actors respond to the pushes and pulls of discipline is a question of *responsiveness*, where the latter term – minding the pitfalls of assuming "hyper rationality" as opposed to path-dependent "rationalizations" – refers to conditional *reflexes* rather than rational responses. The task is to find out about the conditions upon which these reflexes might be based.

Situating the need, the room and the capacity for discipline at different levels of analysis comprises the essence of a nested games perspective: order and disorder at the regime level is the cumulative outcome of lower level bargains. Endorsing a multilevel perspective avoids two (opposite) sorts of the so-called "fallacy-of-composition". First, a multilevel framework steers clear from the fallacy of "catapulting" micro-motives into meso-arrangements and macro-regimes *without properly deconstructing the mechanics of dissemination, structuration and disordering of institutions*. Catapulting is a specimen of the trap of psychological *reductionism*. Second, our framework avoids the assumption of the *pre-existence* of "systemic imperatives", "compulsive affinities" and similar "aggregates" *without properly identifying and dissecting the filiations among the momentum of macro-regimes, the movements of meso-arrangements and the moves and countermoves at the micro-level*. Postulating, instead of explaining, macro-characteristics as a causative force is a specimen of what might be called the fallacy of socio-economic "parachutism" (like the "effectiveness-is-efficiency" illusion lurking in beliefs in the "competition" between, respectively the "convergence" of institutional regimes or the "osmosis" of market-and-state in modern capitalism as foreseen by Galbraith, 1968).

By stressing the *nestedness* of the negotiated political-economic order, we are bound to disentangle the turns by which lower-level responses to inherited or anticipated conditions of interdependence may imperceptibly drift into non-intended, eventually counter-productive escalations of commitments and sorts of regime transformation at higher levels; levels that sooner or later are bound to backfire at lower-level arrangements and stratagems – like a river unknowingly feeding the cascade waiting around the corner.

A convincing way to examine these assertions and conjectures is to forge a laissez-passer to the corridors where the actual decisions and non-decisions are made. However, in order to *understand* what one may come across there, we first need an interpretative framework, inspired by the best that the (divided) academy of political-economics, sociology and institutional analysis has to offer on the "state of the art". This is what I endeavor to do hereafter: to look at the games organizations play through a new prism, to wit: a theory of nested games that might be helpful for a better understanding of the lessons organizations learn or (for reasons to be spelled out later) can *afford not to learn* on account of their own maneuverings.

Regarding the lessons to be learned from models, invented to detect order in a reality that presents itself *from the balcony* as a disorderly theatre, writers seasoned in the fabrics of fact and foible offer assistance. Borrowing from Umberto Eco, a renowned master of spurious epistemological matters, we dare not trifle with a wink from William to Adso (respectively the principal and agent in Eco's *The Name of the Rose* (Eco, 1983: 492):

> *William:* "I behaved stubbornly, pursuing a semblance of order, when I should have known well that there is no order in the universe."
>
> *Adso:* "But in imagining an erroneous order you still found something..."
>
> *William:* "What you say is very fine, Adso, and I thank you. The order that our mind imagines is like a net, or like a ladder, built to attain something. But afterward you must throw the ladder away, because you discover that, even it was useful, it was meaningless."

Believing William (and Adso), I propose to mount the rungs before considering abolishing the ladder. In this fashion the first segment of the ladder is devoted to the construction of a *model* on the orchestration of capitalist discipline (the "view from the balcony"). A second segment details the *parameters* of the games organizations play ("on the floor"): the conditions, codes and commitments. The final segment reconsiders the consequences of corporate games for the swings of capitalist discipline in dynamic terms: a reinterpretation of nested games and the resulting negotiated order as a cyclical phenomenon. If these are the segments that constitute the folding ladder, the *rungs* are the chapters in this book. Hence in **Chapter 1 "The Quest for Discipline"** I outline the contours of our expedition, that is, envisaging the swings of capitalist discipline at the macro-regime level as a consequence of micro-choices and meso-arrangements.

Chapter 2 "The *New Industrial State* Revisited" contains a retrospective on the organization of "modern" capitalism according to some, highly influential classics in the descriptive economic-institutional literature. This interlude is intended to give an impression of what has changed in the ordering of economic life since the last quarter of the past century.

Chapter 3 "The Masks of Rationality" reviews the range of rationality assumptions underlying the prevailing (academic) interpretations of the organization of economic life. I propose an alternative grid in which the prism of the negotiated order of capitalism is seen as a *set of nested games*.

In **Chapter 4** "Cohabitation" I analyze two archetypes of the "logic-of-cohabitation" in nested games: accommodation and containment.

Chapter 5 "The Framing of Discipline" shows the dual use of the concept of framing: as an analytical *construct* and as a self-fashioning *social activity*. The closer the two meanings of the term coalesce the more realist, I think, is a *verstehende* (interpretative) theory of the negotiated order. I document the causes of regime change, that is, change as the consequence of the *re*framing of discipline. This reframing refers to changes from "first-mover/market *sharing*" to "footloose-mover/market *transforming*" games, and from discipline based upon direct "*conduct*-control" to the indirectness of "*context*-controlling" stratagems. I use the study of so-called "neo-corporatist regimes" as a comparative litmus test of the explanatory power of game theory, since both neo-corporatist and game theory – more than its pluralist and comparative-institutionalist counterparts – focus explicitly on the arch-dilemmas of "collective action".

Chapter 6 "Conditions: The Anatomy of Negotiating Power" refines the basics of nested games along two lines: the *structure* of negotiating power and the *structuration* of order. I will address the multilevel manifestations of political-economic order and redress the omission of arena and agenda-*substitution* and the negation of *temporal* asymmetries in the mainstreams of game theory and strategy-analysis.

Chapter 7 "Diplomacy: Houdini meets Ulysses" sketches the contours of a centerpiece in the analysis of the logic of cohabitation among rival firms and rival states: the *shuttle* diplomacy of modern capitalism. The chapter provides a taxonomy of negotiated orders in a comparative set-up by translating mobilization and mobility differentials – the bases of negotiation power – into a taxonomy of (for instance, sector-specific) games. The thrust of the analysis can be summarized as follows: the more lopsided the distribution of mobility and mobilization options, the less representative and reciprocal are the commitments among states, sector associations and firms, and thus the more precarious are the "pyramids" constructed from them.

Chapter 8 "Commitments: The Essence of Discipline" is key to the orchestration of corporate games. I address a forgotten chapter in the analysis of competition, cooperation and compliance, i.e. the issue of strategic "responsiveness". *Under-* versus *over-*responsiveness are considered to be the drivers of the swings of capitalist discipline. As it turns out, these are not psychological phenomena but specimens of organized *intelligence*: they identify the causes and consequences of the innate propensity of organizations to influence, to outguess or to adapt to the most *adjacent* links of their chains of interdependence, rather than to take the chain-as-a-whole as their strategy compass.

Chapter 9 "Consequences: On the Drift of Discipline" concludes the William–Adso "ladder". Stripped to its essence the thrust is a three-step, "nested" spiral: *thrift* at the micro-level ("economizing-on-commitments") triggers shuttles at the meso-level ("horizontal and vertical partner switches"); *shuttles*, in turn, generate drift at the macro-level ("the non-intended/cumulative consequences of intendedly rational choices"); and *drift* reinforces thrift ("recycling the cycle"). The swings of capitalist discipline are the cumulative outcome of the *displacement* of collateral hazards, which arise from imbalances in the creation versus capture of economic value. The benefits of the imbalances accrue to the players with superior negotiating power, which builds upon a combination of the powers of creative destruction *and* creative obstruction. Both are subject to the elementary thrift axiom: "minimizing the costs to oneself of binding *others*". Chapter 9 corrects for the static bias in the taxonomy of disciplinary games presented in Chapters 7 and 8. This is done by reconsidering the games in cyclical terms and tracing the impact of the divides between value creation and appropriation for the recycling of collateral hazards. Hazard-free societies do not exist; what does exist, however, is the possibility of countering the cycle by a more balanced division of the capacity to reciprocate the hazards. The chapter concludes with the most inarticulate corner of our framework: the identification of the determinants of organizational self-discipline – the urge to bind *oneself* – and its foundation: organizational responsiveness.

In the **Epilogue** I invite the reader to reflect on some normative implications of the notion of responsiveness and to look ahead at possible research directions in which to extend the explanatory reach of my work on the "nested" games organizations play. Envisaged this way Umberto Eco's "ladder" may turn out to be an extendable one – thereby rejoining the Wittgensteinian wit resounding in the William–Adso dialogue above. As W. H. Auden writes in his *At last the Secret is Out*: "There's always another story – There is more than meets the eye." Envisioned this way it remains to be seen whether it wouldn't be unfortunate to do away with the ladder too *early*.

2
The *New Industrial State* Revisited

Introduction: on errant spirits

How firms and nations handle the antinomy of chauvinist versus comprehensive rationality varies with the spirits of capitalist evolution. These spirits vary with structures of ownership and control, that is, with what controlling interests perceive as critical resource dependences. Critical or vital are those dependences that are seen as directly related to the core competences of organizations, which are defined by the dominant coalitions of interests that decide the course of an organization. An organization's sense of direction, derived from its self-defined core competence, leads to a selection of core competitors, that is, a selection of rivals that serve as a benchmark for comparing and assessing the organization's performance and the sustainability of its ambitions. The selection of core competitors, in turn, leads to the identification of core *complementors*, that is, the dominant alliances of a private, public or semi-public signature with whom organizations think they can preserve or strengthen their identity and ambitions or, more fundamentally, to alter their course and competence and to recast the rules of rivalry and cooperation.

Whether this three-step sequence of competence, competition and cooperation is self-made, that is, autonomously selected by "sovereign" players, or should rather be seen as superimposed from the outside (e.g. dictated by "technological imperatives", "market imperatives" or some other driving *meta*-force), constitutes one of the puzzles to be addressed in this study. Our earlier sketches of the "strategy trap" and the paradoxes of egoist versus comprehensive rationality suggest another way of looking at the duality of subjective choice and objective outcome. One way of clarifying this point is to look at historical variations in the methods, and unexpected outcomes, of handling the strategy trap. No longer than a generation ago the typical recipe for handling the dilemmas of path dependence and competitive anticipation were epitomized as the logic of "coordination by *annexation and hierarchization*". A.D. Chandler, the icon of this currency of thought, ascribes the growth of the giant enterprise at the start of the last century, though "invented" primarily in the United States rapidly spreading across the rest of the Western world, to the relentless search for "efficiency". According to this business historian the efficiency drive was inspired by cost-based competition. The "imperative" of cost reduction is supposed to have been the response to the evils of "cut throat" or "ruinous" competition. During the upswing of the business cycle, according to this account, the more cost-efficient firms accumulate a reservoir of slack resources that grants them a larger staying power than their less efficient rivals during the downswing. Costs can be reduced by increasing throughput, that is, by accelerating the speed and increasing the volume of production flows. In this view size is not a cause but a consequence of speed and volume: "decreases in unit costs (often identified with economies of scale) resulted far more from the increases in the volume and velocity of throughput than from a growth in the size of the factory or plant" (Chandler, 1977: 281).

Volume and velocity could only be achieved by introducing new devices of organizational control, that is, "by creating an administrative hierarchy operated by many full-time salaried managers" incorporating the complete chain from basic resources to production and distribution, from retailer to the ultimate consumer (ibid.: 236, 283). In Chandler's account the need for vertical chain control is reinforced by the incidence of excess production, especially in industries with firms that face high fixed costs. These costs, combined with overproduction and sticky wages (in the case of well-organized labor unions), are bound to end in cutthroat competition, that is, in price wars and profit squeezes. The only way to counter the downward spiral of this "tragedy of the commons" is external discipline by chain control and internal discipline by hierarchy. Hence the rise and spread of the large, vertically integrated firm.

The Chandlerian canon of coordination by "annexation and hierarchization" has found its sequel in John Kenneth Galbraith's eloquent account of the rise and ramifications of the "techno-structure" in modern capitalism. The author of *The New Industrial State* (1968) takes advantage of a broader conceptualization of the embeddedness of market dilemmas and response dynamics by stressing the role of the state and organized interest groups in the solution of competence and competition dilemmas, thus offering a more explicitly *political-economic* interpretation of the transformation of capitalist order. While Chandler describes the size-follows-efficiency sequence and the subsequent rise of managerial hierarchy, Galbraith stresses the size-follows-technology nexus and the subsequent rise of planning hierarchies. The bridge between the two can be formulated as follows. Where the efficiency drive inspires to size combined with mass production, and the latter to the introduction of large scale technology, it is technology that in turn asks for the domestication of external resource dependences. Summarizing the causal chain, it is the search for efficiency that generates the quest for control and it is control that transforms the game of competing-for-*competence* into the game of competing-for-*dominance*. Earlier and subsequent studies (Piettre, 1955; Chamberlain, 1962; Shonfield, 1969; Jacquemin, 1977; Chandler, 1984; De Jong, 1992) can be seen as preludes and variations on the thesis that competitive pressures foster collusion and centralization, the more so when switching and anticipation costs appear to be high (as in capital- and technology-intensive industries). The origin of the thesis can be reduced, borrowing Galbraith's (1968) grammar, to the iron laws of "the technological imperative".

Technology means the systematic application of scientific or otherwise organized intellectual capital to practical tasks. From this principle follow six "imperatives" (Galbraith, 1968: 23–32). First, an increasing span of time associated with the need to divide and subdivide tasks separates the beginning from the completion of any task. The more sophisticated the production process, the farther back the application of knowledge will be carried, and the longer, accordingly, the time between the initiation and completion of any task. Second, and apart from variations in output, there is an increase in the capital that is committed to production. The application of knowledge to subdivided tasks involves machines, and machines involve additional investments. Third, with increasing technology the commitment of time and money increases the inflexibility of productive tasks. Knowledge and equipment are useful only for the tasks as they were initially defined. Changing tasks require new knowledge and new equipment. Fourth, technology requires specialization which requires the ability to organize and employ information or to apply experiential routines. Fifth, the inevitable companion of specialization is organization since the need to bring the tasks of specialists to a coherent result requires coordination. So complex, indeed, will be the job of coordinating specialists that there will be an increasing number of "specialists on organization".

Technology, organizational complexity and fixed routines go hand in
hand. Sixth, from the combination of the time and capital that must
be committed, the inflexibility of this commitment, the need for larger
organizations and the problems of market performance under conditions of advanced technology comes the necessity for planning:

> The more sophisticated the technology, the greater, in general, will
> be all of the foregoing requirements...Planning is both essential
> and difficult. It is essential because of the time that is involved, the
> money that is at risk, the number of things that can go wrong and
> the magnitude of the possible ensuing disaster. It is difficult because
> of the number and size of the eventualities that must be controlled.
> (Ibid.: 29–31)

With the need for controlling the number and size of eventualities
enters the *state* for sharing and absorbing major risks. The state can provide or guarantee demand, directly or indirectly. It can underwrite the
costs of research and development. Or it can make skilled and scientific
labor available. "Technological compulsions, and not ideology or political wile, will require the firm to seek the help and protection of the
state" (ibid.: 32). "Compulsions" compel the state to assist in stabiliz-
ing demand and supply. Irreversible commitments of time and capital
mean that the needs and whims of consumers must be anticipated – "by
months or years" – and that resources, skills, materials, equipment,
dealers and so on will be available in due time, long enough and at
remunerative costs. Exercising control over demand and supply means
substituting planning for the market.

According to Galbraith there are three ways of replacing the market
by the "authoritative determination" of prices and of quantities to be
sold or bought. First, there is the incorporation ("vertical integration")
of suppliers and outlets, thus converting the uncertainties of external negotiation to the certainties of internal decision-making: "nothing...better explains modern industrial policy in regard to capital and
labor than the desire to make these highly strategic cost factors subject to purely internal decision" (ibid.: 39). Second, markets can also
be controlled by reducing or eliminating the independence of action
available to those to whom the planning unit sells or from whom it
buys. Large and technology-intensive firms always have the possibility of supplying a material or component to themselves. The option
of internalizing upstream markets is an important source of power for
controlling non-internalized markets. And vis-à-vis consumers, large

technology-intensive firms share a common interest in securing stable prices: "it is to the advantages of none to disrupt this mutual security system. Price reductions...might provide further and retributive price-cutting. No formal communication is necessary to prevent such actions; this...arouses the professional wrath of company counsel...Thus do size and small numbers of competitors lead to market regulation" (ibid.: 41).

Third, there can be a "matrix of contracts" by which large firms eliminate market uncertainty *for one another*. In a world where exacting technology with extensive research and development means long production runs and large capital commitments, state procurements and grants guarantee fixed returns for main producers. The main producers share their secure returns with a selective circuit of suppliers, as long as this "extended family" abides to the rules of the system. Thus, "industrial planning is in unabashed alliance with size...Reciprocal absorption of market uncertainty by contracts between firms all favor the large enterprise" (ibid.: 43).

Whereas scholars in the Chandler tradition hold that size, annexation and hierarchization are in the service of volume and velocity – epitomized in the dictum "structure follows strategy", where "strategy" essentially aims at "efficiency" – in Galbraith's capitalist logic size, annexation and accommodation with the state, organized labor and other firms are said to follow the imperative of "effectiveness", that is "size...is (not) in the service of monopoly or the economies of scale but of *planning*. And for this planning – control of supply, control of demand, provision of capital, minimization of risk – *there is no clear upper limit to the desirable size*" (ibid.: 87–8; my italics).

In Chandler's chronicle, efficiency losses that might follow from (over)sizing and hierarchy are kept at bay by "revolutionary" new organizational devices, such as "diversification" and "multi-divisional control" structures (Chandler, 1977). In Galbraith's view, alternatively, there are virtually "no limits" to corporate growth because size is believed to be a *precondition* for effectiveness. "Effectiveness" means ascertaining "freedom from outside interference" (Galbraith, 1968: 97), where the "outside" ranges from labor and the state to suppliers of capital, customers and rival oligopolists alike. All subscribe to the proverb "size and associated power in one place make it necessary elsewhere" (ibid.: 205), because only size guarantees the new industrial complex the required level of return which secures its autonomy and hence survival. Thus, the discipline of the Galbraithian industrial order is based on an organically shared interest of capital, labor and state in averting anything that may frustrate the indispensable trinity of technology, complexity and size.

The trinity explains the greatest miracle of capitalist discipline (in fact it is Galbraith's "solution" for the "clash of rationalities" that was sketched out in Chapter 1):

> no matter how great the rivalry between firms or how carefully cultivated are the institutional feuds and dislikes…using prices as a weapon of competitive aggression…is exorcised by the strongest canons of corporate behavior. It is a tribute to the social capacity of man that such mutually destructive behavior is so successfully banned. (Ibid.: 202)

As we know now (since, for example, Paulson's complaint in his memorable *On the Brink*, quoted in Chapter 1, p. 2) other social capacities of man have not failed to challenge this backhanded compliment. Galbraith's imagination offers ingenious interpretations of the possibility of an "organic solidarity" between contending interests and of the possible recipes for coping with the intricacies of the "competition trap". What it does not do, however, is provide insight into the forces that "effectively" appear to challenge the logic of the New Industrial State. Again (as in the Marxist and the Schumpeterian tradition of looking for endogenous explications of the sources of regime change) the challenge comes from *within*, and not from "ideology or political wile" (because it is ideology that "merely" rationalizes the machinery of rivalry and accommodation *ex post*, though admittedly eventually adding to its momentum). Stated otherwise, the rhetoric of action and reaction represent the *spinning*; but it is the logic of action and response that constitutes the *wheels* of regime change.

The justification for dwelling at some length upon Galbraith's chronicle of the "inevitable" osmosis of private, public and semi-collective powers is that it can be re-read, in hindsight, as a convincing treatise on the gradual *elimination* of "countervailing forces", forces that in his earlier writings (Galbraith, 1952) he held responsible for the "self-correcting" capacity of capitalism. Returning to his earlier work helps us to spot the principles that undermine the validity of his later generalizations on the putative "ultra-stability" of the New Industrial State. Insofar as we may take the "osmosis" of the state, the unions and the educational estate and their subservience to the "requirements" of the "technological imperative" combined with "corporate canons" as the run up to the *eclipse* of the countervailing forces of capitalism in its early modern years, we may now set out to discover the "requirements" of how a political and economic order may lose its capacity to presage, and thus to respond to, fundamental changes in the conditions and codes of rivalry and cooperation. Not acknowledging the evidence that techno-bureaucratic *overstretch* is bound to breed *financial-economic* escapism and freebooting is the price to be paid for believing in unidirectional rather than dialectical "imperatives". For instance, in his chapter on the "Future of the Industrial System" Galbraith foresees "a close fusion of the industrial system with the state", to such an extent that in due time "the industrial system will not long be regarded as something apart from government" (Galbraith, 1968: 399). Such an extrapolation, apart from underestimating the revealed capacity of financial "systems" to spoil the public–private "harmony" by redistributing the hazards, carries on the tradition of presenting the nation state (and its supranational annexes and ramifications) as a coherent strategic entity invested with a non-disputed identity and authority. This practice, even in the case of large domestic markets, stands in the way of seeing how the international escapism of "the" industrial-financial complex – already taking off around the late 1960s – started to erode, slowly but steadily, the capacity of the state to perform precisely that which, in "modern capitalism", it is required to perform. How the *old* discipline – by overstretching the recipes of vertical annexation and horizontal accommodation in firms, as well as among firms, the state and unions – sows the very seeds of its own demise and gradually gives way to the *new* discipline, by recombining and leveraging the old recipes, is the subject of this book.

Old versus new discipline

A recollection of the large corporation would not be complete without briefly mentioning the legacy of a third family of explanations of the rise of "organized capitalism". It is an interpretation that sees the spread of the giant enterprise primarily as instigated by the need to construct a check on the power of organized *labor*. Especially in periods of price and profit reductions due to excessive ("undisciplined") competition, firms have an interest in trying to break the resistance of the trade unions to wage cuts and lay-offs. Centralized oligarchic firms operating in concentrated oligopolistic markets are supposedly in a better position to challenge the labor force's fighting spirit than fragmented capitalists. As we will see in Chapter 5, this seems a curious interpretation in the light of the neo-corporatist literature arguing that centralized labor, flanked by macro-Keynesian inspired welfare states, tends to opt for (associations of) centralized managerial capitalism in a trilaterally shared desire for economic stability and social reliability. Both managerial-technological capital *and* organized labor should therefore be seen as co-*sponsors*, rather than as opponents or victims, of the large, vertically integrated and horizontally collusive firm (Shonfield, 1969). Not without irony, it is the allegation of *competitive weakness* that in more recent assessments has become associated with the symbiotic "iron triangle" of state, labor and managerial capital. At variance with ("new") institutionalist arguments on efficiency and effectiveness, and contrary to class-struggle views on the capitalist impetus to the "ineluctable" and "unlimited" growth of the firm, currently favored interpretations envision the go-together of bureaucratic symbiosis, institutional rigidity and competitive weakness as the chief rationale for rethinking and redressing the giant corporation today. Conventional wisdom summarizes the functional prerequisites of "big business" as follows:

- Ascertain *reciprocity* by maximizing the scale of horizontal coalitions between centralized peak associations and vertical alliances, with the central state serving as a *primus inter pares*.
- Ascertain *representativity* by maximizing inclusivity, that is "consonance" in the aspiration of unions as well as financial and managerial-technological capital and the state to internalize their external contingencies.
- Keep *internal* divides at bay by centralization and hierarchization, while accommodating *external* rivalries by sector segmentation and subsidized regulation, such as cartel formation in the steel, ship-building and railway industries.
- Assign the *state as last resort* for defending the sovereignty and supremacy of its own techno-industrial and agro-industrial complexes.
- Ensure a continuous *oligarchization* of the tripartite (Continental style) or bipartite (Anglo-American style) arrangements for serving the "national" interests of the techno- and agro-industrial complexes.

This sort of enumeration has found its way into numerous chronicles, from Robert Michels's (1968) "iron law of oligarchy" to Michel Crozier's (1963) "bureaucratic phenomenon". It has been hammered into the management lore on "corpocracy". Rosemary Moss Kantor (1990: 353–4) popularized vintage corporate bureaucracy as based upon:

- *Position*, in that authority derives from position.
- *Repetition*, seeking efficiency through doing the same thing over and over again.

- *Rules*, defining procedures and rewarding adherence to them.
- *Status*, where pay is position based, positions are arrayed in hierarchies, and greater rewards come from attaining higher positions.
- *Formal structure*, designed to channel and restrict the flow of information.
- *Mandate*, strictly circumscribing the action arena of bureaucratic territory.
- *Ownership and control*, rewarding repetition, rules and routines as opposed to experimentation and learning.

What is reported here about the "inert giants" of corporate capitalism has been told, largely with similar qualifications, about the inertia of trade unions and welfare-state bureaucracies. A widely accepted view holds that these particulars have eroded the capacity of organized capitalism and its companion – the welfare state – to recognize timely early dissenters, to assess their impact on the viability of the prevailing regime and to respond adequately to intelligent escapes from the iron troika of concentration, centralization and routinization. In our grammar, the *old* discipline, by trying to overcome the *competition* trap through annexation – and oligarchization, drifted imperceptibly into the *competence* trap. When pushed too long and on a too massive scale, annexation and oligarchization lead to institutional autism, which, in turn, leads to a loss of "responsiveness" for organizations and regimes alike, that is, to institutional sclerosis.

At the meta- or regime level the phenomenon has been referred to as the competitive or adaptive "weakness of strong ties" (Granovetter, 1973). At the meso- or sector level the documentation ranges from the restructuring rigidities of the steel industry (Grabherr, 1993: 255–77) to the abortive efforts to rationalize and modernize the shipbuilding industry (Wassenberg, 1983). At the micro- or organization level the loss of responsiveness is often referred to as a predisposition in which the exploitation of existing resources and entrenched routines takes precedence over the exploration of new resources and recipes. The reported reasons for the law-of-exploitation forcing out the drive-for-exploration are diverse. They range from competence traps based on technological path dependence (Arthur et al., 1987; Levitt and March, 1988; March, 1991) to the increasing returns on learning-by-using and repetition (Wernerfelt, 1984; Arthur, 1989). Typical industries and sectors exist in which first movers decide upon investing in critical competences without a priori knowledge on how these strategic investments will influence uncertainty in an industry. One of the proponents of this (clearly non-Galbraithian) stand in modern strategy analysis writes: "when the evolution of technology, consumer demand, and production technology cannot be influenced by first-moving firms, whether or not first-moving efforts will be successful is indeterminate" (Barney, 1997: 110). What all these variations seem to unify is the result that "core capabilities" and "competitive advantages" may turn into "core rigidities" (Leonard-Barton, 1992), "first mover *dis*advantages" (Wernerfelt and Karnani, 1987) and "entrenched routines" (North, 1981; Nelson and Winter, 1982), eventually ending in competitive obsolescence and corporate death.

The phenomenon has been observed, moreover, for the level of analysis between micro-organization and macro-regimes, for instance where firms, unions and local authorities work together in long-established, regional networks. In the case of close-knit relationships "strongly embedded regional networks insidiously [may turn] from ties that bind into ties that blind...Too much embeddedness...may promote a petrification of the supportive tissue [of networks] and, hence, may pervert networks into cohesive coalitions against more radical innovations" (Grabherr, 1993: 24–6).

The dilemma is a reminder of the classical sociological discussion on the "duality" of institutional arrangements, simultaneously enabling *and* constraining social choice and change (Giddens, 1979: 69). The competence trap originates from the same duality. How can we exploit current capabilities without losing sight of the need for exploration, that is, the capacity and the will to challenge the comfort of inherited and time-honored competences? This balancing act echoes the related dispute about the functions and dysfunctions of institutional "rigidity":

> In a world of uncertainty, where the probabilistic calculus is ruled out, rules, norms and institutions play a functional role in providing a basis for decision-making, expectation and belief. Without these "rigidities", without social routine and habit to reproduce them and without institutionally conditioned conceptual frameworks, an uncertain world would present a chaos of sense data in which it would be impossible for the agent to make sensible decisions and to act. (Hodgson, 1988: 205)

Not much sympathy with this view on the latent functions of routines, habits and institutions seems to have been retained – at least in today's rhetoric (as opposed to practice). Concerns about institutional rigidities and the secular loss of competitive acumen prevail instead. Apparently, the pendulum is swinging the other way. The result is utter confusion. For instance, whereas uncertainty gathers momentum nationally and internationally, managerial and political lore tends to have a keener eye for the *dys*functions of social routines than for its functions. Or, whereas societies and economies have become more technology and knowledge intensive, the Galbraithian mystique of the "technological imperative", asking for size, centralization and stability, somehow has yielded to the counter-canons of the "market imperative", asking, instead, for downsizing, simplicity, decentralization and, in particular, for the praise of "flexibility". In the meantime, however, *mega*-mergers and acquisitions and ever-widening webs of "strategic" partnerships are at an all-time high.

The resulting intellectual embarrassment leads to caricatural prophecies and precepts. Among them we find the hype called "hyper-competition". In D'Aveni's (1994) idolization the doctrine is based on the idea that such a thing as "sustainable" competitive advantage does not exist. Only "temporary" advantages can be created. Nothing lasts. In a world where sustainable advantages are non-existent, firms (and nations?) know only one recipe for survival and fortune: *disrupting* their own advantages and those of their competitors. In the gospel of "hyper-competition" organizations are constantly identifying and creating new opportunities. The only thing that is sustained is the momentum of building capabilities for speed and surprise. "Punch and counterpunch" tactics have to see to it that, by shifting "the rules of competition, [which] signal strategic intent to dominate, and confuse or overwhelm competitors" (ibid.: 343), competitors' responses are pre-empted, molded or directed to one's own (temporary) advantage. The name of the game is "market disruption" (ibid.: 310–16). Box 2.1 presents D'Aveni's apodictic manifesto.

Box 2.1 Capitalism untamed: the new iconography

Chivalrous age has come to an end. The gentility of tacit collusion and avoiding head-on competition has gone. The days in which it was uncouth to destroy a competitor are gone. The world of strategy has moved to a new view where winners take all and combatants of unequal weight use any tactic available to them.

   The most aggressive firms realize that they are in the midst of a head-to-head, fight-to-the-death, global business war. They are now adopting a new ideology more appropriate to the hyper-competition environment of all-out war.

   The business environment today is as untamed as the Wild West. Entry barriers and deep pockets ride through the sagebrush. It takes a new breed of rugged and fearless competitor to survive: kill or be killed.

Anti-trust laws served to protect the underdog competitor from what was labeled a "predatory" firm. Yet it is this hypercompetitive predatory firm that survives in today's world. Managers must, therefore, reconsider the following strategic frameworks and maxims:

- Commitments tend to make the firm inflexible and predictable. In hypercompetition the flexible, unpredictable player has the advantage over the inflexible, committed opponent.
- Managers need to plan to be opportunistic and flexible because long-term success depends on a series of short-term advantages, the exact nature of which cannot always be seen at the outset.
- Consistent strategies of being a follower or first mover are too static in hypercompetition. Companies shift from being first movers to followers and then back to first movers.
- Even the most persistent entry barriers and strongholds are beginning to fall. In hypercompetition the best barrier to entry by new companies or expansion by existing players is for the company to move aggressively from advantage to advantage.
- Players that have to be treated with care are suppliers and buyers. In hypercompetition the advantage does not go to firms that squeeze dealers and suppliers but to firms that enlist them in the effort to create new advantages.
- During the 1980s American corporations became leaner. Now they must become meaner, adopting a hypercompetitive intent to dominate.

(Paraphrases of quotes from D'Aveni, 1994: 342–55)

It remains unclear, however, whether this portrait of the Rambo-economics of modern capitalism is meant to be an unagonized reappraisal of existing practices or that it is meant to be an (American) idealized design for competitive rearmament. Whether *Realpolitik* or wishful thinking, the message may trigger a chain of self-destroying prophesies. Where capitalists expect that *some* subscribe to the canons of hypercompetition, cooperative agreements will be difficult to maintain. Where *all* decide to follow them, capitalist order comes to a virtual standstill. So does hypercompetition. This is not to say that D'Aveni's cynicism about cooperative agreements in a hypercompetitive world is totally unwarranted. As he argues, "there is room for pacts and treaties in hypercompetition, but these are not an end to competition …; they are, instead, part of the escalation of conflict" (ibid.: 334). Since "hypercompetitors will take advantage of industries with less aggressive players the way wolves attack sheep", and "today's partners…often become tomorrow's competitors", so cooperation should primarily be seen as "an effective part of aggressive hypercompetitive strategies" (ibid.: 338–9) which are apt to:

- *Gang up against other groups*, because this may be the only way to confront larger rivals and alliances with deeper pockets.

- *Limit the domain of competition*, for instance by competing on quality or know-how in exchange for forestalling competition on prices, costs or competition in specific geographic areas.
- *Build resources* from cash to competences that companies do not have in-house.
- *Buy time*, for instance when a weaker competitor cooperates with a stronger one to keep from being swept away or to build up sufficient resources for an attack in due course.
- *Gain access* into a market thus far untried or inaccessible for other reasons.
- *Learn* new competences or get insight into one's rivals' competences and routines.

Whatever the mix of strategic intents, cooperation under the new dynamics of strategic maneuvering "cannot be used to dampen competitive rivalry because the only effective strategy in hypercompetitive environments is one of dynamic, aggressive movement up the escalation ladders" (ibid.: 339).

Skepticism about D'Aveni's talent for separating fact, fantasy and proof stems, apart from the self-destroying potential of his concept of hypercompetition, from more preponderate considerations as well. First, we learn nothing about the internal properties and prerequisites of the players that are invited to join the hypercompetition game. Organizations are black boxes, a *tabula rasa* without memory and without disputes or doubts about a proper assessment of internal strengths and weaknesses and external threats and opportunities. Organizations are hyper-rational, internally undivided and externally perfect lonesome wolves. Second, nothing is said about switching and anticipation costs in this hyper-unstable world of *über*-competition. Path dependences built on past competences and routines do not exist. The competence trap is irrelevant and core rigidities do not count because nothing lasts. Nor is there a competition trap since unitary, rational lonesome wolves have perfect foresight through prompt punch-and-counterpunch responses. Nothing lasts since everything happens *stante pede*. That is, in the *instantaneity* of hypercompetition there are neither anticipation nor feedback costs, for a simple reason: timing drives out time in a world thriving on speed and surprise only.

Subscribers to this kill-or-be-killed scenario live in a world apparently untouched by the lessons learned on the questionability of the under-socialized conception of "economic man" in neo-classical economics and the over-rationalistic conception of "efficient man" in the (admittedly somewhat less unworldly) world of institutional economics. A proper understanding of the problems of past and future dependences and empirical evidence on possible solutions for the dilemmas of exploitation versus exploration have to come from other sources. Two competing approaches can be called upon. One is a *proximate*, the other an *escapist* answer to the odds of the competence and competition trap. To the proximate variety belongs the concept of "flexible specialization" and its subsequent revision and extension under alternative headings such as industrial districts, the new competition, business systems and the embedded firm. Flexible specialization is an alternative formula for industrial modernization that competes with the formula that dictates the *old* discipline, that is, the Chandlerian–Galbraithian canon of mass production. Flexible specialization is (according to Piore and Sabel, 1984: 17) "a strategy of permanent innovation: accommodation to ceaseless change, rather than an effort to control it, this strategy is based on flexible – multi-use – equipment; skilled workers; and the creation, through politics, of an industrial community that restricts the forms of competition to those favoring innovation."

What theories on the worlds of flexible specialization (Piore and Sabel, 1984), industrial districts (Marshall, 1961), the new competition (Best, 1990), business systems (Whitley, 1992) and the embedded firm (Grabherr, 1993) share, in spite of their diversity, is the rehabilitation of the notion of *Wirtschaft und Gemeinschaft*, that is, a sense of "community" as a vehicle for collective action and value appropriation and as a device for overcoming or disciplining the double strategy trap. By bringing the firm back in as a composite actor (rather than as a unitary black box) and realigning firm, industry and patterns of industrial policy in a functional-regional texture of ongoing transactions, the above-mentioned approaches may be called theories of institutional "proximity". This proximity restores what the mainstream in economic theorizing has separated, if not dismissed as irrelevant: the question whether structural entities (webs of *interdependences*) coincide with cultural identities (webs of mutual *understandings*), with a larger capacity for encompassing as opposed to individual rationality – or not. The capacity for encompassing rationality increases when actors operate in clusters of preferential exchange often linked together over the course of decades (Gerlach, 1992: 4). Proximate responses to the strategy trap have in common that they reject the notion of "social atomization" implied by models of perfect competition, where the latter stands for models that conceive economic order as a concurrence of "temporary exchanges of convenience among faceless traders" (Granovetter, 1985).

The entity combined with identity quest is less easy to answer in the *escapist* response to the dilemmas of specialization and competition. To this category belong strategies of cross-national and cross-regional coordination, such as mergers, alliances and other, more informal forms of networking and clustering. Since the latter phenomena represent a more drastic repertory than the proximate response to the dilemmas of the strategy trap – both in absolute and relative terms, such as assets, size, geographical span, technological reshuffles and the reproduction of corporate elites and prerogatives – the analysis of the escapist variety deserves more space.

The escapist itinerary

After two decades of restored belief in the market as a superior recipe for allocating and combining resources for competing uses, the idea of concerted action seems to be recovering its reputation. The reason must be the rediscovery of the deficiencies of the market as a means of coordination. Both intra-regional and cross-national efforts at coordination may serve as an antidote against the specialization or competence trap. But in an internationalizing setting they are arguably *not* an adequate answer to this trap. Due to the troika of liberalization, deregulation and privatization the competition trap, though in design domesticated within its sub-national confines, tends to re-emerge, eventually in a more virulent shape, at the cross-national level. Could this explain the search for new modes of concerted action?

The classical antidote against the competition trap is public and/ or private hierarchy. Experience with the deficiencies of both market and hierarchy must have inspired the rediscovery of a third trajectory: concerted action. The term used to be reserved for the encompassing macro-coordination of public and private preferences and interests. Due to changes in the international political economy, inducing radical changes in the way rival states and rival firms have to manage their dependences, the new recipes for concerted action do not resemble the old. States and firms are indispensable allies, but the substance of indispensability and the codes of coping with them, have changed:

> Firms are competing for world market shares as a means to wealth
> and survival. But whereas the state needs the production for the

world market to be located on its territory, no matter who is organizing it, the firm needs the production for the world market to be
under its ultimate control no matter where it is located ...
   These are conditions that lead to both co-operation and conflict.
There is a complementarity of interest when the state can secure the
location and the firms can establish the control. There is a conflict
when the firm decides that it prefers another location (and can overcome the exit barriers) or when the state seeks to restrict how the
firm exercises its control. (Stopford and Strange, 1991: 211–12)

The antinomy is clear. Yet what remains unclear is *what* precisely firms
and states may want to "control" and, more essentially, what the concept of control exactly means in space and time. Numerous are the
reports on the loss for national states of territorial control over economic activities (Scharpf, 1990; Marks et al., 1996; Streeck, 1996). As a
consequence, some speak of the rise of the "virtual state" (Guéhenno,
1993; Rosecrance, 1996). Equally numerous are the volumes document-
ing the increasing internal and external mobility of firms. Mobility
blurs the boundaries between firms' functional, sectoral and territorial
manifestation. As a consequence some come to speak of the rise of the
"virtual firm". What kind of "concerted action" do we expect when
virtual states meet virtual firms? Virtual governance? What that might
mean becomes clearer when we listen to the advocates of a rejuvenation
of the old practices of concerted action. The novelty this time is that
the advocacy comes from the corporate Olympians themselves – the
European Roundtable of Industrialists.
   The *European Roundtable of Industrialists* is a platform publishing reg-
ularly on social and political-economic issues (it assembles the leading executives of some 40 of Europe's largest companies). Two decades
ago, the Roundtable raised a series of "urgent" European problems and
offered possible remedies for Europe's recovery.

Box 2.2   Europe: how to beat the crisis

Europe has become a high-cost, low-growth economy that is not adapting fast
enough and is therefore losing its competitive advantage to more dynamic
parts of the world. As a result it has too many people out of work. Concerted
action is urgently needed on a wide range of solutions, both short and longer
term. A return to more rapid and sustained economic growth should be the
central target of policy. The single most immediate stimulus to growth would
be to bring the dynamism back into world trade and to stimulate vigorous

action by European industry to penetrate the more open markets. Special interests can no longer hold the global economy to ransom. The second element of growth must be a substantial increase in investment in Europe, which will only materialize when people believe that growth is back on the agenda and that Europe is well placed to win a stronger share of world business. The fundamental issue, if Europe is to return to sustainable growth led by exports and investment, is the competitiveness of European industry.

With respect to competitiveness three factors require urgent attention. First, factor costs are too high: labor, transport, energy, financial and other costs have to be brought down. Plans exist to modernize Europe's infrastructure but there is no sense of urgency to put them into action. Patchworks of national monopolies stand in the way of European efficiency, as though the "single market" did not exist. The single market itself is a vital tool of cost reduction but much still needs to be done to realize its full benefits.

Secondly, there is enormous scope to simplify government and reduce the excessive overhead of bureaucracy: the aim of Europe should be to reduce the degree of control; industry is hampered by cumbersome rules and an increasing burden of employment regulation at both European and national level.

Thirdly, European industry has to improve the quality of products and processes: unless Europe is at the leading edge of innovation and technology, it cannot pay its way in the modern world. Two steps are needed, calling for closer cooperation between government, industry, and the academic world. One is to mobilize Europe's massive scientific resources and put them to work in a more systematic way. The huge cost of technical projects today often exceeds what single companies or even countries can do on their own. The second is to pay closer attention to lifelong education and training.

As regards the role of government and business, the Round Table makes the following observations. Government and industry should try to find a way to work more closely together. Neither can handle the crisis on its own. What government should do is to enable industry to do its job, especially by action leading to the three "supra" goals of lower costs, fewer regulations and higher quality.

Uncertainty is the enemy of investment. Uncertainty is said to be fuelled by exchange rate instability, changing political priorities and unpredictable proposals on trade policy, competition policy, taxation and energy costs. Governments should therefore demonstrate their commitment to consistent economic policies that will generate confidence in Europe as a good place in which to invest. Another task for government is to cut the level of waste which eats away at the economy. Too much output goes through the public sector, too much activity is distorted by state aids and monopolies, too many resources are transferred from the productive parts of society to the unproductive. What is needed to reduce public spending is not public poverty but lean government based on value for money.

Commenting on the role of business, the Round Table sees it as the task of every single company to raise its quality, lower its costs and break into new markets. Governments cannot achieve this, all they can do is create the enabling conditions for stimulating entrepreneurship. The responsibility of industry is to generate business and so to create wealth. Wealth will lead to job creation if the costs are right, the skills are available and the labor markets function properly. While big companies, including the members of the European Round Table, can do much to set the flywheel of the economy moving, it is the small and medium companies which have the greatest potential for job creation.

The Roundtable concludes by formulating a plan for action. To achieve Europe's goals for many years ahead, the continent needs a long-term cooperation between government and industry based on a commitment to common goals. For rebuilding confidence, political leaders are asked to do three things: first, to commit themselves to a "Charter for Industry" setting out a strategic approach to economic recovery and listing specific policy priorities; secondly, to set up a "European Competitiveness Council" representing industry, government and science to advise on and monitor the detailed implementation of the "Charter"; and finally, to put the "Charter" into full effect by means of "practical policy decisions" to rebuild the competitiveness of Europe (ERI, 1993).

Those who remember the "Lisbon agenda" (adopted in 2000 for a ten-year period, on Europe's (renewed) intention to boost its "competitiveness"), the Roundtable's 1993-appeal sounds strikingly familiar. So do the underlying calls for "concerted action". However, how reliable are charters and agreements based on hyper-mobile (rather than hyper-competitive) allies? And what about the scope and duration of the "mandate" that the Roundtable exerts over its members when it comes to solid commitments? An intriguing facet of the Roundtable's assessment of Europe's strengths and weaknesses is the disparity in concreteness between the claims addressed at political leaders and the European Commission *versus* the counter-performance offered in return by the captains of industry themselves. Compared with the requests for firm "political leadership" and clear "public commitments", the specification of the role of industry remains somewhat less firm and clear. The incongruity stems from the contractual logic of capitalist discretion that expects a stronger sense of collective discipline from the *volonté général* than the captains of industry, who see themselves as opportunity-driven *individualists*, are ready to offer in exchange. Such a division of labor may stand in the way of a productive dialogue. For example, the more serious we take the professed delegation of "job creation" to small and medium enterprises, given the prophesized tendency to outsourcing and flexibilization of the big enterprise, the more problematic will become the task of public authorities (and other interested stakeholders) to identify and locate the industrial partners with, or by whom, the proposed "concertation" has to be put into effect.

Rational actors are interested in predictable counterparts. Predictability depends on the nature of the industrial orbit in which companies invite politicians, public officials, unions and others like universities to play their "enabling" role. As long as the non-market players remain insufficiently informed about the responsiveness of the market players, that is, informed beyond the capitalist reassurance that proper conditions will elicit proper entrepreneurial responses, requests for proactive policies are bound to remain a blind date.

European concertation in the formation of industrial strategies takes place in a setting of nested games. European strategies are the result of the interaction of rival states, from within and beyond the European Union (EU), competing for privileged transactions between governments and firms. Government–business transactions are a function of interfirm strategies. The latter, denoting the permanently changing blend of cooperation and rivalry between competitors, suppliers and customers, are governed by the hazards of international competition. National, regional and global industrial strategies, in other words, constitute a multilevel political economy: three distinct, yet interacting, transactional games – played at different levels of interest aggregation with *different time spans of accountability*. Since the protagonists in this multilevel theatre are not symmetrically positioned, neither in terms of their subjective loyalties nor in terms of their objective maneuverability, mutual accountability remains something of an ill-defined flying object. Where strategic priorities and their interactions drift, mutual accountability tends to recede; where accountability recedes, coordination may fail to materialize. Figure 2.1 summarizes the argument.

The specifics of the configuration of maneuverability, accountability and the timing of feedback governs the decision of each of the players as to whether or not to invest in collaborative ventures. Since, in the view defended here, the consistency of (European) industrial-political strategies depends on the substance of *national* strategies – and national strategies, at the end of the day, depend on international *interfirm* strategies – my study proposes to start with inspecting the inner circle of the nested games, that is *corporate* stratagems and tactics (for a similar stance on analytical and empirical priorities, see Cowling and Sugden, 1999). Understanding the micrologic of intra- and interfirm behavior enhances our understanding of the chances of public–private intermediation at higher levels of interest aggregation against wider time spans of accountability. Inversely stated: the farther our assumptions are removed from the empirical texture of intra- and interfirm strategies and tactics, the less likely it

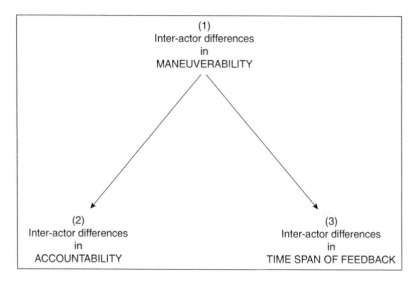

Figure 2.1 Maneuverability and the time span of accountability

is that public *and* private objectives, however rationally conceived, will have the impact that its subscribers profess to be aiming at. Let's look from this perspective at the theory and practice of coordination in European industrial policy-making.

The rhetoric of "common" markets

The discussion on the revitalization of the European economy is embedded in a broader discourse: the reconstitution of institutional arrangements, known under labels such as deregulation, privatization and the harmonization of competitive conditions. The reappraisal and repositioning of institutions mean different things to different stakeholders (Crouch and Marquand, 1990). To some, the exercise amounts to removing the barriers to trade within the EU, harmonizing standards and opening up public procurement programs to European competition. To others, more ambitiously, the challenge should rather be the construction of a coherent European entity able to defend its economic sovereignty vis-à-vis foreign economic powers. Both interpretations may turn out to be mutually supportive insofar as the objective of removing technical, administrative and legal obstacles should be seen as a necessary precondition for the latter ambition of strengthening the sense of European direction and cohesion by promoting the coordination of public policies and private strategies.

Both interpretations prove to be counterproductive in that networks of European–Asian–American interfirm linkages open up the possibility that non-European allies of Europe-based multinationals will benefit as much as the Europeans are said to gain from the leveling of the barriers to trade inside the EU. In the years that immediately preceded the professed 1992 fulfillment ("completion") of the internal market, the available statistics show how European multinational firms met one another in numerous EU-sponsored collaborative R&D programs while cooperating, at the same time, in strategic alliances with non-European multinationals in various sectors: from ICT (Wassenberg, 1991) to a broader array of "core technologies" in which, for instance, Van Tulder and Junne (1988: 233) find a predominance of EU–USA (59 percent) and EU–Japan (23 percent) strategic partnerships, clearly outnumbering the total of *intra*-EU collaborative agreements (18 percent). Box 2.2 and Table 2.1 illustrate how investment inflows and outflows *across* EU-borders – linking European with non-European firms – obtained impetus already as early as the period in which the European Roundtable of Industrialists launched its wake-up call.

Box 2.3   Capital mobility

Direct foreign investments by Asian firms into the EU increased from $100 million in the period 1989–92 to $800 million in the years 1992–94 (*Financial Times*, February 28, 1997). For the period 1992–94 a total of 664 American and Japanese companies, ranging from headquarters, production plants and R&D centers to distribution and call centers, settled in Europe (Buck Consultants International, 1995). Sachwald (1993) concludes from reports on competition policy in the EU that the propensity to cooperate between European and *non*-European firms – through mergers, acquisitions and majority participations – is significantly higher, and has grown ever more rapidly, than their *intra*-European and national equivalents.

Table 2.1   Propensity to industrial interfirm cooperation* in the European Union (1983–90)

Reach	1984	1986	1988	1990	1984– 90
National	0.31	0.23	0.21	0.17	0.21
Intra-EU	0.31	0.38	0.21	0.27	0.25
Trans-EU	1.04	0.90	0.48	0.48	0.70

* Defined as the ratio of the number of companies to the number of mergers, acquisitions and majority participations.
Note: Figures for 1984–90 are averages.
Source: Sachwald (1993: 33).

A couple of years onwards the UNCTAD *World Investment Report 1996* finds for Western Europe that majority shares in cross-border sales of firms amount to $50 billion and purchases to $66 billion in 1995. Though much of the merger and acquisition (M&A) "boom" mentioned in the UNCTAD report can be accounted for by intra-EU deals, a rapidly growing share is due to cross-border M&A operations *across* the Atlantic by leading EU and US firms. The highest cross-border activity was observed in energy distribution, telecommunications, pharmaceutical and financial services. Corporations headquartered in the USA, Germany, the UK, Japan and France accounted for two-thirds of the total global of $271 billion of the outflow and $203 billion of the inflow of foreign direct investment in 1995. The bulk of these activities consisted of cross-regional intra-firm transactions among affiliates of US, Japan and EU-based transnational companies. Intra-firm transactions from US parent companies to EU-located US affiliates amounted to up to 25 percent of US–EU trade.

Table 2.2 shows the cross-border inflows and outflows between the states leading the list.

Table 2.2 Foreign direct investment flows, developed countries, 1995 ($ billion)

Country	1994 inflows	1995 inflows	1994 outflows	1995 outflows
France	17.1	20.1	22.8	17.6
Germany	3.0	9.0	14.7	35.3
Japan	0.9	0.04	18.5	21.3
United Kingdom	10.1	29.9	25.3	37.8
United States	49.8	60.2	45.6	95.5
Total	**132.8**	**203.2**	**230.0**	**317.8**

Source: UNCTAD (1996).

Around this time the 100 largest transnational corporations (excluding banking and financial institutions) had roughly $1.4 trillion worth of assets abroad, accounting for around one-third of global foreign direct investment stock. Before the turn of the century, US-based transnationals considered Europe as the most important future investment location, especially in high technology and consumer goods. Conversely, EU-based transnationals saw the USA as its most appropriate location, whereas Japanese transnationals viewed Asia as the most promising location (their "Atlantic" colleagues would follow suit).

Walter (1994) provides an overview of the participation of US firms in four EU collaborative R&D programs (see Table 2.3). It is worth noting that these very programs – ranging from information technology to telecommunications and advanced consumer electronics – were conceived as a "strategic EU response" to the challenges posed by their US rivals.

Table 2.3   Participation by (European affiliates of) US companies in collaborative R&D programs of the EU, 1984–89

ESPRIT I & II	RACE	BRITE	EUREKA
ITT	ITT	ITT	ITT
IBM	IBM	Donnelly	Captain Video
At&T	AT&T	Ford	LTV
Digital	Hewlett Packard	Rockwell	Covia
Hewlett Packard	Texas	Lee	
Sybase	Instruments	Cooper	
Swift SC	GTE		
Moog Controls	DHL		
3M	DuPont		
DuPont	Ford		
Dow Chemicals			
Honeywell			
Artificial Intelligence			
Babcock & Wilcox			
Cambridge Consultants			
Intersys Graphic			
Peat Marwick McLintock			

Source: Based on Walter (1994).

Opinions diverge on the short- and long-term effects of these company-
led cross-border movements. Do foreign transplants and alliances erode
the industrial integrity and strategic autonomy of the host "community",
ultimately affecting its sovereignty in broader terms; or, to the contrary,
is it a stimulus for corporate and industrial renewal, and thus the only
appropriate response to the "imperatives" of international competition
and technology? Some relate the preference of EU multinationals for non-
European partnerships to the competitive *dis*advantages of "proximity":

> the threshold for European companies to enter a cooperative agree-
> ment [with fellow Europeans] may just be somewhat higher than for
> American or Japanese companies. This may be one of the reasons
> why European companies reach more agreements with American or
> Japanese partners than with other European firms. Negotiations with
> an American or Japanese prospective partner may be more straight-
> forward and less filled with mutual mistrust than...with European
> prospective partners. Negotiations between European firms can also
> be more difficult because their markets may overlap to a larger extent.

As a result competition may dominate in their relationship leaving little room for cooperation. (Van Tulder and Junne, 1988: 221)

Yet, the corporate restructuring of European firms (see Ruigrok et al., 1999) also includes intra-EU alliances. So the question remains: what are the causes and consequences of the enduring *coexistence* of Euro-chauvinist prayers and non-Euro centered practices? Some are skeptical about the possible consequences, for instance for the industrial-technological "sovereignty" of the European IT industry:

> the accelerating pace of technological change in the IT industry, and the major advances being made by Japanese and American competitors in computers, semi-conductors and fibre-optics, puts into question the ability of a program such as Esprit [the European Strategic Program for Research in Information Technology] to build and maintain an independent European technology base. R&D partnerships with world leaders and access to global markets will continue to exercise a counter-weight to a European-oriented alliance strategy for many firms in the IT industry. (Mytelka and Delapierre, 1987: 251)

UNCTAD (1996), admitting the imponderables of the question due to the interaction effects of trade, investment, infrastructure and national–regional particularities, prefers, predictably as a multi-governmental agency, a "neutral" stance and observes the tendency towards an increasingly "trans-national *intra*-corporate orchestration of investment flows". Concerning the impact of, for example, Japanese transplants located in the USA or the EU, some point to the fact that such transplants add R&D facilities, which show the intent to produce products from design to final assembly. Even the affiliated supplier firms move to establish R&D units capable of developing an infrastructure that provides the innovations needed for a dynamic industry (Kenney and Florida, 1993). Others doubt or dispute the intent of the transnationals to build fuller integrated production systems abroad and expect, instead, that transplants will function as branch plants, importing advanced parts designed and developed in the parent country. Japanese firms, standing in a tradition of long-term cooperative relations with suppliers and financiers (Gerlach, 1992), will see little incentive to risk disrupting their domestic networks by shifting core and auxiliary facilities from Japan to the USA. Rather, they will transfer just enough to gain access to the consumer market and the advantages of lower labor costs (hiring non-unionized and less-militant workers only, as for instance is seen in the United Kingdom since the Thatcher governments). As a consequence, the most sophisticated products and production technologies give:

> an enormous competitive advantage in terms of cost, lead time and quality [and] are not being built in-house by the transplants assemblers, nor sourced from outside suppliers in the United States. They are being designed and largely manufactured in Japan in collaborative relationships…The transplants are performing only assembly and stamping [operations]. (Howes, 1993, quoted in Perruci, 1994: 164)

The fear of "hollowing out" haunts Europe as well. As we will see later, the resulting disputes produce a moving mix of intra-union campaigning and extra-union scapegoating. Whatever the difference in their origins, at the end of the day both reflexes merge in a common creed: a strong belief in the "efficiency" of ever increasing economies of scale justifying the "necessity" of further industrial-financial concentration in Europe.

Nested games, played on a non-level playing field, ask for a reappraisal of "European" industrial-economic games in terms of bargaining power. Non-level playing fields arise from the different degrees of freedom of maneuvering for states, trade unions and firms. This is not to say that there are no limits – in the sense of diminishing returns – to the "unreserved" exploitation by firms of the bounds of national and European public powers. The limits reveal themselves in a practice that may be called "strategic dualism". On the one hand, as shown in the grammar of the European Roundtable, firms call for "urgency" in Europe-centered responses to the threats of international competition. On the other hand, as illustrated by the data on cross-regional partner-switches, firms multiply and intensify their pre-emptive efforts in weaving webs of alliances with *non*-European partners.

Repeated demonstrations of the credibility of this *exit* scenario obviously add to the efficacy of the *voice* scenario of multinational firms. In a setting of strategic dualism the *rhetorical* uses of the calls for "concerted action" may be as profitable – as a "perfect fake" – as the *material* uses of asymmetric resource interdependences. The *complementarity* of the two may help to explain what, based on the premises of "rational choice", will likely be dismissed as irrational, or at least as inconsistent behavior. However, from the premises of strategic choice in a nested games perspective, allowing for maneuvering in multiple arenas *at the same time*, the "impurity" and "inefficiency" of the dual use of intra-European mobilization combined with extra-European mobility is a specimen of rational, while demonstrably *effective*, behavior: *whenever contending interests prove too contradictory to handle within a national or regional community of interests, they tend to be lifted out into a web of global alliances, eventually to be used as a leverage for counterbalancing, or escaping from, divides in the national and/or regional divisions of this mosaic of power.*

The paradox in a nutshell is that, apart from providing temporary (precompetitive) exemptions from the strictures of competition law, the access to communitarian funds is used to enter pre-emptive alliances with *extra*-European partners in order to continue or intensify the battle with *intra*-European rivals with other means. The self-defeating logic of this sort of game may be that, however rational from a micro-rational standpoint, winning the battle inside the EU theater may be losing the war at the "Triad [EU–USA–Asia] power" level (Ohmae, 1985). (See Chapters 6 and 7 for more about this specimen of the rationale (in my grammar) of arena and agenda *substitution*.)

Some conclusions

The issue of capitalist discipline seems to be back on the agenda. After more than two decades of love songs about the "market" as a sufficiently efficient device for the organization of economic life, the "mixed market" is recovering a bit from its loss of grace. The reason behind this cursory, if not reluctant, rehabilitation may be the discovery that fighting market "imperfections" at the national level may promote their unsolicited resurgence in a wider, cross-national setting. Long before Henry Paulson's request "to save the free market from itself", Umberto Agnelli, former president of auto producer Fiat and a prominent member of the European Roundtable of Industrialists, stated:

> Europe needs planning capacities. The invisible hand of the market is not enough: we need an extra something (in the form of) major development projects. [European multinationals] have found it easier to reach understandings with American or Japanese companies... They have rarely forged alliances with other Europeans. The result is that a "European industry" does not yet exist. (Agnelli, 1992)

The aim of this study is to find out what the orchestration of conflict and accommodation among rival states and rival firms may look like in a modern form. The canonical response to market failure is the substitution of some form of administered allocation of resources and partners for uncoordinated rivalry. However, subsequent experience with the "imperfections" of hierarchical control and command – especially in an internationalizing and technology-driven world – must have inspired the rediscovery of the merits of mixed arrangements. "Mixed" forms of coordination and governance arise "when there are coordination problems markets in their pure form cannot solve and the pace of change – the rate at which new states of the world are being created – outpaces the adaptive capacities of hierarchies" (Sabel, 1993: 75).

The generic term that has become vogue for these mixed arrangements is "concerted action", that is, arrangements for the orchestration of public and private interests allegedly situated "halfway" between markets and hierarchies. According to academic convention "pure" markets are devices for coordinating interests and preferences among *equals*. In theory *prices* inform us about costs and preferences. Exchanges between competitors, suppliers and customers are based on the *unrestricted* freedom to change counterparts and preferences. In practice, however, there are numerous impediments that entail deviations from the ideals of perfect maneuverability and instantaneous, costless and symmetric information. Imperfections of this kind may be repaired by substituting (public or private) hierarchy for market exchanges. In the same academic idiom "pure" hierarchy stands for devices for the coordination of interests and preferences among *unequals*. In theory *authority* is supposed to inform us about competencies and compliance. Exchanges between superiors and inferiors are based on the *restriction* of freedom to change counterparts and preferences. In practice, again, there are numerous deviations that bring with them contestable competencies and incomplete compliance. The imperfections of hierarchy may be remediated by substituting (public or private) rivalry for hierarchy.

Pure markets and hierarchies do not exist, except in axiomatic fantasy and popular rhetorics. Below the surface there is a lot of hierarchic peddling inside markets, whilst a closer look inside these hierarchies reveals the omnipresence of internal rivalries and coalition formation that one conventionally expects to meet in the market place. The two come and go like high and low tide: the search for remediating market failure leads back to regulatory control (Evans, 1995) just as the search for correcting regulatory failure leads back to the market. Moreover, once created, markets tend to sort out a stratification of players that possess more or less power; and once stratified it is difficult to say where the level playing field ends and the reign of power begins. Where market and hierarchy start to change hands, hybrid forms of orchestration emerge. In theory a "pure" federation of organizations is an assembly of *unequal equals*. In "federations", as opposed to markets and hierarchies, *trust*, instead of prices or authority, is supposed to inform us about coordination and compliance (Bradach and Eccles, 1989; Gulati, 1995; Gulati and Singh, 1998). According to the mainstream literature trust is considered to serve as an antidote against opportunism and other specimens of "rational egoism", such as adverse selection (Balakrishnan and Koza, 1993) and moral hazard (Barney, 1997).

In passing, in the context of the brief excursion into the recent history of the organization of "organized capitalism" in this chapter, it should be noted that it would be a mistake to suggest that the mixed form, halfway market and hierarchy is something recent. It is in fact long standing but has managed to appear, both under stable and recurrent crisis conditions, as a national pact between public and private *hierarchies* – acting as an oligarchic-oligopolist clearing house for the (re)consolidation of the status quo. When, however, unruliness becomes the rule, the mixed form becomes a format rather than a form – not identifiable with a neatly defined set of players, accountabilities and playing fields. It becomes a format for rival firms and rival states to create and appropriate value from *changing combinations of resources and partners*. The mixed form, in short, mutates from an institutional form to a vehicle for exploiting the negotiated order – even if, more and more, this happens without reinvesting the rents of coordination and compliance in the reproduction of that order. The aversion to reinvest the spoils stems from the strategy traps outlined in Chapter 1 – for rival states and rival firms alike. Whenever states and firms are unable to control the collateral hazards arising from their pre-emptive reflexes (the "shadows of the future") or path dependences (the "shadows of the past") they will prefer – as a rule – to shift their concerns about the tensions between value-*creation* and value-*appropriation* to others. Among the tasks of this study is the identification of the determinants of the room for sharing – and shifting the collateral hazards stemming from these tensions, and to trace its consequences for the self-discipline of capitalism. Reduced to the gist, as we will argue and illustrate in the following chapters, the room for sharing – and shifting collateral hazards has to do with the distribution of negotiating power in social systems. Negotiating power, as I will demonstrate below, is the single most important predictor of the way rival firms and rival states search for and select their way out from the contradictions between *joint* value-creation and *disjoint* value-appropriation. In that sense I sympathize with the dictum that "(a)ny theory of negotiation worth its salt needs to address the tension between creating and claiming value" (Raiffa et al., 2002: 86). Intercorporate games and the twists of capitalist discipline are based upon mutations in the external room and internal capacity of organizations for redressing these tensions.

Before delving deeper into the substance and the mechanisms of these mutations we must demarcate, more precisely, our own position in what I designated in Chapter 1 as the Achilles heel of economic order: the *clash of rationalities*. Much of present day analytical interpretations of the organization of economic life rest, implicitly or explicitly, on specific premises about the "rationality" of the processes of search – and selection that are presumed to lead to specific forms of organizational choice and coordination in modern capitalism. By summarily contrasting the strengths and flaws of these interpretations we arrive at a better position to demonstrate the potential merits of another, more *pragmatically* inspired view, the essence of which may be stated in three premises: "rationality" is an *interactive* affair; economic "order" appears to be a *negotiated* order; and negotiated order can best be seen if we look at it as a multilevel theatre, that is as a set of *nested* games.

3
The Masks of Rationality

Corporate rationality: the self as looking glass

In Chapter 1 I outlined the issue of this study as concerning the twists of order and disorder in the organization of economic life. In Chapter 2 I presented a retrospective on the *academic* reception during the last quarter of the past century of the organization of "modern" capitalism. We have also learned how *business leaders*, themselves assembled in the European Roundtable of Industrialists, related the deficiencies in "European" productivity and competitiveness to a lack of "concerted responses" to political and socio-economic "uncertainties". Inspired by the surge of corporate cross-border movements, documented in Chapter 2, I will suggest an alternative interpretation of the links between micro-choices, meso-arrangements and macro-order.

When industrialists assert that "uncertainty is the enemy of investment" they do not refer to the macro stochastic properties of the world in general. What they have in mind, instead, is primarily the uncertainty that follows from the behavior of their concrete *counterparts*, such as competitors, customers, suppliers, banks and others like fiscal and regulatory authorities. *Strategic* uncertainty relates to the quality of unpredictability that is associated with the interdependence of choices by organizations that, for the realization of their own preferences and interests, depend on what others do or choose not to do. In this sense it is not uncertainty as a generalized condition – the "state-of-the-world" – but the *distribution* of uncertainty that counts in situations of interdependent choice. When others are more dependent on a specific organization than the latter is on them, uncertainty can be the *stimulus* (rather than the enemy) of investment. Then, but only then, does the dictum hold that "impredictability is power" (Hirschman, 1970: 50). In all other situations some form of coordination is required to fight the uncertainties of interdependent choice. The preferred sort of coordination varies with the kind of interdependence organizations face, for instance technological, commercial or social contingencies. So next to the distribution of uncertainty, coordination varies according to the *substance* of uncertainty. The responses to the interdependence of choice range from the internalization of external dependences (via the acquisition or encapsulation of competitors, suppliers and buyers) to the externalization of internal dependences when activities are spun-off to the environment and organizations concentrate on their so-called "core" businesses – to the effect of making others dependent on their (self-professed) distinct competencies. In-between internalization and externalization we find a number of less radical alternatives. They are less radical in several respects: the *extent* that partners have a say in each other's choices; the *spectrum* of activities in which partners coordinate their choices; the intended *duration* of the coordination; the *explicitness* of protocols for conflict mediation; the *exclusivity* of the coordination; and the *irreversibility* of collaborative agreements. Examples of tight-knit contractual forms include joint ventures, joint research and development agreements, minority participations, and consortia. More informal, loose-knit forms are collaborations between customers and suppliers, the integration of systems, licensee agreements, cartels and tacit tuning.

Collaborative agreements in information technology, chemicals, new materials, biotechnology, autos and aircraft – negligible before the mid-1970s – have experienced a spectacular spurt since the last quarter of the past century (be it with cyclical ups and downs – see e.g. Hagedoorn, 1993, for the period 1970–93 and Roijakkers and Hagedoorn, 2006, for more recent statistics).

Several rationales for this sort of "strategic alliance" can be distilled from the press releases and annual reports that companies publish themselves (Hagedoorn and Schakenraad, 1990: 13; Gulati and Singh, 1998: 794). Recast in terms of Thompson's (1967) classification of different sorts of interdependence (originally designed in an intra-organizational context, but applicable for interorganizational settings as well), three rationales can be distinguished:

1. *Reciprocal* interdependence, related to (fundamental and applied) R&D, in which collaboration aims at the *reduction and spread of risks and costs*. Additional motives may be tacit learning, synergy effects and keeping up with the evolution of complementary and cross-industry technologies.

2. *Sequential* interdependence, related to the *time lags between exploration and exploitation*. These include interest in the (protected, shielded, tacit) commercial and/or technological skills of a partner, as a way to omit R&D costs or to shorten the time lag between invention and market introduction. The efforts to *slow down* the life cycle of a specific product–market combination may also belong to this category.
3. *Common pool* interdependence, related to *market and technology access*, for instance for the sake of monitoring emerging technologies, internationalization trends and the ease of entering foreign markets.

Harrigan (1988) conducted a survey from joint ventures to less tight-knit forms of cooperation between companies in a cross-sample of all industries in the United States from before 1975 until 1984–86. This survey concludes that the tendency towards the formation of alliances can be reduced to two sets of variables: customer profiles and competitor characteristics. Interaction between the two sets of attributes are said to explain the content and form (focus, duration and residual partners' autonomy) of "effective cooperation strategies". For the demand-side, the bigger the sophistication and negotiating power of customers and the stronger the standardization of markets, the stronger the tendency towards intensive but flexible partnerships. For the supply-side, flexible alliances emerge when intense mutual rivalry coincides with highly specialized asset configurations (mostly intellectual capital) and a high degree of technological innovation and a high capital-to-labor ratio (ibid.: 145–56).

What about the risks of "collaborative failure"? Some argue that failure can be avoided if there exists "complete clarity about goals and strategies of the collaboration and about the relation between the parties involved, particularly the people involved" (Van der Geest, 1989: 1173). Or, alternatively, in case of the public/private collaborative ventures in industrial policy-making we came across in Chapter 2, close and stable forms of concerted action can be expected where "the causal world is well understood … decisions have predictable consequences, and … it is easy to know who has competence and expertise" (Olsen, 1981: 510–11). Are these conditions satisfied in a world wherein rival firms and rival states claim flexibility for themselves while expecting fixed commitments from their counterparts?

It is instructive to confront the *rationale* of the claims of flexibility-*cum*-predictability with (what is usually called) the "rationality" of strategic alliances that we come across in the literature. Porter (1980; 1986), Imai and Itami (1984), Kreiken (1986: 289), Thorelli (1986), Morris and Hergert (1987), Van Tulder and Junne (1988: 244), Harrigan (1988), Jarillo (1988), Jorde and

Teece (1989), Ohmae (1989), Borys and Jennison (1989), Hamel et al. (1989), Van der Zwan (1989), Bowersox (1990), Harrigan and Newman (1990), Hagedoorn and Schakenraad (1990; 1993), Gerlach (1992), Sachwald (1993) and Nooteboom (1999) all relate the formation of alliances to:

- changes in strategic positions that firms cannot achieve on their own;
- technological innovations that lie beyond the reach of individual firms;
- revitalization efforts in mature and new take-offs in emerging industries;
- the shortening of the life cycle of products and processes and the acceleration from research and development to commercialization;
- deregulation and privatization;
- the blurring of territorial and geo-political boundaries;
- the blurring of functional (technological, administrative and organizational) boundaries between industries and sectors;
- the integration of regional markets.

The available statistics suggest that specific (combinations of) factors may be more prominent in the early stages of the evolution of an industry than in later phases. Others point to the salience of differences that originate from the distinction between early adopters (firms, industries, nations) versus late followers (Sorge and Maurice, 1993; Hagedoorn, 1993; Nelson, 1995).

Furthermore, statistical patterns vary with the extent of concentration of industries (Dunning, 1993). Table 3.1 illustrates the spectacular growth of the number of collaborative agreements during the last decades of the past century. It shows how technological complementarity and the reduction of the time lag between innovation and commercialization have become more important over time.

Comparing 1970–79, 1980–84 and 1985–89, the overview suggests that rationales like the reduction of costs/risks, increasing the financial scope, pooling fundamental R&D efforts, accessing new markets and monitoring new technology/market entries hardly gained in importance. Part of this unexpected result disappears when we focus on technology-specific contrasts within and across industries. Technological complementarity appears to be particularly prominent in medical technology, aviation and energy production. On the other hand, market access and market structure seem to be important rationales for collaboration in all industries.

Table 3.1   Strategic alliances compared, 1970–89

Number and motives	1970–79	1980–84	1985–89	Total
Number of alliances	804	1,552	2,630	4,986
High costs/risks	7%	6%	7%	7%
Lack of financial resources	2%	4%	4%	4%
Technological complementarity	14%	27%	34%	29%
Reduction innovation time span	14%	21%	31%	25%
Basic R&D	2%	4%	5%	4%
Market access/structure	33%	34%	31%	32%
Monitoring technology/ market entry	11%	12%	11%	11%

Source: Hagendoorn and Schakenraad (1990: 15).

Summing up the spectrum of self-reported rationales for interfirm cooperation, the following portrait emerges. *Market*-driven agreements prevail in automotives, chemicals, consumer electronics and nutrition; the same holds, be it to a lesser degree, for computers and micro-electronics. *Technology*-driven collaboration, on the other hand, is observed primarily in biotechnology, computer software and aviation/defense (Hagedoorn and Schakenraad, 1990: 18).

Motives for collaboration provide information about essential ingredients of a model of strategic choice: they inform about the *acclaimed* rationality of collaborative action among firms. However, what lacks in this portrait of the "looking-glass self" is at least as important as self-declared motives: firms must have the room and the capacity to convert their ambitions into industrial and corporate realities. For as long and as far as the first condition – the self-reported *need* for concerted action – does not imply or guarantee that the other two conditions – the *room* and *capacity* for concerted action – are also satisfied, we still miss an inclusive, "all round" theory for explaining the factual incidence and variability of cooperative ventures. For arriving at such a theory, two clarifications are in order.

First, it is imperative to be more parsimonious about the *need* for strategic choice and coordination. This is done by reducing the above-listed, non-refutable proliferation of alleged collaborative motives to a narrower set of basic *push* factors that prompt the urge for collaborative action.

As a proxy for the elementary need-to-choose I take the subjectively felt threat of the strategy trap, that is a shared concern about the pending "tragedy of overgrazing" in mature industries that are struggling with excess capacity, price erosion and takeover fights versus its opposite of a potential "tragedy of undergrazing" in emerging industries that are looking for indispensable partners for a successful breakthrough.

Second, it is imperative to determine the *room* and *capacity* for strategic choice and coordination by identifying a shortlist of *pull* factors that enable the search for collaborative action. As a proxy for the latter I take the objectively demonstrated *bargaining power* of the respective players, explaining the robustness of mutual commitments, the perceived equivalence in the allocation of contractual hazards, and other essential features of the way competing interests respond to the subjectively felt need-to-choose. The following section provides an, admittedly rudimentary, overview of a number of disciplines – from behavioral to institutional economics and organization sociology – that profess to inform us about the need, room and capacity for strategic choice and the coordination of economic life.

Theories of choice and coordination: a broken mirror

Two obstacles complicate the intended clearance. First there is the problem of academic fragmentation. The study of corporate conduct and structure is dispersed across several divisions of sub-disciplines that work from completely different premises on agents and agency. Assumptions on *agents* refer to models of organizational choice: what makes organizations search and settle for a particular strategic *trajectory*? Assumptions on *agency*, on the other hand, relate to generative principles, that is models of organizational *causation*: what makes organizations find themselves on a particular *trajectory*? Models are academic constructs, indispensable for the simplification of reality. Model specifications reduce the complexity of social reality by singling out specific variables and their relationships, deliberately leaving out other variables and conditions, in order to explain the "essence" of the phenomenon at hand. Problems arise when models turn imperceptibly into forms of "cognitive capture", that is fail to recognize the declining *empirical* utility of analytical simplifications and what should be done to repair the *explanatory* limits of the selected model and its subsidiary specifications.

The latter leads to a second obstacle. What seems to have been abandoned or just faded away, foremost in the applied versions of social science (say "strategic management" manuals), is the kind of intellectual curiosity that wants to know how micro-strategies feed meso-games and how these games tally up into different sorts of *meta-order* – the "discipline of discipline" – and how, inversely, meta-order feeds back on meso-games and micro-stratagems. To anticipate the conclusion of this multidisciplinary excursus: each of the theoretical models reviewed in this section has its distinctive strengths in "framing" specific parts of the issues of strategic choice and the coordination of economic life, but none of them covers the complete picture of the links between the respective "frames", that is the multilevel, multistage and recursive dynamics – from micro-choices to macro-order and back.

Consider first the problem of academic fragmentation. On the one hand we come across approaches that treat corporate behavior as a matter of purposeful strategic choice, inspired by (ultimately) a unique sort of rationality, e.g. the restless drive for efficiency, which is inspired by the drive for (ultimately) profit maximization. The only limits to maximizing behavior are the cognitive limits to rationality. Internal and external monitoring and metering problems make for imperfect responses to environmental threats and opportunities. An example is the so-called transaction-cost approach in organizational micro-economics (e.g. Williamson, 1975). Another, somewhat older branch within the family of organizational economics, starting from a similar, voluntaristic ("free will") notion of strategic choice, be it constrained by the informational limits of rationality, is the behavioral theory of the firm (e.g. Cyert and March, 1963; Thompson, 1967). In the latter, the assumption of monorationality embodied in the firm as a unitary actor is replaced by more complex details on organizational decision-making. Satisficing (rather than maximizing) and problem-driven search (rather than ex ante rationality) are substituted for maximizing and metering, and dissenting preferences embodied in variable intra-organizational coalitions are substituted for consensual corporate targets and the assumption of unitary command-and-control. In this train of thought, the internal determinants of biases in the mobilization of organizational resources arouse more intellectual curiosity than the rational-choice approach wants to acknowledge. The explanation of the *effectuation* of strategic choice takes precedence over postulating the *efficiency* of organizational choice.

Combining the behavioral and transaction-costs approaches on the basis of their views on "choice" (though admitting for more subtle mixes of unitary versus pluralistic rationality than is shown in our briefing above), the two traditional views may be classified as *Habitus* models. They can be clearly contrasted with *Habitat* models (see Table 3.2 for an approximate classification). In the latter it is the (structural or institutional) *environment* that must carry the burden of causality in explaining corporate behavior and organizational evolution. Habitat approaches range from neo-classical industrial economics, explaining organizational strategy and boundary choice from competitive pressures combined with market structures (e.g. Schenk, 1997; De Jong, 1992), to the business-historical and evolutionary branches of institutional economics (e.g. Chandler, 1977; Nelson and Winter, 1982). The latter explain corporate dynamics from a broader set of environmental pressures and institutional responses than from the structure of competition only. What differentiates "industrial" from "institutional" economists is the allowance for a narrower, respectively broader, set of determinants of corporate performance, that is, for a possibly wider spectrum of rationalities that ultimately decide about organizational search and institutional survival. Again, more subtle mixes or hybrids exist among and between the two (industrial vs institutional) approaches than is suggested above. Besides, we may find a number of authors that feel more or less at ease in or between either of the two divisions of "agency". What complicates this in-between approach, however, is that agency versus agent theories do not subscribe to the same or similar agenda of the kind of phenomena they claim to explain (cf. Groenewegen, 1996). Some attempt to elucidate organizational moves and motives at the micro-level. Others aim at the explanation of meso-movements and the evolutionary momentum at the macro-level of institutional and regulatory regimes. Though authors that sympathize with a "pluralist" stance (cf. Groenewegen and Vromen, 1996) provide useful entries for level-specific parts of this analytical puzzle, they fail to deliver a comprehensive explanation of the processes of institutionalization and deinstitutionalization, that is the *full cycle* of the cross-level repercussions of lower-level choices and higher-level arrangements. What I want to make clear at this point is that there does not seem to be available a coherent and clearly demarcated body of theorizing and research that elucidates how Habitat imperatives impinge, in a selective fashion, on Habitus choices and, inversely, how Habitus particularities accumulate, again in a selective way, into Habitat-like compulsions. What the two modes – Habitus versus Habitat – may learn from one another is how some players in the political economy are *better positioned to select and orchestrate the conditions that imperatively govern the strategic choice of others*; and why

Table 3.2 Theories of choice and coordination: the broken mirror

		Agency	
		Habitus models	**Habitat models**
		Efficient choice	*Market imperatives*
Agents	**Unitary rationality**	Firms "economize" on transactions	Structure of competition "determines" strategic choice
		Effective choice	*Evolutionary imperatives*
	Pluralistic rationality	Dominant coalitions "search" and "satisfice"	Environment "selects" survival of fittest choice

and when the resulting *external* order at the macro-level *(re)conditions the maneuverability of some or all of the players* – leaving aside, for now, the issue of the players' *internal* capacities for strategic choice.

With this juxtaposition of voluntarist (Habitus) versus determinist (Habitat) theories of the organization of economic life, we have landed in the middle of the level-of-analysis dispute. In order to bridge the gap between the two divisions of "agency", and at the same time find a realistic compromise between the methodological rigor of "unitary rationality" and the empirical realism of "pluralist rationality" assumptions, we have to look for a hybrid, that is a paradigm that may restore the "broken mirror". Elements for bridging the respective levels of analysis may come from a more precise specification of the explanatory reach of agent-"sensitive" versus agent-"insensitive" explanations of institutions and institutionalization (cf. Hodgson, 2006: 16–7). Such a specification may start from economic-sociological theories of embeddedness (Granovetter, 1985). Embeddedness provides a useful starting point because attention is paid to the issue of interorganizational dependence, the characteristics and consequences of loose versus tight coupling (Gilsing and Nooteboom, 2005), the role of power and the codes of interorganizational reciprocity associated with loose-knit versus tight-knit networks. Theories of embeddedness sensitize for the "inner circles" of political economic order, such as: the existence of affiliate ties which create zones of economic life intermediate between anonymous markets and vertically integrated firms; long-term relationships, relying on diffuse sets of obligations extending over time; and "symbolic signification" infusing "intercorporate relationships with symbolic importance, even in the absence of formal, legal arrangements or contracts" (Gerlach, 1992: 4).

A serious setback, however, as we will find out later, is that researchers working in this mode appear to be more interested in the embeddedness – of choice, as opposed to the practicalities of the *uses* – of embeddedness. In that sense they tend to subscribe to the agent-"insensitive" legacy of institutionalist theory: they fail to identify how, when and why organizations *differ* in their responses to the *same* opportunities and constraints "imposed" by institutional embeddedness. They therewith lose sight of the privileged role of specific "agents" in the orchestration of corporate games.

A second setback is the "horizontal" bias in the extant interpretations of embeddedness: the concept usually refers to the (density, number, strength, etc.) of the links between organizations. What tends to disappear from this "flat" representation of the world is a third dimension: the stratification of organizations in a world wherein higher-level institutional arrangements condition lower-level organizational responses, and lower-level responses recondition higher-level orderings. Therefore I prefer to speak of the "nestedness" – and the selective *uses* of nestedness or *orchestration* – instead of the "organization" and "embeddedness" of organizational behavior.

For remediating these passive and horizontal biases and, simultaneously, addressing the disputes about unitary versus pluralist rationality – *ideally*: maintain the rigor of axiomatics without sacrificing the realism of both intra- and interorganizational stratagems – game theory might be an attractive serum. The attraction lies in its definitional attributes: "the essence of the 'game' is that it involves decision-makers with goals and objectives *whose fates are intertwined*. They have some control, but the control is partial. Each group of individuals faces a *cross-purposes* optimization problem" (Shubik, 1967: 240; my italics).

This is what interdependent choice amounts to: "each party has partial control over its own consequences and partial control over the consequences of the other party. Payoffs for one cannot be dissociated from choices of the other... In negotiations... the collectivity determines the payoffs for each party" (Raiffa et al., 2002: 82–3). Yet, as will be elaborated extensively later on, in order to make the best of what might be expected from the potential contribution of game theory, several flaws in its current make-up have to be addressed. To mention the most conspicuous of them: in game theory actors are treated as internally homogeneous, undifferentiated parties (though possibly endowed with more than unitary rationality) but with uniform or consensual perceptions of external threats and opportunities, and thus assumed to respond to external challenges and dilemmas with a uniform repertory. In addition, the conditions and codes of the game are assumed to be *fixed*, thus allowing only the resulting "pay-offs" to be the variable outcome to be explained. As will be expounded more thoroughly below, *my* use of game theory starts from opposite ontological premises. In terms of the analytical C-4 scheme (Conditions, Codes, Commitments and Consequences), it is not just "commitments" but *also* "conditions" and "codes" that are considered essential stakes in the game of political-economic ordering, and should therefore be treated as *dependent* variables, open to manipulation for the players – or at least for *some* of them.

In the preceding sections enough has been said about the limits of schools that take exogenous forces – be it "market structure", "techno-structure" or "evolutionary selection" – as a necessary and sufficient explanation for the "imperative" coordination of economic life. More should be said now on the second divide, that is the way received science treats the problems of strategic choice and rationality. The branch that we classified above as transaction-costs economics appears to be the most rigorous corner amid the diaspora of Habitus versus Habitat views, since it considers itself still as fitting in with the methodical strictures and premises of neo-classical reasoning and ontology (Groenewegen and Vromen, 1996: 365, speak of "the new orthodoxy" in the theory of the firm). I therefore propose to start our academic excursion in that corner, in order to see how an infusion with insights from a "nested-game" theory may lead to a more satisfactory model for analyzing the "governance" implications of the spiraling of meso-games from micro-stratagems to the swings of order and disorder in the macro-organization of economic life.

Rational choice: economizing on transactions

Industrial and technological change generate mixes of deliberate and spontaneous changes in the dependence structures of industries, vertically as well as horizontally. Changes in dependence structures alter interfirm relationships. Daems, on empirical grounds (1983: 35–54) and Williamson, on deductive and research-programmatic grounds (1975; Williamson and Ouchi, 1983) predict a transition from market-type contracting (between autonomous organizations) to hierarchical forms (in which the initially autonomous partners are incorporated) whenever interfirm relationships are characterized by (1) uncertainty, (2) recurring transactions and (3) the degree to which durable transaction-specific investments are required to realize least-cost supply.

The discriminatory power of these variables is based on the behavioral assumptions of "bounded rationality" and "opportunism". As Williamson and Ouchi (1983: 16–17) explain:

> Whereas bounded rationality suggests decision-making less complex than the usual assumption of hyper-rationality, opportunism suggests calculating behavior more sophisticated than the usual assumption of simple self-interest. Opportunism refers to "making false or empty, that is, self-disbelieved threats or promises", cutting corners for undisclosed personal advantage, covering up tracks, and the like…It is not essential that all economic agents behave this way. What is crucial is that *some* agents behave in this fashion and that it is costly to sort out those who are opportunistic from those who are not.

One source of opportunism, identified by Williamson as "information impactedness", seems especially informative for our understanding of (the transactional varieties of) the monitoring and sanctioning of inter-organizational conduct. Williamson (1975: 31) circumscribes "information impactedness" as "a derivative condition that arises mainly because of uncertainty and opportunism, though bounded rationality is involved as well. It exists when true underlying circumstances relevant to the transaction, or related sets of transactions, are known to one or more parties but cannot be discerned by or displayed for others". The attention required for *monitoring* this sort of contingency qualifies the transactionalist approach as a potential candidate for, at least partially, explaining the propensity for hierarchization of initially market-like relationships:

> Faced with bounded rationality on the one hand and the proclivity for some human agents to behave opportunistically on the other, the basic organizational design issue essentially reduces to this: organize transactions in such a way as to economize on bounded rationality while simultaneously safe-guarding those transactions against the hazards of opportunism. (Williamson and Ouchi, 1983: 17)

In the case of recurring, uncertain and idiosyncratic exchange relationships – where "idiosyncratic" stands for irreversible transaction-specific *investments* – "hierarchy" is presented as a superior formula for economizing on relational accounting (Williamson, 1979) – as opposed to market contracting between non-integrated, autonomous actors – because incorporation is thought to represent more "sensitive governance characteristics and stronger joint profit-maximizing features".

Daems, working within the confines of the same transactional approach, adds a third organizational formula to "markets" versus "hierarchies", that is, the "federative" form. In terms of (1) the structuring of the conditions of *ownership*, (2) the distribution of joint *returns* and (3) the enforcement of interorganizational *compliance*, interfirm federations (F) represent a different arrangement, somewhere between the Williamsonian extremes of market and hierarchy (M&H). The concept of a "federation" – in my parlance an interorganizational network without clear-cut and undisputed hierarchical prerogatives, but ruled by the more or less compelling, if not coercive rules of a negotiated order, however spontaneously established – comes closer to the real-life practice of corporate and industrial strategies than the M&H extremes. A second reason to dwell somewhat longer upon Daems's extension and refinements of transactionalist economics is the author's use of the term "concerted action" in the disaggregated sense of "interfirm coordination". Extending and applying the term, interchangeably with the traditional meaning of public–private coordination, provides us with a "unified" grammar for exploring the relationships and interactions between the two worlds of coordination.

Reasoning from the three "critical dimensions" of *ownership, returns* and *compliance* structures mentioned above, Daems (1983: 39 ff.) delineates a "market" as a structure of interaction in which there is (1) no shared ownership, (2) separateness in the distribution of returns, while (3) prices play the role of a compliance mechanism. At the other end of this three-dimensional space, we find a "hierarchy" in which there exists (1) consolidated ownership, (2) a pooling of returns for the corporate partners, and (3) formal (legal) rules for the supervision of joint production and distribution by the respective establishments, etc. The intermediate form, a "federation", is defined as a construct in which the respective organizational participants remain: (1) statutorily independent, but engage in (2) pooling returns ("pooling" may take several forms: sharing profits, dividing markets, joint acquisition and allocation of orders, and so on). Concerning (3) the principle of compliance in the federative case, firms rely on "joint decision-making" for coordination, allocation and monitoring of participants' conduct.

Following Daems, "cartels are federations, but not all federations are cartels". Other examples, to be found in Europe and Japan, are firms which are linked through extensive interlocking stockholdings ("financial groups") and/or interlocking directorates. In short, all these varieties of interfirm coordination can be called "federations" as long as the network coordination does not rely on a central administration office to supervise the group members.

Daems supposes or postulates the existence of "institutional competition", apparently not as a nominalist metaphor but as a realist fact of economic life: "institutional arrangements (markets, hierarchies, federations), very much like technologies, compete with one another. In a competitive world with free institutional choices these institutions will survive that promise the highest net return to the co-operating units in the long run" (Daems, 1983: 44). Taken as an *axiom*, the supporting reasoning sounds convincing: "if no benefits can be obtained from concerted actions there is no point to use scarce resources to organize an institutional arrangement be it a market, a federation or a hierarchy for the exchange of information and the enforcement of contract" (ibid.: 41).

Why, then, is it that under certain conditions concerted action is organized by means of hierarchies, and under other conditions federations and markets are used? In order to "organize" his case, Daems points to the same determinants that Williamson used for explaining the emergence of other coordination and compliance mechanisms taking precedence over market contracting as a means of coordination, namely: (1) the degree of uncertainty involved in fully completing the transaction, (2) the size of transaction-specific investments, and (3) the frequency of recurrence of the transaction.

The higher the values of these "independent" variables, the more pressing the need for reliable information exchange and interfirm compliance in that industry. "Hierarchy" may be expected when uncertainty, transactional frequency and the size of transaction-specific investments reach their highest values; "market" is preferred when these variables assume their lowest score; and "federations" in-between. Since Daems assumes that the three institutional alternatives differ in their effect on the "joint return to concerted action" (ibid.), he can formulate his law of the "competition among institutions": assuming (for the sake of simplicity) equal installing and operating costs, H will be preferred to F, and F to M only, and only if the former communicates information better and/or enforces compliance more effectively. As Daems stipulates:

> The greater the amount of resources that is irreversibly committed for specific or transacting-specific purposes the more the need exists for tight compliance. Since hierarchies, for a variety of reasons, have

superior enforcement mechanisms and information networks, it seems plausible to postulate that consolidated ownership and supervision will be more used in industries where the co-ordination, allocation and monitoring processes of concerted actions are subject to considerable uncertainty or require resources for highly specialized and unique uses. (Ibid.: 43)

Yet for some time doubts have arisen about the declared superiority of hierarchy as an unbiased information and enforcement vehicle, for more than one reason. First, we can refer to the growing, rather skeptical, literature on the inertial forces of the "bureaucratic phenomenon". Next, interorganizational stability tends to widen the margins for intra-bureaucratic competition: the external stability reached by oligopolization or cartelization breeds internal rivalries between factions (cliques of functional, professional or sector-specific chiefs with their immediate subordinates) competing for prominence in the "dominant coalition" at the top of the organizational pyramid. Phrased in terms of a paradox: the more effective hierarchy appears in controlling *inter*-organizational opportunism, the higher the probability, *in extremis*, that *intra*-organizational opportunism and "rational egoism" become substituted for its external analogs. Internal opportunism, in turn, tends to destabilize external commitments, in the sense of affecting their credibility and time horizon. As we will see, linking in this manner the contrary dynamics of external and internal "rational egoism" comprises the hard core of a realist negotiated-order theory of the firm, its confines and its external relations (ranging from partners and sponsors to rivals).

Apart from the foregoing, serious doubts should surround Daems's assumption that there exists such a thing as *free* competition among "institutional alternatives" (even if we accept, for the sake of simplicity, his axiomatic proviso of "equal installing and operating costs"). First of all, institutions do not compete; *actors* do (eventually mixing or, more intriguingly, switching between *alternating* institutional alternatives). Besides, there are more implicit assumptions that seem to be questionable, such as: a free floating demand and supply for institutional substitutes, characterized by "complete transparency" of the costs and benefits associated with each alternative; no "hidden defects" or externalities – or at least no information costs for acquiring insight into those defects casu quo effects; uninhibited "mobility" and prompt "delivery" of the substitutes once decided upon (perfect substitutability); and no vested interests in, or oppositions against, the proposed reorganization of existing institutional arrangements. It is not without irony that those who subscribe to the transactionalist view consider the market-based form of contracting "too rudimentary" to be of any help in understanding and monitoring the subtleties of vertical contracting or idiosyncratic exchanges (that is, exchanges in the case of high levels of uncertainty, information impactedness and irreversible, transaction-specific investments). Given such an outlook on the organization of economic life, one wonders how a "market" might ever be able to handle a *hyper*-idiosyncratic transaction such as the "decision" to switch from one institutional arrangement to another. In short, trust in a sort of invisible hand governing the enlightened competition among institutional substitutes does not seem to be readily justified.

The transactional approach professes to explain why certain industries are characterized by higher degrees of concentration and large size. Apart from what was said before, the most serious objection against the transactionalist view remains that more flexible varieties of concertation, for example strategic *alliances*, and variations to horizontal integration, from mergers and joint ventures to mere tactical *coalitions* between competitors, are not mentioned and must therefore remain unexplained. Being disappointing in "width", the transactionalist view seems to miss also something in "depth", that is, the dimension explaining *how* the processes of close versus remote "control" between firms elapse. After all, between a rational insight (identifying the "need" to choose) and the actual deployment of that insight (earlier referred to as the "room" and "capacity" for strategic choice) there are interstitial obstacles and surprises, in particular when firms in a small-number setting either wait for each other (the tragedy of the fallows) or seek to materialize their micro-rational predilections simultaneously or pre-emptively (earlier referred to as the tragedy of the commons) – in short the obstacles versus opportunities that I earlier identified as the *urge* for strategic choice. What lacks, in short, is a proper feeling for the "embeddedness of firms and the role of supporting institutions. Institutional selection and evolution appear to be extremely complex phenomena. Research suggests, to say the least, that 'institutional survival' cannot be reduced to matters of 'comparative efficiency' alone" (Nelson, 1995: 176–7).

The argument seems even stronger in the case of institutional revolution where markets *replace* hierarchies or where federative forms *drive out* market-like transacting. The transaction costs approach gains in realism and explanatory power when the concept of "appropriability" is subsumed under the determinants of the "choice" between M versus H versus F. Appropriability refers to the degree in which firms and states can keep the fruits of their "creative" moves and combinatory movements to themselves and do not have to be apprehensive of "free riders", that is, imitators who try to by-pass the risky/costly stages of research and development (examples may be found in Bhide, 1986, and more principally in Teece, 1990). The main argument for including appropriability in the analysis might be the hypothesis that the urge – to merge or to adopt a centralized "holding" structure (the H-option) increases along with the degree of co-specialization, the frequency of transactions and a decreasing number of potential partners, a fortiori if the "internalization" menu professes to control for the "free rider" temptation.

The issue of institutional "choice" – or closer to practice, changes in the *mix* of institutional alternatives – gains in salience with the introduction of complex new technologies – while asking for standardization, certification and coordination with (future) component suppliers and demanding customers. This is a typical specimen of the "tragedy of the fallows", requiring a critical minimum of parallel and complementary choices by rivals and symbionts alike: *ex ante*, in the form of joint activities related to "pre-competitive" cooperation (for instance in the case of common standard setting), and *ex post*, in the form of "post-competitive" coordination (ranging from production-sharing and market-splitting arrangements in mature industries, e.g. Renault teaming up with Suzuki and Daimler Benz, to "black versus white knight" coalitions in take-over tournaments).

The latter, in order to reap the fruits of "Schumpeterian" creativity, are the players that succeed in finding a workable trade-off between the mobilization of a critical minimum of supporters ("inclusivity") while preserving a maximum of appropriability ("exclusivity"). The trade-off is an instructive specimen of the "mission" of interdependent choice: how to see to it that anticipations (the *sous-entendues* or tacit understandings mentioned in Chapter 1) are coordinated in situations where individual rationality leads to collective irrationalities, while simultaneously *maximizing one's "exclusive" share of the spoils from coordination*. Individual rationality in a capitalist universe encourages proprietary strategies but winner-takes-all stratagems in a *nested* political economy are apt to degenerate into a self-defeating scenario: without proper institutional cocoons competitive advantages are either bound to die in splendid *isolation* or to evaporate in competitive *imitation*.

When, for whatever reasons, neither horizontal concentration nor vertical integration are attainable for "internalizing" the dilemma of inclusivity versus exclusivity, the only practical solution is to *share* appropriability with a critical minimum of others. Sharing appropriability means creating a community – of fate, that is creating interfirm constellations in which enlightened self-interest teaches some modicum of other-directedness. The empirical literature abounds with examples, from horizontal cartels and joint ventures to vertical and diagonal alliances, for instance subcontractor networks or hierarchies, demonstrating that it concerns neither an ephemeral nor a transitional phenomenon. The transaction costs literature does not contain information on this variety of "rational altruism", nor does it provide information about the "federative" solution for the quasi-internalization of external transactional dilemmas (such as the appropriability – versus critical mass of followers' trade-off). Since the "hybrid F" form cannot be equated with fully fledged internalization ("pure H") nor with fully fledged externalization ("pure M") but nonetheless exposes elements of constrained or *contained* opportunism, "orchestration" might be an adequate generic label for earmarking this variety of interorganizational discipline. Joint resources mobilization – ranging from pooled to sequential to reciprocal resource dependences – lies at the heart of a realist theory of strategic choice and order, the essence of which is the *coordination – of anticipations*.

Box 3.1   On the coordination of anticipations: among rational egoists

In more recent writings in the transaction-cost tradition the existence of hybrid forms between "hierarchy" and "market" is acknowledged. Hybrids, however, tend to be treated as something of a transient nature. Williamson, for instance, qualifies forms of interfirm cooperation as "temporary" (1985: 32, introducing the "T" form, where T stands for "transitional"), suggesting that sooner or later either the efficiency drive will prompt a transition towards full integration (the "H" option) or the costs of installing hierarchy, subsequent efficiency losses due to bureaucratic inertia and the diseconomies of scale will stimulate a transition towards arm-length transactions (the "M" option). Apparently, the "federative" cluster or consortium option is not considered to be a serious and sustainable candidate for handling competitive and symbiotic interdependences. The main reason for dismissing the federative form as a viable alternative is said to be the "unsatisfactory state of theorizing on T-forms" (ibid.; see also Kogut, 1988; Williamson, 1993). The latter assessment may turn out to be a self-defeating criticism while stemming from the credentials of transaction-costs theorizing itself, in particular from the way the issues of opportunism and appropriation are treated. "Opportunism" and its derivative, "information impactedness", are said to be based on a "relatively unflattering behavioral assumption" (ibid.: 29), leading to informational asymmetries that may be exploited to the detriment of those who do not know the "true underlying circumstances relevant to the transaction" (Williamson, 1975: 31). It remains obscure as to why the pejorative connotations of opportunism and information asymmetry are emphasized in a theory of opportunism-controlling behavior where explanations in terms of commitments – that is, threats-and-promises, as for instance are normally used in theories of international trade or industrial relations bargaining – seem to suffice.

In international and industrial relations theorizing the management of opportunism is basically considered to be nothing more than the management of the credibility of commitments, especially in situations of info-asymmetry and uncertainty about parties' real stakes and the sustainability of their comparative endowments. From an interaction perspective, the credibility of commitments is based on power. Flattering or unflattering behavioral assumptions are to a large extent irrelevant when power is defined as the capacity of an actor to make the best for him or herself of the room for strategic choice of his or her opponent(s).

Given the relational character of power, especially in a context of inter-firm and market-versus-state interactions, bargaining power can be seen, then, as a function of the (reputational and real) costs to oneself of imposing a loss of strategic and tactical choice upon one's bargaining partner(s). Or, alternatively, in terms of the definition of "strategy" in more adversarial settings, as the costs to oneself of the "art of so moving…as to impose upon the enemy the place and time and conditions for fighting preferred by oneself". No assumptions about the moral predispositions of the transacting actors are required; testable propositions about the material and reputational dispositions of the interacting co-actors suffice to understand the social fabric of credible commitments and to explain from the returns on commitments the sustainability of a specific negotiated order. In later publications Williamson's appreciation of the "state of T-theorizing" may have acquired a slightly more constructive bent (cf. Aoki, 2003, who expects a more "institutionally coherent" reappraisal of the "federative" or "T-form" of corporate governance when "games" are substituted for "transactions" as the principal unit of analysis), but the crux of my argument remains outside of the genetic codes and the empirical scope of "core" transaction-costs analysts, to wit: the increasing *permanence of impermanent relations* in the organization of capitalist order – negotiated order that is primarily driven by the "shuttle" logic of corporate games and the impredictability of the associated "drift" of interorganizational loyalties.

From an *interactionist*, negotiated-order perspective the sustainability of a specific social order has, more than with anything else, to do with the appropriability of the returns on commitments. The meaning of this issue changes radically when – as opposed to what is allowed for in the transaction-costs theory of the firm and its competitive habitus – the quest for appropriation is envisaged from an interaction-costs perspective. Lifting the axiom of rational egoism from the discrete firm to the level of federations of firms (and firms versus non-market players) sensitizes for methods of coordination – among egoists – for instance concerning the safeguarding of relational rents and first-movers' advantages based on tacit "federative" understandings and faster learning routines – that are per definition absent or at best "transitional" in the transaction-costs view on the discrete firm. (As we will see further on, the issues of opportunism and the appropriability of relational rents gain added significance in the recently reiterated debate on different "varieties of capitalism" and the eventualities of institutional "convergence". Where the debaters stand in this discussion, has everything to do with their stance on the federative versus atomist firm.)

Strategic choice: economizing on interactions

The neo-classical heritage leaves us with two more fundamental flaws. First, what is still waiting to be addressed is the unhelpful convention of equating the "M" versus "H" dichotomy with "intra-" versus "extra" organizational phenomena. The convention is unhelpful because *intra*-organizational domains may be dominated by *competitive*, market-like relationships and *extra*-organizational domains may be dominated by virtually *hierarchical* relationships (as exemplified by the tightly orchestrated "pyramids" of sub-contractors, customers and financial intermediaries to be found in Japan and elsewhere in the Asia region). It is therefore more informative to investigate the differing degrees of *interpenetration and contamination* of markets and hierarchies, as well as to explain the *level of aggregation* at which we expect to find a specific "concubinage" of markets-*cum*-hierarchies – rather than continuing to treat the two as mutually exclusive polarities.

The second flaw concerns the preoccupation with *why*-questions, which risks topping a fallacy of composition with the fallacy of functionalist teleology. The first proviso asserts that collective outcomes (such as institutional "arrangements") cannot be directly related to individual motives ("economizing"). The second caveat states that governance *arrangements* that eventually appear to be superior, for instance in terms of the containment of opportunism or the enhancement of appropriability, cannot be equated with the intent of the *arrangeurs* to curb opportunism or maximize appropriation. It is wise to refrain from confusing the apparent outcomes of orchestration with the putative drives or drivers behind it. As stated before, not why but *how* institutional arrangements emerge, respectively disseminate and dissipate must be the organizing question.

Box 3.2   Strategic choice and economic order: a preview

The coordination of expectations and anticipations among "rational ego-ists" and the "capacity to bind oneself" play a key role in the formation and replication of political-economic order. Until recently the neo-classical con-sensus asserted that the "international financial system", including hedge funds, private equity and institutional investors, would ultimately serve as a disciplining force for correcting the problems of excess capacity and over-crediting in the real economy. The first decade of this century has learned otherwise.

Benefiting from hindsight, the coercive deficiency or "veto" power of the nodal players in the international banking system sheds a different light on Galbraith's prediction (see Chapter 2, p. 26) that for the foreseeable future "the industrial system will not long be regarded as something apart from government" (Galbraith, 1968, 400 [italics in the original]: "In time the line between the two will disappear. Man will look back in amusement at the pretense that once caused people to refer to General Dynamics and North American Aviation and A.T.& T as *private* business"). What according to this vision used to be seen as the "osmosis" of private and state interests, may in reality have to do with a (largely inadvertent) escalation of commitments, resulting eventually in an increasingly asymmetric division of obstructive power in modern industrial-financial systems – more than with techno-economic "imperatives" and "compulsive affinities" between market and state players, both allegedly searching for "size and predictability". As we may surmise, the main reason for not discerning these pushes and pulls behind the twists of capitalist discipline is the omission to distinguish between the cumulative but distinct "logics" of actors, arrangements and regimes.

The links missing in the "rational choice" (alias "efficiency") canon can be summarized as follows. First, the canon does not specify the *ante-cedents* of rationality, that is, the full sequence from intent to oppor-tunity to realization. At variance with theories of the firm that relate the imperfections of rationality to the bounds of human cognition, my conception of bounded rationality is based on the (cumulative) imperfections that result from *structural* (as opposed to psychological) impediments in the chain from the ex ante perceived to the ex post *demonstrated* rationality of strategic maneuvers. To avoid confusion with current connotations we may dub this conceptualization of the bounds of rationality "path-dependent rationality", that is rationality as an amalgam of historical investments and "inherited" search and selection routines.

Second, the canons of rational choice fail to specify the *consequences* of path-dependent rationality, that is, how the ex post effectiveness (respectively ineffectiveness) of strategic maneuvers feeds back into a reinforcement (respectively readjustment) of the initial strategic menu (learning versus unlearning). For the sake of semantic symmetry, the latter may be called path-dependent *rationalizations* (rather than rationality in the conventional sense).

As argued above, a full reconstruction of the twist of antecedents and consequences of path-dependent rationalizations is indispensable because, between a strategic intention and its actual implementation, there are numerous obstacles and surprises. By short-cutting intents and outcomes "purist" transaction-cost perspectives are unable to explain why firms under *in*variant transaction-specific conditions (such as "bounded rationality", "opportunism", "asset-particularism", "appropriability", etc.) *do* change their preferred mixes of horizontal coordination (vis-à-vis rivals, from cross-sourcing to collusion) and vertical concertation (vis-à-vis suppliers and customers, from outsourcing to co-makership and co-design). *Firms change their combinatory preferences in response to their rivals' and allies' responses on the formers' initiatives.* Even in the "federative" make-up, transactionalists treat external factors and actors basically as unresponsive entities. The transactionalist paradigm, in short, has an autistic bent.

It makes sense, therefore, to look for a more radical revision of the (new-)institutionalists' legacy. Such a revision has to shed light on two neglected but vital issues in the explanation of organizational strategies and tactics: first, the *quest for remediability* – referring to the desire to minimize the constraints or maximize the renegability of yesterday's choices – and second, the *quest for mimetic control*, referring to the desire to control for the self-frustrating effects of present or future imitators.

Box 3.3   Two faces of the strategy trap

Mimetic control refers to the *competition* trap, arguing that one may occasionally imitate exemplary competitors but that one has to prevent others trying to catch the same train (too soon). Otherwise the tragedy of the commons demands its toll.

Remediability, on the other hand, refers to the *competence* trap: how to see to it that a firm's competence comes to meet a favorable and self-sustaining or expanding architecture of suppliers, customers and non-market sponsors (in time) but does not mutate into an immutable competence (over time). Otherwise the tragedy of the fallows awaits its toll.

For understanding the problem of *remediability* it may be more helpful to envisage transaction costs as a *consequence*, rather than as the cause, of specific institutional arrangements. As will be elaborated more fully in the chapters below, institutional arrangements are webs of tacit under-standings and (pre-)commitments that are a reflection of the distribu-tion of bargaining power in a political economy. If we take as our unit of analysis the webs of understandings and commitments (rather than the discrete transactions, as is done by subscribers to the transaction-costs school) the "costs of transacting" are a function of the degree of asymmetry in bargaining power between incumbent and/or prospective transactors, rather than a function of the intrinsic or "objective" proper-ties of the transactions per se. From a bargaining perspective "asset speci-ficity", "opportunism", "appropriability", "remediability" and "mimetic control" are the consequences of historical decisions by organizations to opt for specific mixes of in- and out-sourcing instead of the anteced-ents of past boundary choices. Historical choices combined with antici-pation of future contingencies lead to path dependences, that is, to the quasi-objectivation – a "matter of faction" – of transactional attributes or dimensions. In other words, the attributes that figure as a priori given or exogenously determined in a transaction-costs perspective become *endog-enized* in an interdependent choice perspective. (Needless to say our argu-ment about the "self-made" character of asset specificity, appropriability and the like has to be read as an assertion of analytical priority and not as a claim of descriptive precedence.) Once endogenized and "empow-ered", the adage "economizing on transactions" comes to mean "econo-mizing on commitments", that is, colloquially, minimizing the costs to oneself of limiting one's own and others' *maneuverability*. By focusing on maneuverability, the analysis shifts from the quest for efficiency to the quest for effectiveness as the foundation of a theory of choice and order. *Effective* choice stresses the basically relational nature of whatever matters in the strategic setting of interdependent choice, such as: the choice of boundaries, competencies, competitors and partners. Both the issues of mimesis and remediability call attention to the elementary datum that transactional efficiencies depend on *inter*actional effectiveness, that is, on what *others* will do (or fail to do) by way of imitative or supplementary responses to one's own strategic or tactical choices.

Box 3.4 Maneuverability

An example may illustrate the difference in the heuristic reach of the two perspectives contrasted above. General Motors has always practiced, from the 1920s to the present, the dual use of external, from time to time even sole-source, suppliers of automobile frames and modules in competition with completely internalized divisions that manufacture exactly the same frames and modules (Coase, 1988). Since the "technical/intellectual/constructive" specificities, and thus the "transactional" parameters, of the situation do not discriminate, explaining the "concurrence" of internalization and externalization must be something of a puzzle to the transactionalists. From a bargaining perspective, however, dual use is a perfectly understandable practice: negotiations with subcontractors are more comfortable when, in case of protracted disagreement about prices, qualities or delivery time, a buyer may credibly threaten to do the job by himself, both in terms of demonstrable in-house expertise (offsetting the "information-asymmetry" aspect of bargaining power vis-à-vis specialized outsiders) as in terms of demonstrable in-house capacity (solving the "immediacy" – alias "ease-of-substitution" – aspect of bargaining power). Galbraith attributes this practice in general to "the need of [the] techno-structure for freedom from outside interference" (1968: 97) and more in particular to the desire of the integrated, large size firm of "eliminating the independence of action of those to whom the [firm] sells or from whom it buys ... Should it be necessary to press matters, General Motors, unlike the dairyman, has always the possibility of supplying a material or component to itself. The option of eliminating a market is an important source of power for controlling it" (ibid.: 39–40). Galbraith further extends his argument to "the provision to itself of its own supply of capital", the "control of the labor market" and the "elimination of price-competition" among rival firms: *"No formal communication is necessary to prevent such actions* ... Everyone knows that the survivor of such a contest would not be the aggressor but General Motors" (ibid.: 41; my italics).

Explaining boundary choice in terms of bargaining power and the search for "effectiveness" in the orchestration of markets seems so self-evident that one wonders why Occam's razor has not driven out the rationalistic overstretch implied by paradigms inspired by the neo-classical firm and its relentless dedication to "efficiency", that is the firm cast as a "Robinson Crusoe" caught in his insular games against nature.

The amendments proposed above do not start from the assumption of "perfect clarity about ends, strategies and resources" of the actors, even less from the presumption that the conditions are met that Olsen enumerates as the prerequisites for successful multiparty collaborative policy-making, to wit: a segmentation of "well-defined and stable interests", "stable rules about who participates and which problems and solutions are relevant" and the existence of arrangements that "prevent policies from becoming large garbage cans (and) from becoming fortuitous results of the intermeshing of loosely coupled processes" (Olsen, 1981: 510–11). My amendments start, instead, from the opposite: the need to accomplish a critical minimum of coordination of mutual expectations in spite of the virtual *absence* of clarity about ends, rules and resources and a generalized strategy of *ignoring* the interaction effects. In such a constellation one may expect, indeed, a sort of "Gresham's law" in which strategic bargaining modes drive out the norms of rational problem solving. Scharpf (1985) has described the displacement effect for the prevailing style of decision-making in European collaborative agreements and its consequences (see Box 3.5).

Box 3.5   Rational versus strategic choice

"In ongoing joint-decision systems, *from which exit is excluded or very costly…* pressures to reach agreement will be great. The substance of agreement will be affected, however, by the prevailing style of decision-making. In its ability to achieve effective responses to a changing policy environment the 'bargaining' style is clearly inferior to the 'problem solving' style. But the preconditions of 'problem solving' – the orientation towards common goals, values and norms – are difficult to create, and they are easily eroded in cases of ideological conflict, mutual distrust or disagreement over the fairness of distribution rules. Thus, reversion to a 'bargaining' style of decision making…seems to have been characteristic of the European [Union] ever since the great confrontations of the mid-sixties. The price to be paid for that is not simply a prevalence of distributive conflicts complicating all substantive decisions, but a systematic tendency towards sub-optimal substantive solutions." (Scharpf, 1985: 40)

The crux, of course, is that in multilevel collaborative games the distribution of entry and exit costs is rarely, if ever, equal for the respective participants. In a world in which strategic aims and resource endowments appear to be contingent matters, organizations do not search for predictable but *negotiable* environments. They avoid or withdraw from non-negotiable environments (when they have "access to exit" opportunities; neither Habitus nor Habitat tell us much about the preconditions, and consequences, of "negotiability" and "responsiveness"). How organizations will take up a position against the environment depends on where they happen to place the boundary of their own competence/mission. Boundary choices are a mixed outcome of the past and future. Where organizations "stand" in terms of competence claims and missionary ambitions depends on where they "sit" (current commitments); and where they "sit" depends on where they *come from* (historical commitments); but the purport of where they come from depends on where they *go to* (anticipated commitments will frame the reappraisal of historical lock-ins). Considered this way environments are created by organizations as much as organizations are created by their environments. The reflexive nature of past and future commitments complicates the analysis of the duality of choice and order. On the one hand, organizations make *use* of their embeddedness in a strategic or opportunistic way. On the other hand, as stressed before, the reflexivity or *nestedness* of the uses of embeddedness can never be left out with impunity under conditions of interdependent choice.

I presume that our capitalist discipline and diplomacy framework, which explains the emergence of negotiated orders from the sequence of nested games, disentangles at least part of the puzzle. One of the assets of the discipline and diplomacy perspective is its tendency to correct for the technology-based and physical capital bias that predominates the literature on "path dependence". In line with the recent revival of interest in the embeddedness of the firm (Whitley, 1992; Grabherr, 1993), the perspective adopted here suggests a broader conception of possible "lock-ins": it includes, besides the technological and financial constraints imposed upon managerial discretion, the intangible assets and liabilities embodied in intellectual and institutional capital ("competence" and "connectedness"). However, in order to trace the consequences of this extended range of lock-ins for the need, room and capacity for strategic choice, it will be necessary to translate the facultative connotations of "embeddedness" into a more directive "theory of entrapment" that explains – rather than postulates or takes for granted – the *making* of lock-ins, that is, a model that demonstrates the (in the cumulative sense) *self-made* nature of historical and future constraints that condition the room for strategic choice and, eventually, *re*condition the future need for coordination. Box 3.6 provides an example.

Box 3.6   Disciplinary instincts

At the end of 1996 the electronics company Philips requested the European Commission to open an inquiry into the lawfulness of a 10 billion (then) francs subsidy for Thompson Multimedia by the French state. The French firm had suffered huge losses in recent years and faced bankruptcy. If the subsidy could not be revoked, Philips, like others around at that time facing a depressed consumer electronics market, would at least press for a substantial capacity reduction by Thompson Multimedia.

Yet, what in this case restricted Philips's freedom to claim full redress or compensation from its (ailing) French rival were the sizeable interests of the Dutch firm in the French market. The turnover of Philips in France, including televisions, semiconductors, mobile telephones and lamps, amounted to 22 billion francs. Philips had to see to it that Thompson's fate would not be relegated to Dutch intransigencies.

Under some conditions capitalist diplomacy teaches containment and accommodation rather than elimination of a rival.

As argued before, under conditions of interdependent choice, entailing a mix of pliable and pragmatic codes of fair play and uncertainty about the returns on commitment, rationality is bound to be a contingent, that is interactive rather than linear, phenomenon. "Contingent" rationality depends on what other organizations do or decide to refrain from – reacting or anticipating what their counterparts (are expected to) do or refrain from doing. Under recursive *cum* small-number game conditions it is non-informative to speak of goal-"directed" behavior. In such a context strategic behaviors are at most goal "seeking" and "suggestive", that is, are meant to provoke "informative" *counter*-behaviors.

Box 3.7   Boeing contra Airbus

For some time the US-based, 60 percent market-share leader in the global commercial aircraft industry, Boeing, confirmed its intention to launch a plus-500 seats "super-jumbo". Its chief rival, the EU-based Airbus consortium, announced a similar ambition. With an eye on the astronomic costs of R&D for developing a super-carrier independently, in addition to entailing a serious risk of excess capacity in the case of double market entry, Boeing and Airbus discussed several times the feasibility of a joint project. The talks failed. ("In hindsight, it was an effective, though not necessarily intentional, move by Boeing to delay Airbus's efforts", "The $1 trillion Dogfight", *The New York Times*, March 23, 1997). Boeing decided to quit on the basis of negative market prospects. Airbus, contrarily, declared to go ahead, reportedly on the basis of positive expectations.

Interpreting the dissenting prognoses as a "chicken game", in which the suggestion of stamina and the power of self-fulfilling prophecies are more consequential than objective staying power and real intentions, two, equally abortive, possibilities remain. Option one is that suppliers and customers trust in Boeing's foresight and will refrain from anticipatory investments in the project. Option two is that suppliers and customers distrust Boeing's foresight and expect, instead, that Airbus's feeling for the future is sound and thus will stick to its initial plans. In the latter case, airlines and suppliers facing a prospective monopolist on the wide-body market may have to decide to refuse Airbus's offer and keep away from the plus-500 seat sector.

Right or wrong, Boeing's message will have the same effect in either case: Airbus's dream, however sound per se, may fail to materialize. Sometimes, what catches the eye of the believer, is real in its consequences. Sometimes, suggestive moves pay. (In the Airbus case it did not: Boeing's deterrence failed, the A-250 was built and passed a successful take-off.) So, again, under what conditions do suggestive moves and countermoves pay?

Towards a new prism

It is only by observing the response of one's rivals and allies that organizations come to learn about the mixed implications of the "imperatives" of competitive and symbiotic dependence. The response of "third" parties provides information about the presence or probability of eventual strategy traps and delineates the room for escape from there. The different guises of "rationality" that we have surveyed in this chapter – from the neo-classical orthodoxy of equilibrium analysis to the sorting out of "efficient governance" forms in evolutionary economics – are not readily helpful in unraveling the intricacies of the *links* between organizational choice, interorganizational coordination and the momentum of economic order. Even game theory (at least in its general make-up) fails to be of much assistance in answering the questions that I have presented as "the quest for discipline" (Chapter 1) and further dressed as the "orchestration" of modern capitalism (Chapter 2). What I propose to replace is the *binary* ("cooperate *or* defect") and *two-actor* logic of elementary game theory by a *three-dimensional* – horizontal, vertical and temporal – and *third-actor* logic of coping with the dilemmas of interdependent choice.

Incorporating in the analysis the *timing* and *sequence* of horizontal moves and vertical movements in three-actor settings allows for switching coalitions and alliances. Since the sheer *threat* of switching may (under specifiable conditions) suffice as a leverage for enforcing discipline, a different spectrum of disciplinary games arises. The spectrum ranges from direct *conduct* control of firm-to-firm and firm-to-state transactions to the more indirect formula of *context* control. In the latter case it is the indirect orchestration of the entry and exit conditions of the *game* that takes precedence over the direct orchestration of the punch and counterpunch of the *players*. Conduct-oriented games follow a *"first* mover takes all" formula in a fixed frame: positioning occurs within a single, self-perpetuating game. *Context*-oriented games follow a *"footloose* mover takes all" formula in a movable world of shifting coalitions and alliances: repositioning occurs *between* games. Conduct control in a triadic setting means embarking on tight-knit, tripartite agreements – or more properly: bilateral transactions "disciplined" by the shadow of a third party. (The *neo-corporatist* repertory that we will meet in Chapter 5 is a prototype.) *Context* control, instead, means entering into non-hierarchical, loose-knit, triangular agreements through impinging upon one's counterpart's maneuverability – that means by manipulating the other's *nestedness* – rather than by disciplining his or her conduct directly. (The *escapist* repertory of European industrial strategy formation, analyzed in Chapter 2, is an exemplary case.)

Conduct-controlling stratagems belong to the sort of regime that I have characterized as the *old* discipline: the gradual annexation and hierarchization of the invisible hand by a *visible* one, that is (à la Chandler and Galbraith, see Chapter 2) a fixed and visibly oligarchic cartel of actors with uncontested internal mandates – operating in clearly marked domains. *Context*-controlling stratagems, then, constitute the *new* discipline: a largely informal, essentially non-recorded ordering – let's call it the "prompting hand" – molding an invisible, movable theatre of powers with ill-defined identities and discretionary mandates – operating in ill-defined domains. For properly understanding the orchestration of the cohabitation of rival firms and rival states under conditions of the old versus the new discipline we need an alternative prism: a theory of games that explains the *framing* of games. When we compare first- with footloose-mover games we see different sorts of stratagems, resulting in different sorts of disciplinary arrangements due to different forms of contractual incompleteness and hazards. Typically, as foreshadowed in the concept of the shuttle logic of corporate games, footloose games organize horizontal discipline by means of vertical alliances, and organize vertical discipline by horizontal divides and the threat of coalitional switches. As we will see more precisely in the coming chapters, the more international the arena, the more credible the threat of partner substitution and, therefore, the greater the salience of indirect instead of direct governance. Stated otherwise, the controlling of the *nodes* of networks – by indirect rule, for example by teaming up with one's partner's rivals or one's rival's partners – waives the necessity of direct rule. And reversing the reasoning, changing the parameters of nestedness entails change in the rules of the game, and changing the *rules* feeds back upon the parameters of nestedness. The following precis summarizes the credentials of the new perspective I propose:

- Organizations shift from strategies to stratagems whenever there exist serious *ex ante* constraints on the possibility of monitoring and sanctioning the behavior of others (e.g. competitors, suppliers, buyers, opponents and others that in any way may facilitate or constrain the discretionary freedom of organizational choice).
- When neither market (M: the invisible hand) nor hierarchy (H: the visible hand) are able to produce an effective solution for the dilemmas of path dependence and the tensions between individual versus collective rationality, *hybrid* arrangements enter as coalitions and alliances. Both M-failure and the inability to arrive at imperatively coordinated H-solutions have to do with combinations of information asymmetry, contested competences and uncertainty about strategic interaction effects.

- Coalitions and alliances are "strategic", not because of their strategic *intent* (more often than not they are driven by signaling considerations for the sake of provoking counter-responses) but because of their *implications*. Implications are "strategic" because of the paradoxes that result from the potential clashes between individual and encompassing rationality: micro-rational moves and movements may be "efficient" but in the case of counter or me-too strategies by others (that is if defensive or offensive anticipations and imitations are the rule rather than the exception), then micro-*efficient* behaviors eventually cumulate into meso- or macro-*ineffective* outcomes, that is outcomes that backfire on the canons of micro-"efficiency". I have dubbed this paradox of self-defeating rationalities the "competition", respectively "competence" trap.

- Inspecting the body of knowledge on strategic management, industrial organization and, more recently, the sociology of the "embeddedness" of firms and federations, surprisingly little energy is invested in identifying the possibly perverse causes and consequences of the "coordination" of strategies. As a consequence we do not learn much about the processes of strategy *drift* that results from firm-to-firm and firm-to-state encounters. Any robust theory of concerted action should therefore start at this Archimedean point: how do strategically dependent organizations cope with the dilemmas of the clash between individual versus shared rationality?

- Coordination is the result of the "structuration" of strategies. In its *external* manifestation structure formation refers to the degree in which past, present and future dependences between organizations represent barriers to horizontal and/or vertical *mobility*. Exit and entry conditions provide information about the freedom of choice organizations have in their strategic positioning and posturing. From the conditions of *maneuverability* follow the codes and commitments governing the games of coordination.

- Structure formation in its *internal* manifestation refers to the degree to which organizations face *mobilization* barriers. Where the external dimension informs us about the discretionary *room* for strategic choice, the latter provides information about an organization's *capacity* to exploit or stretch that freedom, that is the "distinctive" acumen by which organizations effectively *use* the entry and exit options externally offered or imposed on them.

- Note that our view differs from "strategic group" analysis which conceives of entry or exit barriers as clusters of statistical *commonalities*, grouping firms in terms of similar scale, image, capabilities and historical investments (Hartigan, 1975; Hatten et al., 1978; Harrigan, 1985; McGee and Thomas, 1986; Mascarenhas and Aaker, 1989). Our negotiated order perspective focuses on a community of *fates* rather than a commonality of *traits*, that is (1) on the configuration of horizontal and vertical dependences (in terms of techno-financial, intellectual and relational capital), as well as (2) on the intended anticipation costs and non-intended consequences of the interaction effects that condition the current and future freedom of movement of the individual actors.

- Whereas the mainstream literature on organizational behavior stresses the *cognitive* limits of the managerial brain in matters of strategic choice, the capitalist discipline and diplomacy approach stresses the intra- and inter-*organizational* correlates of rationality: an organization's "sense of direction" and "responsiveness" are considered to be a function of the (historical) composition and stability of the dominant coalition within an organization (that is its de facto command and control structure). The composition of the dominant coalition results from what an organization considers to represent its distinctive competence, which in itself is the recursive result of coalition formation in earlier stages of an organization's life cycle. Second, and even more essential, the stability of the dominant coalition, which explains its internal mobilization potential, is the *co*-result of the *effectiveness* of the search for and selection of external partners. Figure 3.1 comprises the hypothesized interactive-cumulative dynamics of coalition, alliance and regime formation.

- As mentioned before, the portfolio of external relations is subjected to specific time/space constraints, that is, "barriers to mobility" that determine the costs of forming new lock-ins and the costs of breaking away from existing lock-ins. Both path dependence and the strategy trap conspire to what is regarded as the basic drive guiding search-and-selection behaviors in small-number games: "economize on interactions". This axiom tells more about the logic of organizational moves and cross-organizational movements than its somewhat narcissistic counterpart in transaction-cost economics; "narcissistic" in that the latter aspires to explain the specimens of strategic choice, like internalization-versus-outsourcing decisions, solely from the point of view of the acquiring or outsourcing firm, that is, without taking into account the countervailing powers and preferences on the side of intra-organizational factions or external actors that fear to be taken over or pushed off, that is, without discounting the barriers to externalization by reluctant internal stakeholders or the

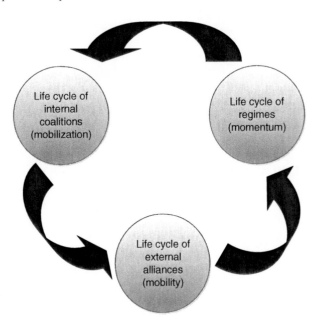

Figure 3.1   Nested games and regime structuration: a first cut

resistance to annexation by those who see themselves chosen as prospective takeover targets.

- On the continuum from tight to loose-knit "solutions", *economizing on interactions* entails the complete spectrum of incorporation,
  encapsulation, satellitization or more Machiavellian ways of coping
  with the inconveniences of past and future dependences. The task is
  to find out which scenario takes precedence when, and why.
- A subsidiary task, as we will see, is to spell out why, in terms of de
  facto commitments, the "subjective" intent of economizing does not
  necessarily always end in an "objective" *economy* of intentions. The
  latter adage is illustrated by the "multilevel theatre" of European
  industrial strategy formation: collaborative agreements at the meso-
  level, initiated for correcting prisoners' dilemmas at the micro-
  level, produce macro-games at the global level, but *once produced*
  the global game starts to restrain, if not undo, the rationale of the
  meso- and micro-games – in the paradoxical sense of becoming the
  "prime mover of its own causal antecedents" (cf. Elster, 1978: 121–2;
  1986: 202–10, 217–18; Giddens, 1979: 211).
- By way of conclusion, a "nested" negotiated-order perspective facilitates the integration of different levels and units of analysis, while

aiming to remedy the odds of academic fragmentation. The first claim argues that the analysis of the processes of search, selection and consolidation should start at the "source", that is with the logic of strategy *formation* (at the micro-level, the actors). However, the latter will not be grasped without discounting the dynamics of strategy *dissemination* (at the meso-level, the arrangements) and the processes of strategy *drift* (at the meta-level, the regimes). Conversely, looking from the point of view of the units of analysis, the *momentum* of a negotiated political-economic order (macro) has to be understood from the interactive/cumulative *movements* of organizations (meso) that result from their intendedly competitive/collaborative *moves and countermoves* (micro).

Summarizing, by looking ahead

The interpretation of disciplinary regimes *as a negotiated order of nested games* intends to offer a springboard for lifting the unfortunate incommunicado that goes with academic fragmentation. *Habitus* models are especially strong in tracing the role of opportunism and eventual hold-ups as a consequence of asset-specific investments. However, they will gain in realism as far as they take into account the possibility of a plurality of interests in the political constellation inside organizations that affect, in a constraining or enabling way, how external threats and opportunities will be perceived and weighted. *Habitat* models, on the other hand, are helpful in the exploration of, for instance, the role of market and technology dynamics, provided they take into account the institutional arrangements that, again in a constraining or enabling way, affect the room and capacity for strategic choice in individual organizations.

What is *empirically* missing in both Habitus and Habitat models, however, is the complete and continuing "cycle of cycles" that is depicted in Figure 3.1. In addition, for a pointed abstract of the *conceptual* incompleteness of the approaches reviewed in this chapter, it may be illuminating to confront the *single*-loop theories of choice and coordination as shown in Table 3.2 with the *double*-loop framework shown in Chapter 1 (see Figure 1.2 on the sequences of Conditions, Codes, Commitments and Consequences – p. 13). Rephrased in that grammar, Habitat models short-circuit "conditions" and "commitments" in a straight diagonal. As a consequence they expose a trained incapacity to see how specific "codes" (for coping with interdependence dilemmas) may lead to non-intended and counter-productive "consequences". Habitus models, on the other hand, tend to conceive of a single-loop diagonal from "codes" to "consequences". They therewith *either* risk finishing up in regulatory illusionism – overlooking the need to explain the possibly wide margins between rule-making and rule-enforcement due to "comply-or-explain" escapes in so-called codes-of-conduct; *or* they risk finishing up in a teleological trap – leaving unexplained the essence of disciplinary regimes, that is the variability of the *credibility* and *duration* of commitments. My *co*-Habitation model avoids both lapses, thus restoring the original mission, to wit: exposing the multilevel and recursive logic of causation between organizational moves, interorganizational movements and what is hypothesized to flow from that: the ordering and disordering of disciplinary regimes. Box 3.8 lists the assumptions and assertions that summarize the kind of synthesis we are looking for.

Box 3.8   Order as a set of nested games

- Disciplinary regimes are the cumulative outcome, and definitely not the ex ante intent, of the push and pull maneuvers among organizations ("ex post rationalizations").
- Push and pull maneuvers are essentially strategies and stratagems for coping with the hazards inherent in competitive and symbiotic interdependences ("interdependent choices").
- Coping with interdependence implies changing the rules of rivalry by changing the rules of cooperation, that is by altering the stakes of the game: "diplomacy" is the continuation of rivalry by other means ("agenda substitution").
- Changing the mix of competition and cooperation means reframing the set of insiders and outsiders ("arena substitution").
- Reframing the set means changing the time horizon of the game (altering the timing of commitments, that is "horizon substitution").
- Manipulating arena, agenda and horizon is a non-trivial option, especially in oligopolistic settings ("small number" games).
- In such settings "economizing on interactions" boils down to economizing on ambitions (agenda), actors (arena) and time (timing).
- An adequate theory of "order as a set of nested games", pretending to explain from *within* the substance and duration of intra- and interorganizational commitments has therefore to conceive of arena, agenda and time as a menu of strategic variables open to manipulation, rather than as a set of preordained or exogenously determined parameters of the games of capitalist discipline and corporate diplomacy.

The dark matter in this storyboard is the question of "manipulation" – my summary term for mutations in the processes of search and selection in the "moralizing and rationalizing" of disciplinary regimes. Compared to the encyclopedia of the Habitus versus Habitat interpretations reviewed in this chapter, my *co*-habitation approach is most at ease with the ontological premises of "institutional theory" – from the founding fathers (Th. Veblen, J. Commons and the Austrian school) to its present-day heirs (D. North, G. Hodgson).

Box 3.9   On the "evolution" of governance regimes

The rapport between the institutionalist legacy and my cohabitation perspective emanates from a shared interest in the evolution of (in institutionalist idiom) "governance" regimes. The grand ambition of institutional theory is to offer a synthesis of the separate traditions in the study of change in the institutions of capitalism, such as theories that take, alternatively, efficiency considerations, technology imperatives, market power and control, the role of culture, or the state as the primary driver of regime change. Among the premises of the integrative-evolutionary interpretation of institutional change that seem to concur most with our cohabitation perspective, are the following:

- Political and socio-economic order are not "spontaneous" things (as for instance in D. Hume, A. Smith or F. Hayek; cf. Hodgson, 2006: 15).
- For the sake of understanding regime change, agent "insensitive" explanations are preferred to avoid a voluntarist overstatement of the role of free will in the selection of institutional alternatives; see my earlier remarks on Daems (this chapter, p. 63) and Hodgson's suggestion (2006: 7, 16): "[to] avoid the conceptual problems of an account based primarily on intentionality ...; face the possibility of the study of markets that focuses largely on institutions and structures, to a degree independent of the assumptions made about agents ... [thus] the explanatory burden is carried by system structures rather than the preferences or psychology of individuals".
- Determinist explanations are equally unadvisable: institutional evolution is a matter of "constrained selection", that is, the interactive outcome of the strategic choices of a plurality of actors responding to one another's choices.
- And finally, for a proper understanding of institutional choice and change, we should not just look at inter- but also at intra-actor controversies and interests (as for instance proposed in Nelson and Winter, 1982; and Hodgson, 2006: 10).

Regarding change in institutional regimes two essential subjects remain under-addressed in the evolutionary economics of "governance" – to the effect of impairing its predictive powers. One has to do with the identification of the *actors* and the other with the identification of the *activism* that is supposed to have – in my framework – a decisive say in the processes of search and selection "behind" the evolution of "governance" regimes. Both relate to the essence of capitalist discipline and the orchestration of corporate games, that is *the manipulation of arena, agenda and time*. As a rule the principal actors in institutional economics are "producer" organizations and the "state" (Campbell et al., 1991). Between these two we find a category called "other organizations", for instance:

> Governance transformations are usually initiated by producers…who respond to new problems and opportunities that are created by changes in economic conditions and technology… However, if the state initiates a transformation, it does so in response to changes in domestic or international political-economic conditions. [Other organizations], including suppliers, labor, financial institutions, public interest groups, and consumer groups…typically respond reactively to producers. (Campbell and Lindberg, 1991: 328–9)

Unfortunately, not only the residual category of "other organizations" but also the "producers" and the "state" are too much of an amorphous grouping to allow for testable propositions on their respective contributions to the transformation of "governance" regimes. It is mainly through historical case studies that we learn – from case to case – about the wildly wide, mostly *sector (policy)* specific variability of *who* more precisely are the "instigators" versus "reactors" in the games of regime transformation. This unsatisfactory state of affairs is partly due to the preferred nomenclature: because of its legalistic connotations, "governance" theorists are inclined to look at the formal codifications of conduct (rule-*making*), while "discipline", due to its sociological and political-economic roots, prefers to look at the informal practices and discretionary margins for rule compliance versus evasion (rule-*enforcement*). Second, and perhaps more serious, not much transpires about the *logic* and the *modes* of operation of the search-and-selection processes that lead to change (or non-change) in disciplinary arrangements. The most we learn is that "selection is…a process of muddling through …, trial-and-error learning …, deliberate negotiations …, [and] elements of coercion through political and economic struggle"; or, alternatively: "the relative resource and power endowments of actors *mediate* the selection process by affording more richly endowed actors with greater capacities to implement the governance mechanisms of their choice" (ibid.: 331, 343).

What is missing in these nearly tautological (and semi-voluntarist) formulations is a rudimentary notion of both the *anatomy* and the *circulation* of bargaining power and its potential consequences for the swings and/or mutations of capitalist discipline. Besides, the units of analysis remain unclear. For instance: *"actors* select new governance regimes" versus *"inter*actions among labor, capital, and the state select the course of capitalist development" (ibid.: 351, 353; my italics). It is one thing to assert that "institutions…facilitate and regulate the resources of power. A definition of institutions that ignores this fact fails to capture part of what is distinctive about institutions, namely that the mechanisms for limiting choices, including contractual choices, reflect the distribution of power" (Levi, 1990: 407). It is clearly another thing to identify the *sources* of this power and the *forces* of its reproduction or change, and more importantly to identify and "locate" the *instigators* of institutional change or continuity.

For this sort of critical link in a *positive* theory, our construct of a nested negotiated order offers suggestions for filling the analytical voids. For a better identification of the processes of search and selection, and what in this chapter (for want of a better term) came to be nicknamed the "prompting hand", we may revert to an older term that – for reasons unknown – was lost in institutionalist translation, to wit: the dynamics of the *mobilization of bias* in the construction of political-economic order. The question relates directly to what we identified above as the "dark matter" of capitalist discipline and the orchestration of corporate games: who are the "semi-sovereigns" that are in a position to take the lead in "moralizing and rationalizing" political-economic preferences and priorities by (Schattschneider's expression, see below) *"organizing in and out"* political-economic controversies? For obvious reasons the most ostentatious players in the game of regime formalization ("endorsement") are the front-stage players, that is, production firms and specific state agencies. However, for reasons suggested earlier, in the study of regime *formation* ("enforcement") it seems to make more sense to look at the *backstage* whips who – for reasons to be spelled out later – play a decisive role in the structuring of the arena, agenda and timing of disciplinary games – in short, those that have a privileged say in the "mobilization of bias" in the de facto orchestration of firm-to-firm and market-to-state commitments.

The original coining of the expression comes from Schattschneider (1960: 71): "all forms of political organization have a bias in favor of the exploitation of some kinds of conflict and the suppression of others *because organization is the mobilization of bias"*. The *empirical* problem with the power "to control the scope of controversy" is that, as a rule, the *backstage* whips constitute a deliberately non-conspicuous and, as it were, amphibious complex – which is neither overtly public nor covertly private. At variance with the officially professed comparative *diversity* of corporate "governance" regimes worldwide (cf. Merlini, 1984), *my* backstage theatre relates to a surprisingly homogeneous and congenial semi-sovereign elite – homogeneous and congenial both in terms of its recruitment and mobility patterns (across public/private interfaces) and in terms of its amoral/professional creed. To paraphrase its tenets: "We have no permanent allies. We have no permanent enemies. We just have interests" (in the words of a US White House lobbyist working on behalf of, among others, the pharmaceutical/biotech and medical-devices industry who was pressing for deregulation in these areas, quoted in Miles, 2001: 90). Or, alternatively, in the words of the US Secretary of Defense, Robert Gates, commenting on the diplomatic discomfort caused by the scandal of leaked US confidential information by Wikileaks, in late 2010: "some...do business with us because they fear us, or because they respect us. But most of them because they need us" (*Washington Post*, December 6, 2010).

Yet the intrigue remains: the *orchestration* of discipline is neither a formal state prerogative nor an informal operation of the visible hand – even less a spontaneous product of the invisible hand. As was argued in Chapter 1, the "semi-sovereign" whips that operate in the backstage of disciplinary arrangements – credit raters and other reputational intermediaries, including law firms, headhunters, investment bankers and pliable regulatory agencies – constitute an essentially *nonrecorded* negotiated order (which definitely does not mean an unstructured, let alone undisciplined, sort of order). While, for these very reasons, the "search and selection" processes behind regime formation are not readily accessible for survey methods or statistical proof, this does by no means imply that the "mobilization of bias" in the orchestration of discipline is inaccessible to empirical inquiry – as the following chapters will demonstrate. There we will see how the social fabric of capitalist discipline revolves essentially along three axes: (1) the containment of controversy, (2) the manipulation of reputation, and (3) the accommodation of risk appreciation. It is along these axes that the remixing of critical resources and partnerships is orchestrated. They are, in my model specifications, the fundamentals of the "politics of cohabitation" in a nested negotiated order.

The substance and stability of firm-to-state commitments is a function of firm-to-firm commitments. Together they breed the stuff from which the negotiated order of the political economy is made. Moves and movements in the "first order", firm-to-firm and intermediary circuits affect the negotiability of "second order" commitments in the market-to-state circuits (cf. Figure 1.1). That is the reason for thinking that the conditions and codes that determine the credibility of *interfirm commitments* deserve analytical priority. As argued earlier, for a convincing explanation of the evolution of market and non-market commitments it is useful to distinguish between the need and the capacity for the coordination of economic activities. As documented in this chapter, *both* neo-classical equilibrium and evolutionary non-equilibrium analysis seem to hold, in spite of their divergent opinions on the meanings of economic "efficiency" and the nature of the underlying "stimulus-response" mechanics, that *"need* sorts out capacity". A *sociological* view of political-economic ordering – starting from the embeddedness of choice and the nestedness of coordination – tends to attach more credence to the opposite: that "need *follows* capacity".

The latter assessment hypothesizes that negotiated orders are typically based on ex post rationalizations rather than ex ante rationalities or, for others, the canons of Darwinian efficiency. The *effectiveness* of ex post rationalizations depends on the positions and reputations of those *who articulate them* – rather than on some allegedly objective demonstration of corporate or societal "needs". Our positional-reputational view, focusing upon critical resource and partner dependences between rival firms and rival states and the mobilization of bias in the rationalization and moralization of the politics of cohabitation inspired by interdependent choice, brings the credibility of commitments – including the shunning or obstruction of commitments – back to the center of the analysis.

As I will argue in the chapters that follow, it is the accommodation and containment of risk assessments that constitute the cornerstones of capitalist discipline. Risk perceptions vary with accountability, and accountability varies with the room for monitoring and sanctioning. Monitoring is related to the codification of conduct. But the *pertinence* of monitoring varies directly with the room for sanctioning. The pertinence of sanctioning varies with the room for the passing on of contractual hazards. As long as the conditioning does not correspond with the codification, monitoring remains largely ineffectual for the control of the swings of capitalist discipline. As we will see later, risk perceptions are typically a short-term affair, whereas the manipulation of reputations and changes in the level of interest aggregation and conflict accommodation are typically long-term affairs. It is this temporal mismatch that has much to do with the main issue of this study: the swings of order and disorder in the organization of economic life. In Chapter 4 I elaborate on these conjectures and propositions by applying them to the economics and politics of industrial policy-making. This application serves as a nearer specification of what we see as two archetypal ingredients of the politics of cohabitation in nested games: accommodation and containment.

4
Cohabitation

Introduction

Social order builds upon reciprocity and representativity. *Reciprocity* tells us about external quid pro quos. It is a derivative of the conditions of dependence between organizations. *Representativity* informs us about the capacity of organizations to act as authoritative identities. Authoritative identity derives from a shared sense of direction, both in the eyes of the members *and* in the perception of an organization's counterparts. Representativity is a derivative of the conditions of reciprocity *inside* organizations, that is, a function of the relations of dependence between the members of organizations and associations.

Representativity and reciprocity are the driving forces of nested games and its collective outcome: the negotiated texture of social order. This chapter delves deeper into the meaning of these concepts. Understanding the principles of social order helps us to understand more precisely what was said in the preceding chapters about the mechanics of compliance and about change and continuity in compliance regimes, such as the transition from the old to the new discipline.

The negotiated order of capitalist games may be summarized as a specific, yet shifting, mix of two complementary stratagems: accommodation and containment. By analyzing the mix it will be possible to explain, first, the way in which market and non-market actors agree upon specific forms of reciprocity. Second, it will become clear, whatever the optical illusion of symmetry on the front stage, how asymmetrical reciprocity sometimes turns out to be on the backstage of capitalist discipline.

The conceptual exercise is made concrete by a "laboratory" example of the workings of accommodation and containment. For that purpose we will look at the Dutch prototype of concerted action in industrial policy-making, from its inception during the interwar period to its gradual demise in the late 1980s. I have selected the Dutch prototype for its "measuredness" and say, "lampedusan" talent for continuation by adaptation. (After Di Lampedusa's novel, *Il Gattopardo*: "If we want things to stay as they are, things will have to change".) The selected time horizon proves to be long enough to illustrate how changing conditions lead to changes in codes and commitments between the architects of capitalist order.

The "architects" are governments, firms, trade associations and labor unions. Industrial order through accommodation and containment is the outcome of negotiating processes at multiple levels of organizational decision-making, that is, the macro-political, the meso-sectoral and the micro-corporate level of handling the puzzles of interdependent choice. As we will see more completely further on, two aspects of the nested games in this multilevel theater deserve special attention. First, the *time span* of strategy formation differs from level to level. Given these differentials it is of vital importance to the actors to control, somehow, the *cross*-level timing of choices and coordination. The capacity to influence the mix of the varying time spans is dependent on the capacity to influence the composition of the arena. The *composition* of the arena includes such questions as: who participates in which stage at which level? Who is excluded? The capacity to influence the composition of the arena defines the capacity to influence the setting of the agenda. Agenda-setting revolves around questions of which issues will be included, when and for how long, and which issues will be organized away at which level, that is, determined to be a non-issue. The latter question refers to a second aspect that we have to pay attention to. Given a specific constellation of the strategic triangle of timing, arena and agenda, the "mobilization" of bias may become a *self-propelling* mechanism. This possibility may have quite radical implications for the way we think about the phenomenon of "*non*-decision making" (see Bachrach and Baratz, 1962; 1963; Lukes, 1974). Moreover, once the mechanism of strategy formation has acquired a momentum of its own, this may have far-reaching consequences for *the extent to which the architects of order want to be held accountable for the logic and the outcomes of the game*. Further on we will see what the latter means for our understanding of the making and unmaking of capitalist order.

Before developing that theme, I will first present a precis of what conventionally is seen as the subject of industrial strategy-making. After that a description and assessment of the Dutch case is given. I will then reconsider the facts from the perspective of a negotiated order of nested games.

The protocols

The official targets of industrial strategy-making cover a broad area. The *scope* may vary from changes in the proportion of the factors of production employed at the level of individual firms, to changes in the horizontal composition and the degree of vertical integration of industries – eventually differentiating large versus small, focal versus peripheral, and import-substitution versus export-oriented firms – up to changes in the relations between sectors of the economy as a whole. At a higher level of aggregation, industrial strategy-making aims at the modernization of a national economy in response to (changes in) the conditions of international competition and employment, quantitatively and qualitatively, and may include such aspects as pollution control, economizing on energy and raw materials, a balanced regional distribution of economic activities and employment, for instance in order to avoid congestion and unacceptable interregional disparities in economic welfare. The *forms* of industrial strategy-making range from direct to indirect modes of firm-to-firm and government-to-industry coordination, alternatively implemented by a varying mix of positive and negative incentives (e.g. withholding financial support) and ranging from macro-generic to micro-specific methods to bring about the varying ambitions listed above.

At first sight, one would expect a high profile for this specimen of strategy-formation, given the *re*distributive nature of the strategy agenda:

- Industrial strategies affect both new and established industries that used to enjoy the status of industrial champions (e.g. shipbuilding, textile, steel, chemicals).
- While absorbing considerable amounts of state finance, it becomes more necessary to find a trade-off between the promotion of promising industries versus the assistance of ailing industries.
- Structural unemployment, even the one that goes with the "spontaneous" reorganization of economies, may be expected to politicize the debate on the appropriate means and goals of industrial policy-making.
- Whether principled or simply opportunist, industrial strategies affect societies as a whole while redefining the status of skills and competences, changing the stratification of pressure groups and interest associations, sharpening the clash between the employed versus the unemployed, and so on.

The Netherlands' variety of industrial strategy-making shows some remarkable *continuities*. In spite of its inherently conflict-prone nature, the Dutch practice has always been low profile, that is, presented in an apolitical, defensive and procedural rather than substantive key. Since the great pre-war depression, arguments and instruments in this area have been by and large variations on a repetetive theme ("If you want things to stay as they are, it suffices to change the semantics and procedures"). What has changed since the last decade is the uncertainty about the rules of the game after a flood of initiatives to "deregulate" state controls, to "privatize" state activities and to substitute independent "expertocracy" for tripartite consultation and consensual decision-making. The latter, however, appears to have done more for the accessibility and the visibility of the size of state involvement than for the transparency and effectiveness of the processes of strategy-making. Apparently, changes in strategy and industrial order follow a logic of their own (not in the Galbraithian sense of systemic "imperatives" or the Chandlerian "efficiency drive" of the visible hand, but in the sense of "mechanisms" (Elster, 1984) that explain how, under specific conditions, the "logic of agency" takes precedence over the "logic of agents"; more about this methodological *interactionist* perspective in Chapter 9).

For a long time the role of the state has been primarily to assist in solving the recurrent problems of excess capacity in a range of industries. This led to a peculiar form of covenants between government and industry. However, the risks and costs associated with crisis-triggered agreements gradually shifted the emphasis from accommodation to containment, that is, to methods for enhancing the discipline of the protagonists. For a remarkably long time the loss of status of erstwhile leading firms did not entail a proportional loss of pressure potential for the former champions. This status incongruence resulted in a growing indeterminacy of firm-to-firm, industry-to-union and business-to-government agreements. How this indeterminacy stems from changing conditions of interdependence between industry, unions and the state can be shown by looking respectively at the front and backstage of the industrial policy-making process.

The front stage

The roots of the politics of accommodation and containment lie in the first and, more recognizably, second decade of the last century. The *inter bellum* years are the formative period for the basic philosophy here, which can be summarized as a pragmatic mixture of ideological ingredients and learning-by-doing. Accounts agree that, from the time when the Department of Economic Affairs embarked on industrial policy-making, it was the captains of industry who taught the Department and not the reverse. At most the Department played a role as a catalyst in accommodating conflicting interests – for instance between industrial and financial capital, between protectionists and free traders, between industrial interests in the south versus the north and west of the country, between the basic industries versus the others, etc. – though both the inspiration and the subsequent implementation of policies agreed upon came, and still comes, from the business establishment itself. Nothing substantial can be accomplished without the explicit fiat (in the case of unanimity) or the informal consent (in the case of non-unanimity) of the strategy subjects themselves. The state has always shown a strong interest in tightly orchestrated, monopolistic representations of its counterparts. Monopolistic representation unburdens the state from dealing with individual dissenters or factional divides. It is only since the end of the 1960s that the labor unions became involved in the co-definition and implementation of (mainly reactive) industrial restructuring policies. The unions were – and still are – non-existent in the *pro*active parts of industrial strategy-making, both constitutionally and practically. As can be seen below, the leadership of the unions proved never to be unhappy with their passive or reactive role in this storyline.

In a meticulous reconstruction of Dutch industrial policy-making during the 1930s and the decades following the Second World War, De Hen (1980) points out three continuities. First, from the onset policy formation has been characterized by obligingness vis-à-vis the industrial establishment. Laissez-faire principles were, so to say, not opposed but guided. 'Guidance' means correcting for the direst consequences of the free play of market forces through state-supported campaigns directed at protecting basic industrial activities like steel, transport (shipyards) and petrochemicals and attracting foreign direct investment into sectors deemed essential for the composition of the economy. A second continuity is the modest degree of planning in the orthodox sense of the word. The third continuity is the virtual absence of any scholarly underpinning of industrial policy-making and strategy formation. "Theories" that were brought up in defense of specific approaches and institutional arrangements can, at best, be qualified as rationalizations of existing belief systems – for instance the harmonic-organicist thought of Catholic origin and the interventionist-contractarian heritage of socialist vintage – rather than as the fruits of stringent political-economic and institutionalist reasoning (for a concise portrait of the religious and secular roots and rivalries behind "neo-corporatist" thinking, see Wassenberg, 1978; 1980a).

Following De Hen (1980), the mixture of ideological and pragmatic ingredients stimulated an "intimate collaboration" between state and industry. The informal understanding between state and business, enacted in the 1930s, makes it clear why the Dutch variety of concerted action never assumed the appearance of formal economic planning and regulation (*ordening*, in Dutch) – except in episodes of massive economic slump during which business temporarily conceded to *ordering* out of sheer self-preservation.

Ordening meant the overt concentration combined with covert centralization of economic decision-making by means of direct cartelization and indirect satellitization, most of the time tolerated if not promoted by the Department of Economic Affairs and not seldom complemented by protectionist practices. However, being a risky recipe for an open, export-oriented economy, protectionism had to take the form of informal, *extra*-legal understandings between selected parts of the industrial establishment and the Department of Economic Affairs. Analogous arrangements emerged between the Department of Transport, Traffic and Waterways, the Department of Agriculture, etc. and their respective clienteles.

The quest for *ordening* fitted in with the drive (observable in all capitalist industrial states around that time) towards large-scale, vertically integrated companies and cartelization. Though never averse to cartels and other forms of restrictive market practices, from the onset of the great depression the Netherlands' government finally came to designate the promotion of cartelization as its official policy. Import restrictions as well as subsidiary financial arrangements became deliberately and effectively oriented at the formation of cartels. After a while the state even acquired formal competence – it could not refuse the industrialists' offer – to *ratify* restrictive agreements and market-sharing treaties (a competence called the Act on *Ordening*). In addition it accepted the complementary competence to impose barriers to entry in most sectors of the economy (the so-called *Bedrijfsvergunningenwet*, an Act on the regulation of the establishing of new firms or plants). So the mixed private–public practice of industrial "concertation" incrementally managed to acquire official status. The accompanying principles of rationalizing and moralizing soon followed.

Apparently unaffected by new acronyms, instruments and agencies, and untouched by the variations in "theories" invoked to rationalize and legitimize the strategies pursued, until the late 1970s every major industrial policy proposal, whether "generic" or "specific", came to be based on an official troika of: (1) a balanced *distribution* of productive capacity; (2) the *prevention* of excess capacity (sometimes supplemented by calls for innovation); and (3) the *reduction* of unemployment. As noted above, the troika was neither based on rigorous analytical reasoning nor supported by any amount of empirical evidence. It just emerged and subsequently was settled on the basis of preaching-by-doing. The objectives continued to be sufficiently non-specific for serving as an efficient vehicle for soliciting state assistance (financially or otherwise, e.g. market regulation, quota rulings) rather than serving as an effective instrument for the modernization of the economy.

Box 4.1   Respectable beliefs

Belief systems make social life predictable, while serving as a means for moralizing and rationalizing compliance (to paraphrase Lowi, 1964). Shared beliefs tend to assume the status of "scientific" theories. Whether the canons of academic orthodoxy confer respectability on this practice or not doesn't matter. What people define as "social order" becomes paraphrased in behavioral maxims. Maxims become axioms and axioms imperceptibly assume the status of sound theory. And what people define as theoretically sound is real in its consequences.

As will be shown below, state officials, unions and firms (and their associations) contribute in a vicious way to the discrepancy between practice and rhetoric. The *rhetoric* is that from now on policies should rather be structural, comprehensive and consistent. The *practice* is that policies remain ad hoc, fragmentary and, by and large, inconsequential. Before trying to understand that – the *back*stage story – let me first round off the front stage storyline.

From 1948 up to 1963 eight White Papers were published on (re-)industrialization, at first to recover from the losses of the war and to rebuild the national economy. After that arguments were put forward to shift the composition of the economy from the pre-war orientation on agriculture/fishery, mining and especially trade towards a more genuine industrial orientation. Around 1963–75 the first signs of a lack of productivity growth, a loss of competitiveness and an overrepresentation of saturated markets in the industrial composition of the economy became visible. From 1975 onwards governmental objectives become more attuned to growing disparities in the development of specific sub-sectors and branches. Concerns arose about growing unemployment, combined with increasing excess capacity, underemployment of capital and the apparent lack of technological and commercial adaptation to changing international market conditions. From the time that these characteristics came to be recognized as structural mismatches rather than as short cyclical deficiencies, pressure mounted for more consistent and finely tuned responses. The first 1973 oil crisis did the rest to drive a common sense of urgency.

Strikingly enough, in spite of the commonly felt urgency of promoting a home-based industry, both as a remedy for balance of payment deficits (import substitution) and as prospective employment for a growing labor force (apart from the need to absorb the shake-out from agriculture), *none* of the White Papers mentioned above spelled out quantitative targets concerning employment and investments. Absent as well were indications of how more precisely these declaratory policy objectives might be communicated to and implemented by the industrial community itself. Thus, in accordance with the low-key legacy from the *inter bellum* years, the immediate post-war character of policy-making remained of a grossly unspecific, aggregate and noncommittal nature ("take-it-or-leave-it"). Apart from two or three more sizeable ventures (such as state participation on behalf of the steel and petrochemical industry and support for the improvement of the national airport, both considered essential for another take-off of the economy) – and apart from facilities and agencies established for the sake of investment promotion and improvement of the technological infrastructure – up to the early 1960s official policy-making remained dedicated to "improving the business climate" and its natural ally, tight wage controls.

Up until the 1980s nothing substantial that diminished the gap between activist rhetoric and reactive practices can be reported. After the specious calm of the 1960s and the first half of the 1970s a collection of official papers appeared on the issues of regional, sectoral and technological innovation. At the end of the 1970s the cumulatively expanded fabric of industrial strategy instruments comprised more than 120 separate regulations, co-administrated by more than a dozen of separate agencies, banks and interdepartmental institutions, fed by a disordered array of partially overlapping, partially incompatible, budgeting systems. To what extent and for how long can a modern industrial state tolerate a growing mismatch between changing political-economic dependences and the institutional matrix construed for governing these dependences? A tentative answer may be gathered from a report published by the highest advisory body of Dutch government, the independent Scientific Council on Public Policy, entitled the *Place and Future of Dutch Industry* (*Wetenschappelijke Raad voor het Regeringsbeleid*, 1980; hereafter referred to as "PFI '80").

PFI '80 advocated the release of industrial policy-making from the institutional ossification associated with the tripartite consultative machinery. As an alternative it proposed a central committee composed of "totally independent" experts who would advise government on selecting promising sectors and industries. The committee would draw its inspiration for "picking the winners" from information provided by a National Development Society, which in turn would be informed by sector committees. At all levels the staff would be experts who, though eventually recruited from business or labor, so having an antenna for what was going on there, would operate independently from interest group instructions or consultations. Government and parliament should have a final say in the selection and financing of projects showing a fair "chance of success".

In hindsight it is remarkable how approvingly business and labor digested the unorthodox shock therapy of PFI '80. As expected, the diagnosis of the structural problems of the economy met with general approval. Rather unexpected was the response to the institutional proposals. Its frankly anti-tripartite thrust caused the least problems for the employers' associations. They declared they were ready to substitute expertocracy for extant neo-corporatist practice, provided expert councils and development agencies would keep aloof from the bogey of binding sector-reorganization scenarios. A second proviso from the employers' side urged the Department of Economic Affairs to preserve its nominal outsiders' posture, that is to maintain an arm's-length position *outside* the tripartite set-up but *without* abolishing the machinery of state subventions.

Even the labor unions were said to favor institutional reform, given their mounting discomfort with the old discipline's division of tripartite liabilities. In their view, however, *central government should take the lead* in formulating industrial-strategical priorities. Once Cabinet and parliament found out what they wanted, negotiations were to be carried out *directly* between state, capital/management and sector associations. During this stage the unions were to stay out lock, stock and barrel. Only when state and capital had reached an agreement and could conclude with concrete commitments, would labor unions consider the external and internal labor-market implications of the proposed agreement and start negotiations according to their interests and insights.

The conclusion was that from the architects of industrial order there was neither head-on opposition to nor outright endorsement of the PFI '80 proposals. First of all, the proposals did not interfere directly with the old discipline's principle of shared "limited liability", a principle that emerged in the late 1960s when the larger part of the labor unions decided to substitute an *ex post* "control" for the *ex ante* "participation" strategy that had prevailed from the 1950s until the early 1960s. In that sense one may say that the "disrespect" of the authors of PFI '80 for the neo-corporatist heritage was not based on courage or fancy. Curiously enough, the hubbub that arose about the PFI '80 proposals came mainly from the *outsiders*. For instance, academic experts on industrial relations predicted that the substitution of expertocracy for tripartism and neo-corporatist forbearance would aggravate rather than remedy the flaws of the old discipline, that is would lead to an increase in non-commitment, free-ridership and collective non-accountability. In other words, independent expertise presented as the way out of tripartite irresolution was not expected to deliver what the social fabric most urgently needed, that is, a new consensus on strategic priorities and binding commitments for the sake of industrial renewal.

In line with the politics of depoliticization and incrementalism, showing an unremitting bias to add new constructs to extant practices rather than replace or alter old customs, government asked the *summit* of the Dutch neo-corporatist pyramid, the tripartite Social Economic Council (*Sociaal-Economische Raad*), for its opinion about the proposal to abolish the premises of neo-corporatist policy-making. Predictably the Social Economic Council answered that it would be quite conceivable to live with the best of two worlds, that is having an expert-based infrastructure for the design and development of focused sector strategies, while maintaining a tripartite infrastructure for the execution of comprehensive industrial strategies. Meanwhile the labor unions insisted on a more compelling articulation of the directive role of the Departments of Social and Economic Affairs in matters of structural, sectoral and corporate renewal. Government, without too many dissenting opinions from parliament, reiterated the argument that politicians should refrain from assuming an initiating, let alone a directing, role since politicians and public officials allegedly lacked the pertinent expertise. Employers' associations, financial institutions and industrial leaders declined categorically to commit the "market" to binding sector scenarios and corporate reorganizations. In the vacuum of this consortium of vetoes, the tripartite machinery of non-decision-making resumed its classical role. Of the projected PFI '80 architecture of Councils and Committees only an expert-based, mixed-financed Agency for Industrial Projects (*Maatschappij voor Industriële Projecten*) was all that survived. After a couple of years even this last flare-up of former aspirations dissolved into silence. With that the subject of comprehensive and sectoral industrial strategy-making disappeared once and for all from the public agenda.

Dutch leniency in handling industrial-political matters can be epitomized in two diametrically opposed documents. On the one hand there is an unusually ambitious White Paper on "selective economic growth", published by the government in 1976 (*Nota inzake Selectieve Groei*), advocating a strategy shift from "sunset" to "sunrise" sectors, including a focus shift from energy-intensive to energy-saving and less-polluting activities. According to this document, focus and strategy were supposed to be based on a solid *tripartite* consensus. On the other hand, as reviewed above, there is the equally prestigious non-governmental canon on the "place and future of industry", articulating comparable aspirations, but this time to be realized by the *non*-tripartite consensus of "independent experts". Since the closure of this episode expertocracy and tripartism continue to live apart together. For understanding this square of the corporatist circle we must quit the front stage and learn more about the backstage of the game of the politics of cohabitation.

The backstage

How to explain the persistence of the gap between rhetoric and practice? In an allegedly rational world it is not the continuity of practices but rather the persistence of elusive rhetoric that intrigues. Part of the answer may be found in the "functional" rationalization of officials warning that a larger degree of transparency of the fabric of policy-making generates unwanted "me-too" precedents. Besides, there is the standard repertory of arguments that points out why it is impossible, however unfortunate, to make the premises of policy-making more consequential:

* Net policy effects cannot unambiguously be established because regulations and policy instruments that perform positive functions for some objectives (for instance economic stability) may have negative effects on other dimensions (for instance industrial innovation or environmental protection).
* The evaluation of the impact of policy instruments takes several years, thus impeding timely feedback and subsequent corrective action.
* One never knows whether the *non*-use of an instrument might have had less favorable results than seems to be the case at face value (windfall effect).
* Instruments may have negative effects for others than the members of the target group for whose welfare a specific measure was designed (displacement effect).

Diagnosing defects of policy-making in terms of rational-technical imperfections – "lack of information", "dearth of proven instruments", "contradictory nature of cross-policy purposes" – tends to look for technical-rational remedies. Allison (1971) has proposed looking beyond this "rational actor" caricature to interpreting deviations from perfect rationality as the consequence of "bureaucratic politics", rather than as their cause. The heuristic potential of Allison's approach can be enlarged when his analysis of intra-bureaucratic politics is extended to strategies among bureaucracies. Treatises that start from a Weberian–Michelsian view on *intra*-bureaucratic politics are trained to see the imperfections of bureaucratic rationality as manifestations of "failing loyalty" or "incomplete compliance" (Weber on "rational-legal bureaucracy") or as a correlate of the "democratic deficit" of voluntary associations (Michels on the "iron law of oligarchy") – which are eventually supplemented with the updated idiom of "bounded rationality" and "incremental decision-making". Game-theoretically inspired interpretations, instead, make us aware of other possibilities: they enable us to see bureaucratic failure and democratic deficits as a consequence of the "rational" search for the *reversibility* of intra- and inter-organizational commitments – as something that has to do with the tactical/temporary advantages of unclearly specified threats and promises among oligarchies and oligopolies. The search for reversible commitments offers a "positive" explanation of the emergence (and persistence) of a less-than-perfect hierarchy and rationality (Schelling, 1956: 282–94) – an explanation that is probably superior to the ones that start from the bounds of rationality and legitimacy as a consequence of the "technical-cognitive" complexities of modern life. Later on we will see how this insight can be extended to the paradox of rationality for "rational egoists" in helping others, including adversaries, in solving *their* troubles with "incomplete compliance" (for instance, due to an undisciplined constituency) and what the perverse consequences may be *for the opponents* of refusing that kind of "offer".

About oligarchy

Among the conventional wisdom about the analysis of bureaucracy belongs the contention that public and private hierarchies have an important property in common: they have a shared stake in the reduction of uncertainty. Both want to minimize instabilities in their environment. However, the modes of coping with uncertainty and achieving stability are opposed. Typically government bureaucracy has to do with the stability of behavior in society at large and amongst and within the departments of the state apparatus. Stability is supposed to be promoted by *standardization*, eventually completed by *stirring up* the competition between client systems and/or competing interdepartmental domain claims. Firms, on the other hand, are said to search for predictable behaviors of competitors, suppliers, customers and governmental actors. Stability, in this stylized juxtaposition, is promoted by *differentiation* and the *suppression* of competition. These are sought by establishing hierarchical relationships in an industry or market and by creating privileged ("clientelistic") connections with specialized ("patronizing") niches in the governmental bureaucracy. Thus, again typically speaking, public hierarchies look for Weberian equalities whereas market hierarchies look for Schumpeterian inequalities. What nonetheless keeps the two "methodologies" on speaking terms is a shared search for limited liability. How do actors reconcile their proper search for limited accountability with the search for predictability of their counterparts? My tentative answer is by *blurring* liabilities.

For quite some time convincing arguments have been put forward that pay more attention to the dynamics of internal bureaucratic competition – which is at odds with the Weberian notion of unquestioned hierarchy or, at the other end, the Anglo-Saxon notion of atomistic-utilitaristic competition between monolithic bureaus and agencies (see for instance Tullock, 1970; Niskanen, 1971). According to Breton and Wintrobe (1982), the mainstream wisdom on public bureaucracy starts from the "monopoly presumption", which assumes that "bureaucracy" may be modeled as a single bureau and that decision-makers within that bureau have a single (set of) objective(s), so that the bureau itself behaves as a "monolithic unit". Breton and Wintrobe (1982: 89–90), instead, see "competition [as] the most general assumption to make about bureaucracy – no less in government bureaus than in private corporations. Impediments to competition do arise in bureaucracies. But we believe that these impediments are best understood as restrictions imposed within a general framework of competition."

In their view intra-bureaucratic competition should not be seen as a struggle by individual bureaus for jobs or budgets (the mainstream view, going back to the earlier classics, e.g. Penrose, 1959; Crozier, 1963; Cyert and March, 1963; Thompson, 1967; Williamson, 1964), but as a competition for positions or membership in bureaucratic "networks" and as the competition for the allocation of resources between networks and bureaus. According to the authors inter-bureau competition enlarges rather than constrains the "capacity for selective behavior", that is the room for managerial or bureaucratic discretion. The question remains where upper and middle public management get their inspiration from when exploiting or stretching their discretionary margins. Explaining the logic of bureaucratic conduct is one thing, explaining the *substance* is another. For understanding the substance a cross-over is needed to "the other side" where private bureaucracies enter and the "circular causation" (Kapp, 1976) of public–private inducements starts. Looking through the public–private screen shows how the negotiated order emerging from the rivalries *inside* public and private hierarchies feed on the negotiated order emerging from rivalries *between* market and non-market hierarchies (to borrow the terminology from Pitelis, 1991).

About oligopoly

As with the analysis of intra-bureaucratic conduct, it appears to be fruitful for the analysis of the stratification of markets to take *games* and *networks*, rather than transactions and firms, as the basic unit of analysis. In Chapter 3 we have seen how a transaction-costs perspective hypothesizes that markets tend to become hierarchized when inter-firm transactions exhibit a high degree of uncertainty, recur frequently and require durable transaction-specific investments to realize least-cost supply. Under these conditions strategic behavior is assumed to be governed by "bounded rationality" and "opportunism". Opportunism refers to "making…self-disbelieved threats or promises", noting that "it is not essential that all economic agents behave this way. What is crucial is that *some* agents behave in this fashion and that it is costly to sort out those who are opportunistic from those who are not" (Williamson and Ouchi, 1983: 16–17).

As we have seen, others, like Daems (1983) and Aoki (2003), have enriched the possible range of institutional options by introducing network-type relationships, such as federations and communes. Butler (1983), starting from similar premises, adds the "vagueness" of transactions as another potential determinant that may influence institutional choice. His concept of "vagueness" reminds one of the role of "difficulty" in Niskanen's explanation of the choice between private suppliers versus public bureaus for performing specific tasks: "the primary reason…for choosing bureaus, rather than profit-seeking organizations, to supply services…is the difficulty of defining their characteristics sufficiently to contract for their supply" (Niskanen, 1973: 10–11).

Plotting the "complexity" of transactions on a qualitative scale from low to high degrees of respectively "uncertainty", "interdependence" and "vagueness", Butler expects that *markets* tend to become *hierarchized* when the first two variables assume high values and the last one is low, whereas networks or communes will replace market-type transactions when the latter exhibit a high degree of "uncertainty", "interdependence" *and* "vagueness".

When oligarchy and oligopoly meet

Applied to the institutional matrix of industrial strategy making, the implications of the (enlarged) transaction-costs perspective look as follows. Uncertainty, interdependence and the vagueness of the stakes of the game of industrial policy-making predict a strong propensity to a more or less "hierarchical solution" for the problems of coordination, allocation and the monitoring of transactions. *Both* the competence and the competition trap (see Chapter 1) will inspire some form of hierarchization of firm-to-firm and government-to-business transactions. Considering the earlier sketch of industrial policy-making as an inherently controversial/adversarial sort of politics, it seems safe to assume a potentially high incidence of opportunistic behavior, information impactedness, recurrent and irreversible transaction-specific investments, large commitments in terms of financial and human resources, organizational chauvinisms, and so on. These qualifications hold both for interfirm, business-to-government and capital-to-labor relationships. Linking the internal and external tendencies to hierarchization, leads to the following propositions:

Proposition I. *The more that "uncertainty", "interdependence" and "vagueness" promote a **quasi-hierarchical** answer to the need for concerted action, and the more that the search for economizing on transactions reinforces the hierarchical impetus, then the more probable is the emergence of the sorts of collusion and mutual respect that we come across in the familiar literature on oligopolistic accommodation and considerateness.*

Proposition II. *The more successful the external politics of accommodation and containment, the more probable that the organizational slack "rents" stemming from external discipline ("cartels") will be spent on internal rivalries, that is the more private and public hierarchies tend to develop **quasi-markets internally.***

This view places Breton and Wintrobe's appreciation of the phenomenon of bureaucratic competition in a proper *context* – thus offering a "thicker" explanation of the competitive *cum* cooperative interplay of internal and external networks.

The next step is to qualify the hypothesized connection between the external and internal dynamics of accommodation and considerateness by introducing a, somewhat unexpected, countervailing tendency:

Proposition III.   *Internal factional rivalries tend to destabilize external commitments, to the effect of diminishing the reliability of the politics of accommodation. Given the (legal, contractual, etc.) limits of "full" hierarchy, and given the presence of other constraints, such as the fear of (re-emerging) opportunism, the most probable net result will be, again, neither hierarchy nor market but (some form of) federation.*

Proposition III is a first try-out to offer a specification of the behavioral axiom introduced in Chapter 3: under conditions of increasing uncertainty about the quid pro quos and the rules of fair play, economizing on transactions will more and more come to mean economizing on *commitments*. This eventuality has consequences for the way we look at the concept of internal reciprocity (a prerequisite for an organization's representativeness) and the concept of external reciprocity – making for the credibility of interorganizational commitments. In the transactional context of industrial strategy-making, characterized by uncertainty, interdependence and vagueness of liabilities in terms of targets, criteria, externalities and so on, we can expect federations to drive out hierarchies, while hierarchies will drive out markets (for more on the distinction between markets, hierarchies and federations, see Chapter 3, p. 61 ff.). Industrial strategies seem to entail the typical features of a "recurrent" prisoner's dilemma. In a self-repeating prisoner's dilemma the will to *orchestrate* rather than the propensity to cheat will be the dominant strategy as long as each actor knows that the other actor(s) can retaliate in the next round. Only at the "final" round, analytically speaking, will a game of recurring transactions become similar to a single-shot game, that is, conducive to cheating (hence the fear for the "*re*-emergence of opportunism"). However, as each player might expect that (at least one of) his counterpart(s) may behave opportunistically in the final round, and as it is costly to find out *who* more precisely it is, it becomes imperative for the other(s) to cheat in the round *before* the end of the game. The latter, trying to pre-empt this "law" of anticipated reactions, will start cheating before the final-round-minus-one, etc. As a consequence the "recurrent" prisoner's dilemma game resumes its self-perverting impetus: pre-emption does not pay. The only solution seems to be the sort of *transient* rationalization by which actors invest – "for the time being" – in each other's interests, that is engage in some sort of exchange of hostages. Again, the result will be a federative rather than a hierarchical or market-type "solution".

Breton and Wintrobe point at an interesting internal mechanism that can be extended to support our hypotheses on the symbiotic interconnectedness of internal oligarchization and external oligopolization. I earlier asserted that a fall in demand, excess capacity, shrinking profits and the loss of status of former "industrial champions" generate uncertainty. The need for certainty is translated into pragmatic coordination, within the industry as well as amongst firms, labor and the state. Sooner or later, in spite of government support and concessions from the side of the labor supply, further cuts on expenditure and more radical reorganization will be needed. Following my Propositions I–III on the predicted rise and consolidation of competing oligarchies (quasi-markets) within private and public hierarchies, expenditure cuts and patterns of reorganization will follow another logic than the one a "managerial-rational" paradigm predicts. As Breton and Wintrobe (1982: 161) hypothesize: "reorganization is … in part, a means of repaying debts and settling accounts within an organization", and "bureaucrats will seek to implement cuts in ways that are least damaging to their long-run capacity for selective behavior" – where "selective behavior" is hypothesized to be a function of and proportional to "past investments in intra-bureaucratic networks".

Box 4.2 Loyalty and trust reconsidered

Assume (after Breton and Wintrobe, 1982: 159ff.) an exogenous fall in the demand for an organization's output, leading to a reduction in its work force. Chiefs – that is, the top of the internal dominant coalition – possess skills that are organization-specific and are consequently less likely to be dismissed when demand is low. In this case, according to Breton and Wintrobe, cuts in the workforce have to come from among the subordinates or lower echelons and "would presumably be made throughout the organization on some formal basis, such as seniority".

Breton and Wintrobe conceive of bureaucracy as a network of internal networks in which from level to level subordinates offer loyalty to superiors and solidarity with colleagues on a competitive basis in exchange for membership in networks in order to acquire network-bound resources and status and to enhance their chances of promotion. The latter is assumed to be dependent on the position of their actual and prospective networks within the organizational stratification (cf. Allison's 1971 "bureaucratic politics" model, not mentioned in Breton and Wintrobe). Subordinates who are members of networks with senior bureaucrats will be aware – in the above mentioned situation of a fall in demand and consequently a fall in organizational resources (expenditures) – "that if they are dismissed, they will never be repaid for the trust they accumulated in the past and for the loans extended" (Breton and Wintrobe, 1982: 159). The network leaders then face a dilemma: formally (à la Weber) they are supposed not to discriminate between those who are in their networks and those who are not. If they do not promote their own clique members, they suffer a double loss: "(i) they lose (the subordinates in) their network; and (ii) those who remain in the organization will observe that network membership did not, in the end, turn out to be worth much" (ibid.).

The consequence is that the very power base – the reliability of the internal exchange system – is undermined for the senior bureaucrats. The corrective reaction on the side of the seniors will be to promote their most loyal clients/subordinates to a "non-dismissible" level in order to *safeguard their own (network) creditworthiness.*

The foregoing opens an amoral view, free from rationalistic overstretch, on the role of trust and loyalty for the preservation or erosion of the capacity of organizations to act as coherent and authoritative entities. It may be the beginning of a decent, "asset-based" theory of the ups and downs in the *representativity* of organizations and interest associations. It may be the foundation for a non-idealist explanation of the capacity of (federations of) organizations *not* to learn from strategic failure or ineptitude. It may be the basis, in short, for explaining – from within – the *fossilization* of strategy.

Summing up, it appears plausible to assume a (time-lagged) correspondence between the *fear of opportunistic behavior* (inducing the recurrent search for containment and pseudo-hierarchization interorganizationally) and the *fear of network insolvency* (generating oligarchization and pseudo-competition intra-organizationally). Intrabureaucratic cliques "invest" in external networks, as external networks are employed to acquire the material and immaterial "rents" to build and preserve intra-organizational cliques. This sort of a political-economic "contingent reciprocity" theory offers inspiration for a realist interpretation of the conservative biases of industrial strategy-making – probably more enlightening for our apprehension of the persistence of the divide between rational *intents* and irrational *outcomes* than either the axioms of technical-rational "imperfections" or the rationalistic assumptions of managerial "learning". A nested-negotiated order perspective makes us aware of a more subtle explanation of the "automatism" of the reproduction of order-in-spite-of-social-discomfort than the explanations built on the intellectually more "lazy" postulates of "institutional inertia" or "the arrogance of power". The next two sections trace some antecedents of the perspective defended here. They review earlier thoughts on the constituent strategies of social and economic order: accommodation and containment.

Cohabitation

Looking at social order from a negotiation perspective brings together what academic convention (for unknown reasons) separates: the logic of bureaucratic action on the one hand and the logic of collective action on the other. By combining the two it may become understandable why there are virtually no serious examples of industrial strategies that fully satisfy the canons that Schumpeter, with the Great Depression in mind, identified as *the* rationale of industrial policy:

> there is certainly no point in trying to conserve obsolescent industries indefinitely; but there is point in trying to avoid their coming down with a crash and in attempting to turn a rout, which may become a center of cumulative depressive effects, into *orderly retreat*. Correspondingly, there is, in the case of industries that have sown their wild oats but are still gaining and not losing ground, such a thing as *orderly advance*. (Schumpeter, 1970: 90; my italics)

In Chapter 1 arguments were put forward to explain why and how the competition trap tends to preclude an "orderly retreat" in the case of declining industries, as well as why the competence trap seriously complicates an "orderly advance" in the case of newly emerging industries. But, apart from that, why is it that in practice orderly retreat and orderly advance seldom, if ever, operate *in tandem*? For answering that we have to focus on a more fundamental puzzle: the remarkable stability of a multi-actor game that one would expect to be inherently unstable because of its contradictory credentials and unequal returns. The following will show that the solution of the puzzle can be found in the junction of the logics of bureaucratic-*cum*-collective action: where the two are allowed to meet in an undiluted way, that is remain unchallenged by any institutional antidote, the result turns out to be the fossilization of strategy. This produces the kind of "compulsion" that reminds us of Lowi's (1970) conception of "institutions" as "the means of moralizing, rationalizing and administering coercion". In my version, however, it is the *anonymity* of coercion – the "masked" prompting hand we came across in Chapter 3 – that causes the compulsion to transpire as less tyrannical, and thus easier to "moralize, rationalize and administer" than unmasked acts of open coercion: the actors come to believe, or say they believe, that they are "prisoners of circumstance", rather than the subjects or objects of exploitation or deliberate manipulation.

The literature on collective and bureaucratic action live in splendid isolation. As a consequence theorizing on bureaucracy misses important insights from the theory of collective action, and vice versa. The lack of correspondence between the two generates a common flaw: both are unable to deduce the essentials of the logic of oligopolistic action and to predict its oligarchic outcomes. For instance, Olson (1975: 42–4), starting from an assertion that "each firm in an industry is not only a rival of every other firm, but also an indispensable collaborator in any collusive action", concludes that in oligopolistic situations the result of strategic interaction – rivalry or collusion – will be "indeterminate". According to Olson, rational members of a group of oligopolists face a strategic problem, but while "the theory of games and other types of analysis might prove very helpful" there seems to be no way at present of "getting a general, valid, and determinate solution at the level of abstraction (pursued here)". Usefully enough, Olson compares the indeterminateness of "oligopoly" in the market place with "logrolling" in parliamentary decision-making: analogous problems of indeterminateness will show up since every potential logroller will pursue the same strategy, that is, insist that his or her counterparts moderate the legislative counter-demands that they stipulate as the price for their support for the special-legislation claims of the would-be logroller that started the bidding. The outcome is predicted to be perfectly Olsonian again:

> Every one of the interests will be better off if the logrolling is done than if it is not, but as individual interests strive for better legislative bargains the result of the competing strategies may be that no agreement is reached. This is quite similar to the situation oligopolistic groups are in, as they all desire a higher price and will all gain if they restrict output to get it, but they may not be able to agree on market shares.

This is a familiar topic, reducible to the divide, introduced in Chapter 1, of value creation ("enlarging the pie") versus value appropriation ("cutting the pie"). Yet, scholars and practitioners working from less sublime "levels of abstraction" report, more than the Olsonian logic of collective action predicts, *determinateness* in the stakes and "tacit treaties" resulting from intra-bureaucratic bargaining. The same can be said for cases of "tacit collusion" in imperfect markets. There is a growing body of empirical documentation on both topics. On the negotiated order inside public and private bureaucracy see: Wildasky (1964); Tullock (1965); Neustadt (1966); Allison (1971); Niskanen (1971; 1979); Halperin (1974); Cowart et al. (1975); Goodin (1975); Aoki et al. (1990); Weissing and Ostrom (1993). See also the numerous case studies that stuff our libraries with documentation on bureaucratic "feuds and fads" from knowledgeable insiders' views: Crossman (1976), Benn (1980), Kissinger (1979; 1982; 1994) and Barofsky's (2012) detailed chronicle of the head-on confrontations between himself – as public prosecutor investigating the $700 billion rescue by Washington of Wall Street banks and the automotive industry – and the Minister of Finance, Timothy Geithner, who reportedly tried to stop the investigations. On the negotiated order inside oligopolistic arenas, valuable observations and insights can be gathered from Richardson (1960), Shepherd (1970), Galbraith (1974) and the scholarly rich overview contained in Jacquemin and de Jong (1976).

However, what remains is the separation between the two academies of theorizing. Models of oligopolistic behavior abstract from the findings of the organizational literature on internal choice processes (strategy formation) and structures of power (internal coalition formation), whereas models of organizational behavior usually abstract from the quest for control of external contingencies, for instance the typical stratagems and spoils that go with oligopolistic behavior. The bureaucratic treasury has an introvert bias excluding the *external* determinants of the rise and decline of *internal* elites. Inversely, the oligopolistic records – even treatises on the Galbraithian "symbiosis" between private and public bureaucracy (see Chapter 2) – systematically underrate the constraints and vicissitudes of the power politics (alias information asymmetries and insider-trading) *inside* large complex organizations and their impact on the stability, that is, the *reliability* of externally negotiated forms of accommodation and compliance. In brief: both fail to grasp the intricacies of the "Faustian" *Wahlverwandtschaft* (elective affinity) between internally negotiated "tacit treaties" and externally negotiated "tacit understandings". Yet it is precisely this "elective affinity" that forms the *hard core* of the anonymous non-recorded part of the mechanics of capitalist discipline. As will be shown further on, under specific conditions the strategies and returns on investment for the actors appear to *follow*, rather than initiate per the rational "design", the escalation of commitments implied by the spillovers from the internal to the external "mechanisms" of social ordering. Rephrased in terms of our strategic triangle introduced before: the *agenda* and *timing* of the processes of strategy formation tend to follow the "framing" of the *arena* rather than the other way around. The under-exposure of the "twin" dynamics of internal oligarchization and external oligopolization in the literature on bureaucratic-and-collective action leaves some striking anomalies unexplained, such as the persistence of reactive practices of industrial politics in spite of the activist rhetoric of politicians, officials and interest groups alike. And perhaps even more surprisingly, when time and again the prophesies of the activists fail, this appears not to impair their *representativity*, that is, to undermine their mandate to act as an accredited actor. How can we explain this act of magic?

The time-honored answer to the paradox of discipline-due-to-adversity (see the definition of "discipline" in the List of Definitions) is the Hobbesian–Lockian "redemption": members of society, *anticipating* the collective tragedies stemming from the unconditional pursuit of individual utility-maximization, will sooner or later concede to some form of compromise between short-term micro- and long-term comprehensive definitions of interests and values. Besides skepticism about the (staying) power of this solution, given the impressive obstacles that stand in the way of finding (and remaining loyal to) this sort of enlightened reappraisals of self-interest (Olson, 1975), there lurks in the reasoning here a fallacy of the functionalist sort: *ex ante* insight into the dysfunctional consequences of the tragedy of the commons (*ex ante* knowledge of the common benefits of cooperative behavior) is invoked to explain the emergence and institutionalization of collective arrangements. Theories that invoke "trust", "loyalty", "unselfishness" or even "false consciousness" as a necessary and sufficient explanation of the paradox of cooperation-in-spite-of-conflicting-interests suffer from the same functionalist assumption of enlightened foresight. As will be demonstrated below there are alternative solutions to the puzzle that neither lean on the meta-rationalistic assumption of functionalist "foresight" nor on the *deus ex machina* of a (visible or invisible) "authority" invoked for disciplining short-sighted rational egoists. What these solutions of the paradox-of-ordering share is the illusion of an idealist or "sentimental" rather than mechanistic or "objectified" explanation of social ordering.

An illuminating example of the problem is Lowi's "solution" of the paradox of a "self-regulating pluralist society". Lowi (1965) starts from Dahl's assertion that when two individuals conflict with one another "they confront three great alternative options: dead-lock, coercion or peaceful adjustment". Following the dimensions of Dahl's model, Lowi discovers the omission of a fourth alternative. Dahl's dimensions are the "likelihood of peaceful adjustment" (ranging from high to low) and the "likelihood of coercion" (from immediate to remote). Combining the two continua generates three alternatives:

- *Deadlock* when *adjustment* is low and *coercion* remote.
- *Negotiation* when the chances of *adjustment* are high and the likelihood of *coercion* remote.
- *Coercion*, that is physical imposition in Dahl's manual, when a low score for *adjustment* coincides with the immediacy of *coercion*.

What about the missing *fourth* logical possibility: the coincidence of a high likelihood of peaceful *adjustment* with an immediate likelihood of *coercion*? For our purposes the latter combination is a relevant one indeed since the politics of industrial (re-)structuring represent par excellence an uneasy mixture of accommodation and compliance in spite of the presence of elements of controversy and coercion that inevitably go with the "disorderly retreat" of industries absent of the promise of an "orderly advance" of new industries that might compensate for the loss of the old ones. Contradictions and coercion arise between capital and labor, between sector associations, between labor unions and the state, as well as among each of them *internally* (e.g. intra-capitalist class and regional conflicts of interest and inter-departmental conflicts of competence). Pluralists hold that a social equilibrium will "automatically" follow from the "dispersed" and "fragmentary" nature of this type of conflict, as a sort of political companion and functionalist equivalent of the Invisible Hand of "perfect competition" economics. As will be exposed below, however, the *fingers* on the hand are perfectly visible. When speaking, nevertheless, of the *anonymous* forces of coercion, we hint at the inertial momentum of once established strategies and definitely not to some sort of spontaneous or self-regulating "intelligence" allegedly governing pluralist accommodation (see my earlier remarks on the omissions in "rational choice" theory in Chapter 3 and the discussion above on the missing "spillover" link in the institutionalist analysis of "disciplinary arrangements"). The intriguing coexistence of "peaceful adjustment" and "immediate coercion" deserves a less mystifying answer.

On the political economics of accommodation

Lowi's "solution" for the puzzling peaceful coexistence of acquiescence and coercion belongs to the idealist family of sociological theories that draw upon an oversocializzed conception of man (Wrong, 1061). The author proposes to call Dahl's "empty cell" – the possibility of peaceful adjustment – inspite of immediate coercion – "administration", includ-ing "all of the governmental processes in which people have internal-ized the sanctions":

> The element of coercion may seem absent when in actuality the par-ticipants are conducting themselves in a certain way largely because they do not feel they have any choice. Since it is well enough accepted to go unnoticed, this coercion can be called *legitimate*. Since it is *regu-lar* and *systematic*, it can be called *administrative*. (Lowi, 1969:52; my italics)

Do those who can't afford to swerve or rebel comply? Treated this way, the paradox is defined away. Schattschneider (1960:72) sees "power as controlling the scope of controversy" — referring to the "mobilization of bias" in favor of the exploitation of some kinds of conflict and the suppression of others — and, more particularly, Michels (1968) offers a less "civic" explanation of the "regularities" and "systemness" by which people come to submit "voluntarily" to coercion. As Michels states in his telling exposé of the "iron rule of oligarchisation": "It is organiza-tion which gives birth to the dominion of the elected over the electors, of the mandataries over the mandators, of the delegates over the delega-tors. Who says organization, says oligarchy" (ibid.: 365).

Yet, the Michelsian explanation tells only half of the story or perhaps even less: leaving Michels's somewhat dated hints of Rousseauean mor-alizing out, his (sound) ideas about the role of functional differentia-tion and professionalization in the making of oligarchy still abstract from the external (that is, *inter*-oligarchic) contingencies affecting, so to say, the hard-as-iron nature of his law of internal oligarchy for-mation. The other half of the story is told by conventional models of the external politics of accommodation: here the rules, means and "functions" of *inter*-elite intercourse play a prominent role (primed by Lijphart, 1975; Dahl, 1966; Windmuller, 1969; Van de Vall, 1970; and miraculously re-emerging with the rediscovery of the model today, now called the (Dutch) "Delta" or Rhineland model of concerted action). Yet again, whereas the *meta*-analysis of the politics of accommoda-tion describes the negotiated order as something that is (re)produced by the political and socio-economic elites at the top of the *zuilen* – the oligarchy of oligarchies – the (re)production of the elite(s) itself at the *intra-zuil* level – that is, the Olson/Hirschman/Michels world of the logic of "exit, voice and loyalty" *within* political parties and inter-est organizations – remains underexposed. As a consequence of that omission, the typical exposition of the "function" of the politics of accommodation reveals the same idealist-teleological bias as the functionalist reasoning behind the assumption of a spontaneous identity between elite and constituency perceptions of the Hobbesian "need" for social order. Cohesion, discipline and Lowi's "administrative legitimacy" are explained as the enlightened co-product of a political culture that stresses a historical tradition of *compromising* and a political elite that responds to the imminent dangers of societal *disintegration*. Again, the paradoxical possibility and *persistence* of the coexistence of "peaceful adjustment" combined with "immediate coercion" is tautologically defined away.

The "idealist" heritage described above is not some sociological museum piece from the 1960s. It resurges in the most recent literature on myopic market and public-regulatory failure, be it today in the shape of the alleged "norm-seeding" and "cueing" role of regulation for the coordination of expectations among rational egoists, to the effect of enabling the emergence and convergence of "efficient social norms" (see Ahdieh, 2003; 2004; 2009, for a review of the state of the art of the "new regulation" wave). Some time ago, Scholten (1980), among others, suggested an escape from the idealist-functionalist trap by rejecting the thesis of the elite's interest in fighting the perils of (religious, cultural, socio-economic) fragmentation. The author hypothesizes, instead, an elite's interest in the sort of system maintenance that we identified earlier as the (elite's) *search for network solvency*. Revisionist evidence on the Dutch politics of accommodation suggests (ibid.: 340–1) that political and socio-economic elites were "more concerned about their own dominance in the subculture (of respectively Catholics, Protestants and Socialists), rather than system performance" and it was neither inter-confessional nor inter-class warfare that they had to worry about, but something else: "It was not that ideological conflicts had developed between confessional and socialist organizations. On the contrary, cooperation and mutual understanding between the unions was excellent; the intention was to abort such forms of rapprochement".

As a consequence, the (fear of) fragmentation and separatism usually associated with the Dutch phenomenon of *verzuiling* should not be seen as "a design to avoid conflict" but rather as the result of the political elites' propensity "to stir up conflict if improved relations threatened (internal) group cohesion" (ibid.: 341). Therewith the logic of "consociationalism" (Scholten's term) is turned upside down and replaced by a (my term) *"rent-seeking"* theory of accommodation: internal network *in*solvency jeopardizes the reliability of inter-elite commitments, just as external commitments are needed to preserve or restore internal network solvency.

In such a resource-based view competing ideologies are *instruments* for the management of internal and external dependences, rather than the opposite view that holds that networks are the medium for absorbing or averting ideological clashes. Once more, applied to the workings of "pillarization":

> Given the important role of structures in the creation and maintenance of values at the mass level, it becomes clear that instead of considering them primarily as the organizational reflection of values, emphasis should be placed on the function of pillarization as a system of social control to enable certain elites to consolidate and protect their position through the manipulation of these values. (Ibid.: 34)

Any society, not just pillarized ones, needs some formula for accommodating conflicts that emanate from internal and external dependencies. A resource-based view on the politics of accommodation conceives of the negotiated order as a set of nested games; interpreting order as a pyramid of nested games makes us aware of the import of a second generic strategy, instrumental to the first: the politics of containment.

On the political economics of containment

Earlier I characterized industrial strategies as "puzzling" because they constitute a game with contradictory features: discipline in spite of undisciplined interests and unequal returns. This featuring summarizes in a succinct way the questions that still wait for a conclusive answer. First, how to understand that regimes and networks persist that demonstrably fail to live up to expectations? Second, how to understand that the "nodal" players continue to respect the rules of the game, in spite of the increasingly unequal appropriation of the returns-to-participation? The first question refers to the *performance* and the second to the *persistence* of industrial order, where that order might be expected to be unstable as a consequence both of system underperformance *and* the (increasing) non-equivalence of the pay-offs. (To simplify the puzzle for a while I leave out another potentially destabilizing force – the game is played by "privileged" players – that excludes a variety of others that might be interested in either becoming an insider *or* changing the mechanics of the game *all together.*)

For clarifying the remains of the puzzle we must know how a disciplinary regime based on *symmetric accommodation* may imperceptibly, and even *unintendedly*, mutate into a regime based on a strategy of *asymmetric containment*. Accommodation and compliance were said to be based on the "elective affinity" between oligarchy and oligopoly. In order to avoid the sentimental (in the sense of "indoctrinating") connotations of the concept of *Wahlverwantschaft*, it may be better to speak of the "chemistry" of accommodation amongst capital, state and labor. A *rent-seeking* view of the mechanisms of tripartite compliance, as exemplified by the old discipline described earlier, substitutes a dependence perspective for the notions of normative "consensus", cultural "affinity" or class "solidarity". In a rent-seeking view the latter is the *product* rather than the cause of how resource-dependencies are handled in the negotiated order of a political economy. Culture may reinforce structure, and eventually explain its immutability, but it does not initiate the "circular causation" of firm-to-firm and business-to-state commitments. From a resource-dependence perspective the stability of order is definitely not based on the (functionalist) assumption of collective foresight or the (historicist) imputation of inherited submissiveness or, even more questionably, the (*über*-functionalist) postulate of the "long-term/*ex post*" complementarity of elite and constituency perceptions of representativity and reciprocity. No more helpful are, as said before, the notions of "institutional inertia", "arrogance of power" or "false class-consciousness", because these are exactly the phenomena that have to be *explained* and cannot serve as explanantia.

The real puzzle, in other words, is to explain the persistence and stability of a "dysfunctional" regime in which reciprocity and exploitation – "peaceful adjustment" and "coercion" in Lowi's grammar – continue to coexist on an equal footing. Gouldner (1960), in his classic on the "norms" of reciprocity and exploitation applied to "political machines" that manage to remain stable and survive in spite of the unequal returns between "bosses" and "clients", has useful notes that may help to clear the ground. As Gouldner (1960: 163) observes, analogous to Elster's (1982; 1984: 28ff.; 1986) even more stringent position, a functionalist explanation of the persistence of the political machine "miscarries because no explicit analysis is made of the feedback through which the social structures or groups, whose needs are satisfied by the political machine, in turn 'reciprocate' and repay the machine for the services received from it."

The argument reminds us of our earlier account of the "circular causation" of (in)solvency within and between (bureaucratic) networks.

Concerning the remarkable fact of the continuation of the "machine" in spite of the institutionalized *non*-equivalence of the returns for bosses and clients, Gouldner asserts:

> Although reciprocal relations stabilize patterns, it need not follow that a lack of reciprocity is socially impossible or invariably disruptive of the patterns involved…The major point is that if empirical analysis fails to detect the existence of functional reciprocity, or finds that it has been disrupted, it becomes necessary to search out and analyze the compensatory arrangements that may provide means of controlling the resultant tensions, thereby *enabling the problematic pattern to remain stable.* (1960: 164; my italics)

Thus, applied to the nested games of industrial politics, apparently enabling an engagement of trade unions, government and firms in spite of their incapacity to turn the tide of industrial obsolescence and subsequent losses of employment, the question becomes: what are exactly the means of "moralizing, rationalizing and administering" that enable the "problematic pattern" to preserve its remarkable stability? It is here that we must look for the "auxiliary" mechanisms that "stringent" functionalists request for a solid answer to the questions posed above.

What follows is the description of the modus operandi of a nested game that, though taking-off as a symmetric game of accommodation, turns out to end in a non-symmetric game of containment. The mutation is "facilitated" by a specific sort of (in Lowi's sense) *transitory* rationalization – in fact an auxiliary mechanism of the kind that "true" functionalists are looking for – and results in specific forms of *exploited* reciprocity between capital, state and labor, in fact the outcome of the political economy of containment that this study seeks to clarify. As will be demonstrated further on this outcome is unexpected, possibly even largely *unintended* (in fact one of Elster's criteria (1984: 28) for a "correct" functionalist explanation). The point can be driven home by taking Offe and Wiesenthal's (1980) "dual" logic of collective action as a seminal point of departure. According to these authors, *employers'* associations operate from the utilitaristic-individualistic logic of collective action – as defined in Olson's essay (1975) – whereas *labor unions* find themselves trapped in a position where strategy and structure not only have to respond to the requirements of an individualistic-utilitarian logic of collective action but also to a more comprehensive, solidaristic/emancipatory sort of logic. Olson's repertory is said to neglect or underrate the inescapable contradictions inherent in this *double* logic of collective action on the side of the representatives of labor. The practical meaning of "selective incentives", "free riders", "side-payments", and other Olsonian keys to the socio-economics of collective action refers to fundamentally different things, even if one has in mind the collaborative strategies of entrepreneurs relative to workers. Lumping the logic of collective action of capitalists and unions together for finding the elementary "laws" of associational behavior *for both* obscures the real underlying forces. Purely formally speaking, interest associations show common characteristics and may be compared in such terms as "voluntary membership", "degree of bureaucratization", "dependence" on material and reputational resources, "commonalities" in the efforts to control for "input" and "output" uncertainties, and so on. Real insight starts beyond this. Offe and Wiesenthal argue that labor and capital show substantial differences with respect to the functioning and performance of their associations in three respects: the *input* factors, asking "what is to be organized?"; the nature of the *outputs*, referring to "the conditions of strategic success that are to be found in the organizations' environments"; and the make-up of the internal processes, the *throughput* following from typical differences in the former two "contextual" factors.

However questionable the authors' underexposure of the opposite corners of the triangle, that is the contradictions of the association of *capitalists* and the benign neglect of the dilemmas of the third party – the *state* – Offe and Wiesenthal's analysis resumes in an inventive way the classical Michelsian thesis on associational democracy turning into oligarchy and corrects for the "lumpy" character of the Olsonian logic of collective action (since the latter abstracts from the internal and external constraints of labor's action relative to the articulation of business and employers' interests). According to Offe and Wiesenthal, trade unions are forced to maintain a precarious balance between the mobilization of *resources* and the mobilization of *activities*, as well as between bureaucracy on the one hand – which allows the unions to *accumulate* power – and internal democracy on the other – which allows them to *exercise* power. None of these dilemmas apply with comparable clarity and urgency to business associations and employers' organizations for the reason that they do not – in the same fashion and to the same degree – depend on internal democracy, collective identity and the need for solidary action "for the very fact that they *already are* in a structural power position which renders complications such as these avoidable" (Offe and Wiesenthal, 1980: 82). The larger the size of a union, the more difficult to reconcile some of the inevitably conflicting interests represented by trade unions. Two typical responses to unions' dilemmas can be observed: either the unions "delegate" the issues that they find too hard to handle (the typical "continental" solution of the problem of the division of "political" labor between unions and socialist parties) and/or they simply try to keep away from irreconcilable sets of their constituency's demands. Thus,

> union leadership is constantly caught between attempting to provide comprehensive representation for all the interests of its working class constituency and being limited in its ability to find a formula that reconciles these partly contradictory interests without endangering their internal acceptability and/or external negotiability. (Ibid.: 83)

Reframed in terms of our analysis of the "chemistries" between oligarchy and oligopoly, it is the trade-off between internal acceptability and external negotiability that conspires to make the unions more of an *accomplice* in this sort of negotiated order than appears to be healthy for their integrity and survival. The complicity is equally operative on both sides of the association – collusion needs two players, at least – but the returns on complicity are of a less self-defeating nature for the associations of business and banking, and therewith for their individual members, than for labor associations. Thus, in spite of the virtual *symmetry* in the strategic conduct of each of the actors – suggesting a symmetry in the *codes* of moralizing, rationalizing and administering coercion – the initial game of accommodation inadvertently mutates into a game of containment that is *asymmetrical*, not only in terms of the strategic intents but also in terms of the final *returns* on commitments for the respective players. In Offe and Wiesenthal's view the unequal returns are, apart from the internal dilemmas of the unions sketched above, more specifically due to a typical difference in the relationships between the state and business interests compared to those between the state and the unions. The former relation is built not upon what capital can do politically via its association, but upon what capital can *refuse* to do (for instance by (dis)investments, being an "exclusive" entrepreneurial competence). As will be shown in the chapters that follow, this observation seems even more to the point in a transnational setting:

> Capital finds it structurally easier than labour to pursue its transnational class interests, since it can do this by either not acting at all, or continuing to act exclusively at national level. Labour, on the other hand, can pursue its transnational class interests only if it manages

to define positive common objectives; build a transnational capacity for collective action; and overcome the logic of non-decision inherent in the intergovernmental system ...

The principal reason for the structural superiority of capital at transnational level is that the interests it has at that level are overwhelmingly negative in character [that is] are best satisfied by *non-decisions...For capital, the very deficiencies of inter-governmental decision-making are therefore a political asset.* (Streeck, 1996: 90–1; my italics)

This asymmetry in the logic of implicit or tacit coercion makes comparatively non-conspicuous forms of communication and interaction between business associations and the state apparatus sufficient to accomplish the political objectives of capital. In comparison, the exposure to more ostentatious and ultimative forms of communicating make the labor unions more vulnerable, in the sense of provoking internal antagonisms and external retaliation, and hence the more liable to the kind of silent complicities that we saw above.

Again recast in our conceptual framework, asymmetry in the *conditions* of discipline leads to the following unwritten *codes* of the tripartite game of cohabitation (cf. Offe and Wiesenthal, 1980: 86). First, compared to the communications between unions and the state, the communications of business associations with the state differ in that they are *less visible publicly* (because there is a lesser need to mobilize the support of external allies). Second, communications are more *technical* (because the insight into the political "desirability", that is, factual indispensability of private investments, can be presupposed as already agreed upon). Third, communications tend to be more *universal* (because business associations can speak in the name of all those interests that require for their fulfillment a healthy and continuous rate of accumulation, which, from the view of capital and the state, is true of virtually everybody and can therefore be exposed as "general interest"). Finally, business communications can afford to be cast almost exclusively in a *negative* form, whether overtly or covertly (because, given the fact that the government has to consider as desirable what is in fact desirable for capital, the only thing that remains to be done is to "warn" governments against "imprudent", "unrealistic" or otherwise "inopportune" decisions and measures).

What begins to transpire is how conditions and codes may "conspire" toward irreversible commitments *in spite of* opposing interests and non-equivalent returns. Accommodation mutates into containment when commitments turn into complicity. The "auxiliary" mechanism harbors the illusion that complicity is a *transitory* phenomenon, and therefore "arguably" rational, and that compliance is the best of a bad bargain. The practice is a sequential game, showing the "traps" that we identified earlier. See Box 4.3 for a recapitulation in consecutive steps.

Box 4.3   Entrapment: on the sequential logic of discipline

- The penalty for overgrazing (as in the tragedy of the commons) or undergrazing (the tragedy of the fallows) is higher and less remediable for labor unions that fix collective wage claims too high or underinvest in collective (re)training programs than the penalty for rival firms and states that collectively overinvest or underinvest (the *competition* trap).
- The asymmetry in the logic of control stemming from structural asymmetries in the threat potential of capital, state and labor increases the latter's dependence and sharpens its internal tensions (the *competence* trap).
- The behavioral axioms pertaining to each of the actors – that is, the search for limited liability, the aversion from unstable allies and the propensity to externalize internal tensions – stimulate the unions' quest for internal oligarchization and external oligopolization (the *solvency* trap).
- The price to be paid is a gradually increasing involvement in a triangular conspiracy – of silence regarding the deficits of legitimacy and rationality in terms of substantive policy outcomes (the *credibility* trap).
- The implicit complicity, finally, tends to increase the unions' external dependences and their internal need for rationalizing and moralizing the unequal returns on accommodation – turning into containment (the *compliance* trap).

The three "privileged" players have a common interest in each other's internal stability as far as it is instrumental to their external reliability. In terms of industrial relations, this kind of *Sonnefeldt* doctrine triggers a self-defeating cycle of mutual "assistance" and "reinsurance": the most dependent players, the unions, are "offered" the brotherly help of the state and business associations to mitigate their internal tensions and to "solve" therewith their internal dilemmas. There are three generic forms of "mutuality" or, as Offe and Wiesenthal (1980: 103) would have it, "three tactics of imposing bourgeois political forms upon unions" – each of them reminding us of Schattschneider's "power to control the scope of controversy". First, there is a *limitation of the substantive areas of interest representation*: a division of labor between the unions and the state, leading to a restrictive definition of the range and type of demands that unions are legally and practically allowed to make. Second, there is *the promotion of the institutionalization of alternative, non-associational modes of working-class interest representation*: work councils, for instance, lead to the uncoupling of the *representation* of interests on the one hand and the *activation* of interests on the other hand; this in turn limits that part of the workers' and unions' interests that can be defended by strikes and other forms of collective action and mobilization. Third, there are the *statutory increases of diversity and conflict*: examples from British and West German industrial relations experience have shown that measures advocated by conservative union "reformers" as a means for promoting intra-organizational "democracy" and "pluralism" are in fact aimed at "strengthening the statutory position of those who wish to criticize the ways in which leaders conduct union affairs" (ibid.). This analysis can be rewritten in the form of a five-stage scenario (see Box 4.4).

Box 4.4 Captiveness: discipline in five steps

Stage 1 represents the formative period of a working-class organization. The life of the organization is characterized by: a collective identity; the cultivation of the members' "willingness to act"; a relatively small size; militant conflict; and a low degree of bureaucratization.

In *Stage 2* the organization has become strong enough to wield some control over its environment: the union's potential power is recognized, that is, concessions are made by their counterparts not because members have gone on strike, but in order to avoid a strike. Here a first dilemma arises: while cultivating its image of being able to exercise power, the union's leadership in fact has to see to it that the members do not prematurely and imprudently actualize their "willingness to act", because that would lower "the price that is paid by the adversary for the reliable avoidance of strikes and other forms of militant action". The dilemma, succinctly phrased, is: "if the organization fails to satisfy the first condition, its survival is threatened; if it fails to meet the second imperative, its strategic chances for success are undermined". There are two possible ways out of the dilemma: either a return to Stage 1 (only likely under conditions of a high level of politicization through class struggle) or a shift to that type of transformation that neither threatens the survival of the organization nor interferes with its chances for success, namely "the opportunist resolution of the organization's dilemma".

Stage 3. Around this time the union tries to make the organization's survival as independent as possible from the motivation, the solidarity and the "willingness to act" of the members. The only way of doing so is to substitute "external guarantees of survival" for internal ones for which the union organization depends on its members: "consequently, the union will try to gain as much external support and institutional recognition as possible. This substitution helps the organization to escape the dilemma of size-versus-power", thus enabling it "to grow bureaucratically without risking its existence and survival, which are guaranteed from the outside". Bureaucratization and professionalization of internal decision-making are

the familiar paraphernalia (cf. Michels, 1968), as are the increasing empha-
ses on individualistic incentives to join (instead of the collectivist solidarity
of the pioneers' stage), the provision of stable career patterns for function-
aries, and the restrictive exercise of control over the means of collective
communication.

Stage 4 comes close to what we earlier identified as "exploited reciprocity", lending a stronger stability to the proceedings of the game of "initial
accommodation-turning-into-permanent containment" than these authors
seem to allow for. Their belief in the *in*stability of the constellation is the
more remarkable because they characterize this stage as follows. Once the
"relative" independence of the organization from its members' willingness
to act is achieved and "internal guarantees" are substituted by external ones,
then the organization *"no longer has any capacity to resist attempts to withdraw
external support"* and to move on without "the externally provided legal and
institutional status" (Offe and Wiesenthal, 1980: 108).

Stage 5 shows the "costs of opportunism" to the effect that institutional
supports have become conditional upon the "cooperative, responsible, etc.
behavior of the organization". It represents the return to the type of collective action and the "willingness to act" comparable to the first stage, but
diverging from that in two respects: "First, because it is likely to be based
upon a faction or division within an already existing organization, and second because it tends to focus on a much broader range of political, legal
and institutional arrangements, which have played such an important and
deceptive role in the prior stages" (ibid.).

Conclusion

Political-economic order is based on the logic of cohabitation, which is
backed by a variety of strategies and tactics that can be reduced to two
generic stratagems: accommodation and containment. These two are
the outcome of a pyramid of sequential games, which is played across
different levels of interest aggregation, each implying its own time horizon. Actors differ in their room and capacity to select the time horizon
that fits best with their self-perceived interests. Speculations about the
lasting impact of the "transitory" rationalizations of the set depend on
how seriously we take the datum that the game is to be played with *three*,
non-monolithic, actors. For some the internal divisiveness – resulting in
unpredictability – is an asset, for others a liability. The scope and stability of the actors' mandates affects the scope and stability of the resulting commitments. Moreover, actors differ in their capacity to influence
the quality of the mandate of their *counterparts*. Finally, they differ in
terms of maneuverability. The latter represents the essence of a three-
actor, multilevel game: the actors differ in their room and capabilities

for shifting alliances and mixing loyalties, thus affecting the net return of their counterpart's connections and commitments.

A puzzling property of industrial politics appears to be the *persistence* of the gap between declaratory intents and effective outcomes. What at face value seems to be the prolongation of an utterly irrational regime, appears to be a rational constellation if approached from another, less academic, conception of rationality. Exploring the underlying forces that breed internal oligarchization and external oligopolization sensitizes for a phenomenon that is systematically underexposed, and thus appears to remain non-explained in the mainstream literature, that is, the elective affinity or "chemistry" of the processes of internal coalition and external alliance formation. The main reason that this chemistry does not attract the attention it deserves is the separation in academia between theorizing on the logic of collective action and the logic of bureaucratic conduct. In this chapter we have made a start on restoring the links. The result is shown in the form of a couple of hypotheses, indicating how two, imperfectly understood, phenomena can be made understandable. First, there are the conditions under which federative or "hybrid" arrangements drive out hierarchy, and there are the conditions under which hierarchy drives out market-like arrangements for coping with the dilemmas of interdependent choice. Second, there are the conditions under which stratagems of containment tend to replace stratagems of accommodation, along with the (ultimately) non-expected and (initially) non-intended consequences of this specimen of strategy *drift*.

It is here that the value of an eventually new brand of game theory begins to transpire. Academic convention, following the logic of *collective* action in describing the interactions between state, labor and capital, casts the story habitually in terms of a prisoner's dilemma. By using this metaphor the sight is lost on at least three crucial tenets of the *real* games of cohabitation ("concerted action" in the official language). First, the metaphor abstracts from the internal particulars of the actors. By leaving out the logic of *oligarchic* action, the essence of the recursive causation ("spillover") of oligarchic and oligopolistic stratagems submerges. Second, a prisoner's dilemma game is played at one level only, suggesting horizontal moves and countermoves, whereas a nested-games perspective respects the essential datum that the game of mutual concertation is played at several levels of the capitalist pyramid – micro, meso and macro – granting some players more leeway for vertical and diagonal maneuvers and coalitional mixing than others. Allowing for horizontal as well as vertical and diagonal moves and movements will inevitably complicate the reconstruction, but enhances our understanding of the agent-insensitive *momentum* of the sequences. Third, in addition to the unity of place or space, the prisoner's dilemma metaphor assumes synchronism for the actors, whereas a multilevel or nested games perspective allows for spatial-temporal differences among them. Allowing for differences in "time horizon" and "time span of feedback" has consequences for our understanding of the *visibility* of the respective stakes and outcomes of the game. Spatial-temporal differences, apart from the assertions above about the internal dynamics of the players, make sense of the "traps" that have been listed on the "dynamics of entrapment" in industrial politics. The latter provides a solid basis for understanding the *persistence* of the phenomenon we are studying: the logic of cohabitation among opposite interests.

In the next chapter I examine the venues for correcting the insensitivities or blind spots of the approaches outlined above. The remedy should serve two purposes. First, the descriptive balance has to be restored by extending the analysis of the dilemmas of concerted action from the unions alone to others that construct the negotiated order of a political economy, such as firms, finance and the state. Second, we need a model that explains where the momentum and mutation of regimes of cohabitation come from. The first is done by scouring the literature on *structures* of concerted action; the second by a paradigm shift that must grasp the essence of the *stratagems* of concerted action.

5
The Framing of Discipline

Introduction

The negotiated order of the modern industrial state is based on "incomplete" antagonisms. Antagonisms remain incomplete when those who constitute the negotiated order know that they will meet again tomorrow. Curiously enough, more often than not the *preservation* of the architecture of social order appears to be the result of the *transitory* rationalizations of its architects. As shown in the preceding chapter, order may be reinforced by rationales that are meant to be a temporary or situational answer to the sordid sides of the status quo. The results may be uncomfortable though. Labor unions, for instance, looking for official recognition in a tripartite neo-corporatist consortium and eager to demonstrate their reliability as a partner by disciplining their constituencies may accomplish something that in the long run appears to be contrary to their effectiveness and survival. The same applies to rival firms and rival states that for reasons of short-term opportunism decide to cooperate – be it primarily in the copycat mode, that is as a defense against the collaborative maneuvers of their rivals. The shared "transitory" inspiration in these cases is that the penalty for symmetric *non-*cooperation is perceived to be worse than the penalty for "temporary" asymmetric cooperation. The result may be *ultra* stable, in hindsight possibly to the regret of some of the architects of that negotiated order.

Usually this type of antinomy is cast in terms of a prisoner's dilemma. I have briefly indicated why this metaphor fails to catch the essence of the dilemmas of concerted action. Alternative metaphors exist that come closer to the logic of the situation. For instance the metaphor of a "chicken game", that is the sort of game in which actors *deliberately* show themselves to have lost control and therefore to be unable to revoke the threat of (mutual) non-cooperation. Imperfect internal discipline or bureaucratic loss of control are *assets* in a chicken game that are of no avail for the internally undivided or "unitary" actors involved in a typical prisoner's dilemma. Consider, for instance, the benefits of irresponsibility or non-accountability typical of a chicken game:

> There is…at least one good word to be said for threats that intentionally involve some loss of control or some generation of "crisis". It is that this kind of threat may be more impersonal, more "external" to the participants; the threat becomes part of the environment rather than a test of will between two adversaries. The adversary may find it easier – less costly in prestige or self-respect – to back away from a risky situation, even if he created the situation, than from a threat that is backed exclusively by…resolve and determination. (Schelling, 1973: 121)

When does a credible demonstration of *ir*resolution or loss of control turn out to be an asset rather than a handicap? Under specific conditions a lack of discipline due to internal strife and divide may *increase* the credibility of threats and therefore strengthen rather than weaken the willingness of others to "chicken out". What the impact of an internal loss of discipline will be in the long run for the stability of regimes of concerted action remains to be seen. Yet, *principally* this eventuality corrects for the *automatism* of regime instability that Offe and Wiesenthal (1980) predict for a constellation in which the trade unions are reported to suffer from a loss of internal legitimacy and cohesion. The heuristic usefulness of the chicken-game metaphor lies in the inversion of some of Offe and Wiesenthal's behavioral assumptions. Typically, in a prisoner's dilemma setting, players are looking for a "focal" point of intersecting interests, although Olsonian instincts may stand in the way of effectuating the "common good" either categorically or temporarily (as in a recurrent game). In a prisoner's dilemma setting it is always *against* the will of the players that the play "degenerates" into conflict, thus eventually making everybody worse off. In a typical chicken game, on the other hand, a rational player will always choose to surrender when facing an opponent who demonstrates in a credible, ultimatum-like way *not* to cooperate; there is no second-best in terms of surrendering, for *mutual* non-cooperation is the worst possible outcome. A second essential difference with a prisoner's dilemma is that in a chicken setting shared interests and arrangements already *do* exist but one or more of the actors are deliberately looking for escalation rather than domestication of the contest:

> In chicken, one party willfully *creates* a conflict by challenging the other and threatens to *destroy* an already enjoyed common interest if it does not get its way in the conflict; the defending party may reciprocate with a similar threat. Typically, the common interest in chicken is something that is manipulated as a means of coercion, not something that is mutually sought. (Snyder, 1971: 84)

Challenging one's counterparts and threatening to destroy the "commons" is precisely what happens when radical changes in technology and the internationalization of competition change the constellation of conditions, codes and commitments that constitute the old discipline between state, labor and capital. Whether the shift of "chicken" from the national to the transnational arena will entail a related shift in the substantive stakes and outcomes of the games of industrial and financial politics requires a specification of the conditions under which a chicken game is expected to de-escalate into the kind of "reciprocity" (out of self-interest) that one typically finds in a prisoner's dilemma:

> It may well be that the best prospects for moving toward cooperation in the prisoner's dilemma super game occur when both parties play the chicken game hard and well. The parties then develop a healthy respect for each other's resolve, vital interests are clearly defined, the prospect for easy coercive gains in the conflict dimension are eliminated, the chicken super game is, in effect, stalemated, and attention and activity shift to the cooperative alternative. (Ibid.: 102)

Contrary to intuition, it is the *symmetry* of dependence in a prisoner's dilemma that makes cooperation unattainable. The main reason lies in the informational parameters of the game: the "prisoners" are effectively prevented from direct communication while a superimposed party, the "judge", may manipulate information about the putative willingness of each of the "prisoners" to confess, thereby pressing his or her counterpart(s) to do the same. The realization of the common interest may well be an honest desire of both parties, but neither can trust the other(s) to collaborate in realizing it. In a chicken game, in contrast, there is ample opportunity for manipulation of information by the players *themselves*, from bluff and concealed intent to unconcealed demonstrations of real intent and stamina. Risk perceptions and brinkmanship play a primordial role in chicken games. As a consequence, the *asymmetry* of dependence and subsequent concessions, eventually leading to the stable but exploited type of "reciprocity" and "compliance" described earlier (see Chapter 4, pp. 120ff.), should be seen as a possible outcome of the game rather than as its necessary preconditions.

Risk perceptions enter the stage in two senses. First there is typically no uncertainty about the parties' basic intentions – some or all are knowingly trying to serve their own interests; it is the eventual misperception about each other's determination and staying power that governs the game: *over-perception may induce unnecessary capitulation* (cf. ibid.: 85). Second, "rational behavior" in a chicken game depends on an ego's expectations about the alter's conduct, *not primarily on the game's pay-off structure*. As a consequence the (im)balance of threats and concessions depends not so much on objective first- and second-strike capabilities, but on the reciprocally perceived readiness to deploy varying levels of selfishness and intransigence (cf. ibid.: 98). From the role of (mis)perception follows the pertinence of *brinkmanship*, that is:

> the deliberate creation of a recognizable risk of war, a risk that one does not completely control. It is the tactic of deliberately letting the situation get somewhat out of hand, just because [that] may be intolerable to the other party and force his accommodation. It means…intimidating an adversary…by showing that if he makes a contrary move he may disturb us so that we slip over the brink whether we want to or not, carrying him with us. (Schelling, 1969: 200)

Dixit and Nalebuff (1991: 214–20) reiterate a telling scene from *High Wind in Jamaica,* a movie picture that Schelling (1973) used to show how brinkmanship works and how to respond to it – especially when the principle of "bounded hands", literally, turns out to work as a double-edged knife (see Box 5.1).

Box 5.1 Brinkmanship

The pirate Captain Chavez wants his captive to tell where the money is hidden, and puts his knife to the man's throat to make him talk. After a moment or two, during which the man keeps his mouth shut, the mate laughs. "If you cut his throat he can't tell you. He knows it. And he knows you know it." Chavez puts his knife away and tries something else.

He could have kept the knife, if only he had seen the Maltese Falcon. There Spade has hidden the valuable bird, and Gutman is trying to find out where it is. Spade to Gutman: "...If you kill me how are you going to get the bird? If I know that you can't afford to kill me till you have it, how are you going to scare me into giving it to you?"

"I see what you mean," Gutman chuckled. "That is an attitude, sir, that calls for the most delicate judgment on both sides, because as you know, sir, men are likely to forget in the heat of the action where their best interest lies and let their emotions carry them away."

(Dashiell Hammet, *The Maltese Falcon*, Pan Books, San Francisco, 1983: 169)

In Chapter 4 a few elementary things were broached about the mechanisms of entrapment stemming from the rationalization of "complicity" rather than "animal spirits" – mechanisms by which parties lose sight of where their best interests lie – as exemplified by the incomplete antagonisms ranging from policies of industrial restructuring to policies aiming at national and international financial regulation. (Note that it was exactly the fear of the US government and the EU for "slipping over the brink" that created the moral hazard and complicity by which states are bound to bail out their banks.) More should be said now about the determinants of perception and brinkmanship that explain where *changes* in negotiated regimes of industrial and financial strategy-making come from.

I began Chapter 1 with the transition from the old to the new discipline. In this chapter I set out to refine the kind of paradigm shift required for grasping the mechanisms of regime change. The chicken-game metaphor in Schelling and Snyder's version was meant to explain the paradox of "adversarial resolve" turning into "cooperative alternatives", though it needs to be made more complete by including the possibility of "exploited cooperation", that is *unequal returns* from cooperation for the "former" or "incomplete" antagonists. So the chicken-game metaphor appears helpful indeed for solving the puzzle we came across earlier (compare our Lowi/Dahl discussion in Chapter 4, pp. 111ff.): that is, the puzzling *persistence* of the living together of "peaceful adjustment" (or: accommodation) are "immediate" coercion (or: containment).

The old discipline

Industrial and financial strategies belong to a broader band of state–market interactions. The interactions are traditionally studied from a variety of perspectives, from neo-Marxist to pluralist political theory and from public choice to institutional theory. A middle course that combines elements from this legacy and offers suggestions for comparing different varieties of political-economic order is the so-called *neo-corporatist* framework.

Until the late 1970s, researchers used to restrict the institutional type-cast "neo-corporatism" to a specific form of conflict management in the realm of class and state relationships. The restriction proved too narrowly cast, for several reasons. First, trade unions, employers, trade associations and financial institutions gradually broadened their agendas from production-related issues to (re)distributive matters such as taxes, wages, employment, labor conditions, social security and vocational training policies. The extension to wider interest areas emerged in reaction to the expansion of the scope of welfare-state intervention. As a consequence, the boundary between strictly socio-economic and broader welfare-state operations blurred. A second condition stems from the drift in ideology and ambitions of corporatist thought. In its "pure" (doctrinary) sense corporatism rests on three dogmas:

• Social order is the harmonious outcome of the complementarity and symmetry of the "laws of organic solidarity", from the micro- to the macro-level of social order.
• State and society interpenetrate to such a degree that practically no distinction between the body politic and society at large can be made.
• Representative interest groups are bestowed with public-legal rights, guaranteeing them externally a representational monopoly in exchange for observing the internal discipline of their constituencies.

As documented elsewhere (Wassenberg, 1982a), the practices of modern corporatism deviate from the original doctrine in several respects. First, more recent manifestations of corporatism are incrementalist and emergent rather than *ex cathedra* designed and implemented, as was the case with orthodox corporatism. Second, modern varieties tend to be heterodox, non-conspicuous and pragmatically oriented, that is, averse to the hegemonic and canonical claims of old style corporatism. Third, remains of the *neo*-corporatist legacy are only found at the meso- rather than the (allegedly *pars pro toto*) micro- and macro-levels where orthodox corporatism was implanted in its heyday. At variance with the "organic" postulate of ancient times, professing "complementarity" between the respective levels of interest representation, growing contradictions in more recent times came to be observed, and accepted, between micro-strategies of interest articulation, meso-structures of interest intermediation and macro-corporatist "solutions" for conflicts of interest. Fourth, historically there may have been a point in distinguishing between "state" versus "bourgeois"-led corporatism. Under non-totalitarian welfare-state conditions, however, the "state-initiated" versus "bourgeois-led" distinction ceases to be of much help because of the exclusively *meso-*, and vertically *non-transferable*, character of neo-corporatism. At that level, privately organized interests and the state condition each other's room for maneuvering to such an extent that it only *analytically* makes sense to distinguish between "first" and "second" movers. The reciprocity between state and market, that follows from mutual "rent-seeking", promotes – under conditions to be specified below – the kind of collusive/coercive coordination that keeps antagonisms "incomplete". As argued before, for understanding this outcome we do not need assumptions of overt coercion or a tacit conspiracy of elites. The "self-evidence" of reciprocity tends to obliterate further the distinction between public and private players.

Summing up, the prefix *"neo"* may more realistically be read as "hybrid". The latter is meant to stress the *two* faces of neo-corporatism, that is, its formal emblems versus its informal practices. In the formal sense neo-corporatism has lost its reputation; informally it has kept its acumen. Against the anti-parliamentarian "consonances" of solidaristic corporatism in earlier times, and the continuation, if not the intensification, of inter-level "dissonances" between micro-intentions, meso-commitments and the macro-output of interest strategies in our days, the once-honored tripartite device for accommodating inter-class tensions, has gradually given way to more pragmatic and less conspicuous recipes for handling firm-to-firm, capital-to-labor, and business-to-state relationships.

The old paradigm

The maiden flight of "neo"-corporatist theorizing took off from an elevated level, that is it described the commanding heights where the peak associations of capital and labor meet the political and bureaucratic summits of the welfare state. Those are the places where interest associations explore the limits of moderating their constituencies' demands "in exchange for" the willingness of the body politic to grant the former a "representational monopoly" and a large degree of "self-governance" in their respective functional domains (Schmitter, 1974; 1977; Schmitter and Lehmbruch, 1979; Lehmbruch and Schmitter, 1982). Cruising at these Icarian heights the *first* generation of researchers was bound to see a rather undifferentiated landscape. After a while the early adopters of the "exchange/monopoly/self-govenance" thesis started to feel discomfort about the growing gap between paradigm and practice.

Box 5.2   Paradigm versus practice

The paradigm: for the implementation of its macro-economic and social ambitions a democratic welfare state requires the support, or at least the complaisance, of internally cohesive and well-disciplined interest groups. The leadership of interest associations, in order to deliver the compliance asked for, asks the state to grant and to guarantee the associations the privilege of (quasi-)monopolistic interest representation. Thus, the strategic interdependence of state, capital and labor produces the neo-corporatist solution for the distributive and redistributive problems of the modern welfare state.

The practice: an astonishingly rapid erosion, from the end of the 1970s onwards, of the institutional arrangements which served as the anchorage of the mixed-market welfare-state politics of accommodation and containment between capital, labor and state.

When academics and evidence are drifting apart, there are two options: either a radical revision of the paradigm or an incremental rearrangement of the theory in terms of its units of analysis. Since intellectual switches incur costs, "normal science" prefers incremental change in the units of observation to paradigmatic revolution (cf. Kuhn, 1962; and, more in particular, Ward, 1972).

A *second* generation of researchers started to look at the workings of the neo-corporatist machinery at a lower level of aggregation. With that the research agenda shifted from tripartite, inter-interest group to *intra*-interest group (firm-to-firm) and *bi*partite (firms-to-government) processes of conflict management and policy coordination. Ironically enough, the shift revealed even more visibly the divergences with other approaches of state–society relationships (such as pluralist versus neo-Marxist theory), the shortcomings of which were said to have inspired the first generation of neo-corporatist theorizing. "Pluralist" political theory was considered to be naïve and idealist because of its assumption of a competitive political market place, its voluntarism and the methodological individualism in its (largely implicit) theory of interests. "Neo-Marxism", on the other hand, was said to correct for the pluralists' naïve and optimistic portrayal of the state as an immaculate, interest-insensitive authority, believed to preserve an institutional and ideological cordon sanitaire between public and private domains. According to "corporatist" critics neo-Marxism suffered from the opposite temptation to reduce political processes to their alleged economic bases only, assuming that political interests are structurally given and driven by economic class relationships only. Hence, in neo-Marxist reasoning, the state is seen as either the "executive" instrument of a dominant class or the arena in which class struggles are fought. As a consequence, the analysis of the "autonomous" impact of the state is left out, as is the impact of the internal divisiveness of class interests in the capacity of (an) economic class(es) to "dictate" state policies.

Cawson (1985) argues that these caricatural features of pluralist and neo-Marxist images of state–society relationships have added to the appeal of a possible synthesis suggested by neo-corporatist theory. The neo-corporatist paradigm builds on the "manifest concentration and centralization of functional interests which in part has been the outcome of the processes of pluralist competition". The "market place" for interest groups is "hierarchical, segmented and asymmetrical, and the organizations within it tend to seek monopoly representation of their constituent interest category" (ibid.: 5). Apart from doubts about the availability of empirical evidence on Cawson's "manifest concentration and centralization" of functional interests, what remains largely unspecified in his follow-up is a realistic definition of "the state". By substituting state "agencies" for the lump-sum notions of "the" state that prevails in neo-corporatist writings, Cawson seems to circumvent terminologically rather than solve substantively the problem that "there has yet to emerge from corporatist writing a distinctive theory of the state" (Ibid.: 6). Consider for example his definition of corporatism:

> Corporatism is a specific socio-political process in which organizations representing monopolistic functional interests engage in political exchange with state agencies over public policy outputs which involves those organizations in a role that combines interest representation and policy implementation through delegated self-enforcement. (Ibid.: 8)

The switch in scholarly interest towards the study of *meso-* ("sector-specific") corporatism resulted in a reframing of the notions of "reciprocity" between interest groups and the state. Much less energy, however, has been spent on opening the black box of "the" state as an institutional complex of competing budgets and contested competences (see our earlier discussion on "bureaucratic chauvinism" and "bureaucratic contests" in Chapter 4, pp. 100ff.). By exploring only the dilemmas of representation and reciprocity on the *private* side of the multi-pronged relationships between state and society, our understanding of the dynamics of "pronging" remains scanty. Indeed, as Cawson admits, the state remains "something of a mystery". Unfortunately, Cawson's suggestion that this imbalance should be repaired by diverting "some of the attention which has so far been given by students of corporatism to interest associations and private interest government ... to the study of the *internal organization* of the state" (ibid.: 20; my italics) does not settle the issue. It is not the "internal" organization of the state as such that deserves compensatory attention, but rather the permeability and management of the "gates" of the state or, more pertinently, the act of the *choice* of the gates of the state. Precisely because of the "modern" interpenetration of state and society, it is the study of (1) the *permeability* of the boundary, (2) the logic of boundary *choice*, and (3) the logic of *association and dissociation* between those that surf on the breakers between the two worlds that deserves to attract primary attention.

Similar dilemmas of private collective action that Streeck and Schmitter (1985) traced in their analysis of "private interest government" apply – as will be shown below – to the dilemmas of *public* collective action as soon as we allow for state, inter-state and regional authorities competing, whether or not in consonance with "their" national *clienteles*, for a fair share in the race for the "competitive excellence of nations". Letting "the" state back in – at multiple levels and with analogous dilemmas about the optimum of its *own* cross-level presences – inevitably relaxes the old paradigm's *parti pris* that

> arrangements are tripartite in form, or that the interests they embrace are restricted to capital and labour ... Other groups are potential partners, including professional and managerial interests, *as long as they have developed the organizational capacity to monopolize the representation of a distinctive interest category.* (Cawson, 1985: 11; my italics)

The "relaxation" of the paradigm brings the question to the center of analysis whether "classes" or "sectors" can be considered to be distinct and concrete enough to be treated as coherent and representative "actors". The rehabilitation of this classical topic has reanimated the search for the conditions under which firms competing in the same market may perceive certain problems as a common sectoral interest *versus* conditions under which sectoral interests appear to be perceived as conflicting with the interests of individual capitalists, or with the interests of capitalists in other sectors, to the effect of weakening sectoral and sub-sectoral "class" loyalties and sapping the cohesion of peak and lower level interest associations.

The corrective value of the meso-corporatist framework has been its capacity to sensitize, more than its macro-corporatist forerunner, for

the probability that classes become *internally* divided by sectoral iden-
tifications and that sectors may be marked by intra-class antagonisms.
However, the question remains open as to under what conditions meso-
corporatist arrangements obtain and under what circumstances the
prevailing level of corporatist intermediation *downsizes* from macro- to
meso- or even lower levels of interest articulation and intermediation. An
exclusive focus on the *intra*-class dilemmas of collective action obscures
our view of the selection of the boundaries and levels of interest articulation as an intended/non-intended outcome of a parallelogram of *four*
(instead of Offe and Wiesenthal's *two*) interacting "logics", to wit: *intra-
class, intra-state, inter-class* and *inter-state* dilemmas of collective action.
It is my presumption that the approach of state–society relationships
from a "shifting boundaries/jumping levels"-perspective, and allowing
for a less ideal-typical mix of voluntaristic and deterministic elements
in the explanation of "level-*cum*-boundary" shifts, will improve our
understanding of the evolution of meso- and micro-corporatist arrangements. The "double" check of the explanatory power of this approach
is to see whether the conditions that are hypothesized to explain the
emergence of lower level varieties of interest articulation and representation can also be held "responsible", in the reverse sense, for the eclipse
of the disciplinary arrangements that, from the early 1950s up to the
late 1960s, emblematized the macro-corporatist ordering of the mixed-
market economy (alternatively labeled "*soziale Marktwirtschaft*", "*économie concerté*" or "coordinated political economy").

On the descent of concerted action

The principal feature of *macro*-corporatism is the involvement of peak
organizations in the articulation and execution of comprehensive policy-
making by "delegated self-enforcement". *Meso*-corporatism, in contrast,
refers to political exchanges between sector-wise or functionally specialized state agencies and sector or function-specific interest associations. *Micro*-corporatism, though less current as a standing expression
in the literature reviewed here, and hence less extensively studied under
that label, refers to the practice of direct bargaining between "the" state
or specialized public agencies and individual (combinations of) firms.
The latter includes restructuring and financial strategies in "sunset" and
financial crisis-struck sectors, which try to prevent immediate collapse
and to temporize capacity reductions (cf. Schumpeter's "orderly retreat";
quoted on p. 107). Alternatively, it may include financial, industrial and
technology policies, which aim at boosting the competitive, innovative

and growth potential of (leading firms in) targeted sectors (Schumpeter's "orderly advance"). Generalizing, the more focused that industrial-political and financial interventions are, and the less generic the levels of policy concertation are, then the more discriminatory is the treatment between sectors in the economy or between firms in a particular sector. In line with arguments developed in Chapter 4 about the discriminatory nature of focused strategies, meso- and micro-corporatist arrangements will be particularly apt to accentuate *intra*-class tensions, horizontally as well as vertically. Horizontal divisions include interests or interest groups occupying similar aggregate positions; vertical divisions include upward and downward shifts of interest articulation within their respective functional domains (business *or* labor *or* the state). Figure 5.1 (which tips over and refines the rudimentary visualization in Figure 1.1) recapitulates the reorientation of the units of analysis implied by this paradigm switch: from a research focus on tripartite, inter-class and comprehensive modes of conflict management – typical for the *first* generation of corporatism studies – towards a focus on bipartite, intra-class and sector-specific modes of interest intermediation – typical for the *second* generation.

The distinctive key of the "multilevel" corporatist approach can be formulated as follows. First, under what conditions (e.g. recession versus growth; capacity reduction versus upgrading of the competitiveness of a sector) do we expect a higher intensity of intra-class antagonisms; and second, how do we expect that the intensity of intra-class antagonism will (co)determine the rise and decline of macro-, meso- or micro-institutional arrangements for addressing (accommodate, contain, displace) these *intra*-class tensions?

The state of the art in corporatist theorizing and research can be summarized as follows (for an earlier version, see Wassenberg, 1982b). First, concepts and case studies are almost exclusively directed at exploring the internal dilemmas and contradictions of private interest associations (capital and labor). Second, the national "state" remains an unidentified object: the black box in the middle of the peripheral right of Figure 5.1 appears as some sort of "pressure" cooker or "converter" of contending forces. Missing is "the" state as a multi-level actor in and through itself with comparably obstinate, cross-level accommodation-and-containment problems *sui generis*. Third, within the confines of a thin body of circumstantial evidence on sectoral and sub-sectoral policies, documentation on "defensive" restructuring policies (in contracting or "sunset" industries) dominates over the documentation on "offensive" strategies (associated with expanding or "sunrise" industries). Fourth,

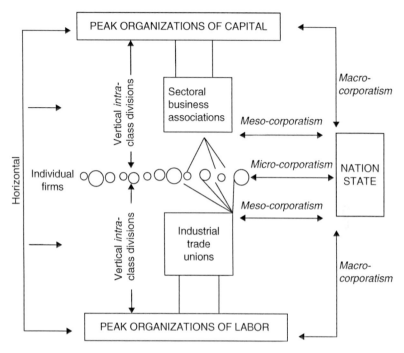

Figure 5.1   Varieties of neo-corporatist policy-making: macro, meso, micro
Source: Adapted from Cawson (1985: 19).

within this biased sample, the evidence on aggregate government-to-business transactions, with or without trade union involvement, surpasses evidence on firm-to-firm, agency-to-agency and union-to-union transactions. Finally, the literature offers mainly comparative descriptions, sometimes with prescriptive connotations, instead of "thick" explanations of government-to-business interactions.

This is not to say that there are no ideas about how to translate the issues of sector- and level-specific variations in the propensity to intraclass contradictions and the rise and fall of institutional arrangements for coping with them into more observable and testable propositions. Atkinson and Coleman (1985) for instance, argue that "sectoral" corporatism may be a "viable option" in the area of industrial policy-making on the condition that, first, sector problems are defined in terms of "the long-term viability of the sector as a component of the national economy" and, secondly, "the" state is willing and able to align, respectively complement sector-specific measures with horizontal policy instruments like competition legislation and (fiscal) incentives for research and development.

This type of proviso, however, neighbors upon a pure tautological exercise, such as: "sectoral corporatism will emerge everywhere affected parties define a problem, like excess capacity or the declining competitiveness of an industry, as a collective problem and apply the appropriate mix of policy-measures". The unknowns, in other words, remain the structural preconditions that generate a capable associational system on the private side, and a centralized, autonomous, state bureaucracy on the public side of the policy arena. Atkinson and Coleman (1985: 28–9) single out three aspects as particularly important for the emergence of a viable sector-specific associational system: (1) the *degree of foreign control* in the sector; (2) the *international competitiveness* of firms in the sector; and (3) the *degree of concentration* in the sector. The coexistence of foreign and domestic firms is hypothesized to entail significant obstacles to unified capitalist action because of the conflicting needs and orientation of these two categories of players. The degree of competitiveness is hypothesized to influence the propensity to associative action insofar as internationally competitive firms do not need the protectionist leverage of a unified front or shelter. Finally, the degree of concentration is supposed to play a role as far as we imagine that oligopolistic sectors will be in a better position to engage in, and reap the benefits of, associative action than sectors populated by dispersed or anonymous competitors (leaving aside for a while the earlier mentioned contentious potential of asymmetry in the divides between shared value creation and non-shared value appropriation).

Following Atkinson and Coleman's review of the literature, the presence of a developed associational system is a necessary, but not sufficient, condition for "sectoral" or meso-corporatism. In addition a significant degree of autonomy or differentiation from society and a high degree of professional competence of the state bureaucracy are required in order to develop and effectively push through a conception of the public interest which is more than the simple sum of particular interests. Without a sufficient degree of state–society differentiation, efforts to induce cooperation among producer groups readily degrade into the type of "privatized" state bureaucracy that Atkinson and Coleman (and, earlier, La Palombara, 1964; Lowi, 1979: 60 and Katzenstein, 1978: 306–23) have referred to as *"parentela"* ("sponsored") pluralism – that is political-economic regimes where both state and sector associations are weakly centralized and the sectoral bureaucracy's autonomy – "the differentiation between state and society" – remains underdeveloped.

The following conditions for state-bureaucratic autonomy and differentiation are mentioned (Atkinson and Coleman, 1985: 30). First, the bureaus involved in a given sector should have a clearly defined conception of their role and a value system that supports that role. Second, the bureau has to administer a corpus of law and regulations that defines barriers between itself and the sector. Third, the bureau *itself* should generate the information, technically and otherwise, which it needs for the pursuit of its mandate – otherwise the bureau becomes (too) dependent on firms or sector associations. The consensus needed for corporatism is most likely to emerge when

> a single agency or bureau dominates, bureaucratically, a given sector. A hegemonic bureau of this kind would be capable of aggregating authority from regional decision points, thus making decisions binding on a nationwide basis ... [However], the presence of a hegemonic bureau in a sector is not a sufficient condition for corporatism ... some stability in the state structure is also highly desirable ... [Structures transforming themselves] frequently to match changes in the sector [are] open to capture by the sector and, in short, fall into the classic pattern of sponsored pluralism. Such a bureaucratic structure ... will lead to a decline in the capacity of the private sector to engage in corporatist decision-making. (Ibid.: 31)

As the authors admit, the proviso of "state organization prerequisites for corporatism" often may be the most difficult to satisfy, and the weakness or absence of a "hegemonic" and "stable" bureaucratic structure might be "the most important reason why corporatism does not develop in a sector that otherwise would appear to be admirably suited to it" (ibid.).

Box 5.3 Sector mobilization

In a follow-up study Atkinson and Coleman (1989) complete the list of "prerequisites" for integrated, public–private concertation at the sector level by supplementing their earlier "market-structure" prerequisites with "the degree of societal mobilization". A "highly mobilized" sector is one characterized by:

A horizontal division of labor within the associational system with separate associations or divisions representing different products, service groups or territories. Such a division of labor implies the absence of overlapping organizations on the one hand, and gaps in the associational system on the other. There will be no competition for members.

One and (normally) only one association will speak for the sector as a whole; either sub-sectoral organizations will belong to this sector-wide association (such that a simple vertical division of labor is sustained) or individual firms will associate directly.

Both sectoral and sub-sectoral associations will have a high density, that is a high proportion of the firms (or of the production) in a given sector will be represented by the association.

In oligopolistic sectors where major firms enjoy the option of direct contact with the state, these firms will retain a high profile of activity in the association, thereby employing both direct and indirect means of securing influence.

Firms and associations will possess considerable in-house capacity for the generation of information, both technical and political.

In a highly mobilized sector, associations will have the capacity to bind member firms to agreements negotiated with the state and to offer assurances of individual firm compliance with policy decisions.

By combining the dimensions of state-bureaucratic "autonomy" and the "concentration of authority" on the one hand, and the degree of business-interest "mobilization" on the other, the authors arrive at *eight* ideal-typical categories of policy coordination (ibid., 1985: 53–4) (see Table 5.1).

However "ordering" in itself, classificatory exercises can never serve as a surrogate for *explanatory* theories on the evolution and devolution of regimes of concerted action – from the old discipline of centralized and comprehensively integrated regimes to the emergence of fragmented, flexible and improvising governance structures of a more recent vintage. For a proper understanding of, first, mutations in the choice of *levels* of interest aggregation and, second, mutations in the choice of the *boundaries* between private and public domains, we need something else than the "structural conditions" of the kind listed above. Classificatory exercises (re)define in comparative-static terms the presence (absence) of (the preconditions for) disciplinary arrangements, rather than explaining, in dynamic terms, the rise and decline of these arrangements. In particular "state"-specific prerequisites – for corporatism, even more so than their private counterparts (that is the "market"-specific conditions that facilitate associative action) – have more of a *definitional* anchoring of the concepts of "autonomy" and "differentiation", and thus of a tautological exercise, than of a theory of strategic *search and selection* explaining the moves, movements and momentum in the relations between state and market.

Table 5.1 Eight types of "policy networks", as defined by state and business associational structures

Mobilization of business interests	Structure of the state			
	High concentration, High centralization	High concentration, Low centralization	Low concentration, High centralization	Low concentration, Low centralization
Low	State directed	Pressure pluralism	Pressure pluralism	Patronage pluralism
High	Concertation	Clientele pluralism	Corporatism	Industry dominant pressure

Reconsidering the requisites of concerted action

The erosion of macro-corporatism has stimulated scholarly interest in lower-level varieties of concerted action but has not – intriguingly enough in the light of accelerating internationalization strategies – resulted in a growing interest in cross-national forms of coordination. Recent studies, instead, extend the earlier sectoral focus to regional analyses of the associability of business interests. Here and there "the" state emerges, analytically speaking, as an internally differentiated actor. Coleman and Grant (1989: 56), for instance, observe that, in the case of conflict between national and *sub*-national state authorities, each level of government "will seek to enlist the support of its corresponding (business interest) association in its struggle with the other level". Unfortunately, however, these observations go by like ships in the night, instead of serving as lighthouses illuminating more pressing puzzles in the current state of our knowledge on these *vertical* reshuffles.

Comparative studies aim primarily at classifying *national* similarities and dissimilarities in bureaucratic and associational structures without answering the question as to what sort of insight it is that we gain from this sort of *cartography* for: (1) our understanding of the strategies of association and dissociation between public and private players; (2) what sort of *impact* these strategies might have for the evolution of government–business relationships; and (3) what the classification of structural similarities and dissimilarities tells us about functionalist *causation*. Lacking in comparative analysis is the identification, and verification, of *independent feedback mechanisms, connecting (mutations in) the structures of resource dependences and partnerships*, with *(mutations in) the representativity and reciprocity* between financial institutions, firms, unions and public agencies. Even analysts – who are more interested in understanding the miracle of "private self-governance" than in endlessly classifying structural (dis)-similarities – do not seem to be in a position to inform us about this kind of causal loop. The phenomenon of "self-governance" is a puzzle indeed, a fortiori when sector boundaries tend to fade away due to technological change and internationalization. In spite of a bewildering variety of organizational representations at the micro-level (documented *in extenso* in regional-territorial studies in corporatism), interest associations sometimes appear to develop a "hierarchical capacity" to transform local interests into aggregate, categorical interests, "thereby making it possible for the sector as a whole to engage in long-term political exchanges with the state" (Streeck, 1989: 89). The intrigue, however, remains how and when interest formations succeed in establishing "long-term relationships" with the state, that is, how, firstly, "private interest governments" succeed in digesting the modern labyrinth of the bureaucratic state *as if* the latter has not experienced a loss of undisputed authority due to interdepartmental rivalries and the rise to increasing prominence of supranational agencies. Secondly, following Streeck and Schmitter (1985) one wonders how "private interest governments" manage to reconcile the "logic of membership" – referring to the problem of attracting supporters in spite of free-rider instincts – with the "logic of influence" – referring to solving the problem of establishing a sufficient degree of credibility by rules of political prudence and norms of reciprocity vis-à-vis state agencies and other contending interests. Finding a realistic trade-off between the two "logics" can be expected to become more complicated the less easy it is to speak of "sectors", "agencies" and their "boundaries" as unambiguously defined socio- and political-economic realities.

The questions raised in the foregoing reviews are definitely not the wrong questions. However, there seems to be a mismatch between the "lead questions" and the respective "logics" that must deliver the correct answers. Consider, for example, the issue of cross-sectoral and cross-regional variations in the preferred level of interest representation. Schmitter and Lanzalaco (1989) have tried to relate the observed variety of regional business interest associations to the interplay of the opposing logics of "membership" and "influence", in addition to two other potentially contradictory "logics", namely the logics of "goal formation" and "implementation". The four are brought home in what Schmitter and Lanzalaco call the (integrated or *meta)* "logic of associability". Their four-logics model is brought forward to predict the "specific form" collective action will take – whether nationally, sectorally or regionally. Collective action, they argue (ibid.: 212–13), faces problems that are intrinsic to all efforts at "organizing complexity" across multiple issues and extensive space – "complexity" means that business interest associations may be "sandwiched" between the often conflicting "imperatives" of

> providing their members with the services and the sense of identity that they desire, and negotiating with their interlocutors for the policy responses and compliant behavior that they are willing to provide, but they also have other generic problems they must deal with ... Interest associations are similar to firms in that they are subject to a set of objective constraints ... that vary according to such factors as the number of members, their spatial dispersion/concentration, the sheer extent of territory covered, the means available for communication, the mix of services proposed and so forth.

Besides, changes in "policy style" may induce changes in "interest representation". For instance Keynesian demand management "designed" to mitigate or offset cyclical fluctuations via fiscal measures and deficit spending was "relatively indifferent to territory". Against that indifference, the

> currently fashionable attention to so-called "supply-side" measures that provide favorable credit, physical infrastructure, worker training, marketing advice and so on to targeted sectors or enterprises is much more selective and site-specific. With declining faith in Keynesianism is likely to come an increasing need to devolve public intervention in the economy from the macro- to the meso-level – and a correspondingly greater role for territorially and sectorally differentiated [business interest associations]. (Ibid.: 217)

Changes in policy "styles" and territorial "sovereignty" are said to inform us as to under which sort of contextual conditions it seems *rational* for business interest associations to change their strategies of "segmentation" and "regionalization". However, regarding the question of how and when business interest associations and "the" state are de facto in a position to opt for such a scenario change – that is asking for the necessary and sufficient conditions enabling or disabling firms, interest formations and state agencies to translate "rational" insights into efficient and effective "solutions" – the "logic of associability" does not provide us with resolute answers. Besides, the problems of organizational and institutional *inertia* remain unaddressed: scenario change involves competing investments clustering around old and new policy "styles" and "loyalties", that is, informal short circuits have to be mobilized to lubricate the transition from old to new commitments (cf. for example the network-"(in)solvency" theorem presented in Chapter 4, Box 4.2). In the wavering assessment of the authors themselves, "neither the 'logical' nor the 'extra-logical' factors predict what specific subnational level will benefit from the choices and trends implied by them...Some combination of...variables should be able to predict not only *where, but at what level* it will occur". After all it does not surprise us when Schmitter and Lanzalaco conclude, in a diplomatic mix of backhanded loyalty to "their" neocorporatist project combined with resignation about the powers of their "associability"-model, that

> the degree of determination [of the model] is probably not great in most cases: hence, the outcome may depend on political struggles

between competing levels of governance and interest aggregation.
All can claim in varying degrees to be the bearers of decentralization
or deconcentration, but which will win out in a given issue arena
will be contingent upon a number of strictly contextual and even
accidental factors that the studies in this [Coleman et al., 1985] volume cannot cover in detail. (Ibid.)

Is this a flexible retreat to the pluralist *perpetuum mobile*, the questionability of which was the very strop on which the first generation of neo-
corporatist theorizing sharpened its anti-pluralist razor?

Scholarly interest and data collection inspired by the second generation of studies in "meso"-corporatism have become increasingly focused
on concrete government–business interactions, rather than on broad
macro- and meso-institutional comparisons of formal regimes of interest
association and intermediation (see for instance Duchene and Shepherd,
1987; Wilks and Wright, 1987; Cawson et al., 1990). One of the off-springs
known as the "policy community" or "policy network" approach demonstrates an advancement (for a critical overview of its antecedents and
ramifications, see Rhodes (1990), and for possible applications see Marin
and Mayntz, 1991). In these studies government–industry relations are
explored at different policy levels and, as a result, attention is drawn to
the accumulating evidence which suggests a disjuncture between conventional characterizations of "national" economic and industrial policies
and processes with what "actually happens" in practice. Reference could
be made, for example, to a comparative three-country study (Britain,
Italy and the then West Germany) on industrial restructuring (Kenis and
Schneider, 1991). The countries were selected for allegedly being antipo-
des in state-interventionist activism: Britain serves as the prototype of
a fragmented, unpredictable and loose-knit network approach; Italy is
exemplary for a top-down variety of "organized capitalism", in which
public and private enterprises, political parties, bureaucracy, central and
regional governments fuse together in a clientelistic but by-and-large
undifferentiated policy network; and Germany somewhere between the
extremes, reportedly characterized by the dualism of a strong tradition
of non-intervention in industry on the one hand, and a long tradition
of bottom-up "organized capitalism" (social partnership) on the other.
Summarizing some findings from Kenis and Schneider (1991: 307–23)
three different kinds of "context" are reported to be significant for the
"absence or presence of policy networks":

- The cluster of *general country variables*, such as the traditional political orientation towards the economy, the level of consistency in how

industrial adaptation is managed, the degree to which industrial adaptation has become politicized, and the role played by public agencies.

- The existence of *general sector variables*, such as personal and/or organizational interlocks and integration within an industry.
- *Structural and situational conditions* of the sector or industry studied: the degree of intra-industry competition and crisis, the presence and activities of trade associations, the frequency and extent of state regulation and influence, the degree of international regulation, and the degree of influence of international organizations.

Again – as observed in our earlier criticism on the proverbial "state remaining something of a mystery" – the absence or presence of certain institutional arrangements is explained by such variables as "the politicization of industrial adaptation", "the role played by public agencies", "the existence of organizational interlocks", "the extent of state regulation and influence", and the like. Considering these as explanatory variables, and hence implicitly as comparatively static *givens*, leads us astray from what they must be in a genuine theory on the (r)evolution of capitalist discipline – in short the essentials that *have to be explained*.

The "policy community" approach aims at cross-sectoral and cross-national comparisons, "with an emphasis on *identifying, comparing and classifying* 'policy networks'" (Wilks, 1989: 30; my italics). The approach classifies and compares networks in terms of their relational stability and continuity, the degree of exclusivity and diversity of membership, the degree of insulation from other networks or publics more generally (including parliament) and the degree of articulation of central–local ("vertical") and territorial ("horizontal") relationships (Rhodes, 1986). The approach has delivered a couple of telling portraits of actors, roles, linkages, informal "rules of the game", insulation from other "communities", etc., in specific industrial sectors – for instance in the chemical (Grant et al., 1988; Martinelli, 1991) and the pharmaceutical industry (Hancher, 1990). It is one thing to believe that the links between attributes such as stability, continuity, exclusivity, diversity, insulation, articulation and so on are "primarily matters for empirical investigation. Consequently ... proliferating definitions [are not] a major problem, provided future research looks for, and appraises, network characteristics and does not seek to preempt, either by definition or by 'ideal-type' formulations, that which needs to be investigated" (Rhodes, 1990: 312). It is another thing, however, to worry about a possible proliferation of *dimensions* that risks shoving away the emergence of an explanatory theory of government–industry cohabitation practices and rent-seeking behaviours. What is needed, in other words, is a radical simplification rather than a multiplication of "dimensions", "logics" and "contextual" or "situational" contingencies that tends to thicken and throttle the scholarly enterprise. The more complex and variable are the empirical realities we are facing, the more urgent is conceptual simplicity and constancy; the more heterodox, hybrid and contradictory the phenomena are that a theory has to carry, the tighter the cargo should be lashed *conceptually*.

Even when admitting that the relationship between public–private "governance structures and state structures is so complicated that it is difficult to confine it to a simple causal and/or linear model" (Kenis and Schneider, 1991: 324), it remains unclear how much we gain intellectually by asserting that "it is not…the structure or activities of the state, nor the structure or activities of policy networks, which are of crucial importance: it is their mutual meeting ground…From a process perspective, one could expect the role of the state to encourage the existence of policy networks – while existing policy networks encourage the state to rely on them, and so on". "And so on", certainly, but this is *not* the answer to the question as to what might be the explanation of the emergence, consolidation or decline of integrated policy networks. It is, instead, akin to the earlier mentioned "rationalist" fallacy, overlooking the obstacles on the way from rational "intent" to actual "materialization" – eventually bordering on a functionalist/teleological fallacy, namely the temptation to "explain" the presence or absence of disciplinary arrangements from their conceivable or alleged "functionality" or "dysfunctionality" for society.

Certainly, when searching for realism in the study of government-to-business relations, impressive difficulties remain – not least because strategies and tactics and, as a result, government–industry relations generally "changed in form and substance and, if anything, [have] become more sophisticated as [they have] become less visible. More sophisticated relationships demand more sophisticated understanding" (Wilks, 1989: 337). Maybe it is too early to know whether the schools reviewed above will provide the foundation that appears to be missing most conspicuously in the current study of state–market relationships, that is: a sound *micro*-foundation of disciplinary regimes, imaginative enough to encircle the phenomenon at hand, at *three* levels (see Box 5.4).

Box 5.4   Order at three levels

1. Strategy *formation* occurs at the level of governance of *individual* organizations, referring to the subjective conception by firms, interest formations, state agencies and other relevant actors of efficient boundaries between themselves and their critical environment;
2. Strategy *diffusion* occurs at the level of *inter*-organizational governance, that is the intersubjective quest for effective levels of interest aggregation that, for each of the players, are the co-result from boundary and level choices made by their *counterparts*;
3. Strategy *structuration* occurs at the *meta*-organizational governance level, that is the objective selection and retention of disciplinary regimes that arise from lower level strategy choices and their diffusion over time.

Processes of strategy *structuration* are "objective" in the sense of being clearly beyond the discretionary control of the respective transactors, while being the result of strategic interaction effects. This is a reminder of the earlier mentioned "incompleteness" and "indeterminacy" of the *coordination* of boundary and level choices in a world in which transactors are bound to anticipate how their counterparts will anticipate the choices of the former, but will be seldom if ever in a position to perform that Herculean task in an exhaustive, comprehensive way. A foundation of this kind should be "elastic" enough to bridge the intellectual gap between micro-strategical intentions, meso-structural commitments and macro-evolutionary outcomes. The gist of that enterprise must be the specification of the spillovers intermediating between these – equally consequential – manifestations of social reality.

The lures of simplification

Capitalists must simultaneously play several games: vis-à-vis one another, the state, organized labor and the consuming and voting public. This means that, depending on the salience of these different games, "business associative action may use different structures and strategies in response" (Coleman and Jacek, 1989: 218). The still-unsettled question is which structures and strategies will be used and when? For finding an answer we have to return to the "origin" of the games of industrial and financial restructuring, that is to the elective "communities of fate" that bring together capital, labor, state, *i tutti quanti* ("and all that").

As the crux in nested games I designate *interdependent choice* (with its usual associates, the traps of over- and *undergrazing*). The question of interdependence reiterates a time-honored topos: under what conditions will coordination emerge in a universe of "rational egoists" with contending interests, as long as no undisputed authority comes up to reconcile their competing claims? Since Adam Smith and Thomas Hobbes the quest for social order in a universe of rational egoists has been answered in different ways. The answers appear to lie between two extremes: those who assume that societies are equilibrium-seeking systems – *eo ipso* – versus those that try to be a bit more specific about the feedback mechanisms required to travel from enlightened "self-interest" (considered to be a sufficient equilibrium condition in the former approach) to the effective realization of "collective interests" (mostly in terms of necessary conditions in later approaches). The two polar types are the functionalist (rational-choice) school of thought. Contrary to sociological wisdom (see for instance Granovetter, 1985) it seems unjustified to reduce the two to an "over"-versus-"under" socialized conception of man.

The functionalist tradition holds that interdependence teaches self-restraint and promotes cooperation. Interdependence refers to situations in which contending parties will discover – or foresee – that they gain more by cooperation than they stand to lose by defecting. Society is seen as a sort of "ecology" of games which accomplishes unplanned but largely functional results. It is considered a "chess" game-of-games: the players in one game use the players in another and are, in turn, used themselves. For instance:

> the banker makes use of the newspaper man, the politician, the contractor, the ecclesiastic, the labor leader, the civic leader – all to further his success in the banking game – but, reciprocally, he is used to further the others' success in the newspaper, political, contracting, ecclesiastical, labor and civic games. Each is a piece in the chess game of the other, sometimes a willing piece, but, to the extent that the games are different, with a different end in view. (Long, 1958: 253)

Why is it possible, for instance in restructuring an industry, that a wide variety of purposes is subserved "when no single overall directive authority controls it" (ibid.)? In the *pre*-1960s the typical functionalists' answer would have invoked a mix of past learning and future anticipation: the interrelation of stakeholders in an industry develops over time, generating general expectations as to the interaction, as there are also generalized expectations as to how politicians, contractors, newspaper men, bankers and the like will utilize (in this example) the restructuring situation in playing their particular game in the future:

> In fact, the knowledge that a banker will play like a banker and a newspaper man like a newspaper man is an important part of what makes the situation calculable and permits the players to estimate its possibilities for their own action in their particular game … Some general public expectation of the limits of the conduct of the players and of a desirable outcome does provide bounds to the scramble. (Ibid.)

In the *post*-1960s a counter-current in the behavioral sciences breaks radically with this belief in spontaneous "bounds to the scramble". Where functionalists believe that individuals are "rational within limited areas and, pursuing the ends of the areas, accomplish socially functional ends", though the miracle appears to be "largely ecological rather than a matter of conscious rational contriving" (ibid.: 254–5), more recent theorizing, known as the "rational choice" approach of cooperation among "rational egoists", though starting from a similar assumption of limited rationality, arrives at diametrically opposed conclusions. Rational-choice theory maintains that there may exist a persistent gap between, on the one hand, individuals' *insight* into the potentially destructive outcomes of mutually non-cooperative behavior and, on the other, individuals' factual *capacity* to cooperate as long as each of them is uncertain, while too costly to find out whether the other(s) will reciprocate in a cooperative fashion or not. If, in a situation of interdependent choice, one side selects the cooperative option whereas the other defects, the former will lose more than he would if he had assumed – and reciprocated – a defection by his counterpart. Given the unreliability of information and the possibility of self-disbelieved behavior, *all* actors, in what we identified earlier in this chapter as a prisoner's dilemma setting, are predicted to select the non-cooperative option. As rational pessimists will say: in order to minimize potential losses, rational egoists will always defect even when they *know* that the failure to reach a mutually benefiting solution makes everybody worse off.

One of the latter-day exponents of this approach, Axelrod (1984), has stipulated, on the basis of experimental computer tournaments among trained game-theorists, that this type of low-trust dynamics can be broken and that even hard-nosed rational egoists may succeed in transforming the retaliatory potential of a non-cooperative game into the mutual benefits of a cooperative one. Curiously enough, the preconditions for this unexpected outcome echo the provisos that the abused functionalists identified as the "bounds to the scramble": for the emergence of a cooperative equilibrium actors must have the capacity to learn from negative and positive experiences – the "shadow of the past" – and actors must take into account the chance that they will have to meet again and that the heavier is this "shadow of the future", the lesser is the actors' propensity to discount distant events and the more probable the emergence of a mutually constructive outcome. The difference, however, with the functionalist approach lies in a more punctual specification by game theorists of the role of the *time* perspective in the dynamics of learning and anticipating. By introducing the dimension of time, disarticulated metaphors, like the functionalists' "ecology" of games, are replaced by articulated treatises on the requisites of monitoring and sanctioning behavior, that is on the pre-eminent role of the *accuracy* and the *promptness* of positive and negative responses for the evolution of (non-)cooperative strategies. For instance, in the grammar of Axelrod (1984: 182):

> Just as the future is important for the establishment of the conditions for co-operation, the past is important for the monitoring of actual behavior. It is essential that the players are able to observe and respond to each other's prior choices. Without this ability to use the past, defections could not be punished, and the incentive to co-operate would disappear.

More scrupulous followers of this line of thinking have readily acknowledged the limited predictive power of these models of social life – many factors are "not incorporated into the simple Prisoner's Dilemma formulation, such as ideology, bureaucratic politics, commitments, coalitions, mediation, and leadership" (ibid.: 190). Even regarding the heart of this framework – that is, the "ease of monitoring" and the "speed of responding" – the most the model can tell us is that waiting too long to respond to uncalled for defections implies the risk of sending the wrong signal:

> The longer defections are allowed to go unchallenged, the more likely it is that the other player will draw the conclusion that defection can pay. And the more strongly this pattern is established, the harder it will be to break it...The speed of response depends upon the time required to detect a given choice by the other player. The shorter this time is, the more stable co-operation can be. (Ibid.: 185)

Axelrod's phrasing is deliberately cast in conditional terms, because responding too promptly (re)generates, in turn, the risk of provocability. As long as the reversion to a "last resort" central authority is impossible, or too expensive, as in fact is assumed for good reasons in this approach, the response must not be "too great" nor "too quick" lest it lead to an unending echo of defections. Consequently, "limited" provocability is a "useful feature" of a strategy designed to achieve stable cooperation. While tit-for-tat responds with an amount of defection "exactly equal" to the other's defection, in many circumstances "the stability of co-operation would be enhanced if the response were slightly less than the provocation" (ibid.: 187).

Later (see Chapter 8) we will have to find out to what extent the notions of the "ease of monitoring" and the "speed of sanctioning" might be good candidates for explaining what is left unexplained thus far: the "miracle" of *selective* self-discipline by capitalists (and others dependent on them) as against the "natural" current of frustrating one another and inducing a non-intended regress into short-term opportunism (hit-and-run), which leaves everybody worse off. From time to time, capitalists appear to be able to overcome their centrifugal reflexes and find some cooperative type of formal and informal discipline. Under what conditions may we expect to witness that result? Consider, for instance, the need to rationalize an industrial sector (e.g., shipbuilding or the aircraft-industry) or the need to modernize an industry hovering at the brink of losing the game of global competition (e.g. information technology). Symptomatically, these situations are haunted by an impressive imbalance between the capitalist "need" versus the capitalist "capacity" to coordinate industrial strategies and tactics (see Chapter 1 on the competition versus competence trap). By differentiating these instances in terms of the "ease of monitoring" and the "speed of sanctioning" we may find a key to the puzzle that neo-corporatist and policy-network analysts, after all, had to leave undecided: given the absence of a central authority, what will be the level of interest aggregation and conflict intermediation "where both *centrifugal* strains and *centripetal* needs can be balanced" (Schmitter and Lanzalaco, 1989: 228)?

Part of the answer may lie in the concept of boundary-cum-level choice. Boundary and level choices are akin to the concept of "closure", as originally stated by Weber (1978 [1922]), "rediscovered" by Parkin (1979), and subsequently reiterated by Murphy (1988). The concept was recently applied by Cawson et al. (1990) in one of those rare studies in which the (inter)firm level of analysis is taken as a point of departure for analyzing the interactions between state and market in terms of processes of *inclusion* and *exclusion*. The latter refer to instances, including notable "neo-liberal" political economies, of closed circuits of policy-making where unwanted and potentially destabilizing actors are excluded. The distinction between insiders and outsiders in these "closed circuits" echoes neo-corporatist and policy-network characterizations of the politics of reciprocity in which "the state" attributes a semi-public monopoly status to interest groups "in exchange for" a privileged say in the way the latter define, articulate and implement the private interests they choose to represent. What Cawson aspires to clarify by applying Weber's concept of "closure" is why

> state actors sometimes attempt to achieve their objectives through incorporating organizations into policy formation and implementation; and why it is that non-state actors often attempt to pursue their interest through, in effect, "borrowing" the legitimacy and coercive power of the state. At one extreme, actors "capture" the state, and public policy and the public interest become identical with the private interest of the non-state organization. At the other extreme, state actors legitimately coerce non-state organizations into pursuing state-defined objectives. (Ibid.: 7)

What kind of forces or mechanisms generate the specific blend of public and private interests in the making and implementing of "public" policy? To answer that question, Cawson suggests finding out how specific groups, firstly, manage to acquire a privileged status for themselves within the state system and, secondly, how they manage to mobilize to protect their interests as a "closed group". This in turn should be related to "the rules of inclusion and exclusion of the organized groups themselves" (ibid.: 9). However, by repeating his earlier assertion that "the process of social closure is a part of the concentrative dynamic, [considered] here to be the essential *independent* variable in the development of corporatism" (Cawson, 1986: 38; my italics), the explanatory potential of the concept of "closure" slips away once more: what has to be explained – the dynamics of "concentration" and "closure" – is declared to be the "independent" variable, which obscures, conversely, what will be considered to be the "dependent" variable(s) in this (e.g. Cawson's) universe, namely the "rules" of inclusion and exclusion. Certainly, the latter form part of the puzzle to be solved, that is the identification of the *motives* for and the *modes* of incorporation and exclusion, but what should be explained prior to this and independently from "codes" or "modes" of inclusion and exclusion are the *modalities* of associative or dissociative action. As argued before, the latter refer to the conditions of dependence, as these are hypothesized to determine what was called before the horizontal and vertical *boundary* demarcation of organizations – in fact the scale and the scope of inclusion versus exclusion – vis-à-vis the environments in which organizations try to serve their interests. In this perspective the process of closure may be part of a larger process of concentration (and of de facto, as opposed to being imposed formally, centralization). But precisely because of being "part" of what has to be explained, the latter can never be used to explain the former. Maybe the implicit premise, or axiom, of the autonomous ("self-propelling") nature of the "concentrative dynamic" – that is, the arch phenomenon apparently not in need of being explained *sui generis* – owes its inspiration from Weber's own formulation (itself in turn inspired by his never-ending discourse with Marxian postures; see Parkin, 1979, and Murphy, 1988):

> In spite of their continued competition against one another, the jointly acting competitors now form an "interest group" towards outsiders; there is a growing tendency to set up some kind of association with rational regulations; if the monopolistic interests persist, the time comes when the competitors...establish a legal order that limits competition through formal monopolies...In such a case, the interest group has developed into a *"legally privileged group"* and the participants have become *"privileged members"*. Such closure, as we want to call it, is an ever-recurring process. (Weber, 1978 [1922]: 342)

Summing up: the evolution from competitive to collusive, and from collusive to effectively exclusionary strategies – especially when projected against the background of what "rational choice" teaches us about the obstacles on the road from the expected gains from collusion and exclusion and the anticipated losses from mutual defection to the effective mobilization and consolidation of collective interests in a universe of "rational egoists" – *that* miracle still awaits a capable "decoder". Part of the decoding, deriving the codes of inclusion and exclusion from the prevailing conditions of interdependence, rather than taking them as some sort of "iron law" or innate "compulsion", may be done by introducing the discriminatory principles of the "ease of monitoring" and the "speed of sanctioning" in the case of cooperative versus defective strategies. In short, relating situations in which cooperation may be profitable or even a *necessary* condition for collective or individual survival, to the presence or absence of proportionate monitoring and sanctioning facilities, may be helpful in understanding how and when conceivable *necessities* become *sufficient* realities.

In spite of its heuristic potential the "monitoring-sanctioning" framework leaves us with some problems. These problems outweigh doubts about the explicative capacity of Axelrod's pseudo-quantitative suggestions, like "an amount of defection exactly equal to" and the virtual exactitude of "a response slightly less than the provocation". (As we saw on p. 128, quoting Snyder (1971), proponents of the "chicken-game" metaphor abstain wisely from over-specification of the conditions under which "overperception may induce unnecessary capitulation".) Whatever the progress from naïve-functionalist to sophisticated-rationalist theories for the explanation of the evolution of collaborative ventures; and whatever the gain in academic realism by respecting the role of time in explaining the "robustness" of reciprocity – in fact the most instructive part of Axelrod's reconstruction of tit-for-tat strategies – two major flaws remain, which reduce the capacity of rational choice to grasp the essential contingencies of reciprocity in situations of strategic interdependence. First, the insight is missing that, more often than not, quid pro quos in a non-trivial exchange of rewards and punishments – however symmetrical in terms of the accuracy of monitoring and the speed of response – do not necessarily entail symmetrical *commitments* and *consequences* for the parties involved (see my earlier remarks on the divides between value creation and value appropriation, a concrete illustration follows in Box 5.5).

Box 5.5 The OPEC case

Imagine what will haffen when the Organization of Petroleum Exporting Countries (OPEC), a loose-knit collection of non-robust reciprocities, considers increasing its prices by reducing its export volume. In response the oil-consuming countries (OCC) might retaliate by intensifying their search for alternative exploration opportunities (substituting technologies) in order to reduce their economic (and geopolitical) dependences. In this case, however, a *short-term, continuously variable* "tit" (on OPEC's side) is "reciprocated" by a *medium* respectively *long-term, non-discretionarily variable* "tat" (on the OCC's side): even when the shadows of the past and the future urge for a more cooperative solution, retaliatory mid-term and/or compensatory long-term investments by the OCC stand in the way of a simple return to the status quo ante.

Alternatively, when OPEC and the OCC are about to discount the mutual benefits of cooperation ("swimming together") by discovering the costs of mutual defection ("sinking together"), reciprocity may nevertheless fail to obtain – either due to each side's proclivity to break *their* prisoner's dilemma by looking for a power-offsetting alliance with a third party (e.g. multinational oil companies or mineral resource substitutes) or due to each side's talent in exploiting the divisive potential of "rational egoism" *within* their counterparts.

Second (also discernible in Box 5.5) the insight is missing that, in non-trivial circumstances, the number of players is open to strategic manipulation or variation. Relaxing the assumption of a fixed number of participants and allowing for disparities in internal discipline – in fact the robustness of reciprocity *inside* each of the "collective" actors – alters the analysis of *external* reciprocities significantly.

Both annotations refer to one and the same phenomenon: the impact of potential differences in the *maneuverability* of contending interests – functionally, territorially *and* temporally. Both demand a theory of reciprocity in terms of "moves resulting in an escalation of *movements*" – as in a three-dimensional "nomadic" game – as opposed to an approach in terms of "moves and countermoves", as exemplified in the metaphor of a conventional, two-dimensional "chess" game.

The fragility of robustness

Concerted action is, par excellence, a game of "imperfect" coordination among partly cooperative, partly antagonistic, players. Approaches of industrial strategies and tactics in terms of "moves" and "countermoves" – whether of a functionalist or game-theoretical signature – are based on essentially short-term, *exchange*-theoretical interpretations of the competition for *market shares*, assuming (1) competitive "moves" within a fixed arena, with (2) a fixed number of players, and with (3) fixed boundaries between the players and the environment. An approach in terms of "movements", on the other hand, starting from short-term versus long-term, *investment*-theoretical interpretations of interdependent choice, focuses on the competitive struggle for *maneuverability* – allowing for varying degrees of freedom to change (1) the arenas, (2) the numbers of players, and (3) the boundaries between them. Not first-mover, but fast-versus slow-mover, advantages is the name of the game. As I will demonstrate further on, allowing for major or lesser *asymmetries* in the distribution of this triple freedom – to change promises fresh insights into the paradoxes of rationality.

To give a preliminary idea of the paradoxes I am thinking of, consider how economists look at a characteristic topos in the study of industrial strategies and tactics, that is the interrelationships amongst competition, interdependence and innovation. Part of the pertinent literature, especially on the dynamics of global competition, reports an excess of innovations due to imitative or bandwagon effects. Bandwagon effects are prompted by the fear amongst competing firms of losing first-mover advantages by "jumping" too late on a promising technology train and, hence, forfeiting new market opportunities. Imitating "exemplary" competitors becomes a rational way of countering, and countering becomes a form of counter-competitive insurance. The "minimal regret" strategy for instance, asserting that imitators follow first movers even when this requires the investment of billions of dollars in make-believe strategies (e.g. Schenk, 1992), reinforces the self-fulfilling prophecy of the "imperative" to innovate. The pre-emptive nature of the mechanism predicts an excess supply of cosmetic or fake innovations. Evolutionary economists, on the other hand, reasoning from a "rational choice" perspective, arrive at diametrically opposed conclusions: they predict a *shortage* rather than an excess of innovations. Several explanations are suggested for this opposite outcome:

- *Appropriability*: organizations often feel uncertain about the chance that they can keep the result of their innovative efforts for themselves; free riders may reap the fruits of the innovative contribution of others (Olson, 1975; Hardin, 1982; Teece, 1990).
- *Critical mass*: organizations may have doubts about the availability of complementary innovations, indispensable for the viability and profitability of their own innovations, and will only switch from existing practices if they reasonably expect that others – suppliers, clients and those who decide on a supporting infrastructure – will follow; otherwise the pioneers are saddled with prohibitive first (that is, lone) mover disadvantages (Farrell and Saloner, 1985; Nelson and Winter, 1982; Winter, 1988).
- *Path dependence*: organizations risk entrapment in hyper-specialized and long-term investments; dedicated and fixed assets restrain the opportunity to switch by constraining the freedom of organizations to reallocate their financial resources (Teece, 1990: 61–2; Blankart and Knieps, 1991); and, I should add, the other critical resources of competence ("intellectual" capital) and connections ("infra" or "network" capital).

Which of the two predictions will prevail in a setting in which the net benefits of one's own choices are dependent on what others are expected to do: the propensity to imitate or the propensity to refrain? Reasoning from the eventualities of the competition and/or competence trap suggests an answer. As far as the salience of bandwagon effects varies from industry to industry, and as far as pre-emptive strategies more often than not are meant for the *containment*, rather than promotion, of competing technological options, we expect that the escalatory impulses of imitation and pre-emption will not be strong enough to offset the stifling forces associated with the problems of appropriability, critical mass and path dependence. The net result, then, will be *inertia* rather than excess in (pseudo-)innovations. Moreover, the social embeddedness of technological innovation suggests that this may be expected not only for process and product innovations, but for enabling or supporting institutional innovations as well. The rationales of appropriability, critical mass and path dependence can be helpful in explaining the puzzle: the puzzle of the incapacity of a rational society, in spite of being composed of free and self-interested players, to switch to rationally superior processes and arrangements. In theory or, for that matter, computer tournaments, a non-selfish authority governed by the laws of comprehensive rather than local rationality might break the vicious circle. One may think of the state, or a regulatory agency somewhere between market and non-market hierarchies (since, as (neo-)corporatists would argue, in order to be effective, even *"self"*-governance needs the shadow of the state as a lender of support for re-ensuring private compromises). In practice, however, bringing "the" state back in seems to be part of the problem rather than the solution: politicians and public officials know that the authoritative allocation of *values* (which is claimed to be the "core of politics") tends to be susceptible to the same spells of the competition and competence trap as the "core of the market" (claimed to be the competitive allocation of *resources*).

The problem of inertia can be summarized as a mismatch between the conditions of mutual dependence, that is, the objective resource dependences among the players who appear to have a stake in coordinated industrial-financial strategies (firms, state-agencies, organized labor, politicians, trade-associations) and the codes of mutual dependence, that is, the subjective ways of coping with these resource dependences. Formulated the other way around: narrowly framed rationality and limited accountability stand in the way of the coordination of rational and legitimized political-economic responses. To the extent that each of the transactors tends to rationalize its bounded and "transitory" rationality by referring to the imperfect rationality, short-term orientation and limited accountability of *others*, the invisible hand (located at the left side in Figure 5.1) "ratifies" the reproduction of a non-rational and non-accountable social order. An analysis in these terms explains the mismatch between "objective" structures and "subjective" strategies more convincingly than the more current approach in terms of value dissensus and conflicts of interest. Paradoxically enough, it is neither the incompatibility of values nor the contradictory nature of interests, but rather the *parallelism* in values, interests and attitudes of the key actors, that thwarts the coordination of their expectations and the realization of their ambitions. Not deficiencies in value or interest sharing but deficiencies in the balance of power explain the mismatch between structures of dependence and coping strategies. Interpreted this way, the so-called "low trust" dynamics (Fox, 1974; Wassenberg, 1987) underlying the earlier mentioned stifling forces of appropriability, critical mass and path dependence are not the causes but the symptoms of something more elemental: the dynamics of *asymmetries in reciprocation*. Being more elemental, the question of symmetry versus asymmetry in the reciprocity between the architects of social and economic order deserves a central place in this study.

When speaking of "objective" structures versus "subjective" strategies we use these labels in the sense of Olson (1975) where he distinguishes between two types of rationality. Where subjective rationality refers to the imperfections of individual action – that is, to the limits of rationality demonstrated by organizations acting as "rational egoists" – *objective* rationality refers to the limits of rationality demonstrated by interorganizational *networks* – that is, to the imperfections in the collective outcome of the extended *inter*action among "rational egoists". Networks of organizations are formed by subjectively rational agents but once produced the objectively resulting web of commitments may impose additional constraints on the already constrained rationality of the architects of these networks. At higher levels of interest aggregation and interaction, "limits of rationality" assume another quality. Whenever rationality assumes a momentum of its own, it makes sense to distinguish between its subjective and objective manifestations. However, the distinction only makes sense *empirically* if the formal principles of subjective and objective rationality are translated into substantive categories, that is, into the subjective coping strategies of collective actors versus the objective interdependences that "govern" – both in the causative and consequential sense of the word – their reciprocal interactions. The latter formulation derives directly from our three levels of analysis, namely an inquiry into the dependences that structure the logic of transaction *between* "rational egoists" at the interface of the micro/meso-level, and the dependences that govern the logic of interaction *among* collective actors, or "rational *super*-egoists", on the meso/macro-level of the policy-arena(s) where they meet. The distinction between the two – the "logics" of transaction versus interaction – refers to two problems looking for a solution in the negotiated order of a political economy: managing the dilemmas of group formation and managing the dilemmas of the formation of intergroup relations. In order to clarify the distinction and to illustrate the way in which firms, interest associations and state agencies cope with this kind of intra- and inter-organizational dilemma, we realign the discussion to what was said earlier about the transformation of government-to-business relationships from the tightly orchestrated, top-down politics of *accommodation* – emblematic of the old discipline – to the equally seclusive (Weber's "closure"), but increasingly fragmented, politics of *containment* that characterize the rise of the new discipline.

The new discipline

As argued in Chapter 4 and elaborated here, from the late 1970s onwards the paraphernalia of the macro-politics of accommodation have become increasingly irrelevant as an encompassing device for expressing and governing *inter*-class conflicts. Strategies and tactics of accommodation that used to be emblematic of neo-corporatist regimes in many a West European, mixed-market economy kept part of their relevance – be it nowadays more as an improvising and opportunistic device for handling interlevel contradictions of interest representation, originating from the *intra*- rather than inter-class inability to overcome the collectively irrational outcomes of individually rational behaviors. As demonstrated above, the transformation applies as much to capital and labor qua interest associations as to the state in its manifold and multilevel manifestations qua value association. Formulated dogmatically, one can say that the order of mixed-market economies underwent a transformation from a negotiated order initially based on the politics of segregation *between* the classes – a regime of horizontal interclass compartmentalization, the stability of which required a high degree of vertical, *intra*-class discipline across all levels of interest aggregation – towards a negotiated order based on *intra*-class segregation – a regime of vertical compartmentalization, the manageability of which requires horizontal and diagonal, *inter*-class alliances (however opportunistically or temporarily motivated) in order to solve, or less cosmetically said to *export* upward or downward, the *intra*-class dilemmas of "collective action". As indicated earlier, these dilemmas gather in weight, the broader the scope and the more inclusive the level of interests that capital, labor and the state, either willingly or by an inadvertent conspiracy of circumstances, pretend to represent and incorporate. As I intend to make clear in the following chapters, industrial-financial strategies offer a rich illustration of this gradual but nonetheless radical transformation from a predominantly *horizontal* regime of orchestrating interclass divides in an accommodationist fashion to a predominantly vertical regime of orchestrating intraclass divides by a mixed menu of escapist strategies and containment tactics. Rephrased in terms of capitalist "discipline": in the old discipline what prevails is the shared respect for the "sovereignty" of each of the representational "monopolists" – organized capital, labor and the state respectively – flanked by an uncontested oligarchic "mandate" within each of these formations. In the new discipline we see the gradual breakdown of the "monopolists" internal mandate and a shift towards lower-level, ad hoc forms of interest intermediation *within* capital, labor and the state – flanked by ad hoc ententes *between* each of them.

Regarding the strategic interdependences governing the games of industrial-financial politics – both nationally and internationally – the key actors know, as they know that their counterparts know, that coping strategies inspired by rational egoism *tout court* will almost certainly have counter-rational consequences. Yet, not knowing what *others* will do with this knowledge and, more to the point, not knowing how far the internal discipline or mandate of the others will ascertain, or frustrate, a proportionate response to the risks of "rational" short-sightedness, the typical reflex for *all* players, public and private alike, will be to look for internal and external safeguards. Leaving political and managerial rhetoric aside, the latter objective may be the hard core of the strategic "competence" that state and market actors are looking for, namely the capacity to forge an optimal fit between their intra- and inter-organizational discipline.

The search for *internal* organizational discipline takes the form of rent-seeking *coalitions*; the search for *inter*-organizational predictability results in the formation of rent-seeking *alliances*. In this make-up, industrial-financial politics are stratified, triangular games: "stratified" because the players may choose – if they *have* a choice – between different levels of interest inclusion and exclusion; and "triangular", not in the conventional sense of some solidaristic variety of tripartite concertation – capital–labor–state – but in the above suggested constellation of firm-to-firm, state-to-state and government-to-business *reinsurance* games: a strategic calculus in which each player (e.g. capital) at the optimal level (or mix of levels) of interest inclusion "offers" another (e.g. labor) to serve as a shield or leverage against a third party (e.g. the state, or more pertinently, a Department, a financial House Committee or a Directorate General of the European Commission). For the state and the interest associations of labor the same type of strategic calculus applies, though more often than not it results for each of them (for reasons to be spelled out in the next section) in *dissimilar* optimal "subsidiarity" levels of interest aggregation. The strongest players in this stratified and triangular setting are the ones who can afford to *commute* between more than a single level of interest representation and intermediation in *different* arenas.

Arenas vary according to the sector-specific games to be played, ranging from labor-intensive and declining industries to capital-intensive and emerging industries. What matters in all cases is the resourcefulness of the players in terms of their financial, intellectual and relational assets. Resourcefulness informs maneuverability. Maneuverability determines whether an inclusive or exclusive game will be chosen. Following Olson's grammar (1975) an *exclusive* game refers to "market" groups having an objective interest in *minimizing* the size of the group, as for instance oligopolists or a group of firms lobbying for exclusive state subsidies. In an exclusive game the theoretical optimum is a closed representational monopoly. An *inclusive* game, on the other hand, refers to "non-market" groups, that is, stakeholders bent on increasing their leverage by *maximizing* the size of the group of their supporters or clients. The rationale may be the hope of declining costs or increasing marginal returns as in the case of trade-union mergers or industries lobbying for protectionist measures or tax reductions. The theoretical optimum of "inclusivity" is a function of the expected economies of scale, as for instance in pressure politics. Whether the choice between respectively a specific *combination* of inclusive and exclusive forms of associational conduct in industrial strategies proves to be an *asset* (increasing an actor's entry and exit opportunities) or a *liability* (overstretching an actor's dilemma-absorbing capacities) depends on the interplay of two sets of variables: the internal discipline and the sense of direction of the actors versus the strength of the earlier mentioned "forces-of-inertia", namely appropriability, critical mass and path dependence.

The new paradigm

More must be said about this in the succeeding chapters, but looking at the complexities of the interplay of internalities and externalities one conclusion can be drawn in advance. Apart from the shortcomings of the functionalist and rational-choice perspectives, our review of the literature casts serious doubts on the explanatory power of another sociological metaphor that "unifies" the otherwise "pluralist" body of accommodationist theorizing and research, that is *exchange* theory. The ambiguities associated with multi-level moves and multi-arena movements question the realism of such a quasi-synoptic paradigm. Of course, our skepticism about the usefulness of the exchange metaphor may be an artifact of the selected sorts of game – "industrial-financial strategies" – representing less "continuously variable" and "calculable" tit-for-tats than the divisible give-and-takes in the world of wage, income, tax, social security, vocational training policies and the like. It may even be argued that the example of industrial-financial politics represents a perfect case for demonstrating the *limits* of exchange: in industries suffering from excess capacity, cyclical rigidities and mass lay-offs (such as in steel, synthetic fibers, textile, shipbuilding and electronics), capital, labor and the nation state are said not to have any choice but to accept the ineluctable "laws" of the market. Consequently, according to this view, there is nothing to be "exchanged". To assess the pertinence of this kind of objection, it suffices to repeat what was said earlier about statics and dynamics, that is, about the inherently static nature of functionalist and conventional game-theoretical approaches. In these, essentially exchange-theoretical images of society, power and dependence are analyzed in terms of moves and countermoves – aimed at improving or consolidating strategic *positions*, in a "flat" world in which the trinity of arena, agenda and time is assumed to be *fixed*. When we confront these assumptions with the approach proposed here we obtain an analysis of power and dependence in terms of processes of position*ing*, directed at maintaining or improving an actor's strategic *maneuverability*. Add to this a world consisting of more than a single issue arena, and allowing for the articulation of interests at more than a single level of aggregation, then it becomes clear why arena, agenda and time, instead of being treated as fixed parameters, should be considered as first-order targets of strategic search and selection. The question, in other words, is not whether actors are involved in exchanging rewards and punishments or threats and promises – they obviously are – but rather whether this observation is of much assistance, first, in identifying the forces governing political-economic exchange conditions and, second, explaining the cumulative effects of these forces for the "ratification" or "revision" of the negotiated order of industrial-financial strategies. The former question refers to the specifics of bargaining power and its elementary distribution in society. The second issue relates to the intended and non-intended consequences of the division of bargaining power for the evolution of the negotiated order between state and market. Exchange theory falls short on both dimensions. Models of state–market relationships based on the exchange-theoretical paradigm – even those that are less "determinist" than functionalism or less "voluntarist" than rational choice and game theory – fail to recognize the essence of strategic choice in a causally "complex" and political-economically "contested" environment, that is an environment in which public and private actors are engaged in disputes about the normative and practical limits of accountability, which result from uncertainty about (1) the reach of the arenas in which they meet, (2) the division of power and authority in these arenas, and (3) the gates between themselves and the environment wherein they seek to (re)deploy their core interests.

Most of these uncertainties can be recognized as specific manifestations of the subsidiarity principle (recently discovered as something "new" but in fact an old timer stemming from the "organic" orthodoxy of corporatism). Subsidiarity refers to the search for "optimal" levels of interest articulation and policy implementation. More intriguingly than the well-known Olsonian rationality traps *inside* interest groups (encumbering their capacity to internalize externalities in policy areas such as employment, inflation, pollution, infrastructure and vocational training), interest groups differ in their preferences regarding the "optimal" level of interest aggregation for their *counterparts*. Who wins in this "battle of preferences" depends on staying power, and *staying* power, paradoxically, depends on one's *exit* opportunities. In order to grasp the subtleties of the politics of reciprocity, of vital importance for our understanding of the negotiated order as well as for conjectures about the governance structures that may emerge, we need a *third* generation of (what probably, then, has to be relabeled as) *post-accommodationist* respectively *containment* theorizing and research. It is to be expected that the distinctive heuristics of this shift of scholarly curiosity generates a research agenda that can be paraphrased as follows:

- First, a shift from macro- and meso-analyses that takes existing (state and business-interest) associations as a predefined menu from which to choose, to micro-analysis, assuming that capitalists (like governmental actors and contending private actors) prefer a mix of institutional as well as *non*-institutional alternatives and postulating that, ultimately, actors' choices determine the rise and fall of the salience of specific disciplinary arrangements.
- Second, a shift from "institutions", seen as a collective state of mind for handling conflicts of interests, to institutions seen as a moving web of formal and informal *commitments*. Commitments are the outcome of intendedly rational choices, imposed or self-contrived by collective actors (firms, state agencies, trade unions, and so forth).
- Third, a shift from the orthodox view of institutions to a stakeholders analysis in the heterodox sense, that is mixing the rationality

assumptions of evolutionary economics with the strategy-of-conflict insights of the science of diplomacy with the concrete sociology of (inter)organizational stratagems and spoils.

- Fourth, a shift from the causal *linearity* suggested by the "structure-conduct-performance" orthodoxy in industrial economics to the causal *circularity* suggested by a "strategic choice" paradigm in which actors, by choosing a strategy, create commitments, which, once created, tend to predetermine further choices. The latter, by constraining the external maneuverability as well as the internal flexibility of the choosing agents (see the competence trap that follows from the intra- and inter-organizational costs of switching from old to new allegiances), may have non-intended ("agent-insensitive") consequences.

- Fifth, a shift from classificatory and comparative "structures" of states and markets to the study of the "competitive advantage of institutions", which is a sort of survival of the "fittest" commitments (in)vested in coalitions and alliances. The "fitness" of coalitions (*around* a specific "collective" interest) and alliances (the bridges *across* specific "collective" interests) serves as the chief explanation of the evolution of government-to-industry relationships ("concerted action"). Structural changes in the pattern of *commitments* ("disciplinary arrangements") are considered to be a function of changes in the (asymmetry of) entry and exit *conditions*, both at the level of individual organizations (firms, state agencies and interest associations) and at the level of cross-organizational connections (the strategic "communities of fate") between state and market.

Conclusion

The latter assertions about the "competitive advantage of institutions" represent the core of a new paradigm: a shift from the quest for institutional *associability*, based on the *exchange*-theoretical notion of moves and countermoves between interdependent actors in a two-dimensional theater – in which the *arena, agenda* and *time* are assumed to be fixed – to the quest for strategic *maneuverability*, based on the *investment*-theoretical notion of movements – and momentum of concerted action in a three-dimensional theater – in which the *manipulation* of the parameters of arena, agenda and time is assumed to be the quintessence of the play. When we designate the evolution of concerted action between state and business as the meta-phenomenon to be explained (explanandum), then the micro- and meso-properties, respectively concerning intra- and inter-organizational *bargaining power*, must be the explaining variables (explanantia). Box 5.6 summarizes the argument and shows the partitioning of the paradigm.

Box 5.6   The argument: the co-evolution of capitalist discipline and corporate games

The Quest for Discipline

How do strategically dependent organizations cope with the quest for discipline when the *arena* consists of a constellation of

- rent-seeking actors economizing on commitments (the essence of *rational egoism*);
- tied by historical investments (the essence of *path dependence*);
- and facing related dilemmas of anticipation (the essence of *interdependent choice*) but differing in their relative freedom to enter or to leave the arena (the essence of *negotiation power*).

Propositions

1. Horizontal rivals confronted with prisoner's dilemmas will look for *vertical allies*.
2. Vertical allies confronted with "reciprocity" hazards will reiterate the search for *horizontal coalitions*.
3. Movements of this kind generate new dilemmas, invoking a new type of disciplinary repertory: that is, the *recycling* of coalitions and alliances.

The Conquest of Discipline

Concerning the revolving relationship between micro-practices, meso-arrangements and macro-order we can say that strategies emerge from structures of dependence; that interdependent choice induces disciplinary codes and commitments; that the latter arrangements generate regimes; and that regimes (re)ratify strategies and structures.

The approach defended here is a plea for the analysis of industrial-financial games from a rent-seeking, interdependent-choice perspective. The grammar of "games" suggests a deviation from both conventional normative and positive approaches to policy planning and corporate strategy analysis. The units of analysis are strategies and tactics of concrete organizations that can be considered as the main stakeholders in the formation and diffusion of industrial-financial politics: firms, interest associations and state (agencies). The institutional arrangements into which firm-to-firm and government-to-business relationships crystallize are seen as *disciplinary* arrangements. The paradigm is sensitive to the paradoxes of power in situations of neither purely authoritative nor purely competitive relationships. Consider for instance the paradox of the "weakness of strong ties": in a triangular setting a relatively weak but *flexible* player may be highly effective compared with strong antagonists, which are inflexible due to financial, technological or relational path dependences ("sunk investments"). Or consider the paradox of the "strength of weak ties": a weak, underperforming or *defecting* link in a chain of strong interdependences may derive disproportional power from its capacity to disrupt the integrity of the community of interdependent fates. Approaching industrial-financial stratagems from this angle asks for the integration of economics, sociology and political science. The recombination of these disciplines results in a reframing and dynamization of the analysis of *capitalist discipline*, the centerpiece of which rests upon the following premises:

- The conditions and codes of disciplinary games change in ways imperfectly understood by the players.
- The games are performed by at least three players, implying the possibility of switching coalitions and alliances.
- The players are internally non-monolithic.
- Though some of them may operate simultaneously in different arenas, with different agendas and time horizons, the interdependence of choice tends to discourage maximalist strategies.
- The moral "vacuum" will be stronger when there is more uncertainty about the number of negotiators and their "visibility", the intensity of the stakes of each of them, and the room for (re)linking stakes and issues.
- The collective and cumulative logic of the game constrains the negotiability of the game.

This list suggests a crucial difference from the world according to Olsonians and Axelrodians: the "shadows" of the past and of the future are, more often than not, *asymmetric* shadows for the respective players. The proviso of a perfect, that is, spatially and temporally symmetric, freedom to answer tit-by-tat will rarely, if ever, be satisfied.

If we allow for (1) the presence of more than two parties, (2) possible asymmetries in external maneuverability and internal mobilization and, consequently, (3) possible asymmetries in the escalation of commitments triggered by successive tit-for-tats, then it must be clear why functionalist, exchange and game-theoretical notions of conflict and cooperation have to be replaced by another framework, the baseline of which is negotiating power and diplomatic intelligence.

6
Conditions: The Anatomy of Negotiating Power

Introduction

The art and science of negotiation is largely a matter of storytelling. Not a great deal of rigorous theory construction and research is implicated. This state of affairs is frequently justified by the claim that negotiating is, in the final analysis, an "artistic" activity. Yet, ever since Molière's *bourgeois gentilhomme* was pleasantly surprised when his house philosopher confided to him that for the last 40 years he had "been making prose *without knowing it*", we are perhaps allowed to say that there is enough logic in the art of negotiation to call it at least an *object* of scientific inquiry, without offending its artistic practitioners. All appears to depend on the perspective one chooses to look at the orchestration of negotiation games – top-down or bottom-up. In the words of an equity trader alias IT lobbyist, versed in "connecting" Silicon Valley economics with Washington politics (Miles, 2001: 240): "If you go to a rave it looks like chaos, and what appears to be chaos is structured. The old companies are going, 'this is messy, this is overvalued, it doesn't make sense'. Well, yeah. From the *balcony* it doesn't make sense".

It is my purpose to come up with a model of negotiating behavior that explains what the rules of conduct are that may develop between negotiators – antagonistic, cooperative or a blend of the two. In my argument negotiators are invariably treated as (representatives of) more or less *organized* parties (organizations, agencies, interests groups and the like). To be able to make predictions we require insight into a negotiator's anatomy – referring to the structure of his or her decision-making powers – as well as insight into the freedom of movement of the parties – referring to the anatomy of their mutual dependences.

The synthesis of the two I call a primitive or lowbrow game theory: a "game" because we still aim at a stylized representation of reality, and "lowbrow" because we do justice to the real-life "known" unknowns that negotiators encounter in practice. The model proposed here is to some extent the reversal of a "purist" theory of games. In my model the rules of conduct are something to be *explained* rather than being postulated as given or parachuted in from somewhere above. *Highbrow* game theory, instead, seems to have removed the strategic moment par excellence in negotiating processes, namely the possibility to choose – be it under variable strictures, as we shall see – an intelligent *dosage* of adversarial-cum-collaborative rules of the games organizations play.

Negotiating

Negotiating is a meaningful activity whenever two or more actors try to achieve, or oppose, something they cannot accomplish without the concurrence of others. This programmatic definition anticipates three objectives. First, the relative value of the concepts of rationality and legitimacy for our understanding of bargaining behavior is subjected to closer scrutiny. Second, a distinction will be drawn between intentions and results to determine which part of the outcome of bargaining is intended, that is, pursuant to the logic of the negotiators, and which part has to be seen, instead, as the unintended outcome of actors' intendedly rational conduct and/or mores, that is, as an outcome attributable to the cumulative logic of the negotiating *process*. Third, attention is paid to the essence of strategic choice, i.e. the mutual dependence of the negotiators. I will restrict myself to situations where negotiating is both pertinent and purposeful. Negotiating is irrelevant (purposeless) when negotiators are not in touch with one another, that is experience their mutual dependence merely in an *ex post*, lump sum way (the kind of facelessness we find in the textbooks under the heading of "perfect competition").

Alternatively, it is a luxury merely to be found in (bad) dreams when the actors are totally subjected to one another (the kind of subordination we encounter in the manuals under the proverbial condition of "perfect hierarchy"). In other words, negotiating as a generic term is meaningful if and only if, for *each* of the negotiating parties, something can be lost or gained, which is not the case when the actors, or some of them, are anonymous or may take without having to give.

A first cut

What we loosely call "negotiating" ranges from informal and temporary (e.g. lobbying) to recurrent and institutionalized forms (e.g. negotiations between states or between employers and trade unions). When observing negotiations between organizations it is inexpedient to ignore what happens – before, during and after the actual negotiations – *inside* organizations. What is irrelevant in situations of either pure competition or pure hierarchy becomes relevant indeed in the vast area that lies between the extremes. In that zone the adage holds that "there are many things decided by politicians, employers and trade union officials. They have no say, however, in their own resolve, nor in the internal stability of the organizations in which they work and which they represent" (Vos, 1982: 30). As a Dutch White Paper on the strengths and weaknesses of concerted action in the modern welfare state concurs: "Central organizations of employers and workers deliberate and negotiate with each other, and with the cabinet, but they are unable to impose the execution of the agreed-upon commitments on their associated members and organizations" (Central Planning Bureau, 1992: 97–9). The same holds for other than socio-economic entities, even when at face value the latter represent formal hierarchies such as state bureaucracies (see Tullock, 1965; Allison, 1969; Niskanen, 1979; Breton and Wintrobe, 1982).

Dropping the reductionist assumption of internally homogeneous and perfectly self-disciplined players stipulates what we may demand from a lowbrow, non-idealized, negotiating theory. Whether organizations manage to mold their environment is determined as much internally as by their external negotiating capabilities. The first condition relates to the mobilization and monitoring of organizational goals internally; the second to the way external resources and partners are secured to realize the goals selected internally.

As said, negotiating presupposes a setting in which parties somehow need one another, for a shorter or longer span of time. Two kinds of dependence can be distinguished: competitive dependence (a setting in which parties achieve their objectives by pre-empting or frustrating one another) and symbiotic dependence (where objectives are achieved by conceding to a larger or lesser extent to one another). The distinction is not synonymous with "conflict" or "adversity" versus "cooperation" or "harmony". Rivals may cooperate for the sake of disarming a third party and competitive dependence may be used to pressure rivals into cooperation. Conversely, symbiotic dependence may entail tough conflicts, e.g. about the terms of mutual accountability and complementarity and about the appropriation of the spoils of cooperation. What they have in common is that *both* competitive and symbiotic dependence demand coordinated behavior. Coordination poses a dilemma: though reducing or controlling dependences, coordination means that scarce resources – financial, professional and relational capital – are tied down for the sake of coordination. Tying down resources renders organizations less flexible. Loss of flexibility engenders uncertainty as to one's own, as well as one's opponents', strengths and weaknesses. That makes it hard to strike a rational balance between one's taste for independence and the need for coordination. The dilemma becomes more acute when familiar transaction patterns are upset – for instance when pre-existing functional dependences are made obsolete by technological change or when territorial dependences start to shift because of internationalization.

Negotiating processes for controlling the environment and securing scarce resources involve more than the kind of complexity reduction referred to in the literature as the limits of rationality. In addition to cognitive limitations to the gathering and processing of information (the classic notion of "bounded rationality") there are internal and external limits to the rationality of organizations. More often than not the internal division of authority has its imperfections, and the external division of power – defining one's dependence on what others do – will stand in the way of responding "rationally" to internal and external contingencies.

Summarizing: a theory of negotiation not too far removed from reality must respect (at least) *three* kinds of imperfection (for a first try-out of this approach, see Wassenberg, 1985): imperfect gathering and processing of information; imperfect internal discipline; and an imperfect grasp of the scale and scope of external dependences. An adequate negotiator is the one who somehow manages to handle the complications that result from the concurrence of this triad of imperfections. His "intelligence" may start with the awareness that his counterparts are likely bound to struggle with similar imperfections. This may conspire to bring parties closer together: *complexity breeds complicity*. The question is, however, how far an organization may want to go in linking or meshing its own fate with the fate of others. A community of fate may be a useful medicine for reducing internal and external uncertainties. However, as with medicine, it is the dosage that draws the line between intended and unintended effects.

Negotiating: a second take

The question of intentionality requires a more precise definition of negotiating and a terminological clarification of its key elements. I define negotiating as:

> *A process of potentially opportunistic transactions whereby two or more interdependent parties through mutual agreement or commitment attempt to reach a result that is more satisfactory than they might accomplish by other means.*

The threshold for any agreement or commitment, beyond which the rationale of negotiating disappears, is, on the one hand, determined by the alternatives to an agreement or commitment and, on the other, by what parties might achieve on their own. The "potentially opportunistic" element of transactions keeps the possibility open for agreements or commitments to differ from the intended "more satisfactory result", especially in the case of parties displaying opportunistic behavior or suspecting it in others. To distinguish between intentions and results we shall call the first type "transactions" or "transactional moves" – whether or not opportunistic, but always intended, *no matter how involuntary*. The results, on the other hand, we call "interactions" or "interactive effects". *Inter*actions may deviate widely from what was intended by the *trans*actors.

The environment in which negotiators meet is called an *arena*. The arena consists of (Wassenberg, 1980b; 1988):

1. *Structures* of interdependence, determining the *need* to negotiate.
2. *Perceptions* of dependence based on partly incompatible respectively diverging, partly compatible respectively converging, stakes and values, which determine the *room* to negotiate.
3. *Rules* generated by the interplay of needs and perceptions – determining the *capacity* to negotiate.

In what way the players interpret and approach their environment – e.g. in a disciplined or largely erratic way, selectively perceiving opportunities and threats, opting for an antagonistic or conciliatory mode, differentiating friends and foes, responding timely or not to threats and opportunities, and choosing for a specific time horizon for handling these contingencies – depends on the characteristics of the internal arena of actors. The composition of the internal arena determines an organization's *capability* to negotiate. The same structural, behavioral and normative features that we use to describe and compare external arenas can be used to analyze relations and attitudes inside organizations. At that level too there are dependences, collision and collusion of interests and values, specific codes of handling interests and values, and managing dependences.

If we relate the internal and external arena attributes to the aforementioned "imperfections" of organizational rationality, the result is a clearer demarcation of our subject as: (1) negotiating is a process of potentially opportunistic transactions between (2) interdependent actors that try to promote their individual goals by (3) increasing the predictability and manageability of their counterparts, a process (4) that may have intended as well as unintended consequences, not only for the external environment but also for the internal predictability and manageability of the organization or collectivity on whose behalf the negotiators act, as a result of which (5) the potentially opportunistic element may have its "origin" both inside and outside the negotiating entities, which is the reason why (6) the final outcome – the materialization or defeat of the negotiators' objectives – can only be understood by taking into account the totality of internal and external attributes and circumstances.

The spectrum of negotiation

Is there such a thing as a *science* of negotiating when, apart from the conventional notion of cognitively bounded rationality, we also have to deal with the "diplomatic" bounds of organizational and inter-organizational rationality, that is to say, with the limits of rationality resulting from the incompleteness of internal authority and the indeterminacy of external power relations? Maybe there is, lest we end up with two caricatures. On the one hand we must resist the *anecdotic* temptation to pronounce negotiating situations as unique and to see negotiators as a kind of stand-up artist – e.g. the statesman, the trade union boss or the tycoon who is led by his sublime *intuition*. On the other hand we must resist the *rationalistic* temptation to lock the players in the iron cage of maximalist and utilitarian premises. The rationalistic caricature is called a "cage" because the players are alleged to live in a definite time-space framework, condemned to be with each other, gifted with similar utilitarian rationalities and sentenced to a symmetrical clock and calendar. In this type of metaphor – the template in many a part of the literature – negotiators no longer resemble artists but rather prisoners or marionettes, at worst uncertain about their opponent's preferences and hidden agendas, but internally undivided and indivisible. A marionette may be docile or recalcitrant, constructive or obstructive, but never suffers by definition from nervousness about dissenters or defectors *from within*.

What appears unsolvable in the artistic version – "each situation is unique" – and more often than not indeterminate in the rationalistic one – "a prisoner's dilemma" – can be solved when we unshackle the assumptions of symmetry in space and time. Players are not undivided or undividable monoliths; not all of them are condemned to find a solution to their dilemmas at the same time; and in spatial or territorial terms they are rarely if ever sentenced to one another in the same degree. Inter-actor differentials in time and space and variations in internal cohesion allow for more room for *informed improvisation* than the hermetic metaphor would have us believe, as well as more room for *routines* and *conformism* than is allowed for in the "artistic" metaphor. Let's see what this means.

More about magicians and marionettes

The "clinical" literature on negotiating largely consists of wise advice and practical suggestions. There is nothing wrong with prescriptions, as long they are based on something. The practical usefulness of recommendations increases when they are grounded on a solid analytical-empirical foundation. Concerning that foundation there is disagreement. The discussion of the bases of the phenomenon of bargaining varies between two poles: some argue that negotiating is a matter of the "magic eye" and is not a science – if science means looking for refutable generalizations, and something that can be taught. For "magicians" it is only possible to assess the successes and failures of bargaining in retrospect. Supporters of the "magic eye" view are found among novelists, journalists, diary writers and, more conceivably, negotiators themselves. What is meant by qualifying negotiating as a work of art? As an impulsive activity whereby magic, intuition or plain luck play a more overriding role than the canons of logic and science? However, we can think of numerous instances of human creativity not inspired by the laws of science or logic, which nonetheless lend themselves to scientific scrutiny, that is to say, to the discovery and sometimes the explanation of regularities or patterns. Musicology, literature, drama and art history spring to mind. Conversely, we are accustomed to the colloquialism that denotes certain recipes (as in politics), formulas (as in mathematics) or moves (as in chess or the waging of war and peace) as "beautiful" or "elegant": it seems that products of the human mind, in addition to their logical stature, sometimes are seen to have artistic value as well. Consequently, it seems there is no a priori reason why the *aesthetics* of negotiating would be inaccessible with an analytical-empirical reconstruction of its foundations.

At the opposite end of the scale we find those who argue that the appropriate subject of inquiry is not the *sprezzatura* of negotiating, but rather the ingenuity it requires. Theirs is the claim that any theory on negotiating cannot be called scientific as long as it is not anchored in the rigorous grammar of logic. Some aspire to go quite far in this, undaunted by the artificial rather than the artistic nature of their impersonations of social reality. Game theorists reveal the strongest bent for this puritan stand. Rather radical immunizations are called upon to make the intricacies of social reality *mathematically* manageable. The most common assumptions to be found in the "discipline" of game-theoretical modeling are:

- The number of players is prefixed.
- Each player chooses from a given number of alternative strategies.
- Each player knows not only his own strategic options, but those of his opponents as well.
- Each player attaches a certain value to every imaginable strategy mix, the value of which is assumed to be invariable during the game.
- Each player knows not only the value he himself attaches to alternative strategy mixes, but the value his opponents attach to them as well.
- Each player behaves rationally, that is actors will always choose the strategic option that promises the greatest utility.

Though testing the acumen of its subscribers, assumptions of this stature unfortunately do not allow for testing the empirical value of game theory. Yet, mathematical game theory is said to be a valuable tool for complex decision-making alias negotiating problems. It is precisely the "alias", lumping together decision-making and negotiating theory, that exposes the Achilles heel of game theory. Its first deficiency is that it offers no help in answering a host of *preliminary* questions that need to be answered for ensuring that game modeling really becomes a useful tool for the simulation or reconstruction of complex bargaining situations. Summarizing one of the sceptics, conventional game theory appears to leave unidentified such "preliminary decisions" as (Junne, 1972: 142):

1. which opponents need to come under consideration;
2. which coalitions the individual players belong;
3. which rules will govern the game;

4. how much resources are spent on the consideration of different strategy combinations and on the gathering of information to arrive at
   a preferred result and at a realistic calculation of the likelihood of
   that result;
5. what time horizon is chosen;
6. which methods are chosen to play the game and which of the opponents' methods are to be taken into account;
7. which results of possible strategy combinations have to be taken into
   consideration.

The above-mentioned modalities demonstrate "what preliminary decisions have to be made before a strategic decision can usefully be made,
irrespective of the mode of decision" (ibid.: 145; my translation). The
normative undertone of game theory, aspiring to offer practical guide-
lines for negotiations, as well as its overtone of short-term and short-
cyclical rationality – reasoning from individual utilities and immediate
tit-for-tats – are not its sole deficiencies. Even if we know more about
the above-listed unknowns, we would still not have an *explanation* of
bargaining behavior and its (intended versus non-intended) payoffs.
For that we need, first of all, a conceptual framework that describes the
anatomy of decision-making within organizations. However, even such
a non-reductionist "rational choice" model does not equal an authen-
tic "*strategic* choice" theory. For that we need a conceptual connection
between the anatomy of decision-making (based on an *internal* arena
analysis) and actors' objective freedom of choice (based on a network
or external arena analysis). Only by *relating* the "externalized" need and
room to negotiate on the one hand, and the "internalized" discipline and
capability to negotiate on the other, can we begin to approach the core
of negotiating processes among contending, but interdependent, actors.
The core consists of three coordinates – a triangle which one searches for
in vain in game theory: the demarcation of the *arena* (the selection of
allies and opponents), the definition of the *agenda* (the selection of issues
and non-issues) and the *timing* of negotiating processes (both in the sense
of the selection of the periodicity and the time horizon of bargaining).

On the coordinates of bargaining

Arena, agenda and timing constitute a negotiator's strategic *compass*. Its
significance is conditional on such nearer qualifications as:

1. *Elasticity*: bargaining situations vary according to the extent to which
   the arena, agenda and timing can be manipulated at will.

2. *Predictability*: situations vary according to the extent to which each of these parameters, for instance the arena, affects the other parameters, for instance the agenda and timing, in a more or less foreseeable way.
3. *Level playing*: situations vary according to the extent to which the interlinks of arena, agenda and timing are equivalent for each of the negotiators or not.

Distilling the practice of negotiating processes into an *explanatory* theory makes it possible to tighten a rich but predominantly descriptive and classificatory literature to more manageable proportions. An outstanding representative of such a classificatory approach is Raiffa (1982). Portraying himself as a game-theoretical "renegade", Raiffa originally played with "the grandiose idea of devising a taxonomy of disputes, in which the listing would be reasonably exhaustive and in which overlaps among categories would be rare". It turned out this could only be achieved "after developing a host of abstract constructs – and even then the taxonomy was not very useful" (ibid.: 11). He decided on a "partial" classification in the shape of a number of "organizing questions" to distinguish amongst various negotiation modalities. Paraphrasing the list, the questions are (ibid.: 11–19):

• Are there *more than two parties* and how sharp are their *demarcations*? As soon as there are more than two players coalitions can be formed. This points to the contingency of playing actors off against one another and, more pertinently, to the fact that negotiations are held on who the negotiators are and who in fact will excluded or "organized out".
• Do parties reveal *internal homogeneity*? Often negotiations between two parties mean that agreements have to be reached at two levels: between the two parties, and within each of the individual parties. Sometimes internal consent consumes more energy than external compromise. Consequently, aligning and synchronizing external and internal negotiations may be a delicate and complex affair.
• Is the game *repetitive*? There is a world of difference between parties that only meet once and parties that have to live together for a given amount of time: in the second case reputation, credibility and information (a)symmetries play an important role. Repetitiveness does not necessarily lead to cooperation: stakes in long-term rather than short-term gains may encourage rather than mitigate confrontational attitudes.

- Are there *linkage effects*? Call this the "material" complement of the "temporal" community of fate suggested in the preceding item: negotiating behavior is influenced by the possibility to link and trade-off matters that, strictly speaking, are unrelated.
- Is it *imperative* that an agreement is reached? This aspect refers to what we identified earlier as the "need" and the "room" to negotiate, that is as a proxy for the objective interdependences and the subjective interests or values at stake.
- Are there *temporal constraints* or *costs*? Negotiations are affected by the degree of the players' need to reach an agreement quickly. Sometimes the law prescribes the term, sometimes other circumstances make delays impossible or simply too costly.
- Are the negotiations conducted *publicly* or *behind closed doors*? Premature media exposure or grassroots interference makes for different negotiating dynamics. Sometimes public statements or press leaks are an autonomous element in the construction of the credibility of promises and threats. Sometimes the main target of premature disclosure or (dis)information may be to internally divide one's opponents.
- What are the *mores* of the game? The normative scale ranges from loyalty and trust via opportunism to unfettered cheating and rivalry.
- Is it possible for *outsiders* to intervene? Sometimes outsiders may serve as referees. Arbitrage will not fail to affect the benefits of opting for a (specific mix of) provocative versus conciliatory positions during negotiations.

Raiffa talks of a "partial" checklist that gives an impression of "the complexity, the pervasiveness, and the importance of our subject. The questions are obviously overlapping and are far from exhaustive" (ibid.: 19). However, for our purposes the real problem is not that the list is "partial", "overlapping" and "far from exhaustive". I surmise, somewhat on the contrary, that the list is not *tight* enough to produce verifiable propositions on the structural determinants and outcomes of negotiating dynamics.

The *intelligibility* of bargaining

The science of negotiating consists of two kinds of intelligence. The first is about the gathering and framing of information; the second is about the interpretation of that information. Information gathering is subject to the principles of bounded rationality (in the conventional sense). In addition, as argued before, the framing of information is influenced by imperfections in internal authority and external power configurations. The art of negotiating demonstrates itself in the way these imperfections are dealt with in ordinary life. Between the true to life but inchoate world of circumstantial evidence and the rigorous but unrealistic world of game-theoretical exercises lies a beckoning wasteland. The literature makes it clear that no single discipline has a final say in this area. We might speak of an interdisciplinary game theory as far as we benefit as much as possible from insights provided by game theorists' *substantive* neighbors such as the sciences of sociology, politics and economics.

In deciding how far one should go in adopting an interdisciplinary perspective, science must negotiate with itself. What, for instance, distinguishes a political-economic game theory from its mathematical counterpart is a trade-off between axiomatic elegance and explanatory power. The loss of axiomatic rigor is compensated for by an increment of empirical expressiveness. To demonstrate what the distinction seeks to explain and with what instruments to proceed, I turn to an example: the Iraqi invasion of Kuwait and the ensuing confrontation between the Western–Arab coalition and Iraq. The case makes two things clear: in the Western–Arab coalition both "doves" and "hawks" appeared to use political-economic and sociological considerations when deciding on military intervention, although the (not insignificant) difference remains that the soft-liners – those favoring peace enforcement – tended to issue threats to force the opponent back to the negotiating table, whereas the hard-liners seemed to do so to *preempt* negotiations or even to make them utterly ineffectual – as in a "chicken" game (see Box 6.1).

Box 6.1 The *ratio* of collective irrationality

We go back to the breath-taking eve preceding the expiry of the United Nations ultimatum after which using force against Iraq was allowed: the military preparations of "Desert Shield" were in full operation but the dramatic operation itself, "Desert Storm", had yet to commence. Richard Nixon, former president of the United States (1969–74), commenting afterwards in a press release on the military operation under his successor George Bush Sr., justified the American presence in the Gulf on two grounds. It had nothing to do, he says, with restoring democracy ("apart from Israel there are no democracies in the region, and none can be expected in the near future"), nor with the notorious cruelty of the Iraqi leader Saddam Hussein ("if our policy would be to punish cruelty we would not be allies with [Syria's] president Hafez al-Assad"). To Nixon the only reasons "that 400,000 American soldiers spent the Xmas season in the Saudi Arabian desert and may be at war at a fortnight's notice" were economic motives and the discouragement of armed aggression as a political instrument between states. Tellingly, the former president hinted at two sorts of externalities, a political-economic and a political-military effect.

(a) Pre-empting a *political-economic* domino. "If we had not intervened an international gangster, Saddam Hussein, would by now control 40 per cent of the world's oil reserves. Although the United States by imposing a stricter energy policy could do without oil from the Middle East altogether, Europe and Japan could not. What happens to the economies of other great industrial nations has immediate repercussions on the American economy. We cannot allow Hussein to blackmail our allies into accepting his aggressive objectives."

(b) Pre-empting a *political-military* domino. "Because Saddam Hussein has oil he has been able to purchase the weapons he needs for his aggression towards his neighbors, including in the end nuclear weapons. If he gets what he wants in Kuwait he will attack other countries... We may also assume that if Hussein reaps the harvest of his aggression, other potential aggressors in the world will be tempted to wage war on their neighbors. If, in agreement with the UN resolution, we succeed in removing Saddam Hussein from Kuwait and in liquidating his ability to wage future wars... we will increase our credibility when at a later point we want to deter aggression without sending in American forces. The world will take American warnings against aggression seriously."

According to Nixon, economic sanctions imposed earlier by the UN could never have been an alternative to the proposed military intervention. The most important reason for this was *not* doubt as to the demoralizing effect of economic exhaustion of Iraq ("the Iraqi army will be spared as long as possible"), but rather the problem the allies had in maintaining the unity required for the boycott to be successful. Besides, "domestic support for the military obligations we have taken upon ourselves will almost certainly melt away if the operation goes on too long" (all quotes and paraphrases of Richard Nixon's words from a Dutch newspaper *De Volkskrant*, January 12, 1991; my translation).

Analysis. In hindsight there appeared to be more at stake than concern about the cohesion of the allied forces and the potential decline in popular support for US involvement in the Gulf War. Apart from possible fissures among European allies, there were signs of moral and practical irresolution in the American Congress as well. Support for President George Bush Sr.'s course, shortly before the ultimatum was about to expire, amounted to 250 against 183 in the House of Representatives and 52 against 47 in the Senate. As Democratic Senator Paul Simon declared at the time: "This is the smallest margin in favour of the use of force in our country since the 1812 war" (*International Herald Tribune*, January 14, 1991). Another reviewer pointed at yet another contingency: the fissures within the US military-bureaucratic complex that was to carry out the operation. On the one hand the Pentagon and the State Department were fighting over who of the two was to be in charge. On the other hand the various military disciplines were arguing about who had the primacy in the operation. "The result [was] a complex, obscure and uncontrollable decision-making process. It is hard to predict its outcome, because it is the outcome of a power struggle between the bureaucracies that are most involved...All of the four American disciplines will have to take part in a possible military intervention...Not because this is what the most effective strategy dictates, but because it is the only way to secure the relative position of each discipline."

Technically speaking, as the latter commentator (H. Tromp, *De Volkskrant*, January 12, 1991; my translation) observes, merely a *surgical strike* conducted by the air force would be so "effective and decisive that ground force, navy and marines would hardly have to participate", but such a scenario "violates the interests of the other disciplines". Consequently, the most likely result is a "combined operation", which in turn will result in a head-on confrontation, exactly where the Iraqi army is considered to be at its strongest, namely *"protracted warfare* instead of a *surgical strike"* (ibid.; my translation). Unintended and paradoxical results of this sort are reminiscent of the risks the French president François Mitterrand pointed out, barely three weeks after the Iraqis' invasion of Kuwait: the risks of a self-propelling *logique de guerre*.

The foregoing suggests that an adequate analysis of bargaining – even as a prelude to unconditional confrontation – should take account of the credibility of threats and promises not just in terms of their feasibility, but also of their containability (what often means *revocability*). The transactional logic of protagonists is no sufficient guarantee that they remain masters of the interactional logic of war. The *intelligence* of threats and promises is based as much on the extent to which commitments can be built-up as on the extent to which they can be revoked: what counts in intra- and inter-organizational bargaining is the dosage of demonstrable firmness and flexibility, that is *governability*. Reduced to its analytical essence the story recollected above can be condensed into the two dimensions of "mobility" and "mobilization".

Mobility

Organizations are interested in creating and sustaining as much maneuverability as possible (backing-up and backing-off). Maneuverability is a function of the mutual dependence of the protagonists; it refers to the entry and exit options at the network level. Expressed in terms of resources (and illustrated by the "Gulf" experience above) the main indicators of dependence are:

- *Nodality*: both directly (the indispensability of oil) and indirectly (the geopolitical and economic repercussions worldwide of an oil shortage).

- *Substitutability*: both directly (the presence of alternative suppliers of oil) and indirectly (the availability of other energy bearers).
- *Timing*: directly (the time it takes to find the kind of substitutes listed above) and indirectly (the time it takes before the wider, geopolitical and international economic repercussions will be felt).

Nodality, substitutability and timing are the objective, external bases of credibility. They represent an organization's potential room for using others' dependence for its own objectives by demonstrating its relative *in*dependence. Independence means the ease or toil to switch from an existing partner and/or resource constellation to another. Entry and exit conditions at this level determine actors' *room to reciprocate*. Reciprocity, both in terms of threats and promises, is related to the phenomenon of interorganizational governance. The emergence of *network* or *chain* discipline can be explained by it – without having to assume either inter-organizational trust or the presence of an ultimate decision-making authority presiding over the "chained" network as a whole.

Mobilization

Whether organizations are able to exploit their external mobility ("switch") potential adequately and timely depends on their internal mobilization capacity. Mobilization depends on internal cohesion. Cohesion has to be defended against the short-term temptations of membership egoism and free-rider opportunism. Cohesion is a problem that all kinds of complex organizations face internally: firms, states, interest groups, departments within a government and so forth (see Chapter 4 for our earlier excussions on "intra-bureaucratic/oligarchic competition" and "internal network/chain solvency"). Cohesion is a function of the entry and exit conditions at the micro-level of individual organizations. *Ceteris paribus*, entry and exit conditions at this level determine an organization's capacity to act as a coherent (composite, collective) actor, that is its *license to operate*. Coherence is directly related to the representativeness of organizations/associations and of the mandate of agents acting on behalf of them. The eventuality of organizational or associational *self*-discipline can be explained by it – without presuming solidaristic or other moral sentiments in the bosom of an organization or assuming unitary, undisputed corporate or state authority. Where *reciprocity* refers to the external, "objective" foundation of an organization's credibility as a bargaining agent, *representativeness* refers to its internal, "subjective" foundations (and the perception of that attribute by relevant *others*).

The approach to the phenomenon of negotiating in terms of the entry and exit options at the network and individual organization level promises to have a number of practical and theoretical merits. First of all, it is an approach that seems to be applicable to a large variety of phenomena. It throws light not only on political-military maneuvers (as with the Gulf War), but on less violent ones as well, e.g. in the areas of trade policy (GATT), energy policy (OPEC), business strategies (mergers, acquisitions, alliances), industrial relations (employers, trade unions) and industrial-financial politics (the restructuring of industries and banks). Second, the explanatory potential of the approach justifies a certain loss of axiomatic strictness when compared with game-theoretical orthodoxy. This need not be too tragic if the claim holds that the *empirical* scope of the theory is broadened without overstretching its analytical complexity. The rich, but – in terms of its empirical refutability – *over*-richness of Raiffa's "organizing questions" is reduced to what we designated in the foregoing as the "essence" of bargaining: the interaction of organizational mobilization and mobility conditions. On the other hand, as I hope to demonstrate, the empirical scope of my model might have a reach comparable to that of Raiffa's list, because the comprehensiveness of the concepts of "mobilization" and "mobility" opens a window for bridging a rich, but inconveniently fragmented, research literature: from the sociology of organizations to the economics of state and market behavior and the politics of national and international relations. To these claims we will return later. Let's first look at the finesse of the model.

Refining the model

Mobility is the ability to reduce existing dependences or replace them with more favorable and negotiable ones. As argued above, the main indicators of dependence are the nodality/centrality and substitutability of the resources parties need from one another and the time for which this sort of dependence holds. However, for a more complete grasp of the workings of dependence, we need to introduce an additional set of characteristics, such as the *number* of players (defining the density or concentration of a network), the *manipulability* of the number of participants (defining the degree of "closure" or exclusivity of a network) and the *duration* of these characteristics (defining the stability of the resulting community of fate). Nodality/centrality, substitutability, concentration and closure, adjusted for the "staying power" of these characteristics, are the conditions that determine the *reciprocation* potential of the parties – that is, their (positive and/or negative) sanctioning power. However, as said before, the extent to which this external potential can be made "manifest" depends on parties' internal mobilization potential.

Mobilization is the ability for parties to counter the strains of internal opportunism and other centrifugal forces, and to stay on a given "collective" course for a longer period of time. There are two classic problems here: recruitment and maintenance. Recruitment problems have to do with what Olson (1975; 1986) calls "the logic of collective action": how to persuade potential group members to join when they suspect that free-riding outsiders will benefit as well. Or conversely, seen from the free riders' point of view: why join and concede a deal of individual freedom of movement when the "collective" objective will be achieved anyway? The extent to which this "rational" abstinence or aloofness can be overcome, for instance by side payments or evasion, determines an organization's or association's *recruitment* potential. The latter, in turn, determines the *scope of the mandate* of the representative(s) acting on behalf of the "collective" interest of the (would be) members. Once recruited, however, the problem with members is persuading them to stay within the confines of a collective venture. This is the second problem: the art of organizational or associational *maintenance*. How to keep members loyal to a common course against the current of particularistic sub-goals, the temptations of internal free riding and the contingencies of internal "network-solvency"? This second question reiterates the "exit, voice and loyalty" repertory (Hirschman, 1970) and the internal quests for power, competence and control as conceptualized by Hickson et al. (1971) and March (1988: 101–15). Emblematic of the latter's perspective is the reconceptualization of organizations, for instance a business firm, as a coalition of pluralist interests, the maintenance of which requires ongoing bargaining processes, not only to satisfy the individual, short-term claims of the coalition members but also to induce the creation of a *surplus* ("slack resources" or "rents") needed for the long-term "solvency"and survival of the currently "governing" organizational coalition as a whole (cf. Breton and Wintrobe, 1982: 11ff.). In that sense we can subscribe to the assertion that

> A business firm is a political coalition and…the executive in the firm is a political broker. The composition of the firm is not given; it is negotiated. The goals of the firm are not given; they are bargained…The executive-political problem is twofold. On the one hand, "brokers" must select a coalition that has relatively low costs of maintenance and relatively high returns from the environment.

On the other hand, they structure the payments made to the coalition members in such a way that shifts in demands conducive to increasing the difference between total demands and total resources are made. The theory to this point becomes well-defined when we can specify the dimensions of participant demands, some measure of their complementarity, the functions by which they change over time, and the short-run internal constraints on the bargaining process by which goals are formed. (March, 1988: 110–11)

The prerequisites of the art of coalitional maintenance are even more impressive when we switch from coalitions between individuals or officials within "unitary" firms to those acting on behalf of coalitions of *organizations*, as in the case of multi-divisional firms, collective interest associations and other complex organizations such as mature state bureaucracies. There we may say, even more pertinently: where organizational entry or recruitment conditions influence the *scope* of a coalition's mandate, exit conditions will determine the *stability* of that mandate. However, it takes more than the scope and the stability of a mandate to assess the effective credibility of a "rent-seeking" coalition. For that we need to know an organization's relative freedom vis-à-vis others in the wider network or chain of outside dependences and interests.

The two faces of credibility

The interplay between mobility and mobilization determines an organization's net credibility as a bargaining agent. We say "net" since there is no reason to expect that the two dimensions will always *vary in the same direction*. A lack of external maneuverability may undo the comparative advantage of enjoying a high internal mobilization potential, just as a lack of internal mobilization may leave the benefits of external maneuverability underexploited. Credibility means to be taken seriously by others. Seriousness, in a negotiating context, is based on the credibility of promises and threats. Credible threats and promises are called commitments. To commit oneself to a specific course of action, or reaction, is not a categorical imperative. In its elementary representation, a credible commitment is a functional or situational imperative: it is the expression of the demonstrable capacity to do what is announced – both in the case of promises and threats. Doing what is announced incurs costs. In that sense we may define bargaining power as the costs to oneself of imposing a loss on others, that is as the costs of not keeping a promise or having to effectuate a threat. By stressing the cost to *oneself* of disadvantaging others, the relational character of bargaining power is accentuated: in situations of dependence the actual imposition of will is seldom if ever costless.

Credibility is a somewhat ambiguous concept. The ambiguity has to do with the *contrary* implications of mobility and mobilization in the case of positive versus negative commitments: mobility tends to support the credibility of threats, a fortiori when backed by a high degree of internal mobilization of the threatening party; but it tends to diminish the credibility of *promises*, a fortiori when accompanied by a low internal mobilization profile on the side of the promising party (due to, for instance, grass roots obstruction, free riding incentives or factional rivalries). Only in the case of major external mobility restrictions (due to high entry and exit thresholds at the network or chain level) and a sufficient degree of internal mobilization (due to high entry and exit barriers at the organizational level) may we expect symmetrical values for the credibility of both promises and threats: in such a constellation the costs of not keeping promises *and* the costs of having to effectuate threats seem to be equally prohibitive. As a consequence we may expect that under these conditions both inter-organizational or "chain" discipline and intra-organizational or "self"-discipline will reach its culminating point. As we will see later the problem of credibility appears to be more complicated, and thus less manageable, as soon as we allow for *asymmetries* in mobility and mobilization – either between the actors or between the entry and exit conditions prevailing at the network level compared with the entry and exit conditions at the level of individual organizations.

What the foregoing should have made clear at least is that credibility must not be mistaken for trustworthiness or loyalty, and even less for legitimacy. Organizational credibility refers to the readiness or preparedness of others to regard a counterpart's threats and promises as believable commitments. Practically speaking, this implies that a credible negotiator has to give up, demonstrably, some of his exit opportunities – that is, to demonstrate his internal capability and external willingness (for whatever reasons) to enter into long-lasting commitments. This, of course, is not to deny that credibility may be *complemented* by conditions of trust or legitimacy. However, what matters in negotiations is the predictability of players' moves and countermoves. As far as the genesis of negotiating power is concerned, apart from the few additional points proposed above, it can be seen as the co-product of mobility and mobilization, and will be – ultimately – the *(a)symmetry* in these dimensions that decides on players' credibility. In such an amoral universe cultural predispositions – like trust and codes

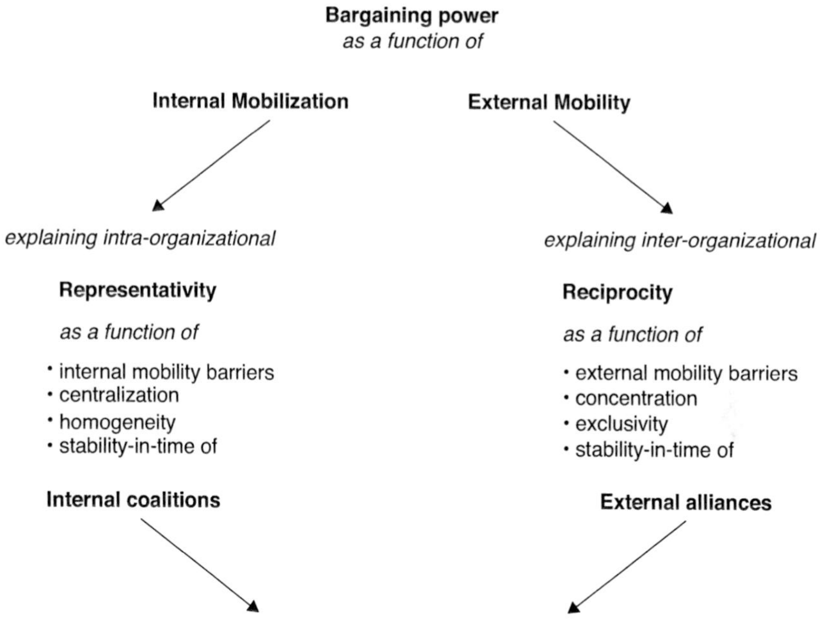

Bargaining power
as a function of

Internal Mobilization   **External Mobility**

explaining intra-organizational   *explaining inter-organizational*

Representativity   **Reciprocity**

as a function of   *as a function of*

• internal mobility barriers   • external mobility barriers
• centralization   • concentration
• homogeneity   • exclusivity
• stability-in-time of   • stability-in-time of

Internal coalitions   **External alliances**

Figure 6.1   Credibility, commitments and bargaining power

of fair play, and the *enhancement* of credibility that may result from trust and fair play – should be seen as the *consequence* rather than as the cause of mobility and mobilization.

Figure 6.1 summarizes the argument: (1) the credibility of commitments is a function of *bargaining power*, where (2) bargaining power is a function of (inter-actor differences in) *internal mobilization* and *external mobility*, even though it is adjusted for two sets of additional conditions, namely (3) the centralization, homogeneity and stability over time of intra-organizational coalitions which define actors' *representativeness*, and (4) the concentration, exclusivity and stability over time of inter-organizational alliances, which define actors' *reciprocity*. Reciprocation, then, is the co-product of conditions (3) and (4).

Arena, agenda and timing

The essence of bargaining is the effective management of the interplay between internal coalitions and external alliances. The stability of both determines the ultimate respectability of commitments. Sometimes the ambiguity of the agenda and the instability of the policy arena(s) and,

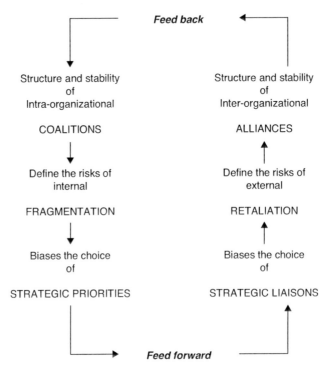

Figure 6.2   Structure, choice and strategy: the cyclical links

consequently, doubts about the time horizon of concluded commitments, are due to *intra*-actor instabilities, rather than to inter-actor conflicts of interest. Ambiguity and dilemmas originate from external as much as from internal sources, that is from intra-actor fragmentation or rivalries, generating unreliable responses to critical *inter*-actor dependences and vice versa. This was the reason behind my earlier argument that in the explanation of organizational responses to environmental contingencies, the risks of internal opportunism and fragmentation deserve as much attention as the risks of external opportunism and retaliation. The former may have a far-reaching impact on the selectivity and the degree of "incorporation" of external allies for restoring *or* challenging the internal balance of power – an insight conspicuously missing in mainstream game-theoretical as well as transaction-cost explanations of the formation of strategic ententes and other kinds of organizational responses to environmental contingencies (such as in insourcing and outsourcing decisions). Figure 6.2 summarizes the links between the internal and external determinants of strategic conduct.

Further refinements are meant to improve the predictive powers of the framework without spoiling the rigor and compactness we are aiming at. Reinterpreting the diplomacy of organization–environment relations, as the ambition to control the interplay between internal coalitions and external alliances, introduces an unexpected connotation of "other directedness" in the discussion: more often than not effective negotiating boils down to securing commitments by affecting the internal mobilization and external mobility of one's *counterpart(s)*. In this sense it may not be too difficult to understand why negotiators, the more so when acting on behalf of unstable coalitions on their *own* side of the bargaining table, are not just interested in the external mobility of their counterparts but also, if not primarily, in the internal mobilization potential, that is the scope and the stability of their opposites' mandate and "responsibility". This is the essence of the *intelligence* of bargaining. Box 6.2 illustrates some of the paradoxes of the interplay between internal mobilization and external mobility. There we see how, somewhat counter-intuitively, the quest for recruitment and coalitional maintenance, that is *representativeness*, may reduce rather than increase an actor's negotiating power by constraining his or her capacity to *reciprocate*.

Box 6.2   When negotiating power fails

An epitome of negotiating power is *leverage*. Porter (1984) applied the term in his analysis of the annual corn negotiations between the United States and the Soviet Union. He tried to establish the validity of the idea (commonly accepted in the mid-1970s) that "with tighter controls (on corn deliveries), the United States would have real leverage for both foreign policy purpose and for economic advantage" (ibid.: 114). Rephrasing Porter's analysis, summarily, in terms of arena, agenda and timing, appears to be elucidating.

The United States is a major corn supplier and the Soviet Union a major customer. For one of them to have effective leverage vis-à-vis the other, three conditions should be met: the supplier must largely control global supplies; demand must be relatively inelastic and no substitutes such as rice must be available; and the costs facing the supplier of persuading the customer to give in must not outweigh the damages facing the customer (hunger, bread riots, starving livestock, meat shortage) as a result of refusing the other side's conditions. According to Porter (1984: 115) 1975 was a year when all these conditions were met. The American harvest promised to be plentiful, expectations of crops elsewhere were neither exceptionally high nor exceptionally low, and the expected shortage in the Soviet Union started to materialize in the months prior to the negotiations. To determine what this meant for the United States' *leverage* we need to know more about the structure of the *external arena* and about *timing*. In our grammar: the scene is "concentrated" (essentially two dominant players) and "exclusive" (the probability of new entrants or joint operations by alternative suppliers is low); furthermore, the degree of "centrality" is high (due to an inelastic demand on the side of the

Soviets) whereas the "substitutability" (for instance, rice for corn) is virtually zero; and the "duration" of the community of fate is fixed (since it will take at least a year to prepare a new crop). In short, in terms of *mobility* we may safely conclude that the Soviet Union has little or no room for maneuver, since it cannot conceivably, at least not within the relevant span of time, trade existing dependences for less captive ones.

However, history takes an unexpected turn once – we epitomize Porter's story again in our parameters – the *internal arena* and *timing* are introduced. Now a revaluation takes place of what is actually on the *agenda*. The Americans want not just the highest possible price for their corn. They also want, in addition to a long-term corn agreement, a profitable oil contract and a guarantee from the Soviets to improve their storage capacity (so as to anticipate fluctuations in American corn supplies). Initially the Russians appeared to opt for a cooperative stance. Notably, at the start it was *their* suggestion to conclude a longer-term contract and to include escape clauses covering the eventuality of disappointing American harvests in such a contract.

However, they refused to supply oil at reduced prices or improve their storage capacity. After a while, their obstinacy paid off: after protracted deliberations only the corn contract was signed. What might have caused this agenda stripping and what might have limited the leverage of the Americans? Whatever the head start the Americans may have had in terms of external *mobility* – for the reasons listed above – appears to get lost in the scope and stability of their internal negotiating mandate, that is to say in terms of their representativeness and hence in the staying power of their *mobilization* potential at home.

Giving in to the Americans was perceived by the Russians as a loss of face. As Porter argues, in a situation like that the latter may be willing to accept a great deal of domestic hardship – such as reduced livestock, lower quality of bread and postponed oil revenues – and the authoritarian nature of the Soviet regime (as of the mid-1970s) allowed it to impose on its people "belt-tightening measures...with little public outcry" (ibid.: 116). Whereas the negotiating mandate of the Russians was not restricted by domestic pressures, their American opposites had to do all they could to maintain a united front in the face of domestic opposition to the intended linkage of oil-for-corn, while corn farmers threatened a mutiny if there were any further delay, which was "a politically costly consequence to the president during the coming election year...The Russians knew it, and the United States *knew the Russians knew it*" (ibid.; my italics).

In this case, the combination of the *internal arena* – characterized by restrictions and instabilities on the American side – and *timing* proved to be decisive. Time in particular was on the side of the Russians. It gave them the opportunity to look for alternative suppliers, to prepare their Eastern European satellite states for import reductions, and, above all, to watch the American home front fall apart. Porter concludes: "Leverage involves at least two parties and, as the 1975 grain negotiations reveal, an open, democratic society inevitably places greater constraints on using leverage than is the case in authoritarian regimes" (ibid.: 117).

What is said above about the *conditions* of the game of international trade also holds true for other types of organizations and agencies – government departments, labor and employers' associations, branch organizations, agro-lobbies, hospitals or multinational firms negotiating public–private technology programs – that is for all those who need others so as to get what they want (or steer clear of what they fear). In all these instances the dictum holds: representativeness and reciprocity – the license to operate and the capacity to reciprocate – determine *leverage*, while leverage, in turn, determines the *codes* of the game, that is to say, the *dosage* of obstinacy and compliance.

Discussion

The "art and science" of negotiating is dominated by treatises taking the rules of engagement and ententes between parties as the *explanantia* rather than as the variables *to be explained*. Instead of analyzing the machinery itself – that is, internal authority structures (the "license to operate") and the external power figurations (the "capacity to reciprocate") that explain the "manners" of the game – the latter are postulated or assumed to be given, as in standard game theory. For instance, the distinction drawn by Walton and McKersie (1965: 4–6) between "distributive" and "integrative bargaining" still appears to be highly influential. In distributive bargaining – analogously to zero or constant-sum games in game theory – one party's loss equals another party's gain. Integrative bargaining, on the other hand, is associated with common or complementary interests where the nature of the conflict allows for a solution whereby both parties benefit, or at least one party's loss need not be equal to his or her opposite's gain. Walton and McKersie, not surprisingly since their work dealt with labor relations and the behavior of trade unions vis-à-vis employers' organizations, added a third type: "*intra*-organizational bargaining". This refers to the process of internal consensus-building whereby negotiators are faced with two, potentially clashing, sets of aspirations: those of their opponents and those of the members of the organization they represent. Though the authors provide instructive illustrations of the three types of bargaining, and pay extensive attention to the interaction between them, they do not come up with an integrated, predictive model: their work is more of an elaborate *typology* of conflict situations larded with illustrative cases (cf. Raiffa's initial aspirations) than an *explanation* of the why and when of adversarial, cooperative or "mixed" behaviors.

In spite of its explanatory deficit, the look-alikes of the distinction of "distributive" and "integrative" bargaining have remained quite popular

since its original coining, be it under varying labels, occasionally supplemented by more intermediate types of bargaining like "coercive" versus
"utilitarian" versus "normative" (Etzioni, 1961), or "politics" versus "bargaining" versus "problem solving" (March and Simon, 1958), or "negative" versus "positive coordination" (Scharpf, 1972; Mayntz and Scharpf,
1975) or "confrontation" versus "bargaining" versus "problem solving"
(Scharpf, 1989, after Olsen et al., 1982). There are two vital questions that
remain unanswered in this topsy-turvy world ("topsy-turvy" because the
more or less confrontational nature of actors' conduct is always exposed
as something *given* – historically, accidentally or imported from elsewhere. As a consequence, only *ex post* assessments rather than *ex ante*
predictions can be offered for the confrontational or cooperative signature of negotiating regimes.) What, in other words, remains obscure is:

1. The *origin* of the codes of bargaining: why do some treat an issue as
   "distributive" whereas their counterparts perceive it as an "integrative" one?
2. The *permutation* of the codes of bargaining: when and how is it that a
   "distributive" conflict becomes an "integrative" one and vice versa?

Favorite responses to these elementary questions are mostly variations
on the gospel according to Hobbes – either in the utilitarian outfit of the
invisible hand ("selfishness naturally selects the common good"); or as
a specimen of evolutionary learning in repeated games (Axelrod, 1984:
"cooperation pays, defection defects"); or as the miracle of pragmatic
foresight ("selfishness makes everybody worse off"). Unfortunately, all
of these remain pseudo-solutions as long as no indication is provided as
to *when* the Hobbesian epiphany is expected to materialize, how long
the enlightenment may last and what eventually may cause it to disappear. Neo-Hobbesian "explanations" fit into the (typically Western)
canon of "rational choice": apparently, what is at stake "determines" the
rules of discipline.
  In the light of what has been advanced above about the structural determinants of bargaining power, there is much to be said in favor of a reversal
of the dominant paradigm. The reversal is given by a "strategic choice"
approach that respects the imperfections within and between organizations identified at the beginning of this chapter. Formulated succinctly:
not the mores nor the stakes of the game but the structural properties of
the *arena* ("conditions") determine the *time horizon* of the negotiations;
and the *timing* determines the *agenda* – that is the mores and the stakes of
the game ("codes and commitments"). In reality, of course, the sequence

of conditions, codes and commitments represents not a unidirectional, but a recursive sequence: conditions determine codes; codes determine commitments; commitments lead to certain intended and unintended consequences that, at the end of the day, feed back to the "origin": the conditions and codes of the game. As set out earlier, the *conditions* are the "imperfections" in the internal distribution of authority (that is, the degree of collective actors' mobilization, related to their recruiting and retention capabilities) *versus* the "imperfections" in the external distribution of power (that is, the degree of mobility in the network of collective actors, related to the exclusivity, concentration and symmetry of entry and exit options in the network). The internal distribution of authority *filters* the perception of external dependences and hence their translation into threats and opportunities; the latter will determine the selection of strategic responses. Conversely, the external relations of an organization determine the way it will seek to solve its internal recruitment and retention problems.

It must be clear by now why I think that the rules of the game – the variable blends of confrontation and cooperation – are determined by its conditions: the codes of conduct are the co-product of an organization's internal license to operate and external capacity to reciprocate. Conditions and codes in turn lead to commitments, that is to say, to the readiness, however unwillingly, to enter binding agreements. Commitments can either be negative (threats) or positive (promises) or, more often, a combination of the two: promises gain credibility when they are backed by threats in the same way as threats assume added diplomatic clout when they can be replaced or redressed by promises (*reciprocation* covers both meanings). The quality of the commitments, in the end, will decide on the *ratification* of the negotiated order, that is on the reproduction of the material conditions and the moral codes that shaped, at the onset, the constitution of the game. (In passing it should be noted that, in line with what was said at the end of Chapter 4, pp. 120 ff., on the paradox of "order" under conditions of "transitory" rationality, it is more accurate to speak of *pre*-commitments rather than binding agreements. In the next chapter I will make clearer why the distinction makes sense.)

Recapitulation: the science and art of negotiation

I began this chapter by arguing that organizations under less than purely competitive or purely hierarchical conditions will attempt to make their environment more predictable by negotiated agreements. Since negotiating only makes sense in situations of interdependence, that is situations in which parties are bound, however asymmetrically, to allow for some kind of reciprocal commitments, we can define a *credible* commitment as "some voluntary but irreversible sacrifice of freedom of choice". That is to say that "commitments rest on the paradox that the power to constrain an adversary may depend on the power to bind oneself" (Schelling, 1969: 282).

In fact, this chapter should be seen as an inquiry into the causes and consequences of the "power" of organizations to bind themselves. On the *causal* side, organizational "self-discipline" was said to be a function of the need, room and capacity to negotiate, that is to enter binding agreements. On the *consequential* side, looking at the contingent phenomenon of "network discipline", I have argued that the choice of strategic action and reaction – the variable blend of confrontational and cooperative strategies and stratagems – may bring about unexpected results. The credibility of commitments in the "imperfect" world we are talking about is based on actors' mobilization potential (which tells us about the scope and stability of the respective negotiating mandates) and on their mobility potential (which enables us to gauge the prevailing reciprocities, provided we know more about the relative closure, concentration and stability of the arena). Whether they are credible or not, even tactical threats and promises may have *strategic* consequences. In a cyclical model these are twofold:

1. Commitments frame the *constitution* of the game, that is they confirm or change the determinants of bargaining power.
2. Continuity or change of the constitution of the game reframes the *dosage* of rivalry and cooperation in subsequent rounds of negotiations.

I consider this cycle of conditions, codes, commitments and consequences as a blueprint for an explanatory theory of negotiation. It may help to explain specific rules of conduct (for instance "distributive" versus "integrative"). The same goes for permutations, cyclical movements and the evolution (structural transformation) in the types of games: the dosage of rivalry and cooperation will change when internal licenses and/or external dependences change. Paradoxical though it may sound, taking the imperfections of collective actors' mandates and the limits of their freedom of movement earnestly – as in a "strategic response" theory – does more justice to the *ratio* of negotiating agents – no matter how irrational the outcomes – than seems to be done in conventional "rational choice" theory. In the latter paradigm, actors' performances are allegedly only limited by imperfect, that is, "bounded" rationality and informedness.

As a result, the main object of actors' choices is taken away, placing the phenomenon that must *be explained* out of view, that is variations in the blends of rivalry and cooperation as implied by arena, agenda and time.

In this chapter I have argued that representativeness and reciprocity have a mutually conditioning effect. In practice this means that negotiating organizations aim for *congruence*, i.e. representativeness and reciprocity have to be "matched". Alternatively, if representativeness is below par, reciprocity may compensate (and vice versa). Second, negotiating organizations aim for *synchronization* – the congruence between representativeness and reciprocity has to be on time so that they can live up to their full potential. The temporal-spatial connectedness of representativeness and reciprocity creates a twofold dilemma, that (crediting its inspirers) might be epitomized as an "Olson–Schelling" theorem. This theorem consists of a double trade-off:

1. The *"logic of collective action" (alias "mobilization") trade-off*: how to see to it that enlarging a coalition's representativeness (by broadening an organization's recruiting potential and hence the scope of its negotiating mandate) will not impair the *solvency* of the coalition by inadvertently sapping its cohesion and thus forfeiting the stability of its mandate (the issue of internal fragmentation);
2. The *"sacrifice of freedom" (alias "mobility") trade-off*: how to see to it that the desire for *reciprocity* (by promoting the strength of a community of fate by the closure and concentration of a network of coalitions) does not interfere with the search for *flexibility* by promoting the contrary tendency of switching and recombining alliances *across* coalitions (the issue of external retaliation).

It is the latter, that is the risks of internal coalitional frictions and its impact on the selection and continuation of external alliances (see Figure 6.2), that is conspicuously absent in the mainstream of the empirical and theoretical literature on organizational responses to environmental threats and opportunities. Insofar as a proportionate response to the first trade-off (informing about the optimum of credibility for a coalition from within) may collide with an adequate response to the second dilemma (informing about the optimum of credibility for cross-coalitional alliances), negotiating remains a contradictory pursuit. The more complex are the trade-offs, the more practical is a theory that simplifies the pursuit in a tight manner.

7
Diplomacy: Houdini meets Ulysses

Introduction

Industrial and financial strategies change when states and firms discover that they are wound up in a world in which centrifugal tendencies are gaining ground on centripetal forces. Centrifugal forces are the result of the displacement of dichotomous power constellations (state versus market, labor versus capital, market versus hierarchy) by polycentric dependences. Polycentrism enlarges the margins for shifting alliances and coalitions. However, changing coalitions and alliances tends to increase the uncertainty they are supposed to check, that is, the strategic uncertainty produced by tactical rationality under conditions of mutual dependence. In this chapter I again take the EU as an internally sufficiently diverse arena for sketching the way games of industrial politics deal with the new contingencies. In the case of interdependence, firms, interest groups and state agencies face two questions: how to sustain *representativeness* (a question referring to the credibility of organizations as a function of their internal cohesion and governance) and how to handle *reciprocity* (referring to the credibility of organizations as a function of the external demarcation and connectedness or "density" of the domains in which they meet).

Permanent activism

The signing of the Single European Act (SEA), in early 1986, provided the European Commission (the EU executive) for the first time with a legal framework for codifying its ambitions in the area of industrial policy-making. This is not to say that nothing happened before then: from 1983 projects on information technology, telecommunications and biotechnology, known under such acronyms as Esprit, Brite, Race and Bap, were launched and a framework was outlined for the recovery of Europe's competitive potential (starting with the First Framework Programme in 1984–87). However, a formal authorization was missing until the SEA, title VI, article 130F, stipulated that:

> [The] Community's aim shall be to strengthen the scientific and technological base of European industry and to encourage it to become more competitive at an international level. In order to achieve this it shall encourage undertakings, including small and medium sized undertakings, research centers and universities in their research and technological development activities; it shall support their efforts to cooperation with one another, aiming, in particular, at enabling undertakings to exploit the Community's internal market to the full, in particular through the opening up of national public contracts, the definition of common standards and the removal of legal and fiscal barriers to that cooperation.

Those familiar with the semantics of *communiqués* on European political-economic integration will recognize the exercise in idiomatic agility. The call for closer interfirm cooperation is deftly steered past the pitfalls of European competition legislation and the rules that exclude state subsidizing (articles 85–94 of the Treaty of Rome, which comprise anti-cartel clauses and restrictions on government financing). Second, the European Commission phrases its "picking the winners" terminology in such a way that no reminiscences are evoked of the previous restructuring episodes in the 1970s and 1980s, when the predominant philosophy resulted in one of "backing the losers". Third, the Commission offers both interventionists and non-interventionists an alibi with which to embrace the SEA: with its freshly acquired powers the Commission demonstrates it understands the needs of the time but on the other hand pays tribute to the faith in the self-regulatory abilities of the market. Finally, the Commission lends both large, international corporations and medium-sized and small companies a helping hand as they venture into the international market.

After an institutional, legal and diplomatic steeplechase the European Commission managed to establish a firm industrial-political *acquis* for "Brussels". It would be wrong, however, to think of the Commission as a monolithic body. Backstage rivalries among the respective Directorates General, each of them claiming primacy in European structural policies, went on for a while. That no clear victor emerged from the bureaucratic contests must be attributed to the fact that the leading edge of European multinationals – initially benefiting from a constellation of privileged entries combined with free exit opportunities (arena), a selective menu of policy priorities (agenda) and an unprecedented pace of decision-making (timing) – gradually started to disintegrate.

This is only part of the story. A balance of power among rivals in one policy domain is influenced by (temporary) alliances that are the product of conflict and cooperation in other domains. Alliances are forged across domain boundaries when players need one another to further their vital interests (which essentially means that they are in a position to obstruct each other as well), *especially when these interests threaten to be frustrated by intra-domain rivalries*. Internal rivalries erode the license to operate of those who pretend to speak on behalf of that domain. The consequences this has for the relationships with other domains depends, among other things, on the structure and resolve reigning in the opposite domains. Later I will illustrate how internal representativeness and external reciprocity affect one another. For now, let it suffice for us to indicate in what way players attempt to increase their internal representativeness. Euro-patriotism has always played a summoning role in the restoration of unanimity, both within and across domains. This "adhesive" use of industrial politics can be illustrated with an example from the final decade of the past century.

Scapegoats à la carte

Around that decade waves of anti-Japanese sentiments flooded Europe. Hard feelings were fed by the fear that Europe's key industries would be wiped out by Japan's staggering post-war success, reducing the complete internal market to an industrial colony. Germany and France set the tone in what the *International Herald Tribune* fetchingly called "Nippophobia". Yet, warning against the Japanese threat is one thing, responding to it is quite another. While the European Commission tried to steer a fragile course between protectionism and free trade, at the *shop floor* of Europe's industrial establishment deals were constantly being made with the non-European "intruders". More often than not the deals got a *nihil obstat* from the Commission. The cooperation between Philips and Japan's Matsushita (aimed at standardizing consumer electronics) may serve as an example. Because the Philips–Matsushita case, though restricting competition "also leads to technical progress and will possibly benefit consumers", the Commission declared itself to be willing to "make an exception for this joint venture" (*NRC Handelsblad*, August 28, 1990). Exemptions like this, however, make some industries and member states rather nervous because the industrial samurai invaded the fortress of Europe not only indirectly, that is, via the boards of their European allies, but through direct foreign investment as well. The fact that the abolition of intra-EU barriers was intended to create a 340 million consumer market was not the sole reason for Japan's interest in the emerging "Common Market". At least as important was Japan's hope of bypassing by direct and indirect ways the threats of levying and other, less visible, restrictive practices (like import barriers based on artificial product and location-of-production requirements).

Some expressed their nervousness less circumspectly. France's former Prime Minister Edith Cresson compared in her inaugural speech the Japanese with "ants" raiding the Western world: "They sit up all night thinking of ways to screw the Americans and the Europeans...They are our common enemy". In an interview she compared the purport of a publication by Sony's president Akio Morita, *The Japan That Can Say No* (in which the latter called Japan "the rightful leader of a new world order"), with Hitler's intention toward the world: "It is exactly the same thing as the real *Mein Kampf*...That is to say, this book describes everything that is going to happen" (*International Herald Tribune*, June 17, 1991).

American alarmism paralleled European concerns about the Asian Trojan Horse. Choate (1991) catalogued the ways Japan "infiltrated" the United States commercially via "dealer networks", culturally via "educational institutions", politically via "lobbies" and bureaucratically via the "recruitment of American former government officials". Japan's "propaganda machine" was reported to make efforts to counter mounting overseas resentments by a variety of reassuring messages (ibid.: 87–103): "Japan creates jobs for the Americans", "Japan's critics are racists", "It's America's fault", "Globalization:...national borders are disappearing, along with such outdated concepts as national pride and national security", "Japan is unique...and...changing...because of political reforms instigated by corruption scandals" (for example the "recruit scandal" around share holdings offered by Japanese firms to government officials in exchange for preferential treatment). All of this has brought about a "Japanese government far less beholden to its corporations and more concerned about consumers".

At the other side of the globe France, Italy and other southern European countries joined the anti-Japanese chorus (with incidental cheers from the north-west by individual firms like Philips and the trade unions). Even notorious "free traders" like Germany were in favor of creating a web of defensive alliances – notably between European and

American firms (see Chapter 2, pp. 39ff.) – to withstand the Japanese invasion. Understandably Europe feared especially for its automotives and electronics because Japan, after having agreed on "voluntary" trade restrictions with the United States, might redirect its expansionist focus on the old Continent instead.

Yet, in spite of widely shared concerns, centrifugal forces kept the "Community" from formulating a unified response. To some extent the lack of unanimity might be attributed to traditional differences in the attachment of the respective member states to the principle of free trade. Besides, disputes about the degree of "Europeanness" of specific products stood in the way of a solid European response. Britain, for instance, insisted that Toyotas and Hondas manufactured in the United Kingdom were seen as genuinely *European* products. Others, not housing Japanese transplants, disagreed. Furthermore, a growing number of European suppliers, dealers, fiscal and legal advisors, financers and, of course, consumers were said to feel wronged by the exclusion of Japanese products. In short, Europe's internal solidarity continued to remain a moving target. The reason is that two types of dependence are at play here, which are opposites in principle but difficult to tell apart in practice: competitive and symbiotic interdependence.

Moving targets

Theoretically the distinction is clear. We are used to speaking of *competitive* interdependence when for instance Japanese competition, in order to be successful in its penetration efforts, takes into account its European (or, for that matter, American) rivals' ability to come up with a sovereign, coherent and united response to the "common" threat of foreign intrusion. Group cohesion and mobilization potential versus group divides and collective indecision is a familiar dilemma facing "rational egoists", who know that coordination serves their collective interests but who are unable to reach a measure of internal discipline and external synchronization as long as they can't be sure that everybody will pay their due share in the defense. As seen earlier, that surety leaves something to be desired – when capitalists have to be "organized" (Bowman, 1989) – though eventually it is not that different from states competing as much as capitalists for securing their "market share" of national and cross-border private investments (Strange, 1992). On the other hand, mutual dependence is called *"symbiotic"* whenever Japanese companies – as a logical complement to their penetration and crowding-out strategies – manage to create situations in which the fate of suppliers, services, local administrators, tax authorities, consumers and employees becomes entangled with their own fortune, a situation that, paradoxically enough, may result in a community of fate where each needs the other to calibrate his or her *own* independence. This is an effective method, whether intended or not, to mislead or disorient rivals through a combination of positive and negative incentives and signals. Once an "opponent" finds himself in this position it becomes hard to decide whether, practically speaking, he is dealing with a partner (denoting a "symbiotic" relationship) or a rival (meaning a "competitive" relationship). Box 7.1 illustrates the implied ambiguities.

Box 7.1   Catch-22

In 1986 Japanese chip manufacturers (holding a 45 percent world market share) for the first time surpassed their American counterparts (at the time holding a 43 percent share). Earlier the US Semiconductor Industry Association (SIA) had complained about Japan's dumping practices. The American government, mobilized by the SIA, reached an agreement with the Japanese Government: Japan would stop its dumping and, moreover, American semiconductor manufacturers would be granted greater access to the Japanese market. However, when, by the second half of 1987, the trade restrictions led to an unexpected shortage of chips in the US, another "collective actor", the Computer and Business Equipment Association, representing the interests of the industrial consumers of semiconductors such as Hewlett Packard, protested sharply. Typical of the confusion on the American home front was the fact that Hewlett Packard not only complained to Washington, but directly to the Japanese Ministry for Trade and Industry, in order to *revoke* the restrictions and the inevitable price increases. American consumers by that time had already noticed that the price of television sets and electric drills had gone up by 100 percent as a result of Japan's "voluntary" import restraints. Whether an intended divide and rule or not, the Japan–US chip case illustrates the ambiguous implications of "competitive-cum-symbiotic" interdependences.

Variations in stakeholders' perspectives and levels of analysis are not the only complications that make it difficult to draw a sharp distinction between the two types of dependence: what is called symbiotic dependence at the local or regional level can manifest itself as competitive at the national or supra-national level (and vice versa). Empirically more interesting, however, is the possibility of *converting* competitive into symbiotic dependences. The conversion can be observed both for private and public players insofar as each, according to his or her specific predisposition and self-perceived "core competence", will be interested in establishing a more or less sustainable domain boundary. The redefinition of domains and switches between levels of interest aggregation can help to solve or alleviate intra-domain strains, that is, the type of Olsonian contradictions that one expects to find inside associations that try to unify or "aggregate" the interests of (competing) equals. The stability of such "solutions" is of later concern. What matters here is that competitive and symbiotic relationships may either neutralize or reinforce one another. They *neutralize* each other when intra-domain and/or intra-class rivalries – for instance among companies or rivaling levels of government competing for the primacy in matters of industrial policy – trigger a search for symbiotic partners. Alliances are formed beyond the boundaries of a coalition's domain in order to alleviate or "bypass" the strains of competition *within* the domain. Competitive and symbiotic dependence, on the other hand, *reinforce* one another whenever rivals break into existing alliances of their counterparts or try to pre-empt prospective ones. A persistent lack of cohesion and mutual trust *within* coalitions reinforces the remedial search for alliances *across* coalitions. However, when *all* try to evade intra-class divides in this way they will, sooner or later, meet again in their original constitution. The only difference is that the object of their rivalry has shifted, by then, from competing for market *shares* to competing for allies and market *transformation*. To what extent the conversion of competition into sym- biotic dependence appears to be a real remedy, or a pseudo-solution, for intra-domain rivalries and dilemmas depends on the symmetry or asymmetry of the prevailing dependence relations. As we shall see later, differentiating constellations of symbiotic and competitive inter- dependence in terms of (varying degrees of) symmetry and asymme- try will increase our grasp of the logic of intra- versus cross-coalitional action. The latter duality, interpreting coalition-*crossing* alliances as a way of coping with *intra*-coalitional strains, will help to explain what has been designated above as a "moving target": the wavering solidarity among European firms as well as among state agencies, and the vary- ing robustness of government–industry reciprocities that follow from these intra-coalitional strains – both at a national, interstate and cross- regional level of inclusion.

Reconsidering industrial politics

What we mean by the "relationship" between the business community and government refers, first of all, to the inside knowledge public and private players have of the strengths and weaknesses of their counter- parts and the sort of industrial-political ambitions that are built upon them, and, second, how each of them *uses* that knowledge in practice.

Officially the term "industrial policy" pretends to span several levels of intervention. As outlined earlier, industrial politics aim at changing the proportions of production factors (labor, capital, knowledge) – from the level of individual firms to the horizontal differentiation and vertical integration of the economy as a whole. The official ambition is to increase the productivity and competitiveness of the economy and/or particular industries by means of "the infusion of goal-oriented, strategic thinking into public economic policy" based on the belief that "industrial policy is the logical outgrowth of the changing concept of comparative advantage" (Johnson, 1984: 8). With industrial policies, states strengthen the "strengths" of the economy and remedy its "weaknesses" by:

> accelerating the structural transformation of domestic industry in a desired direction, improving the international competitiveness of designated products, encouraging the development of new technologies, smoothing the phasing out of chronically depressed industries, assisting the rationalization of a weakened industry that is judged to have a chance for recovery, and protecting domestic employment in a particular industry. (Ozaki, 1984: 48)

The *instruments* used to achieve these aims range from protectionism, export subsidies and financial aid (research and development) to competition and fiscal policies, government purchases and infrastructural investments. In the comparative literature a distinction is made between Japan, Europe and the United States, suggesting a dichotomy of state-to-market profiles from "liberal market" to "coordinated market" regimes. In the latter, "firms coordinate through information sharing, repeated interactions, and long-term relationships, all sustained by institutional arrangements that make the stability of these commitments credible" (Gourevitch and Shinn, 2007: 52; see also Hall and Soskice, 2001). In Japan the interplay between public bureaucracy and the business community is reported to be the most centrally directed and instrumentally diverse, with the United States representing the opposite. The EU is said to find itself somewhere in between (Dyson and Wilks, 1985; Wilson, 1985; Audretsch, 1989): state intervention ranges from France, Spain and Portugal on the side of those in favor of an activist stance, to Germany and more outspokenly the United Kingdom on the side of the skeptics, if not outright opponents (see also Merlini, 1984). Smaller economies including the Netherlands, Austria and the Scandinavian countries – sometimes designated as "corporatist consensus" systems – occupy the middle ground. In the latter figure centralized "peak associations" of employers and workers and financial institutions that aggregate and intermediate conflicting cross-class interests into formal, polity-endorsed "grand bargains". The contrast has been classified as "interventionism" versus "non-interventionism". Table 7.1 shows the typological attributes of the two sorts of states.

It is not clear whether this type of labeling must be considered part of a somewhat outdated academic lore inspired by the historical self-image that nations pass around on official occasions, for public and patriotic consumption mainly. However, as soon as we take a look behind the symbolic screens of politics, from the mid-1960s to the early 1980s, the alleged radical differences amongst, say, "interventionist" France, "non-interventionist" Britain and the "pragmatically" or "informally interventionist" Netherlands tend to vanish. (For detailed evidence on the *parallelism* in sector-specific specimens of industrial restructuring in France, Britain and the Netherlands, compare Hogwood, 1979; Wassenberg, 1983; and Cohen, 1989.) In all of these cases interest groups and government alike deploy tidings of mischief and similar calls for saving a so-called "strategic minimum" needed for preserving the "industrial integrity of the nation". In all three countries for a considerable period of time public funds used to be funneled into "sunset" industries only; and in none of them did trade unions demand a substantial say in longer term restructuring and modernization programs (the role of the state in the so-called "sun*rise*" industries, indeed, differs from nation to nation state, be it more in terms of the backstage affinities between industrial elites and state officials than in the front-stage priorities selected by them). Finally, a last parallel is that in all three countries attempts to assign one or more firms as prima donnas to serve

Table 7.1   Interventionist versus non-interventionist states

Interventionist states	Non-interventionist states
Discriminatory policy	Even handed non-discrimination
Firm-level intervention	Industry-level intervention
Proactive government	Reactive government
Business cooperation	Business suspicion
Regular and stable contact	Irregular and ad hoc contact
Informal consultation	Formal consultation

Source: Wilks and Wright (1989: 278).

as a booster or pacemaker of the rationalization process proved to be a fiasco.

Again, regarding the selection of "sunrise" priorities in industrial and technology policy the analogies among the EU member states are more conspicuous than the differences. Public and private opinion makers and sponsors seem to agree, for instance, on the need for a further increase in scale and for industrial and financial concentration in Europe. The European Commission, individual member states and European multinational firms may not see eye to eye on the need for a more prominent role of "Brussels" in industrial policy-making; however, whenever it comes to "concentration", "economies-of-scale" and the selection of "key" technologies, they think and act virtually in the same key. Against the above-mentioned "divergences" in interventionist legacies and the "contrasts" in corporate governance regimes among, say, Britain, France and the Netherlands – this concordance may surprise. The correspondence is the more surprising since the "official" contrasts in interventionism and governance among the member states of the European Union are usually believed to be associated with stark differences in "economic efficiency" and "competitive agility" – predicting for the long run the Darwinian survival of the efficient and agile only (for a critical review, see Fligstein and Choo, 2005). Even the presumption of "institutional convergence" does not likely explain the concordance (for the ill-founded illusions around "convergence", see Gourevitch and Shinn, 2007). The main reason to expect *di*vergence instead of convergence is because industrial restructuring or renewal is always *redistributive* (in practice), and therefore discriminatory (in disguise). As noted earlier (Chapter 4, pp. 91–2), whenever choices have to be made and conflicting priorities selected one would expect individual nation-states to react differently, for a number of reasons:

- Industrial policy is about the expansion of new sectors and the fading out of old ones. The fading out is often accompanied by a loss of status, as was the case with the demise of many major post-war industries: shipbuilding, textile, steel and bulk chemicals.
- Government–industry relationships become unstable due to status incongruencies which result from the uneasy combination of a loss of reputation in terms of economic performance and a continued power to pressure in political and social respects.
- The greater the amount of public money involved, the stronger the need will be to compare the costs and benefits of promoting new industries versus upholding or revitalizing old ones.

- One would expect the debate about "suitable" means and ends of industrial policy to become politicized by mass unemployment, particularly when the latter is regionally concentrated.
- Industrial policy, whether it turns out to be coherent or erratic, is bound to have a restructuring impact on the wider economy and society: inter-sector relations and the rise and fall of skills, professions and the social stratification – all of them are affected.
- "Coordinated market" (alias "interventionist") states are said to respond differently to these challenges than "liberal market" (alias "non-interventionist") states, given their divergences in the prevailing constellations of interests of workers, employers, owners and intermediary polities.

If this is a commensurate summary of the potential sources of dissonance in the play of industrial politics, how can we explain the above-reported consonance with which the *players* in more or less concurrent terms preach the triple gospel of "scale", "concentration" and "technology push"?

Industrial strategies and stratagems

In order to understand the gospel, it may be fruitful to shift our vantage point. More can be learned from observing the concrete maneuvers of the players than from formal institutional arrangements and officially proclaimed policies. From the outset the official promise of European integration states: *the completion of the internal market will bring about series of positive scale and spiral effects* (Emerson, 1988; 1989; Cecchini, 1988; Pelkmans, 1988). From the onset, however, economists expressed their doubts. Their skepticism focused on three topics: the assumption of scale and domino effects, the geopolitical reach of the policies proposed, and the perception of vested industrial power structures.

- Regarding the *assumptions*, economists questioned the promise of (ever increasing) homogeneous markets and emphasized that, instead, an increase in product differentiation and heterogeneous markets was a more likely outcome of the campaign for an "undivided" market than an increase in scale and homogeneity of markets (Dornbusch, 1989; Peck, 1989; Usunier, 1991).
- Regarding the *reach*, the prophesies of Europe's becoming a true "community" also met with skepticism, both in terms of scale and scope. In *scale*: "Despite the almost hysterical conviction of many

business analysts that markets in the 1980s and beyond are inherently global, the fact is that most of them are not even national, much less pan-European. It follows, then, that however respectable the case for a European industry policy is, it is quite a limited one" (Geroski, 1989: 25). And in *scope*: "Any policy whose domain is less than that of the economic market will not span the activities of those to whom the policy is applied, and any attempt to restrict their activities and bring them within the boundaries of policy application will, of necessity, be doomed to failure" (ibid.).

- Regarding *power relations*, the last verdict preludes a non-trivial divergence in the expected discretionary margins for public versus private strategy makers; a divergence that will not fail to affect the nature of commitments emerging from the meeting of private and public powers.

Divergences manifest themselves along three dimensions, serving as a proxy for "power differentials":

1. Divergences in the *span-of-geometry*: multinational companies can to a large extent ignore the boundaries within which political agents and public agencies operate. When firms are in a position to move their investments and production while nation states (or confederations of them) cannot, the result is an asymmetry of power:

   > Maybe the strongest lure to spread its activities internationally is that the managers of a firm can free themselves from the bounds of a national state and its authority. By spreading multinationally the firm can become a "state outside the state"; it is the denial of the limits restricting it to the power of a national state and the creation of its own power, to be exercised freely, if not unreservedly. (De Jong, 1972)

Furthermore, the comparatively larger "internal" monitoring and sanctioning capacity of firms operating transnationally tends to reinforce the asymmetry:

   > Trade is managed by the transnationals: most trade is intrafirm and is therefore directly controlled by these corporations, and much of the rest is directly controlled by them via subcontracting, licensing and franchising arrangements. This control gives power to these organizations which can then be used to secure their own objectives at the expense of communities which have no say in such decisions. (Cowling, 1990: 171)

2. Divergences in the *span-of-gravitation*: multinational firms show a tendency to situate their "nerve centers" in one another's proximity, thereby creating major imbalances between on the one hand urban centers with a high concentration of cash (financial capital), competence (intellectual capital) and connections (relational capital: politico-economic access, media exposure, etc.) and on the other hand marginal regions that have to make it without the synergy of these assets. Feagin and Smith (1987) describe these centers of privilege as "world command cities" with "extraordinary concentrations of top corporate decision-makers representing financial, commercial, law and media corporations", which are not subordinated to any of "their" respective national polities.

3. Divergences in the *span-of-timing*: another asymmetry between private and public powers in terms of their maneuverability is the fact that national and community funds are usually tied down in path dependent ("sunk") and long-term projects such as infrastructure, education and other collective facilities, whereas multinational firms are usually in a far more movable position.

Given these asymmetries in choreography, some are tempted to believe, on practical grounds, that industrial policy is doomed to fail (De Jong, 1985: 192–7; 1987: 13–28). Their opposites argue, on normative grounds, that the imbalances resulting from "transnationalism, centripetalism and short-termism" (Cowling, 1990) make a strategic response all the more urgently needed as a means of counterbalancing the odds of transnational capitalism.

Let's refrain from choosing between the two sides until we know what the proponents and opponents of an activist stance think about a problem that the former leave largely implicit and the latter seem to consider of no avail: the *anatomy of the modern state* in mixed-market economies. In this respect two problems must be tackled. First, both in "interventionist" and "non-interventionist" regimes competitive and symbiotic dependences have become interwoven to such a degree that it becomes difficult to separate, empirically, *market-pushed* instances of "antagonistic cooperation" (e.g. coalitions among rival firms in an oligopolistic setting) from *state-pulled* instances of "cooperative antagonism" (e.g. rival state–market alliances competing for market shares in cross-regional investments). Second, neither pessimists/opponents nor optimists/proponents in the interventionist debate seem to consider a related problem: the difficulty, be it now categorically speaking, to indicate the border line between, respectively the primacy of public versus private agency in the orchestration of industrial politics. By not delving deeper into the creeping implication or *capture* of the two powers, skeptics and optimists alike reproduce the myth of a dichotomy of state versus society and tend to underrate the fait accompli attributes, rather than the premeditated or "designed" character, of industrial politics.

Both problems relate to the same phenomena: the coexistence of dissonance and consonance, and the interpenetration of state and market. Hence we can argue, prior to the question as to whether or not interventions in industrial structures and processes can be considered a "viable option", that we first of all have to know:

1. How *private* objectives, without an intelligent design ex ante, happen to become *public* priorities through the uses of private power (more often than vice versa).
2. How, despite the discriminatory nature of these priorities, a veil of *self-authorization* moves these priorities above or beyond the industrial-political agenda, thereby substituting tactical accomplishments for strategic choices: the latter may be called *der normative Kraft des Faktischen* – a *factuality regime* of escalating commitments that after some time tends to obscure its origins and eventually even to elude the control of its instigators.
3. How, in turn, this may create ex post communities-of-*fate* that makes it possible for irrationalities to co-exist in communities-of-*practice*, and even to reinforce one another – apparently without any innate pressure to get released from them.

The state of the interventionist state

Old caricatures never die. Despite empirical evidence supporting the claim that in modern capitalism industrial-political regimes differ in degree rather than kind; and that differences emerge gradually rather than abruptly; and that the degree in which they differ from one another tends to *fluctuate* in time – scholars persist in speaking of "interventionist" versus "non-interventionist" regimes and, correspondingly, of "strong" versus "weak" states. Intervention, whether provoked indirectly by those having a stake in getting the state involved, or imposed directly by the state autonomously, as a distinct "third party", always implies a certain degree of entwining public and private interests:

> He who intervenes *commits* himself, lets himself become part of a situation from which it is harder to withdraw than it is to get involved

in…Given the nature of the intervention the notion of "strong" or "weak" states disappears. *An interventionist state's variability moves along another axis, viz. that of a high versus a low level of entanglement.* (Van Doorn, 1984: 12; my italics)

The *implications* of the mutual entanglement, however, are not obvious. Van Doorn has it that a higher level of entanglement increases both the state's options *and* its commitments. Besides, no matter how intendedly rational the "start" of the entanglement of power and authority may have been, the moment the dynamics of scale and scope tend to get their own momentum, "a series of bilateral activities give the interventionist state a dialectic that is extremely hard to shake. Disentanglement may be considered desirable by everyone, but it has become a very laborious, almost unimaginable operation" (ibid.: 13). To explain the "dialectic" we may refer to a less metaphysical hypothesis, formulated earlier, about the mutual conditioning of horizontal ("intra-coalitional") dilemmas and vertical and diagonal ("cross-coalitional") alliances. Firms try to reduce their exposure to the actions of their (present or future) rivals by exploiting the interdependent relationships between government and the business community; government institutions on the other hand try to control their own internal rivalries by winning the support of external client groups (often rivals among themselves). The cumulative outcome can hardly be seen as a rationally designed and comprehensively controlled phenomenon. This obviously has to do with the sheer quantitative scale of the phenomenon. A more pertinent explanation, however, is to be found in its *quality*. Our earlier "catch-22" example of the American chip manufacturers springs to mind. The USA–Japan agreement on import restrictions, inspired by sector or "locally" rational considerations, after some time turned out to have non-intended, "comprehensively" *non*-rational consequences. Subsequent attempts to undo these unintended consequences led to an *increase* rather than devolution of firm-to-state *and* state-to-state involvement. This is how the wonderful "chemistry" of entanglement gets started. Is this a demonstration of power or rather a demonstration of its counterpart: the *Uberfremdung* (estrangement, expropriation, displacement) of power? To answer that question we will have to obtain a more precise understanding of two auxiliary mechanisms: first, in what way do these processes lead to a "gross" reduction in strategic options? Second, to what extent does this reduction imply an "equivalent" loss of maneuverability for all the parties involved? The first question relates to the *production* of power; the second to the extent to which the dividends of power are reinvested in its *reproduction*.

Strategic choice: Houdini versus Ulysses

De Jong (1972) states that multinational firms derive discretionary power from their superior maneuverability vis-à-vis their counterparts (such as state, labor, national suppliers, vendors, and so on). As quoted earlier, it is a power that is said to be "exercised freely", though not, we think, "unreservedly". In the context of the dependences discussed above, the residual *reserve* or self-restraint companies show when wielding their power may be regarded as "non-consumed" or "reinvested" relational capital: a prudent deployment of interdependence *capital* yields dependence *dividend*. In this vein it must be possible to refine the image projected by Van Doorn and others of the "vagueness" of power relations and of the "dialectical" impetus of entanglement processes in the interventionist state. Actors for whom exiting from present and entering future arenas is easiest – in terms of the parameters mentioned above: their span of geometry, gravitation and chronology – can afford to pursue a paradoxical dual strategy: as shown in Chapter 2 they profess to be *loyal* to their "European" mission, yet remain free to join competing alliances that *obstruct* that mission at the same time. The result is an intriguing mix of centripetal and centrifugal stratagems.

Discipline-seeking stratagems

Every now and again occasional coalitions are formed in Europe between parties that otherwise remain each other's rivals or contenders. Campaigns are triggered by the identification of external threats. "External threats" can be effectively called upon to defend "temporary" protectionism and to obtain dispensation for so-called pre-competitive cooperation, that is a "temporary" postponement or relaxation of anti-trust and competition law. Since the main objective is the *mobilization of parallel interests*, one may expect that the usual dilemmas of "capitalist collective action" will obtain. The art of defining a "sufficient" collective interest is to muster an exemplary constituency while at the same time keeping the coalition as manageable as possible. The "ideal blend" would be to have tight entry barriers (in order to ensure a representational "monopoly") combined with loose exit conditions. This blend facilitates a coalition's internal monitoring and at the same time reduces the chance of fights over the fair distribution of the benefits or the sacrifice of (part of) one's autonomy. (A sacrifice of autonomy is inevitable when rivals, for the time being, put aside their rivalries.) In order to maximize such a coalition's *representativeness*, that is, satisfying the internal prerequisites of credibility, the *size* of the coalition becomes decisive. The

212 Capitalist Discipline

optimal size of a coalition is determined by two *criteria:* minimizing the costs of monitoring each other's behavior and minimizing the costs of sanctioning, that is, rewarding kept promises and punishing disloyalty. In addition, as argued in Chapter 6, there are two supplementary *external* conditions that determine the ability for rivals to form a coalition: the degree of concentration of "their" market domain and the fierceness of the competition in that market domain. Irrespective of the outcome, the "cement" of such a coalition will be ruled by the device that:

> bei einer solchen Konstellation [haben] die privilegierten Gegner bei aller Gegnerschaft zugleich aus das gemeinsame Interesse, nicht privilegierten Gruppen von der Beteiligung an der Kontrolle der zentralen staatlichen Machtmonopole und an den Machtchancen, die diese Kontrolle bietet, auszuschließen.

> in a constellation of this kind privileged antagonists [have], in spite of their antagonisms, a common interest in keeping non-privileged groups from taking part in controlling the power monopoly of the central state, and from benefiting from the chances that this control offers. (Elias, 1969: 403; my translation)

Discipline-shunning stratagems

In the case of alliances *across* boundaries of parallel or collective interests we are dealing with a different kind of "common" interest. The (potential) partners are private or public organizations who are at least not in the *direct* sense one another's rivals. Only at a distance – functionally, geographically or in time – they may challenge each other's domain or competence. Cross-coalitional alliances serve to reduce the risk of retaliation by introducing the possibility of *ménages à trois.* The first type of bonding – the *mobilization* of a coalition – is about what goes on within a class or category of collective interests; the second one about what goes on between classes or categories of interests. The second type of bonding depends on the *mobility* of organizations, that is to say the possibility of swapping allies. Contrary to the type of bonding in coalitions, in the case of *alliances* the "ideal blend" is the one in which it is easy to join, but hard to leave. A bond of the latter kind has two things going for it. First, liberal entry options may increase the requisite diversity of the alliance internally – the richness of its complementing or symbiotic "content" – whereas, secondly, by erecting strong exit barriers the alliance reduces the risk of cannibalism (the selfish exploitation of one's partners' resources – cash, competence and connections). The risk of cannibalism is determined by the intensity and asymmetry of mutual dependences. The latter are defined by the relative criticality of the resources/partners that bind the parties (*centrality, nodality*) and by the ease with which resources/partners can be replaced (*substitutability*). Here too, as in the quest for intra-coalitional mobilization, actors have to face a trade-off.

As far as they anticipate that their counterparts will preserve their exit options there is not much room for the second prerequisite of credibility, that is, *reciprocity*. Reciprocity seems best guaranteed by as little cross-coalitional overlap as possible, and by maximum complementarity. Complementarity means that each partner is "dedicated" to specialized assets (financial, professional or otherwise) in which he or she will try to obtain a quasi-exclusive position. Specialization, however, makes for "inverted" dependence, and exclusivity attracts fellow riders. The risk of fellow riding echoes Schumpeter's adage that "the position of a single seller can in general be conquered – and retained for decades – only on the condition that he does not behave like a monopolist" (Schumpeter 1970 [1943]: 99). Exclusivity, in other words, is a relative *and* temporary phenomenon. Analogous to the case of "organizing" for a coalition's representativeness, when "organizing" for cross-coalitional reciprocity the optimal *size* of a web of alliances will be governed by the law of diminishing returns: the costs of monitoring and sanctioning limit the benefits of alliances between coalitions. Where the toll of coalition formation around parallel interests implies a loss of autonomy, with alliances among complementary interests it is the loss of autarky that is implied. Whilst *entry* barriers provide the cement for coalitions of *parallel* interests – let's call this the "Houdini" principle since options to free oneself are kept open – alliances of *complementary* interests, while indifferent or positive vis-à-vis new entrants, are held together by *exit* barriers. Let's call the latter (following Elster, 1984) the "Ulysses" principle. The latter stands for "some voluntary but irreversible sacrifice of freedom of choice. [Commitments] rest on the paradox that the power to constrain an adversary may depend on the power to bind oneself" (Schelling, 1969: 282).

Boundary choices

The assertion that the qualifications "adversary" versus "ally" are relative and reversible labels, all the way up from corporate stratagems to industrial politics, can be substantiated by elucidating why strategic choice in the games of coalition and alliance formation is a matter of *boundary* choice, that is a choice related to the optimal demarcation between actors (firms, interest associations, states) and their competitive alias symbiotic environments. In both coalition and alliance formation the trade-offs between keeping distance (at the extreme: "isolationism") versus proximity (at the extreme: "annexation") are governed by *the minimization of costs involved in monitoring and sanctioning*. The "double thrift" element encoded in this axiom offers an explanation for the nexus between the size and sustainability of coalitions and alliances. The more costly the creation and maintenance of discipline-seeking coalitions, the stronger the tendency to minimize their size and to seek compensation for the associated loss of autonomy in discipline *shunning*, that is *cross*-coalitional alliances. This is the mechanism, varying according to the prevailing conditions of symbiotic alias competitive interdependence, that determines the urge and differentiates the room for capital, state and labor to commit to one another.

The mechanism starts at the bottom of the pyramid, that is at the micro-level of interfirm relationships: it governs the quest for remote versus close control between a "core" producer and its specialist subcontractors ("co-production") and launching customers ("co-design"). It may be seen as an escape – forwards, backwards or sideways – from intra- to inter-organizational strains.

Box 7.2 The shuttle in action

An instructive example is offered by changes in the nature of tactical *coalitions* among established pharmaceutical companies on the one hand, and strategic *alliances* between them and small, innovative, biotechnology firms on the other. *Tactical coalitions* refer to shifts in the *horizontal* division of power: they aim at the postponement or obstruction of the introduction of generic medicines by means of side payments offered to the new entrants, the producers of generics, by the established majors that see the patent protection of their products running out. *Strategic alliances*, on the other hand, refer to shifts in the *vertical* division of power. From the infancy of bio-pharma in the mid-1970s until the 1980s, biotech firms, backed by venture capitalists, played the instigating role in R&D partnerships with established pharmaceutical firms. Alliances at this stage were typically joint ventures, that is newly formed equity-based enterprises. After a newcomers' breakthrough in the 1980s the large pharmaceutical firms reassumed their dominant role as nodal players in increasingly extending and denser networks of first and second-tier R&D suppliers and subcontractors (from biotech upstarts to universities). From then on *equity*-based alliances were replaced by *contract*-based partnerships. Compared to joint ventures backed by short-term oriented venture capital, contractual relations have (at least) two strategic advantages for the pharmaceutical majors, both of them satisfying the rationale of "economizing on commitments": they keep the majors informed about promising *and* (for their standing investments) potentially threatening new pharmaco-medical trajectories, while absolving them from the necessity to commit substantial sums in asset-specific and relational investments (all the way down, from FDA [Federal Drugs Administration] – submittance to upstream licensing and downstream commercialization). Under conditions of shortening product and technology cycles, the "advantage of contractual partnerships over equity relations is that the former...provides research partners with a high degree of flexibility and enables them to switch from research in one technological field to another" (Roijakkers and Hagedoorn, 2006: 434). However, given the *outsourcing of critical research* by the major firms themselves (known as the "Pfizer" doctrine) and the absence of the *possibility of crossovers* from one technology to another for the biotech minor firms, the question arises as to whether both parties-to-the-party will prefer the "flexibility" of contracts over equity to the same extent. All depends on the equivalence of entry and exit opportunities for the alliance partners. In that respect equity-based alliances are more "equitable" and thus (in Ulysses' sense) self-disciplining than contract-based alliances (reiterating the issue of "contractual hazards" and the divide between value creation and value *appropriation*).

What these mixed modes of horizontal moves and vertical movements learn is twofold: what the *games* have in common is their purpose, namely the consolidation of power; what the *players* distinguish, however, is that the major firms may have a heavier hand in claiming the rents from this Schumpeter/Schelling menu than the minor firms. As a consequence, at least three substantial obstacles may erode the distributive fairness and the stability of interfirm collaborative agreements (see Wassenberg, 1990, and Box 7.3).

Box 7.3 The fragility of cooperative arrangements

First: "A cooperative agreement is a compromise between a desire for collaboration and an intention of maintaining independence, so that the organizational structure reflecting such an ambiguity is usually complex. Various clauses of the legal structure express this concern and imply heavy transaction costs of negotiation, especially for transnational ventures. Partner selection and the possibility of defining well-balanced contributions is the first barrier. An especially important fear is that one partner will be strengthened by the cooperation in such a way that it will become a dangerous competitor. This situation is of course more probable for horizontal agreements than for vertical ones. In the latter case, complementarities allow the benefits to be distributed according to the respective activities and products. In the case of cooperation between competitors, a geographical partition is the most obvious system of trying to solve the problem but has a side effect on existing competition."

Second: "The management of existing cooperative agreements is also costly, especially in R&D where technological conditions are changing rapidly and unpredictably. As it is not possible to maintain complete control over the functioning of the cooperation, it is necessary to construct complex contracts containing explicit clauses concerning confidentiality and transmission of information; and patent, trademark and copyright licenses. In fact, in joint R&D, there are fundamental limits on the ability to protect intellectual property, especially when technology advances at a rapid pace and competitors can invent around existing patents."

Third: "It is not easy to divide the benefits of a cooperative agreement in R&D given that scientific knowledge has many aspects of a public good and that its results are not often easily incorporated. Disputes about joint appropriation, exclusivity and sharing (*ratione loci* or *ratione materiae*) of the results are often the source of disagreements."

Conclusion: "All of these elements suggest that even in the context of a very tolerant antitrust policy, without positive public actions, European cooperation in R&D will remain a limited and unstable phenomenon."

(Jacquemin and Spinoit, 1986: 492–4)

The "Houdini" mode is not a one-way principle, that is a formula for converting the strains among parallel interests into relief between complementary interests. The mechanism works both ways. Like interest-grouping coalitions, interest-*crossing* alliances have monitoring and sanctioning costs too. "Rational egoists" will try to back out of both, preferring the risks (and possible benefits) of a free-rider stance to the risks of defection in a universe where the number of triangular relationships (*ménages à trois*) tends to grow faster than the number of potential allies (due to increasing concentration).

Though the *shuttle* between discipline-seeking coalitions and discipline-shunning alliances may be hard to capture in deterministic terms, it is intuitively plausible that the two have a mutually conditioning impact. In our framework the conditioning works along two axes:

1. The freedom for entering and exiting an assembly of *parallel* interests (firms, state agencies, interest associations, each considered *sui generis*) affects the costs of monitoring and sanctioning *aggregates* of interests. The costs of monitoring and sanctioning determine the optimal size of the coalition. The size of a coalition, by affecting its mobilization potential and credits (internal "solvency"), determines its representativeness, that is its *license to operate*.

2. The freedom for entering and exiting an assembly of *complementary* interests determines the costs of monitoring and sanctioning

alliances. The latter determine the optimal size of an alliance. The size of an alliance, by defining the mobility potential and external credits (external "solvency") of the allies, determines its *capacity to reciprocate*.

We think that the axiom of "double thrift" (economizing on coalitions *cum* alliances) and its behavioral implication (the "shuttle" between discipline-seeking *cum* discipline-shunning arrangements) provide a clue for some of the incongruities of the European game of industrial-financial politics, such as the remarkable adherence to the categorical "imperatives" of scale, concentration and centralized control – despite economists' doubts and a lack of coherent industrial-strategic justi-fications, and the puzzling concurrence of Euro-chauvinism living harmoniously together with a monotonously increasing number of alliances with notoriously *non*-European allies. From a "monogamous" standpoint these things are at best a puzzle, or, in Olsonian parlance, the "irrational" outcomes of "the logic of collective action". Before pro-posing a more satisfactory interpretation, based on the "polygamous" dialectics of the politics of representativeness *cum* reciprocity, it may be helpful to insert a concrete example of coalition and alliance-formation processes, and to illustrate how the "shuttle" operates in practice (see Box 7.4 and also Chapter 2, pp. 39–45).

Box 7.4 Houdini meets Ulysses

The phenomenon of coalition formation in European industrial politics can be substantiated by looking at the remarkable "bias" in the mobilization of finan-cial resources for specific technology projects. Table 7.2 (adapted from Roscam Abbing and Schakenraad, 1990) illustrates the way a lump sum of 5,617 bil-lion ecus was distributed among various technology projects sponsored by the European Commission (from 1987 to 1991). As can be seen the bulk of the financial efforts went to the area of information technology. Figure 7.1 gives an impression of the (in Elias' idiom) "privileged antagonists" comprising the coalition of European major firms in information technology. A distinc-tion has been made between Esprit (an IT project sponsored by the European Community, with an outspoken *techno-push* orientation) and Eureka (a *non*-Community project sponsored by individual member states, based upon alter-nating sub-coalitions within the same overall coalition of European major firms, but this time operating closer to the *demand-pull* side of the market).

Typical examples of coalition-*transgressing* alliances, on the other hand, are found in worldwide networks in which "most favored" Euro-partners appear to collaborate with their "most feared" non-Euro (e.g. Japanese and American) colleagues. Figure 7.2 shows how multinational firms involved in the international technology race try to deal with the contrary "demands" of the *mobilization* of a European coalition of parallel interests on the one hand – demanding stringent entry barriers combined with permissive exit conditions (the "Houdini" principle) – while simultaneously pursuing their worldwide freedom of movement, that is, a high degree of *mobility* beyond their parallel interest coalitions on the other hand – requesting permissive entry combined with stringent exit conditions (the "Ulysses" principle) – even if the latter means that the quest for unfettered mobility implies that the major firms happen to meet again as "proto"-antagonists with the *same* overseas allies.

The shuttle between regional coalitions looking for discipline and global alliances looking for compensation for the disciplinary escapes in the regional "logic of collective action" – enlarging rather than mitigating the "net" disciplinary deficits – illustrates the perplexities involved in the sandwiching of competitive and symbiotic dependences. The shuttle may be interpreted as an instance of addressing *complexity* by forging *complicity*: that is as an example of the belief that perplexities produced under conditions of competitive dependence by the "logic of parallel action" can be offset by reciprocities under conditions of symbiotic dependence – assuming that symbiotic relationships are self-monitoring (less costly) and, in a universe of rational selfishness, easier to sanction (while inflicting self-losses upon the egoists). However, when do these efforts to escape from the "complexities" of *intra*-coalitional rational egoism (as exemplified by the free-rider trap) lead, inversely, to an increase of the *cross*-coalitional risks of "complicity" (as exemplified by the cannibalistic trap)?

Table 7.2 The politics of mobilization: the European Commission's R&D framework, 1987–91

Traject/projects	Expected budgetary commitments 1987–91 (millions of ecus)
1. Quality of life	
1.1 Health	67
1.2 Radiation protection	60
1.3 Environment	292
2. Towards an information society	
2.1 Information technologies (Esprit)	1,534
2.2 Telecommunications (Race)	462
2.3 Applications of IT (including transport)	105
3. Modernization of industry	
3.1 Manufacturing industry (Brite)	396
3.2 Advanced materials	205
3.3 Raw materials	65
3.4 Standards	188
	(Continued)

Table 7.2   (continued)

Traject/projects	Expected budgetary commitments 1987–91 (millions of ecus)
4. Biological resources	
4.1 Biotechnology	121
4.2 Agro-industrial	88
4.3 Competitiveness of agriculture	56
5. Energy	
5.1 Fission	472
5.2 Fusion	902
5.3 Non-nuclear	190
6. Science (S) & Technology (T) for development	67
7. Exploiting the seabed and marine resources	
7.1 Marine S & T	42
7.2 Fisheries	25
8. European S & T cooperation	
8.1 Stimulation	176
8.2 Large facilities	25
8.3 Forecasting, assessment, etc.	22
8.4 Dissemination of results	56
Total	**5,617**

Source: DTI, *A Guide to European Community Industrial Research and Development Programmes*, as referred to in Sharp (1990).

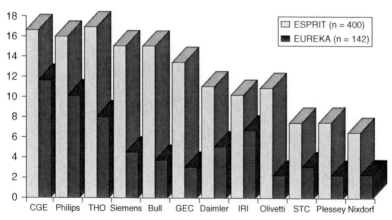

Figure 7.1 Discipline-*seeking* stratagems: Europe's "big-12" coalitions in two information-technology programs

Note: Figures on the vertical axis represent the percentage of relative "shares" of the participating firms in Esprit or Eureka.

Source: Adapted from Roscam Abbing and Schakenraad (1991: 211).

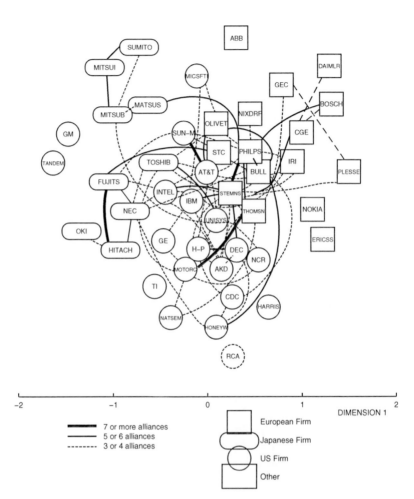

Figure 7.2 Discipline-*shunning* strategies: information-technology alliances worldwide, 1985–89

Source: Hagedoorn and Schakenraad (1990: 170).

Discipline

Two recent developments in the literature may offer help in answering this kind of puzzle. First, let's look at more fine-grained versions of the notion of "transaction costs". As elucidated earlier (see Chapter 3, pp. 59–68), the transactional rational-choice approach tries to predict under which conditions organizations decide to *internalize* part of their external contingencies (Reve, 1990; Scheiberg and Hollingsworth, 1990). Besides, use can be made of a late offshoot of the "neo-corporatist" school (see Chapter 5, pp. 142ff.) in which the relations between government and industry are no longer cast in the ideal-typical terms of tripartite institutions and the mores of corporatist polities. Instead, capital, state and labor are analyzed in terms of strategic *network* relationships (cf. Wright, 1988; Peterson, 1991; Martinelli, 1991; Marin and Mayntz, 1991).

The two approaches are complementary. The "neo"-transaction-cost approach can be used to repair a weak spot in "network" theory – i.e. the underexposure of the *processes* underlying the formation of intermediary structures between hierarchy and market. The "network" approach, on the other hand, may benefit from the credits given to "uncertainty", "frequency of transactions" and the role of "specialized assets" in transaction-cost (Tce) analysis of the rise and transformation of integrated institutional arrangements. The advantage of the latter approach is that relations between organizations, in terms of *type* of dependence (competitive versus symbiotic), *intensity* of dependence (strong versus weak) and *changes* in type and intensity of interdependence (concentration versus fragmentation), may be translated into a model that clarifies when and why organizations tend to incorporate (e.g. in the case of free-rider risks) or to put one another at arm's length (as in the case of cannibalism risks). In other words, it helps to explain how organizations will mark their boundaries vis-à-vis their (competitive versus symbiotic) environment. It remains to be seen, however, how far the combination of the two sheds any light on the processes of association versus dissociation between players with *parallel* (as opposed to complementary) interests, or, not less urgently, on the processes of entanglement versus disentanglement between actors "belonging" to distinct and divergent functional domains (like capital, state and labor). To find out if it does we have to come up with a broader politico-economic explanation of the quest for domain control. This inevitably means bringing the dimension of *power* back in.

Power, as we saw, is a concept that is granted only secondary status in the explanation of interorganizational behavior in Tce orthodoxy (compare Chapter 3), which takes us back to the network approach. In recent network theories a central position is given to the degree of *interpenetration* of state and market (Grant et al., 1989; Hancher and Moran, 1989; Cawson et al. 1990; Martinelli, 1991; Peterson, 1991). The problem with the latter, as argued above, is that it appears to be unable (or of no concern) to explain the *processes* of association and dissociation between state and market organizations. Conversely, the Tce approach, although helpful in explaining the preference organizations have for arm's length relationships versus merger or annexation, is one sided if not naïve in sticking to the motive of "economic rationality" in the overly narrow, neo-classical sense.

Discipline at work

We have to look for models that grant the tactical and offensive features of organizational behavior the space it realistically deserves. The starting point of the analysis is what in the general management literature is called the "strategic core" of an organization, that is, the notification of its (alternating) specific "identity", unique "competence" or "strategic mission". It is claimed that without such a core competence organizations lack an economic or socio-political *raison d'être*. Looking from its self-defined "core" organizations face four types of dependence: (i) *downstream* they see customers or clients; (ii) *upstream* they have to do with suppliers and subcontractors; on their *flanks* they find two kinds of competitors, (iii) those that do exactly the same, thus serving as a substitute or stand-in for themselves, and (iv) newcomers that may try to enter, or even take over, their task domain or market (potential invaders posing a more radical challenge). The argument can be reformulated in terms of stakeholders. Every organization – whether profit or non-profit – has to deal with players that are *affected* by its actions, either in the symbiotic (upstream and downstream) or competitive sense (substitutes or invaders). Each type of dependence asks for its own governance recipes. In the *competitive* arena the risks associated with the presence of rival producers may be countered by "horizontal" coalitions, that is by tacit or explicit collusion among rivals looking for possibilities to keep their antagonisms at bay. This is the response to one type of environmental uncertainty: the quest for control of competitive dependence by means of coalitions in search of mutual self-restraint or discipline. In the *symbiotic* arena, on the other hand, the uncertainty associated with the dependence on suppliers, customers or policy "takers" (in the case of a state agency or interest association) is countered by "vertical", that is upstream and downstream, alliances respectively. Together they constitute a repertoire aimed at controlling a second type of environmental uncertainty: the quest for control over the suppliers of critical resources and the attempt to bind customers or policy "clients" through the creation of alliances. By charting the question of environmental control in this manner (Figure 7.3 is a graphical representation) I hope to shed light on the following issues:

1. The essential strategic choice facing an organization that wants to maintain or improve its position in a specific environment is the choice of its boundary: the organization has to decide which dependences it prefers to "internalize" and which to place or keep at "arm's length".
2. The choice of its boundary may either be active/offensive or passive/defensive: to minimize their symbiotic and competitive dependences organizations will look for corresponding centrifugal alliances and centripetal coalitions.
3. Symbiotic dependence is not necessarily a synonym for "harmony" or "cooperation", nor is competitive dependence synonymous with "conflict" or "avoidance". Interfirm and interagency collaboration is competition with other means (and vice versa). Every pact – between rivals and symbionts alike – has its price. Moreover, both coalitions and alliances are subject to the law of diminishing returns on dependence-controlling arrangements. Consequently, organizations will try to economize on both recipes for coping with their environmental contingencies (I call this the "dual thrift" rule).
4. Control deficiencies of coalitions may be compensated by opportunities offered by alliances. In terms of Figure 7.3: when horizontal coalitions with "invaders" or "substitutes" are legally ruled out or are too costly to ward off the threat of competition – thereby leaving unchecked the risks of excess capacity, free rides and other specimens of opportunism – organizations may attempt to survive by forging vertical (producer–supplier–customer) or diagonal (market combined with non-market) alliances. Conversely, when alliances entail too many new uncertainties – e.g. when mobility promises the liberation from intra-coalitional free riders, but, instead, introduces the cross-coalitional risks of cannibalism – organizations may prefer horizontal coalitions to vertical or diagonal alliances as their second-best option (I call this the "shuttle" rule).

Strategic *choice* in the above-presented trade-off – comparing the "marginal utility" of coalitions *versus* alliances – is a function of four (sets of) attributes:

- The *concentration of the arena*, that is the number of organizations or collective actors constituting the competitive environment.

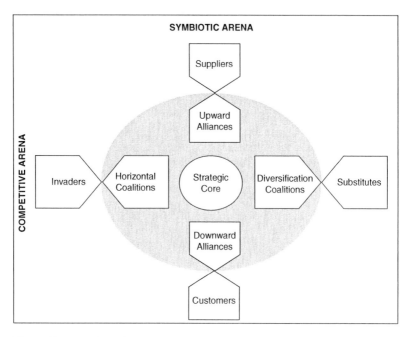

Figure 7.3 Boundary choices in a two-dimensional arena

- The *strategic core of the actors*, defining the "indispensability", that is the relative "centrality" and "non-substitutability", of each of them vis-à-vis their counterparts.
- The *centralization of the arena*, interpreted as a function of the uncertainty, frequency and degree of co-specialization that characterizes the transactions between the players (in terms of the Tce approach: the independent variables that predict the transition from "market" type to "stratified" relationships *between*, or "hierarchical" relations *within*, organizations).
- The *power equivalence of the actors*, understood as a function of the symmetrical or asymmetrical distribution of the internal mobilization ("license to operate") and external mobility potential ("capacity to reciprocate") of the players.

The *mobilization* potential of an organization – whether a firm, state agency or interest association – refers, first of all, to its "strategic core", that is, to its indispensability for the realization of the interests or values of others and to the degree that stand-ins or substitutes for performing this role are available or not. Second, it must be obvious that the degree of *centralization of the arena* and the internal cohesion of an organization, seen as a precondition for the latter's mobilization potential, are interrelated phenomena: the more uncertain, frequent and specialized the transactions between organizations, the more they will operate as a quasi-hierarchical rather than a market-like "organization of organizations" and the more undisputed the "mandate" or "solvency" of such a formation will be. The *mobility* potential of organizations, on the other hand, is related to the *concentration of the arena:* the sheer number of players will have a negative impact on the ease of coalition formation among rivals and on the stability of a representational monopoly for such a coalition – though it may positively influence the chance of finding alternative allies among symbionts. Interpreted this way, it is the *spillover* between cohesion/mobilization on the one hand, and the type and degree of dependence/mobility on the other, that in the final analysis will determine the bargaining power of organizations.

Considered individually, the attributes listed above are necessary conditions for the wielding of power; taken together, they are considered to be *sufficient* conditions. Bargaining power, then, explains the phenomenon we wish to clarify: the "strategic choice" of the boundary between an organization and its environment. What assistance does this precis offer us for comprehending the shuttle dialectics of coalition and alliance formation?

Regimes and games: from accommodation to guerrilla

To be respected, state agencies, interest associations and firms have to control in an *efficient* way the values and interests they pretend to represent. The representativeness of this type of collective actor – in fact coalitions of parallel interests – is said to be a function of their internal cohesion and mobilization potential. Next, in order to be *effective*, collective actors have to arrange for a critical minimum of reciprocity vis-à-vis their primary counterparts. Reciprocity, as said before, is a function of collective actors' mutual dependence and mobility potential. Representativeness and reciprocity are considered to be the two essential coordinates of the politics of networking between interdependent organizations. Combining the two parameters yields a fourfold classification that can be used for the comparative analysis of *regimes* of capitalist discipline and the orchestration of corporate games (see Box 7.5).

Box 7.5   A typology of disciplinary *regimes*

Type I: Regimes in which – due to entry and exit barriers, both at the micro-level of interest *parallelization* and the meso-level of interest *intermediation* – neither the representativeness nor the reciprocity of collective actors are seriously disputed.

Type II: Regimes in which – due to ample entry and exit opportunities at both levels – both the representativeness and the reciprocity of the collective actors tend to fall below some critical minimum.

Type III: Regimes in which – due to entry and exit barriers at the level of collective interest *parallelization* – coalitional representativeness is beyond dispute, but – due to entry and exit opportunities at the level of interest *intermediation* between collective interests – *cross*-coalitional reciprocity tends to become deficient.

Type IV: Regimes in which – due to the lack of entry and exit opportunities at the level of interest *intermediation* – there is no alternative but cooperation among collective actors, and hence a sufficient degree of reciprocity, but in which the representativeness or internal "credit" of the respective coalitions remains insufficient due to ample entry and exit options at the level of collective interest *parallelization*.

Let us summarize the preceding. Competitors joining a cartel, firms forming a trade association, trade unions subsumed in a larger federation, districts in a trade union, ministries within central government, divisions within a company, and so forth can be seen as coalitions of parallel interests. The scope and stability of a coalition's mandate is determined by its *inclusivity*. Inclusivity determines a coalition's license to operate vis-à-vis third parties. However, since the scope and the stability of a mandate tend to affect one another – that is: the more many-sided or variegated the scope, the less stable a coalition will be – the pursuit of inclusivity is subject to diminishing returns. The consequence is a loss of representativeness: players no longer grant their counterparts a representational monopoly or will even try to take advantage of their opposite's credibility deficit due to the latter's internal divides. Alliances, on the other hand, represent symbiotic relationships between collective actors that need one another to further their own (not necessarily parallel) interests and values. The *exclusivity* of an alliance (for instance between suppliers, producers and customers, or between trade unions and employers' organizations, or between state and industry) is determined by their centrality and non-substitutability vis-à-vis their counterparts, which in turn determines the expected differentials in their capacity to reciprocate. However, *mutatis mutandis*, the pursuit of exclusivity has its built-in limits too: as far as allies

		INTER-ACTORS RECIPROCITY = f (entry and exit barriers at domain level)	
		Strong	**Weak**
ACTOR'S REPRESENTATIVITY = f (entry and exit barriers at organization level)	**Strong**	Consolidation: *Captive cooperation*	Conversion: *Pre-emptive cooperation*
	Weak	Containment: *Exploited cooperation*	Co-optation: *Serial cooperation*

Figure 7.4 Discipline as a function of the interaction between representativeness and reciprocity

continue to search for alternative partners – more than they are willing to grant their allies – alliances remain unstable constructions too (see Figure 7.4).

Whereas an actor's representativeness is determined by the entry and exit conditions at the organizational level of interest *aggregation*, inter-actor reciprocity is governed by the entry and exit conditions at the interorganizational level of interest *intermediation*. In order to comprehend the *interaction* of the dynamics inside and between collective actors – the shuttle dialectic we introduced before – we must not only pay attention to the extent of entry and exit barriers in and between collective actors per se, but more consequentially to the *asymmetries* among them in terms of their entry and exit options at both levels of analysis. Not everybody pays the same toll for joining or leaving a coalition or alliance. Sometimes joining is foreclosed, or leaving is too costly. The significance of this elaboration (for an earlier version, cf. Wassenberg, 1992a: 437–41) becomes clear by indicating how the four industrial-political "compliance" *regimes* distinguished in Figure 7.4 correspond to four different sorts of diplomatic *games* (see Box 7.6, a more accurate labeling than the original, used in Wassenberg, 1992b: 437–41).

Box 7.6 A typology of diplomatic *games*

- *Consolidation* games: the kind of accommodationist stratagems and strategies we may expect when collective interest coalitions do not suffer from internal centrifugal strains while profiting at the same time from strong coalition-crossing interdependences (resulting in relatively low monitoring and sanctioning costs for both dimensions). Under such "idyllic" conditions the license to operate and capacity to reciprocate seem guaranteed. Typical examples are "mature" neo-corporatist regimes backed by large hierarchical firms, comprehensive interest associations and central state authorities (under conditions of unquestioned discipline internal to each of them) and centrally coordinated negotiations between stable private and public oligarchies, with high entry and exit barriers for all the parties involved. Illustrations are found in the period of the large-scale rationalization and restructuring of "sunset" industries like textiles, shipbuilding and the offshore industry in several European countries during the second half of the twentieth century. We call them consolidation games because "closed coalitions" meet "closed alliances".

- *Conversion* games: the type of stratagem and strategy that will occur when firms, interest associations and the state *internally* are still governed by the "iron rules of oligarchy", but externally suffer from decreasing symbiotic dependences (caused by technological change, deregulation and internationalization, offering entry options for new entrants and exit options for one or more of the incumbents). Power differentials associated with asymmetries in the freedom of movement make the risk of cannibalism more real, causing the costs of monitoring and sanctioning of alliances to go up, at least for the more dependent, that is more *immobile*, parties. Typical examples after the demise of the neo-corporatist framework are industries halfway through their reorientation from "sunset" to "sunrise", such as information technology, software, telecommunications and pharmaceuticals. We call them conversion games because they feature "closed coalitions" mixed up in "open alliances".

- *Containment* games: the kind of tactical search and coordination behavior we may expect when firms, interest associations and state agencies become increasingly uncertain about their self-acclaimed "core competence" and face an increase in competitive pressures combined with shifting symbiotic interdependences (resulting in a growing number of entry and exit options and consequently a more frequent switching of partners). Recent examples are what in an era of global, "demand-pulled" competition are called multi-tier "strategic alliances" in, for example, aircraft manufacturing, airlines and automotive industry. Characteristically for this type of cooperation are the increasing differences between, on the one hand, the "biotope" of multinational firms (associated with a declining interest in their domestic trade and employers' associations) versus state agencies (facing increased rivalry and hegemonic aspirations inside the European Union framework), and trade unions (associated with a decrease in loyalty to their federations and the loss of traditional respect for horizontal, intra-federation, domain boundaries) on the other. Containment is the name of the game when "open coalitions" meet "closed alliances".

- *Co-optation* games: the kind of cluster of sequentially complementary allies we expect in the case of potentially high symbiotic dependences – bringing with it lower cross-coalitional monitoring and sanctioning costs and, thus, a reduced risk of exploitation *within* networks – combined with "unpredictable" switches across competing clusters – meaning increasing monitoring and sanctioning costs *across* networks (the result of the cobweb-like nature of international "technology-pushed" competition). Typical examples are the rise of vertical and diagonal alliances – from the Japanese *Keiretsus* and the Korean *Chaebols* with their international transplants-cum-satellites, regional "industrial districts" such as Silicon Valley, Baden-Wurttemberg, northern Italy and the south-east of France (Best, 1989; Sabel, 1989; Cowling, 1990; Saxenian, 1994) and the pharmaceutical industry vis-à-vis biotechnology ventures (Roijakkers and Hagedoorn, 2006). Cast in terms of our premises, co-optation games feature sequences of "open coalitions" meeting "open alliances" in parallel circuits.

Encounters of the "co-optation" and "containment" type represent *shuttle capitalism* in its purest form because of their tactical-offensive *use of coalitions as leverage for controlling alliances, and alliances as a leverage for disciplining coalitions.* The transformation from "sedentary" consolidation games, with the central state as a hostage of trade unions and "sunset" sector associations (the old discipline), to the largely "nomadic" coalition and alliance movements of the present day (the new discipline) constitutes a regime change that becomes comprehensible when its evolution is envisaged in terms of structural shifts in negotiating power; shifts that appear to be the product of a *symmetrical* loss of the sense of direction and mobilization potential of firms, interest associations and the central state, combined with *asymmetrical* changes in mutual dependences and mobility potential: a decreasing *license to operate* confronts increasing asymmetries in the *capacity to reciprocate.*

Recapitulation

In the foregoing I have tried, first, to build a methodological bridge between three levels of analysis: a strategic "choice" theory (micro) explaining how actors draw their own boundaries, followed by an outline of how a web of commitments between actors is expected to evolve from these choices (meso), resulting in an explanation of regimes that are seen as the logical though unintended outcome of these intendedly rational *choices* and *commitments* (macro). Second, I have offered a theoretical elucidation of the contrasts between disciplinary regimes by indicating the elementary rationale behind organizations' boundary choices (the *"dual thrift"* axiom); as well as asking how this rationale under shifting conditions – that is mobilization and mobility differentials as the primary drivers of change – entails change in the mixed modes of interorganizational games (the *"shuttle"* hypothesis).

In the final two chapters I propose to elaborate on a phenomenon hinted at only too rudimentarily in my discussion of the logics of game and regime formation, namely the *recycling* of discipline and diplomacy. Understanding the cyclical characteristics of choice, commitments and the resulting negotiated order helps us to understand the apex of the puzzle: how rival firms and rival states, despite the fact that all of them are bound to follow the *"diktat"* of internal and external conditions, appear to differ dramatically in the *"hand"* they have in the exploitation and transformation of these very conditions. What obscures the *visibility* of that *"hand"* is the fact that both the locus and focus of the circuits that preside over the orchestration of dependences and the (re)distribution of the spoils shift from stage to stage in a cumulative fashion. Such a *non*-determinist stance is enabled by the substitution of a cyclical perspective for the comparatively static view underlying the *"genealogy"* of regimes and games presented in this chapter. The obvious drawback with genealogies is that they offer punctuations or "stills" in the evolution of disciplinary arrangements, suggesting a quasi-linear and unidirectional sequence of episodes, though they unfortunately fail to specify the driving forces behind the *beat* of regime and game change, as in a motion picture.

8
Commitments: The Essence of Discipline

Introduction

After having landed at the coordinates of the *modalities* of games and regimes, what can we say about the checks and balances that explain the *transitions* among them, that is mutations in regimes as the outcome of changes in games? Though the preceding suggests where to look for the answers, we cannot afford to be conclusive. What defies straight answers is the concurrence of specific movements, the cumulative impact of which has begun to transpire only recently.

New technologies change the composition and the boundaries of organizations, and the internationalization of competition changes the boundaries and the composition of the circuits in which rival states and rival firms meet. Though remains of the older principles of discipline and diplomacy persist, they are increasingly sandwiched in the outbidding of rival states competing for the location of rival firms, and competing firms looking for the most receptive nations and regions. Instructively enough, the outbidding inspires firms and states to diametrically opposed responses to the ensuing dilemmas: states tend towards nationalist or crypto-protectionist reactions whereas multinational firms intensify their cross-national allegiances – precisely because of the benefits they reap from the *intensification* of the competition of nations.

Box 8.1 Moving targets

For instance, when, after a series of corporate accounting scandals, the so-called *Sarbanes–Oxley* regulation on corporate disclosure practices became stricter in the USA, financial firms started to migrate to less stricter locations

---

like London. After a while they appeared ready to leave the City again when pressures for re-regulation mounted after the 2007 commencement of the American crisis in finances – the origin of which can now be traced back to an April 28, 2004 meeting when a successful lobby of five leading US investment banks persuaded the US Securities and Exchange Commission to exempt them from the standing regulation that limited the amount of debt they were allowed to take (see the "regulatory pendulum" described in Chapter 1). As we know now the granting of the bankers' wishes ended in the meltdown of once formidable Wall Street financial institutions, crippling in their slipstream major parts of the real, non-financial economy worldwide. As the survivors of the scramble keep moving, the reshuffle of codes and commitments will follow – be it always a couple of steps behind. The proof of regulation is in the eating and in the role of the *cooks* that are entrusted to check for compliance with the rules of regulation, such as credit rating agencies and their sponsors.

States, regions, firms and affiliate interests try to curb the odds of the relay race by advocating the principle of "mutual recognition". However, even inside the family of the European Union the leveling intentions behind the mutual recognition principle are unable to create the hoped-for backlash against European *and* foreign-owned firms shopping around for the most permissive and pliable environment among the Union's member states:

> The history of the [European] community suggests that its reactions to problems such as these is likely to be restrained, as different member states weigh in on different sides of the issue. In short, the possibility seems real that the "mutual recognition" principle will precipitate a new wave of competition among governments for enterprises that serve the European market. (Vernon, 1991: 3)

Though the targets of the regulatory steeplechase may have shifted over the last two decades, more than once due to the elusive *semantics* of regulation and corporate governance, the elemental principles of the shopping game still hold sway. As frequently observed, unless banking regulation is identical across frontiers, there remains plenty of scope for "regulatory arbitrage". Besides, there is ample room for yo-yoing with

> capital-adequacy requirements by manipulating how capital and assets are *defined*. Indeed, investment banks like Goldman Sachs and Barclays Capital, are already inventing new types of securities to reduce the capital costs of holding risky assets. (Robert Skidelsky, Project Syndicate, *The Guardian*, July 27, 2009)

The two-pronged search for *front*stage strictness to end "regulatory shopping", while *back*stage there is a preserving of the loopholes for "regulatory capture", can also be found in the less "virtual" world of the real economy. For instance, on the eve of an international climate conference held in Bali in December 2007, the *Financial Times* published a two-page advertisement in which some 150 publicly listed international firms called upon government leaders to arrive at *more compelling* regulations on environmental protection, full disclosure on carbon emissions and so on. What the advertisers called for was not more or stricter rules, but rules that obtain *equally* for every nation, under the adage: "if you don't live uphill on the mountain of competition, ask for a level playing field".

The search for this sort of *contingent* "strictness" ranges from the intra- to the international level. On the one hand, to give an example, we come across a Dutch association of insurance companies issuing a "position paper" in which the Dutch Central Bank is exhorted to impose urgently on insurance companies a ban on risky investments and to press for *European* surveillance over the observance of the ban by *national* surveillance agencies (*Financieele Dagblad*, May 2, 2009) – in brief: a coalition of players following the *Ulysses*-principle. On the other hand there are the European member states, following their instinct of economic patriotism in the wake of the worldwide financial and economic crisis, which bitterly criticized the European Commission for stalking and stalling their "innovative" efforts to give preferential treatment to *their own* financial and industrial institutions – that is, a private–public alliance following the *Houdini*-principle.

In that sense one wonders what will appear from a renewed call by the European Commission (February 6, 2010) for an independent European credit-rating agency to correct for the power of international credit-rating bureaus, while leaving the certification of each of the existing agencies to the national member states.

Firms need states, and states need firms, to realize their ambitions – respectively, public welfare and private prosperity – but they differ in their capacity to pose as sovereign actors. Problems of coordination that once were controlled for in a national framework re-emerge in a cross-national setting – be it now *without* the institutional, organizational and financial backing that "disciplined" the older arrangements.

This study set out to presage what sort of capitalist discipline has taken the place of the older arrangements. My analysis subscribes to a secular tradition that envisages politico-economic order as a profane co-product of intra-group coalitions and inter-group alliances. In that sense my study diverges from "summit-level" studies that approach business–state interactions from the degree of centralization and differentiation of state and society. *Summit*-level studies are not perceptibly fit to inform us about the *sources* of mutation in the substance and forms of concerted action. The main reason is that they fail to identify the sort of resources that enable actors to influence the rules and results of the games of economic change and continuity. Summit-level studies, designed for comparing and assessing cross-national differences in policy styles and competitive performance, tend to take institutional settings as fait accomplis; that is they focus on ideal-typical contrasts and similarities rather than on the necessarily fuzzy mix of *proto*-typical and (re)emergent properties that characterize living societal arrangements. Endogenous forces explaining the rise and fall or, sometimes, the miraculous revival of institutional arrangements remain unidentified. "Floor-level" analysis, instead, takes the strategies and tactics of the actors (whether tangible or *perfect fakes*) as its point of departure, tries to identify the causes of action and response, and traces the consequences for the continuity or discontinuity of the effective reach of "summit-level" arrangements.

Part of the problem is that both mainstreams in the current academy of political economics – institutionalist and rational-choice theory – tend to work from an over-organized conception of "the" state as opposed to a disorganized conception of firms and interest groups. Conceivably the notion of the over-organized state is a remnant of the, by and large, non-contested Weberian legacy, which holds that democratic systems are legitimate – though periodically relegitimized – monopolistic arrangements for moralizing and rationalizing coercion on behalf of the "authoritative allocation of values". Of course, due to a steady erosion of national sovereignty, the secular decline of the bases of authority domestically, and the uncertainty about the (multipolar?) future of international hegemony, the status of "the" state is not what it used to be. Nevertheless, in most impersonations of its transactions with interest groups and individual firms, the state remains, basically, an internally undifferentiated black box negotiating with a differentiated and increasingly ungovernable, while selfishly-oriented, collection of external stakeholders. The latter, on the other hand, especially since the academic proliferation of the Olsonian rational-choice perspective, are typically seen as disorganized aggregates of rational egoists (alias free-riders) due to a lack of rational foresight pinched between instinctive tit-for-tat and herd behavior ("animal spirits").

Practice shows, however, that public actors have learned from their private counterparts about the principles of free-riding and competitive imitation, be it usually presented in the stately idiom, or desiderata, of subsidiarity and matching. Private interest formations, on the other hand, demonstrate time and again – contrary to theoretical forecasting – a miraculous flair for finding a more or less astute modus vivendi for coping with their own ("Olsonian") intra- and inter-group dilemmas of collective action. An opposite image seems therefore more plausible: states, as yet somewhat inexperienced with methods for compensating for their loss of standing and sovereignty, tend to become more *un*disciplined, while interest groups and individual firms, discovering the perverse effects of rational egoism and the costs of selfishness, seem to become more and more disciplined – the more so when there is room to displace *the costs of group discipline and unselfishness to others.*

Our search for a streetwise middle course between the state-versus-market caricatures is frustrated by the continuing absence of a shared *micro-foundation* for understanding the dynamics of interfirm and firm-to-state interactions. (For recent audits of the *academic* failure to link (inter)corporate strategies and macro-economic analysis see Bailey and Cowling, 2006; and Colander et al., 2009). As a consequence we neither know how well state actors are informed about the dilemmas of capitalist coordination nor to what extent firms and interest groups are familiarized with the (intra- and inter-)state dilemmas of coordination. As a consequence we do not know how public and private actors make the best of what they profess to know about themselves and their counterparts.

The literature offers no ready-made solutions that might serve as an antidote to the nominalist and comparative-static bias of institutionalist analysis. Of course, strategic management theory and organization analysis examine micro-interests and actors' capacities to "choose", but they conventionally forget about the rest of the task at hand, that is, to explain how micro-choice leads to meso-commitments, how meso-commitments crystallize into meta-structures, and how these meta-structures subsequently constrain or enable future choice. (It is not without irony that the disciplines most devoted to "methodological *individualism*" – from neo-institutional economics to rational-choice and game theory – find themselves unable to relate the birth of institutional arrangements and the evolution of social order to the acts of individual agents.) The aim of my study has been to find an umbrella perspective that synthesizes the best of both institutional and strategy

analysis while removing its typical blinkers. The "umbrella" we are looking for may be called a politico-economic "game theory", though one
amended in such a way that it fulfills its main mission, namely restoring the forgotten links between (1) the logic of actors, (2) the dynamics
of games and (3) the making and unmaking of social order. The name
I have suggested for the micro-foundation of this realist game theory is
corporate or *organizational* diplomacy. Organizational diplomacy tries
to trace a middle course between the reification, respectively narcissism
of institutional organization and strategy analysis.

Organizational diplomacy is about the art of exploring and probing the limits of *sovereignty*. Sovereignty is always a relative prospect:
self-interest in situations of mutual dependence teaches restraint in the
pursuit of self-sufficiency. Questions of sovereignty re-emerge whenever dependence relations change. The central argument of this study
has been that changes in the patterns of business-to-state interactions
tend to follow changes in the patterns of interfirm dependences, whilst
changes in interfirm dependence are the result of increasing asymmetries in the mobility of financial, intellectual and relational capital.
Since relational assets ("network" capital or "connectedness") tend to
be more sticky than organizational brains ("intellectual" capital) and
intellectual assets are less migration prone than financial resources
("financial" capital, in old and new guises), it is – as a rule – the latter
that set the pattern and pace of change in firm-to-firm and business-to-
state reciprocities. In that (paradoxical) sense one might say: structure
follows mobility.

The soaring volatility of international finance precipitates the disentanglement of large financial holdings and conglomerates of unrelated
businesses that emerged in the 1960s and 1970s. In popular parlance
the disrepute of the defensive practice of interfirm cross participation
and the rebound from unrelated diversification to more focused forms
of enterprise have been fashioned as the return to undiluted "shareholders capitalism", euphemistically rationalized as a forced return to the
rediscovery of the "core competence" of the firm. With this assessment
an intriguing question poses itself: Are the waves of corporate break-
ups, buy-outs and external realignments a *consequence* of the renewed
search for "core competences" and "cost-efficiency"? Or should one say,
instead, that the surge of new combinations of old resources and partners is the *cause* for reconsidering the competence of the firm? In the
latter case, the declaratory search for "core competences" may be seen
as an *ex post* rationalization of *the gradual insolvency of internal coalitions*
due to *the radical reshuffle of external alliances* that goes inevitably with

corporate break-ups and take-overs – that is to say: as something else than the alleged *ex ante* rationality of the search for economies of synergy and the putative blessings of lean-and-mean production.

This chapter assesses the balance. The causes and consequences of change are briefly reviewed and illustrated by examples that demonstrate how government–business interactions follow interstate rivalries, and how the latter follow the changing terms of engagement in interfirm rivalry. For grasping the causal chain, contrasting assumptions on the emergence, diffusion and crystallization of strategies – from rational to embedded and diplomatic models of economic man – are compared and assessed. The chapter ends with a couple of suggestions for where to look for completion of the most incomplete track of our expedition, that is, the question as to what strategic "choice" exactly means in an otherwise "dependences-driven" world (inspiring investment bankers and the like to Kafkaesque alibis – "there was no choice" – when testifying in US Senate Committee hearings; see, for instance, Cohan, 2011).

The latter puzzle preludes a tempting research agenda: the development of a theory of strategic *responsiveness*, based on the distinction between organizational dis- and pre-dispositions. The latter are indispensable concepts, since they serve as a necessary antidote against the deterministic flavors of a model otherwise arguing that (firm-to-firm, state-to-firm) codes and commitments "inexorably" follow the conditions of mutual dependence. Otherwise said, disposition and predisposition sensitize for the unmistakable margins of *discretion* in the diplomatic uses of nestedness (as we have come to term behavior in a setting of interdependent choice). The margins of discretionary choice can be explored by looking more sharply at the "bottom-up" workings of the mobilization of bias in the causal chain linking actors, games and the resulting negotiated order. That will be the contribution of this chapter: first, to learn more about the margins of discretion; second to identify the sources of strategic selectivity; and third, to assess their combined impact on the logic of change in the orchestration of disciplinary regimes. The latter includes the ambition to understand the *co*-evolution of diplomacy, discipline and order, in short to ascertain what more precisely drives the logic of change in the orchestration of nested games. The latter amounts to, among others, a revision of current corporate governance discussions, substituting the *Realpolitik* of corporate responsiveness for the deontology of corporate responsibility. (The latter is a serious affair but remains gratuitous without a proper understanding of the former.)

When structure follows volatility

Around the turn of the past century analysts pointed to several tendencies that deranged the familiar texture of resource dependences amongst producers, suppliers, customers, substitutes and new entrants, therewith altering the codes and commitments of the negotiated order of firm-to-firm and state-to-business relationships. The first of these tendencies is called *deindustrialization*. The label refers to the alleged decrease of the share of manufacturing activity in the gross domestic product and structure of employment in developed (Western) economies, and to the increasing centrality of service-based and knowledge-related industries. In order to place the tendency in proper perspective it should be noted, first, that the growing knowledge intensity of production – when considered in the narrow sense, that is, as the intensity of research and development activities – is evident as much in agriculture, forestry and mining as it is in the manufacturing industry and, within that sector, across industries from textiles to telecommunications (Mytelka, 1991: 15–16). Second, the notion of deindustrialization tends to underrate the lasting importance of manufacturing in two respects: the relative decline of employment through productivity increases does not imply a net decline in the centrality of manufacturing as such; and service and knowledge-intensive activities remain vitally dependent on the continuation, if not expansion, of industrial activities, both within the domestic economy and elsewhere. What nevertheless *did* change, and will continue to change in the foreseeable future is, first, the overall composition of developed economies and, second, the *boundaries* between its constituent sectors.

The latter relates to a second tendency, called *deintermediation*, referring to the impact of technological innovations that redefine dramatically inherited patterns of intermediary routines and relationships amongst suppliers, producers and customers. The tightening and uncoupling of intermediary links upset established "communities of practice" within and between firms, as well as between sectors of the economy as a whole.

A third tendency is usually called *delocalization*, including the regional and inter-regional migration of economic activities to places where substitute markets emerge or existing markets expand more rapidly and where investment and production conditions – from pollution control and labor relations to competition legislation and industrial-financial nepotism – appear to be more lenient than in economies based on stricter rules of financial regulation, social justice and environmental protection.

Box 8.2   Icarus' flight

- Each era entertains its favorite iconography. "Iconographies" are sets of imperative beliefs about order and its requisites. Order and requisites are usually presented in terms of logical "necessities". *Counter*-logical aspects of order are wiped off as "frictions" or "transitional" inconsistencies. Only when frictions and inconsistencies become too obtrusive and persistent to be overlooked or negated any longer, are frictions renamed *in*fractions or *sub*versions of social order. By qualifying contradictions as a distraction or subversion of the "realms of necessity", iconographies resume to do what they were erected for: *moralizing and rationalizing disciplinary arrangements.*

- The iconography of more recent times, known as the "Washington consensus", consists of two icons: the stripping of the state and the rehabilitation of the market (eventually followed by the stripping of corporations). The two are presented as logically complementary "necessities". State and market are said to respond, in unison, to a common imperative: the globalization of local and regional economies. After the "Washington Consensus" the ineluctable response to globalization is: liberalization, deregulation, privatization, and the retreat of the state. Despite the quietist, if not fatalist, TINA mantra ("There Is No Alternative") that goes with this "consensus", at least two alternative recipes (re-)emerge from the ruins of the 2008 global credit crunch: westward some argue to look again at the merits of the *mixed market*/welfare state; more eastward another form of capitalism manifests itself: an update of authoritarian, *state-driven* capitalism.

- "Globalization" is the catch-all for the cross-border mobility of intangible competences (organizational "brains" or "intellectual" capital), cash and more tangible assets ("financial" and "plant" capital) and interorganizational connections ("relational" or "network" capital). In the global race of rival states and rival firms it appears to be the *most mobile* resources and players that serve as the catalyst in the cross-border movements: they decide about the *new combinations* of intellectual, financial and relational capital. It is the latter that decide about the competitive fate of nations.

- The dislocation and recomposition of national economies affect moral and rational registers – registers that under more stable conditions are *taken for granted* while operating largely implicitly: a fine-grained web of interlaced interests combined with a critical minimum of understanding and routines for coping with the dilemmas exposed above. The cross-border mobility of tangible and intangible assets is bound to upset the taken-for-granted orchestration of public and private stakes, both inside and across national entities. The result echoes Icarus' fate: wings that once lifted the flight of the "new industrial state" have gradually melted away (Guéhenno, 1993; Rosecrance, 1996). Let's look at a concrete example (see Box 8.3).

Box 8.3 Icarus illuminated

The commercial aerospace industry is a showcase for what happens in knowledge-intensive, financially and relationally interlinked sectors. The two main producers, *Boeing* (USA) and *Airbus* (Europe), are examples. Airbus recently announced to dislocate parts of the production to Asian, American and Arab subcontractors. Reportedly the dislocation was caused by rising labor and supply costs, exchange rate disadvantages (producing in euros while selling in dollars), shrinking international demand due to soaring oil prices, slowing economies and the shakeout among Wall Street institutions that finance aviation companies. As of 2009 it was announced that part of the production of A-320 planes would be transplanted to China. Meanwhile, sophisticated components of the central fuselage of the A-350 would be produced by a former Boeing subsidiary – the same subcontractor that also participates in the assembly process of Airbus's *most feared rival*: Boeing's Dreamliner 787. The level of airframe outsourcing on the wide-body A-350 is estimated to amount to 50 percent. Airbus union officials and even an Airbus chief executive were reported to consider "the fear of [Airbus] losing control of its critical operations [as] a legitimate concern…That would be a danger if we didn't know what our core competencies were. But we've done studies into what should be core and what non-core. There are risks to this concept, but I'm optimistic we can manage it" (*International Herald Tribune*, September 26, 2008). Industrial experts, though, tended to be less optimistic: they predicted within five to ten years an "irreversible transfer" of core technology and associated relational assets from Airbus's headquarters to its Chinese and Indian partners (*De Volkskrant*, March 1, 2007).

Apart from concerns about the migration of brains and preferential partnerships, mention should be made of the role of international financial capital in the self-propelling movement of geopolitical relocations. The bulk of the fleets exploited by international airlines is bought by lease finance firms. ILFC, the US-based, world's biggest, plane lessor by fleet value, and the most important customer for *both* Boeing and Airbus, is up for sale after the Wall Street collapse since its *owner* – the insurance giant AIG (American International Group) – had to raise cash to pay back a lifesaving $85 billion US Federal Reserve loan. Immediately the shares of both Airbus and Boeing went into free fall as investors worried about the outcome of the sale and what the eventual collapse of ILFC – the biggest buyer of Boeing's Dreamliner 787 and Airbus's A-350 superjumbo – would mean for the industry. The only buyers with adequate muscle to pull off a deal with ILFC are expected to be, again, sovereign wealth ("state") funds from China and the Middle East (*International Herald Tribune*, September 19, 2008).

The commercial aviation case demonstrates how the "spillover" of locational, intellectual, relational and financial capital operates – in a world in which the *supply-chains* of each of these resources become increasingly disjuncted.

The trilogy of deindustrialization, deintermediation and delocalization coalesces into "modern" uncertainties about the displacement of public prerogatives and private competences. The uncertainty is a consequence of the intensification of inter-state and inter-regional rivalries: everywhere states and regions look to minimize the odds, respectively maximize the benefits of shifts in the composition and territoriality of national economies. Whatever their separate and combined impact, the trends *do* have significant consequences for the ease of monitoring and sanctioning interorganizational relations, and thus for the credibility of firm-to-firm and business-to-government commitments. The uncertainty, associated with changes in the configuration of dependences, induces change in the repertories for coping with dependence: from accommodation to containment, from centralized to relational control, and from direct annexation to indirect orchestration. The transition from the old to the new discipline may be summarized as the transition from the administration of the *nuts-and-bolts* of national industrial complexes to the orchestration of the *hubs-and-spokes* of the cross-national ramifications of formerly national complexes. In the latter constellation it is not the (functional, sectoral or geographical) location of the ownership and control of resources but the focus and the locus of the *instigation to migration* that count. As will be elucidated in the next sections, the "power-to-instigate" is the capacity to set into motion a chain of moves and movements – by obstruction, pre-emption, inducement or containment – though without the slightest temptation or aspiration to "own" or "control" – even less to be held "accountable" for – the *momentum* of the systemic spillovers.

The *focus* of instigation shifts from Schumpeter's tenet "the threat of competition disciplines before it attacks" towards Schelling's tenet "the threat of partner-substitution disciplines before it materializes". Competing for market shares comes to be mixed with, if not overruled by, competing for *partners*. As far as the latter contest is more and more driven by pre-emptive and expeditionary considerations, fast-splitting and first-quitting rather than first-entry and scale advantages decide about the fate of corporations. In that sense one can say: *volatility follows versatility*.

As a consequence of focus shifts, the *locus* of instigation changes as well. The focus of Schellingian competition varies closely with the locus of Schumpeterian competences. Inversely, *shifts in the locus* of Schumpeterian instigation are a sure foreboding of *switches in the focus* of Schellingian skills. Increasing disparities in the mobility of financial, intellectual and relational capital tear apart the identity of organizations and the domain over which organizations factually exercise control, or aspire to. Identity tells the subjective tale, recounting what organizations think they are, whom they represent and where they want to be held accountable for. Identity informs about the demarcation of insiders and outsiders, and about reputations and self-believed capabilities. Domain, on the other hand, renders the objective story, gauging where organizational "dominion" begins and ends: it informs about the reach of resource dependences and their objective leverage. Whilst identity builds on internal discipline and the *claim* of representativeness, domain control rises from external maneuverability and the *practice* of reciprocity. The two complexions may widely diverge, announcing a radically different sort of corporate "schism" than the classical divide of "ownership versus control" (Berle and Means, 1932). It is the *match* between representativeness – the "license-to-operate"– and reciprocity – the "capacity-to-reciprocate" – that constitutes the credibility of organizations. Credibility is at stake as soon as the two "realities" tell another tale, while possibly widening the mismatch between subjective impersonations and objective practices.

Whatever the possible sources of the mismatch, and its net impact on credibility, the desire for exploiting extant or forging new balances of internal and external commitments induces organizations, sooner or later, to reconsider their "competences". Reconsidering an organization's competence entails the insourcing and outsourcing of activities; outsourcing in turn prompts new forms of *cross*-sourcing, that is to the shared acquisition and exploitation of resources not belonging to an organization's own core and command. The spreading flood of corporate break-ups, used as a leverage to undo old and finance new waves of mergers, takeovers and realignments (Schenk et al., 1997; Schenk, 2005), affects both the nexus of commitments built around the internal core resources of the firm and the nexus of commitments built around its external core of partnerships. Against the inflated uses of the term "strategy" in general, considered from this vantage point the choice of an organizational boundary is a matter of "strategic" concern indeed.

Second, as a result of the shifting boundaries between core and periphery, organizations are forced to reconsider the *level of aggregation* at which they prefer rivalry and cooperation to become "fixed". Whilst transaction costs and institutional economics profess to link the "decision to internalize *or* externalize" to considerations of transactional specificities, thus presenting boundary choice as a matter of *efficiency* (whether inspired by neo-classical purist or bounded rationality assumptions), the choice of a particular level of aggregation, linking arena choice to possible *inter*action considerations, should be seen, instead, as a matter of *effectiveness* (at best based upon a fuzzy mix of negotiated rationality and expeditionary intuition).

Both specimens of strategic choice – inside-out versus outside-in – explain the remarkable renaissance of the debate about questions of *sovereignty* – a summary term for the search for "efficient" boundaries of organizational strategy formation – and *subsidiarity* – summarizing the quest for "effective" levels of strategy aggregation. The search for efficient boundaries alters identities; the quest for effective levels of aggregation redefines arenas. Organizational diplomacy owes its topicality to the wickedness of the problem of "fixing" identities and arenas when the functional and territorial boundaries of both organizations and domains begin to shift and when the articulation of interests appears to be more a matter of maneuverability *across* levels of aggregation than the pay-off of institutionally fixed *single*-level games. Though the two phenomena are clearly interrelated – organizations redefine their boundaries in response to arena mutations and arenas mutate due to organizational boundary shifts – the two follow their own logic: the boundaries of arenas change as a consequence of cumulative *interac*tion effects; the boundaries of organizations change as a consequence of punctuated *trans*actions. Following their own distinct logic, there are arguably neither theoretical nor practical reasons to expect that organizational and domain boundaries will change at the same pace and proportion. The lack of synchronism and proportionality unsettles the "correspondence" of internal pretensions and external practices. Once unsettled, two sorts of intelligence become of strategic avail: *private* intelligence, asking what boundary and arena choice fits in best with what rival firms know about the competences (and dilemmas) of their rivals; and *public* intelligence, asking what rival states know about the predilections (and dilemmas) of rival firms, and what level of decision-making and strategy aggregation would fit best with that reciprocal knowledge. The fit, or misfit, of the two "intelligences" determines the form and substance of the evolution of concerted action.

Box 8.4 Europe's concert revisited

European industrial strategy "agendas" – from the European Roundtable of Industrialists to the Lisbon consensus – illustrate the point. A negotiated order is based upon credible commitments. Credible commitments among rival states and rival firms are only feasible and sustainable as far as firms and states are willing and able to define their *lower limits of sovereignty* – a matter of *organizational* boundary choices (delineating their "representativeness") – and to define with similar clarity the *upper limits of subsidiarity* – a matter of choosing the boundaries of the *arena* in which firms and states seek to solve their dilemmas of collective action in order to arrive at credible commitments ("reciprocity"). When uncertainty about sovereignty and subsidiarity prevails or, more recently, increases, the trade-off between the two is bound to remain an unsettled affair, as will be the case with the solvency of "European" strategy agendas.

Concerted action may be seen as the art of trading sovereignty for subsidiarity. An ideal trade-off serves both efficiency and effectiveness desiderata. As an administrative device, subsidiarity may be invoked to check for coordination deficits due to market (and state) imperfections, whereas sovereignty may serve as a remedy for coordination deficits due to hierarchical overstretch. The *doctrinary* roots of the debate on the trade-offs between sovereignty and subsidiarity reach back to the organicist-solidarist genealogy of Catholic and (later) social democratic thinking on the "vertical" division of competences between (lower level) *private* and (higher level) *public* interests (see our excursion on [neo-] corporatism in Chapter 5). The reanimation of the subsidiarity debate around 1989, refashioned into a discourse about the competences of the European Community vis-à-vis its member states (Geelhoed, 1991; Santer, 1993), was codified in the 1992 Treaty of Maastricht, where article 3B stipulated (italics added):

> The Community shall act within the limits of the powers conferred upon it by this Treaty and of the objectives assigned to it therein. In areas which do not fall within its exclusive competence, the Community shall take action, in accordance with the principle of subsidiarity, only if and in so far as the objectives of the proposed action cannot *sufficiently* be achieved by the Member States and can therefore, by reason of the scale or effects of the proposed action, be better achieved by the Community. Any action by the Community shall not go beyond what is *necessary* to achieve the objectives of this Treaty.

Since its reincarnation in terms of public competences only, much judicial-casuist quibble has been put in for finding a workable definition of "subsidiarity" and delineating the matching confines of "sufficiency" and "necessity". The persisting semantic fuzz prompted Jacques Delors, a former chairman of the European Commission, to offer a reward for anyone who could explain the real meaning of "subsidiarity", characterized by himself off the cuff as "a way of reconciling what for many appears to be irreconcilable ... the need for a European power capable of tackling the problems of our age and the absolute necessity to preserve our roots in the shape of our nations and regions" (Santer, 1993.). The fuzz remains unsettled until today. It is safe to assume its perpetuation as long as sovereignty and subsidiarity remain the favored hunting ground for two (at first sight) opposing kinds of rhetoric: those who believe that any form of human intervention in the natural course of things inevitably leads to social mischief versus those, though subscribing to the pessimist camp on matters of "social engineering", nevertheless expound a panglossian belief in the powers of *"strategic* engineering". For a concise portrait of the first species I follow Hirschman (1991), who epitomizes the messengers of doom's agenda as the rhetoric-of-reaction, based upon three articles of faith: "perversity", "futility" and "jeopardy".

Box 8.5   The rhetoric of reaction

The doctrines of perversity, futility and jeopardy assert that human aspirations for change invariably lead to either disaster or inverse results or, at best, to nullification: *plus ça change, plus ça reste le meme.*

The *perversity* doctrine

Historical proofs for the occurrence of perversity range from retrospective reports on the "denaturation" of the ideals of the French Revolution and the Age of Enlightenment to modern portraits of the "failures" of the welfare state. The latter are exemplified by: unemployment insurance allegedly reinforcing unemployment by discouraging workers to search for new jobs; aid to non-working mothers with dependent children which not only assists broken-up families but allegedly eventually encourages family breakups; speed limits and the compulsory use of seat-belts causing drivers to relax their vigilance and to drive more recklessly; irrigation projects leading to the loss of irrigated acreage through waterlogging and the increase of conflicts over access to water. The examples are variations on the topos of "unintended consequences of intended action". As a rule, the subscribers of the perversity doctrine ignore or obscure the illustrations and evidence that the intellectual fathers of the thesis, from Adam Smith to Robert Merton, provided about the potentially beneficial effects of activities that actors never had in mind when preparing for or performing specific acts (Hirschman, 1991: 38).

The *futility* doctrine

The second pillar is the epitome for thinkers that hold that political or economic interventions – from the promotion of democracy and egalitarian values to the redistribution of income and wealth or the readjustment of the market mechanism – inevitably come to naught because these efforts disregard some "law" whose existence has allegedly been ascertained by "science". The intellectual genealogy runs from Mosca, Pareto and Michels to modern monetarists, anti-Keynesians and other chroniclers of the "[laws] ruling the social world...and acting as an insurmountable barrier to social engineering" (ibid.: 71). The law of futility ends, at best, in a self-defeating prophecy.

When assessing the first two sub-doctrines in terms of their social impact, Hirschman presages that the futility thesis is more malicious in its premises and devastating in its consequences than the perversity thesis. The advocates of the *perversity* claim speak "condescendingly" and in the spirit of "forgivingness" about the lack of anticipation and the surplus of good intentions on the part of those who start the chain of events that leads to perversity; the architects of perversity are seen as incurably naïve, while lacking an elementary understanding of the interactive complexities of social and economic life. The advocates of the *futility* thesis, on the other hand, start from the *parti pris* that the architects of policies for empowering the powerless and for helping the poor are themselves, in fact or by intent, the beneficiaries of these policies, and therefore by no means all that innocent or well-intentioned. Social justice and all that "are nothing but smoke screens hiding the most selfish motives... Far from being naive and full of illusion, 'progressive' policy-makers suddenly come to be perceived as cunning schemers and nasty hypocrites" (ibid.: 77).

The *jeopardy* doctrine

Whereas the futility thesis thrives on demonstrating the inconsistency between proclaimed purposes (promoting democracy and welfare for the masses) and actual practice (continuation of oligarchy and mass poverty), the third pillar, the jeopardy thesis, cherishes the belief that intended change, though perhaps desirable in itself, involves unacceptable costs or consequences of one sort or another. What rises is invariably prophesied to fall. Underlying the jeopardy thesis is the irrevocable belief that any fortuitous gain in one direction, for an individual or a group, is bound to be balanced and therefore in fact erased by an equivalent loss in another. Upon looking more closely "we lose and we gain, but what we lose is more precious than what we gain. It is a case of one step forward, two steps backward: what first looks like progress is not just illusory, but outright impoverishing" (ibid.: 122–3).

Though less condescending than the perversity and less outright reactionary than the futility claimants, the subscribers of the jeopardy thesis share with the other two a consistently non-empiricist bias towards affirmative evidence only, a fact-resistant belief in some mythical, more noble, antecedent, and an equally non-empiricist disinterest in the occurrence of cases in which their prophesies of tragedy fail, that is where the rise of something is not followed by its subsequent fall, or where the rise *and* fall of something end in net progress and increase of the common wealth.

Though each of them declines the possibility of comprehensive or system-level rationality, the three siblings of the rhetoric of reaction arrive at their gloominess for contradictory reasons. At first sight both perversity and futility seem to be based on the notion of collectively unanticipated consequences of individual social action. Upon closer inspection, however, the two are based on almost opposite views of the social texture of purposive human and social action:

> The perverse effect sees the social world as remarkably *volatile*, with every move leading immediately to a variety of unsuspected countermoves; the futility advocates, to the contrary, view the world as *highly structured* and as evolving according to immanent laws, which human actions are laughably impotent to modify. The comparative mildness of the claim of the futility thesis – human actions pursuing a given aim are nullified instead of achieving the exact opposite – thus is more than compensated by what I earlier called its insulting character, by the contemptuous rebuff it opposes to any suggestion that the social world might be open to progressive change. (Hirschman, 1991: 72)

The currently favored cure whenever individual rationality is believed to end in collective irrationality (or worse) is provided by the canons of rational individualism. The neo-liberal fellow traveler of the rhetoric of reaction is the rhetoric of strategic activism.

Box 8.6 The rhetoric of activism

The activist doctrine of strategic engineering delivers a variety of corporate recipes for "breakthrough strategies for seizing control of industries", "creating the markets of tomorrow", "shaping and scanning the future", and so on (cf. Hamel and Prahalad, 1994, and the spirits of strategy regeneration and corporate renewal who pervade the columns of the *Harvard Business Review*). In brief, what distinguishes this train of strategy thinking from positive science are: a large dose of self-complacency stemming from a prescriptive rather than an analytical orientation; an under-socialized, über-rational and slightly narcissistic "model" of economic man, not taking into account the *embeddedness* of organizational practices; a linear and unidirectional conception of strategy design, implementation and learning, not respecting the iterative and interactive nature of strategic moves and countermoves; and an ahistorical, single-loop view of strategy making, which is insensitive to the "thickening" character of strategies and which escalate or accumulate into (unforeseen) commitments that these daring "designers" possibly never had in mind.

Curiously enough, this *winner-takes-all* doctrine of "strategic engineering" faces an internal contradiction that parallels the antinomy we observed in its virtual antipode, the negativist doctrine that is devoted to fight the "fakes of social engineering". The volatility caused by the international troika of deregulation, liberalization and technological turbulence is said to make the universe radically different from what it used to be. Remarkably enough, this unruly state of affairs appears to strengthen rather than weaken the advocacy of gilt-edged recipes for "creating the future", "out-performing the neighbors" and "securing the market of tomorrow". So, in the latter liturgy, volatility should be seen as a blessing in disguise, because those who read reality in a proper way will arrive in a world that is structured enough to outbid the competition. Apparently there is order in the chaos of hyper-competition (see the iconography of "untamed capitalism" in Chapter 2, pp. 30–1) – though the kind of order we may expect remains unspecified. The rebuffing fatalism of the reactionary rhetoric stands in sharp contrast to the exhorting self-conceit of the managerial rhetoric. The former inspires to the arrogance of collective *im*potence, justifying the sufficiency of individual choice; the latter inspires to the arrogance of individual *omni*potence of the self-declared "masters of the universe", who are not concerned about the nested nature of strategy and structure and thereby ignore the necessity to take into account the eventually self-frustrating or *collectively* counter-productive effects of individual rationality. Thus, curiously enough, in spite of their opposite *partis pris*, at the end of the day both the reactive sorcerer and his proactive apprentice come to ground in a shared illusion: the triumph of rational individualism.

As long as sorcerers and apprentices assemble apart together, the parallel implications of their contradictory premises remain unnoticed, hence leaving the real intrigue unaddressed: How do organizations cope with the shadows of the past that tie them to fixed routines and competences to the effect of limiting their (ache for) strategic leeway – the "competence trap"? On the other hand, how do organizations cope with the shadows of the future that teach them that the net pay-offs of strategic choice depend on what others are preparing to do in an imitative way – the "competition trap"? The best one can say about the rhetoric of reaction is that its teachings on perversity, futility and jeopardy help in making understandable the dismal outcomes of "atomistic" rationality. However, the remedy proposed for the dismay is not particularly helpful when the noise of the rhetoric of individual action is called in to fill the void of the rhetoric of collective reaction. Both sorcerer and apprentice fail to inform us about the *practical* solutions that the capitalist aptitude for improvisation, however inadvertently or in vain, invents for addressing the traps of competence and competition. In that respect, our analytical trilogy of diplomacy, discipline and order seems to have a stronger hand.

Rather than joining the chorus line of doctrinarian specialists, our diplomacy framework favors a focus on the praxis of rhetoric. As argued before, in practical usage sovereignty and subsidiarity constitute the dual axes of the quest for coordination: sovereignty relates to competence-based *organizational* boundary choices that tie down the relationships among organizations – firms, states and interest associations vis-à-vis their opposites – while subsidiarity relates to *arena* choices, that is the levels of aggregation at which firms, states and interest groups attune their trade-offs between the desire for "selfishness" on the one hand and the need for (still self-serving) "unselfish" forms of self-restraint and discipline on the other. The two are inextricably interlinked: subsidiarity implies the transfer of sovereignty to higher or lower levels of interest aggregation; but by shifting sovereignty upward or downward, horizontal links between the *iso*-"sovereigns" alter as well. With that we are back at the center of this study: the choreography of interdependent choices among organizations whose fates are intertwined – whatever the direction, duration and degree of the formal codification of the means of orchestration.

Volatility follows versatility

What may be considered novel in this study? The empirical objective has been to unravel the intricacies of the spillovers of "nested" dependences and to identify the forces that alter the form and substance of their orchestration. Theoretically the aim has been to find a bridging grammar for the various disciplines that are helpful for gaining insight into interfirm and business-to-state relationships, but unfortunately fail to benefit from one another's insights and findings. Sometimes one gets the impression that *academic* divides are susceptible to the same forces as the ones that favor "stasis" and "cognitive capture" in corporate and industrial practices, that is:

> large sunk costs represented by the development of well-practiced routines, supported by locally efficient information codes and the establishment of common knowledge-like expectations, [which explains why] it is less costly to eschew revolutions and favour

ameliorative and essentially conservative modes of response to any dysfunctional aspects that may be noticed in the existing arrangements. (David, 1994: 215)

This view on the conservative bias or inertia ("path dependency") of *business* routines resembles the view of critical economists on instances of *academic* inertia that explain the trained incapacity of mainstream economics to understand, let alone predict, systemic crises due to the "blindness" of macro-economics "with respect to the role of interactions and connections between actors", which induces "self-reinforcing feedback effects within the profession [that] may have led to the dominance of a paradigm [with] no solid methodological basis... [nor] empirical validation" (Colander et al., 2009: 14).

Among the objectives of this study is to address the dysfunctionality of the academic convention of considering the strategies and tactics of actors (micro), the dynamics of games (meso) and the evolution of order (meta) as disjointed intellectual ventures and, instead, to trace the intricate conjunctures between these three "productions" of social reality. The generic term for the stratagems reviewed in this study is concerted action (with different protagonists), the medium is organizational diplomacy (in different settings) and the result is capitalist discipline (in different shapes).

As argued before, there are two generic imperfections of capitalist self-regulation, both springing from the canons of rational choice:

1. The *competence* trap, referring to the loss of strategic flexibility due to switching costs as a result of historical commitments (Arthur, 1988) – from the "lock-in" of specific asset combinations (cf. Williamson, 1983 on "hostages") to the "inertia" of operating routines (Nelson and Winter, 1982).
2. The *competition* trap, referring to the loss of strategic advantage due to an overdose of imitation (Schenk, 1997) *or* its opposite: the absence of strategic advance due to a *lack* of complementors or sponsors (whereas "excessive" imitation is a matter of maximal, the latter is a question of minimal critical mass for converting potential privileges into real ones).

The need for concerted action – Schelling's "antagonistic cooperation" – arises from the shadows of the past (*path* dependence in its manifold manifestations) and the shadows of the future (*partner* dependence in its potentially self-perverting or paralyzing manifestations). Both tend to tie organizations to status quo routines and therefore to limit the room for "free" responses to changing threats and opportunities. Neither the rhetoric of reaction nor the narcissistic rhetoric of strategic activism provide plausible clues to the question as to how – *in a non-authoritarian setting* – states and firms cope with this sort of dilemma in practice. In a "schizoid" world characterized by increasing interdependences among increasingly commitment-*averse* players, versatility becomes a strategic assignment.

The issue of versatility – "responsiveness" in our short-hand notation – can be looked at from different angles that traditionally claim a say on the subjects of corporate strategies and industrial change. The claimants can be divided in two broad divisions: first those who address the question as to *what* is supposed to drive the firm – a so-called "agency" perspective – which ranges from comparative "modes of organizing" (inside-out looking) to "environmental imperatives" (looking outside-in); second, those who address the question as to *who* drives the firm – a so-called "agents" perspective, which ranges from those who interpret the firm as a black box (that is treating the firm as an undivided "unitary actor") to those who envisage the firm as a nexus of potentially diverging orientations and contending interests (that is seeing the firm as a "composite actor"). By confronting agents and agent approaches (for the initial presentation of my arguments see p. 57) a four-fold partitioning of the literature results that covers the academic gymnasium from corporate strategy to industrial dynamics (see Figure 8.1).

As proposed in Chapter 3, the *left* part of the matrix can be summarily seen as harboring schools in the *Habitus* key, since organizational behavior is interpreted as the result of *habit* formation – ranging from the axioms of rational choice and the search for efficiency (e.g. transaction cost theories of the firm) to the issue of problem-driven and "satisficing", instead of efficiency-driven and "maximizing", routines and the role of dominant coalitions in defining these routines (e.g. behavioral theories of the firm).

The *right* half of the matrix represents schools in the *Habitat* key, since analytical priority in this corner is granted to what the *environment* dictates as "efficient behavior" (e.g. industrial economics) or selects as survival-enhancing, respectively constraining institutions (e.g. evolutionary economics) – thus explaining the (possibly counter-rational and/or non-efficient) mixes of adaptation-cum-inertia in the behavior of (imperfectly rational) organizations (e.g. neo-institutional economics).

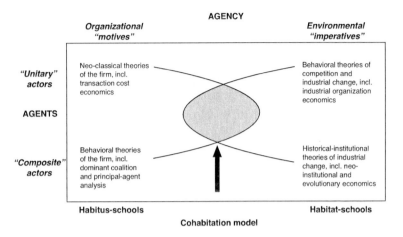

Figure 8.1 Corporate strategy and industrial change: the two premier leagues and their academic associates

Each of these schools has its merits in terms of explanatory scope. However, *combining* them compensates for what their opposites leave out categorically or dismiss inadvertently. Where the two can be made to meet – the shaded overlap in Figure 8.1 – fresh options emerge for uniting the best of the insights and predilections of the two divisions. Such a *"Co-habitation approach"*, as I proposed calling it, is expected to come to grips with the issues of versatility and the underlying dilemmas of "antagonistic cooperation" – more consequentially than what can be expected from the left and right side as long as the latter continue to work in mutual separation and neglect.

A *co-*habitation framework centers directly on the puzzles and paradoxes of capitalist coordination. The *quest* for coordination arises from the need to face the limits of capitalist rationality (the "competence" and/or "competition" trap). The *room* for coordination varies with the structure of the various games of "competitive cooperation", that is, with the symmetry or asymmetry of vertical, horizontal and diagonal dependences. The *capacity* for coordination refers to the question of versatility or "responsiveness": that is, the capability to cope with the problems of path and partner dependence by distinct mixes of "skill, strength, or luck" (see the *Concise Oxford Dictionary* for definitions of "game"). Firms respond to the shadows of the past and future by selecting – or getting mixed up with – specific boundaries of actors and arenas.

Let us list some conceivable gains that may be expected from bridging the academic divides presented in Figure 8.1. The *Eastern* regions, granting priority to environmental conditions and evolutionary dynamics in the explanation of corporate and intercorporate strategies, will benefit from importing elements from the West. For instance, competition analysis and the role of path dependences in the evolution of industries will gain in explanatory power when, in the case of cooperative and competitive strategies, micro-level behavioral specifics are inserted, such as the willing misrepresentation of the value of skills and connections brought to a partnership ("adverse selection"), or a less-than-promised contribution of skills and resources in a cooperative venture ("moral hazard"), or the unfair exploitation of the transaction-specific investments made by others in a partnership ("holdup") – typically the behavioral specimens of opportunism that figure prominently in the world according to transaction-cost economics. More sociologically oriented behavioral theories of the firm would additionally explain how (changing) dominant coalitions in the upper stratum of organizations affect the (changing) way in which corporate partnerships respond to competitive pressures, while taking into account the constraints of "free choice" in the case of irreversible commitments and the inertia of organizational routines.

Western regions, on the other side, trained in the axioms of rational choice and the search for efficiency – be it here and there allowing for the realities of "bounded" rationality, "satisficing" instead of maximizing behaviors and possible biases in the definitions of efficiency or performance – will certainly profit from absorbing elements from the East. Both transaction-cost and behavioral theories of the firm gain in explanatory power when including particulars of the competitive and symbiotic arenas (as for instance is shown in Figure 7.3) and granting a more prominent role for the way in which shadows of the past ("path dependence") and future ("partner dependence") affect the rise and fall of "dominant coalitions" inside complex organizations, thereby providing a "thicker" explanation for (Schattschneider's) "mobilization of bias" in the search and selection of corporate responses to external threats and opportunities.

Keeping an oblique eye on East and West, *both* will gain from inserting elements of game-theoretical analysis, provided the "orthodoxy" of formal game theory is prepared to concede to the axiomatic "permissiveness" that inevitably slips in when the paradoxes of competitive or antagonistic cooperation and discipline are looked at from the *co*-habitation perspective advocated here. The tolerance for a measure of indeterminateness in matters of strategy and tactics will vary with one's attachment to the respective gestalts of strategic rationality that each of the above-listed academic regions espouses (see Box 8.7).

Box 8.7   The four Gestalts of "strategic rationality"

- At the upper-East side of the spectrum we come across a *reactive* actor, who listens to the adage *"where you stand depends on what the environment imposes"* and who believes that open competition selects and reinforces best practice; under perfect conditions the future is for those who read the invisible hand properly.
- The lower-East end lodges a *captive* actor, who knows that *"where you stand depends on where you sit"*, which means: an actor captured by institutional settings and inherited procedures; institutional fit and organizational routines decide conduct and performance, whether rational and efficient or not.
- At the upper-West side lives an *opportunist* actor: *"where you stand depends on where others stand"*; since it may be difficult if not impossible to know beforehand, or only from hearsay, who will behave opportunistically, it will be rational to assume opportunism everywhere and efficient to assimilate and internalize the associated problems of incomplete contracting and imperfect monitoring ("agency costs") by vertical integration and hierarchical control.
- For seeing the problems of opportunism *inside* hierarchies, and the non-contractual aspects of contracts plus the supervisory biases within organizations, it may be wiser to descend to the lower-West end of the strategy spectrum. There we are promised to meet players versed in the internal politics of complex organizations, say a *fixing* actor, that is a power broker who knows how to read the visible hand correctly while living according to the adage *"where you stand depends on wherever a minimal winning coalition can be found"*.

The foregoing can be summarized as a menu of four "models of man" figuring in each of the schools of thought that claim to have a say on the primacy of man *or* the selection environment in the explanation of "strategic choice" (see Figure 8.2).

Orthodox game theory appears not particularly helpful in reconciling the incompatibilities of the four "models". The main reason is that the scraps of political and economic realism still to be found in each of them are washed out in formal game-theoretical axiomatics and deduction – e.g. when actors, both in cooperative and non-cooperative games, are assumed to meet in a setting where, first, the arena, agenda and timing are fixed; second, the actors are symmetrically similar in

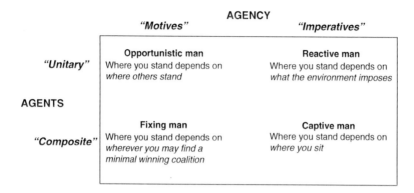

Figure 8.2:   Models of man: the strategic choice-menu

terms of their criticality, substitutability and the time span of mutual indispensability; and third, the players are assumed to measure up to one another in terms of stamina and resolve. These leveling assumptions, though "flattening" the calculus of gaming, succeed in effectively killing the need and the room for improvisation and probing, which is associated with the non-level playing fields that breathe life into the games covered in this study. Another genus of game theory can be imagined, however, in the shaded space where Habitus and Habitat views overlap (or can be refashioned to do so). In this area – say the habitat of the politics of *co*-habitation – figures another persona, a *diplomatic* actor, who operates according to the maxim: *"where you stand depends on your entry and exit opportunities"*, that is on the *costs of switching* from where you sit ("path dependence") and aspire to move to ("partner dependence") *and* on your position in the dominant coalition inside "composite" actors – the latter as an echo (cf. Cohan, 2011) to the adage (Sadler, 1992: 29):

> Many would like to think that board-level decisions are made on the basis of rational argument and in the best long-term interests of the stakeholders. However, the boardroom is often the arena in which a struggle for power takes place and the principles of management are abandoned in favor of the law of the corporate jungle.

Looking back at the particulars of the symbiotic and competitive arena (Chapter 7), and the specifics of internal mobilization, representativeness and the role of internal dominant coalitions in all that (Chapter 5), it is not the "embeddedness of choice" that counts in a diplomatic actor cohabitation framework but the *"choice* of embeddedness", be it still *constrained* by the confines of past and future commitments (including *internal* commitments: cf. Chapter 4 on rivalries inside "oligarchies" and the related contingencies of "network solvency"). This is what is meant by the notions of "recursive" causation and *ex post* "rationalization", as opposed to the assumptions of "linear" causality and *ex ante* "rationality", that pervade the literature on strategy matters and dynamics. It is neither organizational "habits" nor "habitats" as such that explain strategic choices. It is, instead, the difference in the time spans of financial, intellectual and relation-specific investments that defines the essence of strategic choice, to wit the room for converting past commitments into future ones.

Box 8.8   Nested games

In October 1997, South Korea's government announced it would rescue by *nationalization* the troubled Kia Motor group by asking the state-run Korea Development Bank to take a controlling 30 percent stake in the failing car maker through a debt-for-equities swap – after placing the car and truck units under court receivership (guaranteeing that creditor banks could begin recovering their loans from a near or definitively bankrupt company). The Kia group, around that time the nation's third-largest car maker, is part of Korea's eighth-largest *chaebol* (a Korean version of typically Asian, tightly knit networks of producers, banks, equipment supplies, trade companies and state agencies which are bound together through cross-shareholdings, technology agreements and interlocking directorates and are considered to be the pillars of the economy; thanks to state-guaranteed direct lending to the *chaebols*, banks and financial institutions had no qualms about lending to them, whatever the health of the indulging business and its phenomenal expansion rates, which were bound to end in excess-capacity).

A report in the *Financial Times*, on October 24, 1997, demonstrates the virtual impossibility of any rescue operation, either by full state control or by dismantling a *chaebol* through selling its parts to the (international) market:

Mazda, a Japanese car maker which has an 8 percent equity stake in the troubled Kia Motors and supplies most of Kia's technology, says "it had not been consulted" about the government's decision to nationalize the company. As a consequence Mazda said it had not had time to consult with colleagues at Ford, which owns 10 percent of Kia *and* is the controlling shareholder in Mazda. Apart from its equity and technological *Verflechtung* with Kia, Mazda also has several license agreements with the company. Many of Kia's vehicles are directly derived from Mazda products.

As Mazda's president says, "I obviously have a concern how we protect our investments and protect our interests," adding that he was basically "neutral" about whether ownership of Kia would pass to another *Korean* car maker. Mazda, he says, would not be "concerned" even if the government allowed the company to be bought by Samsung, a Korean electronics group which is expanding into the motor industry. However, a takeover by Samsung would be widely seen as contrary to Mazda's interest. Samsung has signed a technology deal with Nissan, Japan's second-biggest car maker, so in that sense is a formidable rival of Mazda. Thus *"any control over Kia's destiny would be viewed as ultimately detrimental to Mazda's interests"*.

The Mazda versus Samsung rescue operation is a prototype of a "nested game": what at first sight seems to be a "simple" bilateral (public–private) Korean game turns out to be a trilateral, Japanese–Korean–American game, conditioned by an inextricable interlocking of partly complementary, partly competitive, stakes. The assumption of symmetry (as in conventional game theory) fails to grasp the intricacies of a "nested" game, in particular because the former excludes the possibility of eventually *leaving* the game for another one – for instance by switching partners *within* a circuit or by the *cross*-circuit sourcing of resources – thereby radically reframing the arena, agenda and time horizon of the game. As a consequence conventional game theory seems to pass over the crux of nested games – which is in fact the foundation of our cohabitation framework: the paradox of *staying* power. The paradox stipulates that negotiating power accrues to those who are *free to leave* – the organization or the arena – as opposed to those who are *bound to stay*. The paradox rests on a simple axiom and its behavioral correlates (see Box 8.9).

Box 8.9 Staying power: the premises

1. Imperfect rationality and incomplete accountability are, on equal footing, the basic tenets of the game.
2. Though it may be assumed (for the sake of simplicity) that actors are roughly equal in terms of the *cognitive* "limits of rationality", they are rarely if ever equal in terms of accountability due to constraints and facilities that follow from the mobilization of bias in the organizational-institutional framing of "rational" behavior.
3. The rules of the game (the so-called "pay-off matrices") are not a priori given or postulated as an extraneous input; they are, instead, an endogenous *output* produced by the cumulative logic of the game.
4. The *cumulative* logic of the game, generated by prior conditions of mutual investments – the "bounded hands" we earlier referred to – may deviate substantially from the *individual* logic of the players. The reason is simple: actors act on the basis of their understanding of the situation; but once they have decided to act, they alter the very conditions on which their initial understanding is based.

5. Players are rarely, if ever, equal in their options for entering or leaving the game; if it makes any sense to speak of "pay-off matrices", it must be this: how do players differ in terms of the returns from equal or unequal entry and exit opportunities? The latter we identify as a first "gross" foundation of negotiating power: *mobility* differentials.

6. Apart from differences in external mobility, players eventually differ in their capability to play the game in a consistent and credible manner, due to differences in their capacity to mobilize the required internal support and self-discipline. This we identify, as a second "gross" determinant of bargaining power, *mobilization* differentials.

7. Mobility and mobilization differentials constitute the elemental explanation of inter-actor contrasts in *responsiveness*, that is the capacity of actors to respond to the volatility of their environment.

The notions of mobility and mobilization point to a crucial difference with the world according to "rational egoists" (such as Olsonians and Axelrodians): the "shadows" of the past and of the future are, more often than not, *asymmetric* shadows for each of the respective players. The proviso of a perfect, that is, spatially and temporally symmetric freedom to answer tit-for-tat will rarely if ever be satisfied. If we allow (for the sake of realism) for the (1) existence of more than two parties, and (2) possible asymmetries in their external mobility and internal mobilization potential and, consequently, (3) possible asymmetries in the commitments produced by successive tit-for-tats, it must be clear why rational-choice and game-theoretical notions of conflict and cooperation have to be replaced by another construct, the cornerstones of which are "staying power" and the "negotiated order".

Staying power is the *micro*-foundation; from there follows a reconstruction of the uses of embeddedness, which demonstrates how strategies produce specific (pre-)commitments. From this *meso*-level of analysis follows a reconstruction of the crystallization of strategies into a negotiated order of constraints and opportunities at the systemic or *meta*-level; the latter delineates the room for strategic choice, that is the embeddedness of the *uses* of embeddedness. From this "nesting" perspective specific hypotheses are drawn, that is, how differences in types of dependence, each associated with particular sorts of dilemma, lead to specific codes and modes of handling interdependence, such as different modalities of coalition, alliance and circuit formation. "Circuits", as will be elucidated later, refer to the *recycling* of coalitions and alliances. The latter leads to different sorts of commitments and disciplinary regimes. The argument, explananda and explanation are set out in Box 8.10.

Box 8.10 The argument: explananda and explanation

ARGUMENT
The "recycling" of corporate games and capitalist discipline

"The quest for discipline"

How can we explain the oxymoron of capitalist discipline, when the "world" consists of (1) a constellation of actors preferring to economize on commitments (the paradox of *staying* power), (2) while each of them is constrained by historical investments (the essence of *path* dependence) and (3) facing dilemmas of anticipation (the essence of *partner* dependence), but (4) differing in their freedom to renege on past and future commitments (the essence of *interdependent choice* in strategic affairs)?

The "shuttle" hypothesis

1. Horizontal rivals, when facing prisoner's dilemmas (the *"competition trap"*) will look for *vertical allies*.
2. Vertical allies, when facing reciprocity dilemmas (the *"competence* trap") will reiterate the search for *horizontal coalitions*.
3. Binding oneself (the *"Ulysses"* principle), while economizing on commitments (the *"Houdini"* principle) invokes the *recycling* of coalitions and alliances.

EXPLANANDA

Level of analysis:	Micro-moves	Meso-movements	Meta-momentum
Logic:	Logic of actors	Logic of games	Logic of regimes
Units of analysis	Actions ("thrift")	Transactions ("shuttle")	Interactions ("drift")

Conditions

Competitive dependences	Complementary dependences	Cyclical dependences

---

Disciplinary *dilemmas*

Short-sightedness ("myopia") and competitive imitation ("herd behavior")	Pre-emptive ("appropriation") and exploited reciprocity ("lock-in" or "holdup")	Shifting costs (due to "path dependence") and switching costs (due to "partner dependence")

Codes		
Ordering by *coalition* formation: dividing and binding *competitors*	Ordering by *alliance* formation: dividing and binding *complementors*	Ordering by *circuit* formation: *revolving* competitors and complementors

Commitments		
The *horizontal* exchange of threats and promises under competitive dependence: seeking to curb the risks of the *competition trap* ("myopia" and "bandwagoning")	The *vertical* exchange of threats and promises under symbiotic dependence: seeking to curb the risks of the *competence trap* ("appropriation" and "holdup")	The *cyclical* exchange of threats and promises, turning competitive into symbiotic and symbiotic into competitive dependence: seeking to curb the risks of the *captiveness trap* ("path" and "partner" dependences)

Diplomatic *menus*		
The orchestration of horizontal dependences: from market "segmentation" to "annexation" (merger and acquisition)	The orchestration of vertical dependences: from "insourcing" vs "outsourcing" to "cross-sourcing" and "satellitization"	The orchestration of revolving dependences: using vertical alliances as a leverage for horizontal discipline and vice versa

EXPLANATION
"The conquest of discipline"

On the spillover from micro-*actors* to meso-*games* and macro-*regimes*:
"Strategy follows structure, and structure follows cycles"

Strategies emerge from dependence **conditions** ("*structure*"); dependence conditions induce **codes and commitments**; codes and commitments coagulate into disciplinary **regimes** ("*negotiated order*"); and order (re)produces **structure and strategies**, until changing dependences trigger a new turn of the cycle (the "*recycling*" of discipline).

Box 8.10 partly contains a review, partly a preview of the analytical job we have set out to accomplish: explaining (the recycling of) capitalist discipline. The aim of the exercise has been to trim the dilemmas of firm-to-firm and business-to-state interactions to a measure of analytical simplicity. The esthetics of the exercise has been to simplify the complexities of everyday life, without anaesthetizing them – as in symmetrical, fixed and monolithic actor game theory – that is, by eschewing analytical solutions "with a degree of computational complexity that even analysts are unable to cope with in practical applications" (Scharpf, 1993: 140). The latter assessment may explain why skeptics have come to believe that "almost any theory of organization that is addressed by game theory will do more for game theory than game theory will do for it" (Krepps, 1992: 1, quoted in Williamson, 1996: 357). However, as we have set out to demonstrate, there are less sublime "models of economic man" that might be able accomplish the task though.

The *novelty* of what I have done should not be overrated. My work is primarily an essay in realigning a host of useful but scattered insights into a more coherent whole. Organizational diplomacy aims to formulate an answer to the question as to how rival firms and states try to steer a middle course between market myopia and bureaucratic overstretch. Neither marketization nor hierarchization appear to be able to solve the arch dilemmas of capitalist coordination. Hierarchization, "whether technically or by chain of command" (Mayntz, 1991: 11), fails to appreciate the subtlety of the "colligations" between sovereignty and subsidiarity. Hierarchy drives out the impromptu of complex social systems, that is, the capacity for improvisation. The hierarchic "temptation" overlooks a systemic paradox that Simon (1965) hinted at: "the more tightly complex an organization, the closer it moves toward becoming a disaggregative system".

Tightly coupled organizations, though continuing to pose as hierarchies, end up in *fake* hierarchies, that is as organizational constructs deprived of internal cohesion and an external sense of direction. If interdependence between the components of social systems like organizations increases, they become less decomposable; becoming less decomposable means that should one component fail, the whole system either collapses or becomes inoperative. System theory asserts that social systems may escape from the risks inherent in tight interdependence by making use of their "near decomposability". Nearly decomposable systems are believed to be able to resist the spiral of "death by disaggregation" by making sure that (cf. Simon, 1965: 69–70) (i) "the short-run behavior of each component subsystem is approximately independent of the short-run behavior of every other component subsystem", whereas (ii) "in the long run the behavior of any one component subsystem is dependent in only an aggregate way on the behavior of the other component subsystems".

In plain language: *strong ties* make for *weak systems*. But, conversely, when do weak ties make for strong systems? Unfortunately, loose coupling may not provide a solution either: the "design of nearly decomposable structures becomes an elusive goal ... when the frequency, density and volatility of interactions increase beyond a certain level". As the interaction effects among tasks assigned to different organizational units become more frequent and important, hierarchical organizations are confronted with an unattractive dilemma: *either* recentralization, which means that "the advantages of decentralization and selective intervention will be lost, the agenda of upper-level managers will be overcrowded and their capacity for information processing overloaded; *or*, by contrast, decentralization, leaving subordinates to cope by themselves with increasing inter-unit interactions, which means that "the organization loses the advantages of hierarchical coordination, and is left with the complementary problems of horizontal self-coordination which, while qualitatively different, are not necessarily less damaging" (Scharpf, 1993: 136–7).

Decomposition and self-regulation tend to promote the proliferation of sectional and local interests, inducing a regress into short-term opportunism (hit and run), possibly leaving everybody worse off. It is exactly the paradoxical concurrence of aggregate interdependence combined with short-term independence – in substantive terms: *the limited liability of a "composite" constituency for the cumulative effects of the acts of its "constituents"* – that breeds the "ideal" setting for selfish, micro-rational behavior. As we have seen, micro-rational behavior leads to dilemmas of the "rational egoist" type, frustrating a commensurate response to intra- and inter-organizational dependences. Moreover, disjunctions of this kind breed normative uncertainty; and normative uncertainty confers rational and moral standing to the further eclipse of accountability. It is exactly "aggregate interdependence combined with short-term independence" that comes close to a concise summary of the conditions that brought about the financial-economic catastrophe we are still witnessing.

Box 8.11 Runaway securities

Where accountability wanes, anomy enters. How anomy breeds a fairy ring of internal control and external reciprocity losses can be seen in the management of the most volatile specimen of mobile resources, the global trade in securities with its present day variety of financial derivates. Central banks and other institutions, officially supervising private banks and stock exchanges, became concerned – long before the implosion of the financial system worldwide in the first decade of this century – about the incentives that allowed fund managers to embark on increasingly risky and Fata Morgana transactions. An example from the roaring 1990s (in hindsight the trailer for the complete collapse that followed some 15 years later, roughly the average duration of a full cycle) is the spectacular splash-down of the UK's elite bank Barings after the confessions of one of its market-makers. The Barings saga is now generally held to be the vicious result of, first, vanishing internal controls and, second, the eclipse of external checks and balances. *Internal monitoring* fails when, apart from and probably more decisive than the lack of internal socialization by traditional in-company traineeships, the bonuses of the bosses (board of directors and supervisors) are directly linked to the bonuses of the runners (fund managers). And *external sanctioning* vanishes when – apart from the bandwagoning drive of rival banks, who are afraid of missing out for themselves or who are eager to pre-empt others for the next mega-deal – the old informal rule not to entice away one's rival's top-level fund managers has ceased to be adhered to. Merchant banks like US Morgan Stanley and Deutsche Morgan Grenfell, a subsidiary of Germany's largest bank, Deutsche Bank, are said to have served as the catalyst or pacemakers; others felt they could not afford to stay behind. As hindsight shows us: efforts to bind employees by offering them ever more exotic salaries and bonuses accelerates the further break-down of the informal codes of discipline and accountability.

To sum up, individuals gather into organizations, organizations assemble into federations and federations start to negotiate their interdependences. The emerging negotiated order consists of a web of unstable commitments, and unstable commitments press for never-ending renegotiations. Borrowing once again from Schelling (1969), negotiations and commitments among and between organizations are specimens of "precarious partnerships" fed on "incomplete antagonism". No unitary hierarchies nor clear-cut principles of accountability govern these partnerships. Neither do the "laws of the market" – the textbook metaphor for an atomistic assembly of individuals who are symmetrically free to enter and leave the arena without switching costs. What remains, given the objective mutual dependences, is the need to coordinate or somehow share subjective expectations. What, then, will this neither market-fed nor hierarchy-led "clearance" of expectations look like?

Abstract formulations about deficiencies in the correspondence between objective interdependences and subjective perceptions have to be corroborated by falsifiable propositions. Instead of testing the "correspondence" thesis in the quantitative sense, this study focuses on a qualitative exposition of the arenas in which governments, firms and private interest groups meet, on a regular basis, each of them haunted by the ambiguities listed above – short-track independence ("sovereignty") combined with long-term interdependence ("subsidiarity") – and which is to be dealt with under conditions of imperfect rationality and limited accountability, and embedded in an institutional setting in which the *bottom-up* articulation of sectional interests and short-term demands proves to be easier than the *top-down* mobilization of long-term supports for collective purposes. Yet, there is more coordination in developed industrial society than is plausibly explained by the classics of rational egoism or Hirschman's countervailing forces of exit, voice and loyalty. Extrapolating from the empirical and theoretical material documented in earlier chapters, the solution to the dilemmas of subsidiarity and sovereignty may be sought at the intermediate or meso-level of governance. That level is believed to be the "cog wheel" between the micro- and macro-level where we may look for varieties of

> negotiated self-coordination [that] increases the scope of welfare maximizing "positive coordination" and create conditions under which externalities are inhibited through "negative coordination". In combination, these mechanisms are able to explain much of the de facto coordination that seems to exist beyond the confines of efficient markets and hierarchies. (Scharpf, 1994: 27)

Assessing the pertinence of this kind of conjecture requires the identification and operationalization of the micro- versus meta-conditions "between" which credible meso-commitments may arise. Starting from below, we must know how firms, state agencies and interest associations think about their *own* optimal levels of interest representation. More consequential, however, than the Olsonian *idées reçues* about the rationality traps *inside* public and private interest formations, may be the premise that states, firms and interest formations differ in their preferences about the optimal level of interest aggregation and reputation management of their *counterparts*. As noted before, who tends to win in these "battles of asymmetric preferences" depends not on the morality but on the *staying power* of the respective players, where staying power depends on the configuration of exit and entry opportunities from incumbent to substitute and emerging arenas. One of the novelties to be learned from the approach adopted here is that staying power is primarily a sociological specimen of "nestedness", rather than an instance of economic rationality or political stamina:

> Extraneous features of...initial conditions, the historical context in which institutions or organizations are formed, can become enduring constraints. They can result in the selection of a particular solution for what is then perceived at the time to be the crucial generic function ... the resulting quid pro quos...can limit the design of other rules and procedures, so that even if the organizational rationale were to become irrelevant, altering the organization's...policy would possibly disturb many other aspects of its operations and so impose considerable readjustment costs. In this way the organizational structure can become "locked in" to a comparatively narrow subset of routines, goals and future growth trajectories. (David, 1994: 214)

Assessments of this kind fit in well with our earlier observations on the anti-functionalist *cum* anti-teleological implications of interpreting "path dependences" from a wider than purely techno-economic perspective. Organizational "routines" and institutional "trajectories" show similar inert tendencies – in other applications sometimes called the "liability of newness". The latter explains "the possibility of persistent and systematic error-making and thereby non-optimising behaviour" (Hodgson, 1996, 265) – more convincingly than, for instance, explanations in terms of "animal spirits" and the like.

Routines and institutions are as indispensable for our understanding of the evolution of organizational "competences" and interorganizational "commitments" as stories about the evolutionary consequences of the techno-economic constraints of choice. Just as the sheer survival of organizational-institutional arrangements does not tell us about their efficiency, the decline or eclipse of governance structures does not demonstrate their *in*efficiency in the narrow sense of economic rationality. The "thickening" evidence on the micro-economic and sociological conditions underlying the meso-dynamics of institutional continuities and the evolution of macro-order (David, 1985; 1988; 1993; Arthur,

1989) shows how arbitrary choices and random events in the early days of a process may settle outcomes independent of any – past, present or future – demonstration of efficiency:

> In these path-dependent processes, one sees increasing returns to scale because once one of several competing technologies has a temporal lead in the number of users, this lead makes it profitable for various actors to improve it and to modify the environment in ways that facilitate further use. This further use again spurs improvements and reduces the profitability of improving competing but less-adopted technologies. Eventually, less efficient technologies may be locked-in by this train of events. What appear to be "random" events from an economic frame of reference can often be systematically treated in a sociological account. (Granovetter, 1992: 50–1)

"Economic theory can tell us a lot about policy alternatives, but unless our economics contains an understanding of power, it will not tell us enough to understand the choices actually made" (Gourevitch, 1986: 17). Economic models of efficient choice turn into empirical explanations of *effective* choice when economic doctrine is supplemented by sociological and political analysis. Economics is about the need, sociology about the room, and politics about the capacity to choose. Power is the outcome of the interplay of these three "agencies". Unless we combine need, room and capacity we will fail to understand why efficiency is rarely a sufficient, and seldom a necessary, precondition for the effectuation of choice – including the question where the systematics of *non*-choice come from. Those who have the capacity to manipulate the room to choose are in a position to define the need to choose. The room to choose is determined by the structure of the arena. Varying the *arena* (the "conditions" of the game) alters the agenda (the "codes" which define the stakes of the game). Changing the *agenda* affects the cohesion and versatility of the players: new divides may arise or old ones may resurface; loss of cohesion impairs an actor's versatility by weakening its sense of direction and resolve (the "mobilization" of bias) in the uses of entry and exit possibilities ("mobility"). Cohesion determines representativeness, and representativeness moderates reciprocities. Inter-actor inequalities in representativeness and imbalances in reciprocity determine the *timing*, that is the actual need for and urgency of reaching an agreement (the "commitments" of the game). *Diplomacy*, then, is *the capacity to play upon the interplay of arena, agenda and time* – a mix of positional strength and organizational skill, be it always moderated by a modicum of luck in choosing a specific mix of sovereignty and subsidiarity.

Box 8.12 The interplay of arena, agenda and timing : USA–EU negotiations on the "reciprocity of chemicals control"

The following example illustrates what we mean with "playing upon the interplay of arena, agenda and timing". In this case the definition of "reciprocity" appears to depend, first, on what the USA and the EU considered to be "representative" negotiators, as the latter qualification depends, inversely, on the kind of "reciprocity" each of the parties were aiming at. The chemicals control case is instructive indeed because it shows the subtleties of the trade-offs of subsidiarity and sovereignty – that is the workings of a nested game *in action*. In order to act as a coherent actor rather than as an ad hoc aggregate of member states with diverging corporate and trade interests, the European Union – in fact the European Commission – had to negotiate the necessary legal resources for acquiring a full mandate to engage in bilateral negotiations with the USA. For that "vertical" mandate the Commission had, first of all, to persuade the respective EU-member states to suspend their "horizontal" leanings toward sovereignty, that is to give up their chauvinist predisposition to advance their own interests in a multi-government setting. In addition, the Commission had to negotiate, this time *intra*-bureaucratically, a "horizontal" pact among the various Directorates that stick to their "sovereign" bureau-chauvinisms in a multi-aspect policy arena – including the environmental protection, health, trade and competition aspects of chemicals control policy. Only after the preliminary manufacture of this intra-European negotiated order, *on top* of the negotiated order *inside* the member states between government officials and corporate leaders of the national chemical industries, could horizontal negotiations with the USA take off.

According to Kenis and Schneider (1987), the Commission's competence to initiate policy in the control of toxic matters is split up into two competing domains. First, since 1973 the Environmental Action Program charges the Commission with measures to harmonize and strengthen control by public authorities over chemicals before they are brought to the market. Second, since diverging national regulatory preferences and practices within the Community may seriously affect the functioning of the Common Market as a "Union", Community action is also grounded in the treaty provisions for common trade policy in which the Commission, as opposed to environmental and health affairs, has far-reaching legal competences. In the inter-directorates' (continuing) rivalry in the toxic substances domain it is not the environmentalist's coalition which happened to win the intra-bureaucratic battle. As Biles (1983: 55, quoted in ibid.: 443) concludes:

It often has been stated that the basic policy objective of efforts to harmonize the US and European laws is the achievement of consistent and effective protection of health and the environment. However, economic considerations – in particular the avoidance (or minimization) of non-tariff trade barriers – constitute the principal force behind virtually all of these multilateral efforts.

However, in spite of the EU's legal powers to act as a representative player in trade affairs – its subsidiary "license to operate" even against the interest of individual member states – its resources in the chemical controls dispute were limited in the sense that the Union could criticize and challenge the US position but did not have anything to offer in the initial rounds of negotiation, because it had first to invoke, negotiate and legislate the "implied powers" principle for engaging in external relations in a domain (environmental and health policy) in which the Union had no immediate authorization according to the Treaty (ibid.: 444). As a consequence, it appeared relatively easy for the US to practice extensively the art of *re-*"nesting" the game to its own competitive advantage: while preferring to consider the negotiations within the Union as purely informal, the USA proposed to "locate" the formal negotiations within the broader OECD framework. The gains, for the USA, were twofold. First, by designating the OECD as the "relevant" arena for negotiating reciprocity, EU members could be reranked as "merely" a pack of nations among some 24 others; second, the OECD could be put on stage as truly "representative", because it included "all relevant" chemical producers (ibid.: 445).

Thus, by the elementary act of arena *substitution*, an initially bilateral small-number game, with concomitant monitoring and sanctioning contingencies, is transformed into a multilateral large-number game – benefiting the internally most coherent and externally more versatile player(s) on stage.

Earlier we marked the paradigm shift required to grasp the concentricity of order, games and actors, where credibility and commitments constitute the *substance* of a nested game and arena, agenda and timing its *parameters*. Instead of reiterating the details, it is more informative to recapitulate briefly the main assumptions and assertions that shore up the proposed construct:

1. In the circuits figuring in this study it is *economizing on commitments* (the goal), rather than on transactions (the means), that constitutes the basic drive behind firm-to-firm and government-to-business ententes and tacit understandings.
2. Economizing on transactions is based on efficiency considerations – inspired by the distrust of agents internally and the hazards of opportunism externally - governed by the *cognitive* limits of rationality – whereas economizing on commitments centers on the intended and

unintended consequences of the search for remediable or reversible interorganizational arrangements – governed by the *negotiated* limits of rationality and accountability. The two lead to diverging interpretations of the urge to hierarchize compared with the logic of in-, out- and cross-sourcing, and thus to different interpretations of the orchestration of corporate games.

3. Game theory, as a rule assuming a *fixed make-up* of the arena, agenda and timing of the game, is replaced by an approach that assumes a fuzzy make-up of this parametric "triangle", because it is only in the latter layout that the contingent and trial-and-error character of the links between *conditions, codes, commitments* and its *consequences* – that is, the (re)constitution of the negotiated order – will become apparent.

4. In this revised game-theoretical perspective firms, states and affiliated interest formations have to be treated as *composite* actors, each governed internally by "dominant coalitions", as opposed to the monolithic, black-box treatment that predominates the literature – from micro-game-theory ("representative/ unitary actor") to macro-system-level ("weak state/strong state") treatises.

5. In addition, the static and introvert conceptualization of "dominant coalitions" has to be replaced by a dynamic and extravert interpretation, stipulating that players' choices, games and order are the cumulative yield of a *two-way traffic*, that is "internal coalitions, (pre-) selecting external alliances" and "external alliances, (re)conditioning internal coalitions".

6. Internal coalitions generate the mobilization – of bias that underlies organizational *predispositions*. External alliances are the *biased* (while internally filtered) response to externally perceived threats and opportunities, that is organizational *dispositions*.

7. Predispositions and dispositions are the cause and consequence of organizational boundary and arena-spanning activities. *Intelligent* players are those who manage to find an appropriate mix of consolidation and in-, out- and cross-sourcing activitities – where "appropriate" means creating a (moving) mix of horizontal, vertical and collateral commitments that enables organizations to keep options open without forfeiting its internal and external prerequisites of credibility (like a critical minimum of internal coherence and the willing suspension of "unconditional" selfishness – as for instance when embarking on relation-specific investments with external parties).

Box 8.13   Unidentified flying objectives

Note that "market intelligence" in this make-up is at odds with the demand-side oriented and overtly prescriptive notion of "core" competencies that prevails in the strategic management literature. In that part of the literature "competence" figures as an organization's "dynamic capability" of "infusing products with irresistible functionality" or, better yet, "creating products that customers need but have not yet imagined" (the reader is invited to reread the overblown proclamation of "the new standard" in an award-winning article by Prahalad and Hamel (1994) that triggered the "core competency"-hype in trendy management journals and monographs). Once adopted by the rhetoric of the executive boardroom, however, "core" competencies appear to be sails set according to how the wind blows. For example, the former Belgian–Dutch bank *Fortis*, confronted with a dramatic, more than two-thirds, dive in its market value after having bitten off (together with two other consortium partners) more than it could chew, its share of the Dutch *ABN-AMRO* bank, announced in summer 2008, with an eye on bolstering its crumpled balance sheet, that it would sell "non-core assets" worth about €2 billion. Incidentally, barely three months later, it had "identified" again another bunch of "non-core assets" worth up to €10 billion – such as its "private banking" or "clearing and asset management units" (*The International Herald Tribune*, September 27–28, 2008). After such an abysmal reappraisal of a corporation's "core" competences, "products with irresistible functionality", or, better yet, "products that customers need but have not yet imagined", start to taste differently.

Our *supply*-side conception of "intelligence", instead, is a descriptive, as opposed to prescriptive, amalgam of strength, skill and intuition – luck sides with the prepared – referring to the Schumpeter/Schelling legacies on the ability – however precarious – for creating (new) resources and/or partner combinations. With this "double face" of intelligence I reiterate our earlier discussion on the coordinates of bargaining power and the credibility of commitments. By linking power and commitments a *positive* (testable) canon of governance comes within reach: as has to be demonstrated, governance – according to its etymology defined as *the art of navigation* – is the ability to mobilize the winning internal coalitions for mobilizing external allies, which is required for the realization of new value-creating combinations. The mobilization of internal coalitions is a (resources-based) *entrepreneurial* competence and the mobilization of external allies a (partners-based) *diplomatic* skill. Neither ownership nor formal control entitlements but the de facto *range of command* over critical resources and partnerships decides about the "direction" of organizations, that is, about the credibility – in terms of substance and duration – of their internal and external commitments.

Versatility: a primer on strategic responsiveness

The transition from the old to the new discipline represents a contrast in the *modes* of coping with commitments. Culturally, the contrast represents a three-step change in dominant *beliefs:* from a historical belief in the virtues of tight-knit ties ("neo-corporatism") to the presumption of the weakness of strong ties (the "competitive advantage of nations" adage), and for the last decade or so to a settled and sublimated belief in the superiority of weak over strong ties (the "corporate governance" dispute, ranking the "contrasts" between "Anglo-American" versus "Asian" versus "Rhineland" regimes). What seems to be missing, thus far, is insight into a fourth possibility, that is the strength (or weakness) of *revolving* ties. Structurally – when switching from an evaluative to a matter-of-fact approach – the above-sketched sequence of beliefs may be reinterpreted as the outcome of growing divergences in the room, need and capacity of firms and states to form strategic and tactical combinations. In our study the need, room and capacity are hypothesized to be related to inter-firm, inter-state and firm-to-state mobility and mobilization differentials. When we designate mobility and mobilization conditions as the explanantia, the stability and substance of the resulting negotiated orders is the *explanandum*. Mobility and mobilization differentials refer to the variability of the openness of the boundaries of organizations and arenas. In this set-up the strength or weakness of interorganizational ties is not an (irreversible) *historical* but a (comparative) sector-, technology- or economy-specific phenomenon – where more than anything else changes in the life cycle of technologies, sectors and so on, are hypothesized to entail changes in the sort of prevailing (stage-specific) negotiated order. Figure 8.3 summarizes the possibility of the *coexistence* of different regimes of concerted action *within one and the same national or regional "business system"* (see Chapter 5 and my earlier comments on the flaws of "system-level" studies in Chapter 7).

Figure 8.3 should be read as the complement of Figure 7.4. The labels of the games of "ordering" in Figure 8.3 differ from the labels used in Chapter 7, since the focus in Figure 7.4 is on the classification of different forms of *regime discipline*, whereas Figure 8.3 focuses on the modes of coping with different mixes of competitive and symbiotic interdependence, that is on different modalities of corporate *diplomacy*. Clearly, the two are interrelated, and are needed for the next step: the classification of different sorts of strategic *responsiveness*.

A classification of different sorts of corporate games as a function of contrasting mobility and mobilization conditions is definitely not

		Arena boundaries	
		Fixed	Variable
Organizational boundaries	Closed	Ordering of the game based on *Segmentation* of dependence[1]	Ordering of the game based on *Pooling* of dependence[2]
	Open	Ordering of the game based on *Nesting* of dependence[3]	Ordering of the game based on *Rotation* of dependence[4]

Figure 8.3 Corporate diplomacy: sector-specific modes of coping with interdependence

[1] E.g. shipbuilding and extraction industries; [2] e.g. information-technology and telecom industries; [3] e.g. aircraft and automotive industries; [4] e.g. pharmaceutical and bio-technology industries.

sufficient to qualify for a comprehensive *causal* explanation. As regards this, a formidable task remains: we have got to clarify how "gross" associations between contrasting mobility and mobilization with (1) fixed versus variable arenas, and (2) open versus closed organizations, can be made "net" by connecting them to an underlying set of more specific parameters. The latter include two broad categories. First, there are objective *arena* characteristics that affect organizational dispositions to competitive and collaborative moves. As will be outlined hereafter, I think that the most critical characteristics under this heading include: (1) large versus small-number game attributes that affect the *observability* of threats and promises ("observability" defines the objective *room* for mutual monitoring); (2) the presence and duration of (financial, organizational and institutional) *lock-ins* that affect the *credibility* of threats and promises (credibility defines the objective *need* for mutual sanctioning). Second, there are subjective *organization* characteristics that explain variations in *pre*dispositions, that is the mobilization of bias in subjective organizational responses to the above-mentioned objective dispositions (i.e. the "room for monitoring" and "need for sanctioning").

Coupling dispositions and predispositions points to an underexplored territory at the crossroads of strategy and institutional analysis and the theory of games: the issue of corporate responsiveness, that is the comparative *capacity* of organizations for exploiting variations in the room for monitoring and the need for sanctioning. As will be discussed later, the main modalities of responsiveness include the way organizations handle the (interrelated) choices of competence, competition and concerted action.

The concluding sections of this chapter are devoted to each of these topics. The distinction between dispositions and predispositions opens a venue for upgrading the "mechanistic" interpretation of social order into a genuine causal explanation (in the sense of Elster, 1989b: 3–10): considering games and strategies as a function of mobility and mobilization conditions offers a more precise articulation of the modus operandi of the generative principles of political economic order. The following is a summary of the research agenda ahead of us.

Diplomacy: back to basics

There exists a lavish library on competitive and collaborative strategies, ranging from descriptive surveys to in-depth case studies. Nothing of comparable quantity and quality is available on the variables behind the processes of strategy formation that might explain why organizations, in spite of similar exposure to environmental pressures, differ in their *sensitivity* to those pressures and why some of them respond more promptly to external threats and opportunities than others do. Even less adequate is our understanding of the structural impact of these response variations on mutations of the environment itself. The sum of the two unknowns leaves us with a poor understanding of the *drivers* of corporate and industrial change.

Explicit attention for the causes and consequences of organizational responses may serve as a corrective for the typical flaws that we found earlier in the mainstreams of strategy thinking, game theory and institutionalization analysis. First, finding out about the determinants of variability in responsiveness will serve as an antipode to the solipsism of strategic management approaches that neglect the pre-committed (while path-dependent) and indeterminate (while interactive) nature of strategy processes. Second, attention for the variability of strategic responses corrects for the over-socialized and deterministic leanings of institutional analysis, which asserts that embeddedness "cements" structure and that structure "fixes" strategic choice. Third, allowing for variations in responsiveness nuances the leveling axiomatics of "minimax regret" and bandwagoning or "imitation" theory – all of them implying that more often than not uniform responses and herd behavior determine the bulk of strategic conduct, and that strategic "conformism" should be held accountable for much of the (waves of) "irrationality" of, for instance, merger and acquisition practices. Alternatively, and perhaps even more importantly, a nuanced theory of strategic responses renounces a curious feature of strategic, institutional and game-theoretical analysis alike, that is the propensity to treat actors as a black box, saddled with a largely uniform (though not perfect) rationality, living in a largely fixed (though not uniform) environment. A theory of the *variability* of responses, instead, may help to get rid of this sort of academic simplification, and may be instrumental in restoring the triple assignment of positivist theory, to wit: first, *explaining how internal nexuses of coalitions and compromises precondition the selection of external allies and commitments*; second, *how these external nexuses of alliances and commitments, recondition the fate of internal coalitions and compromises*; and third, *how this cycle of iterative causations explains the co-evolution of corporate games and capitalist order.*

The analysis of response variability touches upon the stock themes of organizational diplomacy and discipline, set out in the first chapter (on the "tragedy of the commons" and its complement, the "tragedy of the fallows") and epitomized in the topos of Chapter 3: how to explain the emergence of concertation among rational egoists in the absence of hierarchy? As outlined earlier, rational choice theory, though starting from the "universals" of selfishness and short-termism, allows for transitions from adversarial ("zero-sum") to cooperative ("positive-sum") games, provided actors learn from earlier experiences ("the shadows of the past") and/or anticipate the typical characteristics of a game that has got to be repeated ("the shadows of the future"). Learning and anticipation are believed to assuage selfishness and to check for the potential damage of low trust and mutual defection dynamics. The gain from this line of reasoning lies in its explicit attention to how the "accuracy" and "promptness" of reciprocation affect the eventual evolution of cooperative versus non-cooperative games. The accuracy of monitoring and the speed of responding with proportionate sanctions (positive *and* negative) were said to influence the chances of cooperation. For example: waiting too long – assuming symmetry in monitoring – may suggest that defection pays; on the other hand, responding too promptly – given the risk of misinterpreting the other's choices – may trigger uncontrollable cascades of retaliation, and so on. Generally speaking, the more transparent the terms of exchange and the shorter the timing of response, the better the chances for stable cooperation.

Though certainly instrumental for an elementary feeling for the *consequences* of transparency and promptness, we learn little to nothing from this perspective about the *causes* of the accuracy of monitoring and the proportionality of responding. Social science, as a rule, approaches questions of cooperation and order by relating monitoring and sanctioning to "proximity" in its various meanings – from physical closeness to cultural affinities and the socio-psychological correlates of *Gemeinschaft*. The closer a community, the denser its communication system; the denser the communication, the more transparent and accountable, and thus the more credible, the threats and promises. The reasoning sounds plausible, regardless of whether one subscribes to a rationalist, a norm-based or a reputational perspective. (Even to invest in a reputation for being *ir*responsible pays more in a close-knit community than in an anonymous world.) As Elster argues:

> Tit-for-tat arguments work best in small and stable societies, in which there is a high probability that the same people will interact over and over again. Conversely, in modern societies interaction is often too ephemeral for implicit promises and threats to ensure cooperation ...
> Traditional communities enforce cooperation in three distinct ways: by promoting stronger emotional bonds among the members, by providing more effective sanctions for promise breaking and by increasing the scope for long-term self-interest. (Elster, 1989a: 285–6)

In spite of its intuitive plausibility, many a treatise on social cohesion and order tends to concede that

> the partial answers ... provided are several sizes smaller than the questions. Altruism, envy, social norms and self-interest all contribute, in complex, interactive ways to order, stability and cooperation. Some mechanisms that promote stability also work against cooperation. Some mechanisms that facilitate cooperation also increase the level of violence. (Ibid.: 287)

However deservingly as a stance, it must be possible by now to be less inconclusive about the numerous instances of both order – *without* proximity – and disorder *in spite of* proximity that we have come across in these chapters. (It is not without irony that the damages of the tragedy of the commons and its mirror, the parable of the "undergrazed" fallows, are both – metaphorically speaking – locked up in the face-to-face encounters of a *proximate* community.) The notion of proximity, therefore, seems too primitive for understanding the links between the immediacy of monitoring and sanctioning and the emergence of order and discipline. For our insight into the role of monitoring and sanctioning – and, thus, in the causes and consequences of responsiveness – for the evolution of disciplinary arrangements, more can be learned from looking at *disparities* and *changes* in proximity, than by focusing on the role of proximity *as such* (as in a comparative static set-up that is leaving processual variables out). Moreover, successive revolutions in electronics and telecommunications tend to attenuate the importance of proximity and to promote *virtual* proximity as a substitute for physical nearness, thus making "reachability" and "likeness" more pertinent candidates for explaining disciplinary arrangement than proximity in the spatial, cultural or psychological sense.

For a first approximation of the forces that influence the speed and substance of responses in a competitive adversarial setting, we have to turn to those parts of the non-mainstream literature that go into the real-life complexities of information seeking and processing, the interpretive uncertainties that go with signaling and bluffing, and the interactive effects of the timing, number and nature of the rival's responses. A meticulous example is provided by Smith et al. (1992). Their research avoids the coarse-grained analysis of aggregate industrial economics and, on the other hand, allows for aspects of bounded rationality that are not well "hosted" by conventional game theory and micro-economic analysis. Smith et al. work from a sequential stimulus-response model containing the following components: the actor (the firm that takes a competitive action); the action (a new product, a price cut, an advertising campaign); the responder (the actor's rival); a communication channel connecting actor and responder (such as a common supplier, common customer or public reports of the action); noise in the environment (influencing the manner in which the responder decodes the competitor's actions); and a feedback loop (signifying that the rival's response will act as a new stimulus evoking new responses). Further refinements in these categories include the *reputation* of the actors in terms of market leadership, management experience and past competitive behavior. The *action* is differentiated in terms of radicalism, magnitude, scope and implementation requirements, since these characteristics will affect the credibility of a competitive threat. The *responder* is characterized with criteria such as its external orientation, structural complexity (affecting information processing capacities), organizational slack and management experience. Competitive *responses* are assessed in terms of number of responders, response firm, response likelihood, response order and the room for controlling rivalry. The latter has to do with general characteristics of the *environment* in which actors and responders operate, such as (information on) the structure of an industry and the overall context of competition. A central tenet of the authors' approach is that firms rarely know what the outcome of their competitive moves will be, since the successfulness of action and response depends on complex combinations of the above listed factors: "Given this complexity, we assume that the outcomes of competitive actions and responses are virtually always uncertain to managers at the onset" (ibid.: 22). What about the follow-up, when competitive moves, instead of being a one-shot affair, become part of a *repetitive* or sequential game?

For a broader understanding of the determinants and outcomes of corporate *responsiveness*, the evidence from this piece of research on competitive responses may serve as a starting point. In particular the observations on the ease and speed of imitation by actors' rivals and the role of reputation of first movers are of special interest for gaining a better insight into the dynamics of competitive (and collaborative) behavior. Both have to do with the timing and order of moves and countermoves.

Box 8.14   Imitation and reputation

The size of first mover advantages is influenced by the relative ease with which rivals can imitate incumbents' moves. The possibility of imitation increases first movers' *dis*advantages. Seldom do first movers know, a priori, how successful their actions will be. First movers get locked into advertising campaigns on which account later movers may take a free ride. "Incumbent inertia" may block first moving firms from improving product and processing designs. Being a "fast second" mover may mitigate this sort of "first mover" disadvantage. Fast followers may realize cost savings derived from superior information, ranging from imitative learning to seeing the environment more clearly by observing responses to first movers' initiatives. Thus, timing and order in competitive rivalry have a significant impact on firms' performance, because waiting – the willing *suspension* of imitation – allows more time for market uncertainty to clear (Smith et al., 1992: 138–58; for some forerunners of this approach, see Teece, 1986; Wernerfelt and Karnani, 1987; Lieberman and Montgomery, 1988; and Scherer and Ross, 1990).

Timing and order of response enter in yet another way as a function of players' reputation. When a firm's reputation for predictability increases and its perceived aggressiveness decreases, competitors tend to respond more slowly. Reputed price predators elicit faster responses than do their less aggressive counterparts. Having a reputation for moves of greater magnitude or strategic potential appears to slow down rivals' responses. As the scale and implementation requirements of a competitive move increase, response time also rises; but as the threat potential of a move increases, response time declines. Responses tend to be slower, when the radicalism of a move and the importance of information on earlier moves, rise (Smith et al., 1992: 178–81). The net effect of imitation and reputation on the propensity to respond on competitive moves is furthermore influenced by intervening variables like structural complexity, length of top management's industry experience, the size of organizational slack, profit-maximizing orientation at the cost of other corporate goals, an industry's life cycle being in the emerging growth rather than the mature and fragmenting stage – all of these conditions appear to attenuate the propensity to respond in an imitative manner to competitive moves. Summing up, "a slow second strategy for easy-to-imitate moves is preferable to being a first mover, a fast second, a slow third, and a late mover" (ibid.: 181).

However instructive, for several reasons the foregoing is just a first step in the construction of a fully fledged model of strategic responsiveness. It is, first of all, a story about tactical maneuvers (as in tit-for-tats in pricing behavior) and tactical imitation (as in advertisement campaigns), so definitely not about strategy (e.g. investment decisions) and strategic imitation (such as mergers and acquisition and resources and partner switches; for an update and upgrading of their framework over the last decade, including future directions in the study of the impact of corporate strategies on changing resource configurations and industry structure, see Smith et al., 2001). Perhaps though it is even less than this story, since data on signaling, bluffing and other specimens of the familiar arsenal of competitive stratagems are left out. Since the analysis does not start from the elementary determinants of strategic dispositions – such as the observability and the structure of dependence among firms – we are left in the lurch with our questions about the need, room and capacity for strategic responses. The *need* – to respond derives from competitive and technological pressures, the *room* – for response from small versus large-number game characteristics, historical lock-ins and future holdups and the *capacity* – to respond from organizational governance attributes (that feed back on the *perception* of the need and room to respond). Missing these basic distinctions, nothing useful can be said about the causes and the interaction effects of slow versus rapid responses. Being ignorant about the sources of dispositions and the consequences of responsiveness, nothing can be said about the way firms handle their dilemmas of the competence and competition trap.

A proxy for answering these questions in a more systematic mode may be sought in a realignment of game theory and transaction costs analysis. With that the puzzles of disorder and discipline among rational egoists re-enter – from competitors in their horizontal moves and countermoves to producers in their vertical exchanges with suppliers and customers. As shown before, private ordering rests on credible threats and promises – so thereby the explanation of competitive dispositions and organizational responsiveness turns into an analysis of the preconditions of credible firm-to-firm commitments (with concomitants spillovers to the credibility of semi-market and business-to-state commitments). The literature working at the crossroads of game theory and transactional analysis offers numerous entries for understanding the repertoire by which rivals or suppliers and customers may arrive at credible commitments – such as the exchange of transaction-specific assets that, though increasing a firm's exposure, at the same time may attenuate the risks of mutual opportunism and misappropriation. A widespread, but under-researched example is hostage or bond posting by the mutual exchange of dedicated assets:

> Dedicated assets [are] discrete additions to generalized capacity that would not be put in place but for the prospect of selling a large amount of product to a particular customer. Premature termination of the contract by the buyer would leave the supplier with a large excess of capacity that could be disposed of only at distressed prices. Requiring buyers to post a bond would mitigate this hazard, but only by posing another: the supplier may contrive to expropriate the bond... reciprocal trading supported by separate but concurrent investments in specific assets provides a mutual safeguard against this second class of hazards. The hostages that are thereby created have the interesting property, moreover, that they are *never exchanged*. Instead, each party retains possession of its dedicated assets should the contract be prematurely terminated. (Williamson, 1983: 532)

The unmistakable advance of this sort of approach is that it goes back to the heartland of capitalist coordination dilemmas. First, microanalytical interest in "asset specificity" helps to sow the seeds of the *competence* trap: specialization is inevitable in the perennial gale of competition but poses problems of path dependence and competitive inflexibility that may result in bargaining disadvantages ("holdup"). Second, cooperative agreements, both among competitors and between suppliers and customers, pose the problem of the *competition* trap: either there are too many followers or the necessary complementary investments fail to materialize – for instance because would-be partners fear (mutual or unilateral) defection. All of these may be seen as variations on the paralysis-by-parallelism adage of the prisoner's dilemma.

Yet, looking at the frequency of cooperative agreements in everyday life, both of the horizontal and vertical sorts, two observations seem to the point. First, for explaining the occurrence of cooperative behavior in-spite-of selfishness, a too premature appeal is made to the (mostly *ex post*) imputed presence of "exogeneous norms of cooperative behavior" (Hirschman, 1982: 1470). Williamson, instead, presumes that due to the micro-analytic neglect of the real-life practices of bonding and other, more subtle, ways of organizing for mutually reliable commitments, the "practical significance" of the allegedly frustrating effects of the "prisoner's dilemma to the study of exchange has been vastly exaggerated" (Williamson, 1983: 538). Scharpf, equally on empirical grounds, seems to adhere to a similar position, although his "solution" of the miracle of "cooperation – without hierarchy" rests on the somewhat more *civilized* idea that positive coordination may emerge (and last) whenever the criterion of a so-called Kaldor optimum is met: that is, cooperation may result when the benefits for those who gain are large enough to compensate as fully as possible the losses of those who stand to lose by cooperating (Scharpf, 1991: 624; 1994: 38–40). Whether and under what conditions the latter criterion will be satisfied *in practice* – when the *deus ex machina* of hierarchically imposed (re)distributive justice is ruled out (as is done in the rules of the game of Axelrodian game theory) – has to do with a second observation. An immediate and profane reason why "rational egoism" *under*-predicts competitive and complementary collaboration lies in the rationalists' trained ignorance of initial and self-reinforcing disparities in bargaining power. As will be further explained below, disparities in bargaining power have everything to do with a variable I hinted at earlier: (mutations in) *disparities in proximity*.

By letting power back in, the mystery of "cooperation" loses much of its mysteriousness. Among its earthly characteristics belong the *observability* of moves and countermoves and the relevant *range* of dependences – from customers to competitors and from firms to states – since it is only in this extended make-up that we may see how horizontal dependences come to be used for the orchestration of vertical dependences (or how vertical dependences may be used as a leverage for domesticating horizontal dependences); it can even be shown how horizontal actors eventually turn into vertical or lateral players and vice versa. To this should be added a reassessment of the narrow meaning of "asset specificity", by including in its scope the relation-specific corollaries of organizational ("brains") and institutional assets ("connectedness"). Extending the scope from techno-financial to organizational and institutional specificities alters our conception of the dynamics of cooperation and competition quite radically. In the following two sections I will spell out the implications of observability and dependence for the credibility of cooperative and competitive commitments, and trace the consequences of credibility for the logic of actors, games and social order. These digressions on policing and sanctioning enable us to mark more sharply what remains to be done for crafting a genuine theory of concertation that covers the full "ladder": from micro-dispositions and predispositions to macro-consequences, and back.

A digression on monitoring

The room for policing hangs, primarily, on the visibility and causal understandability of actors' moves and countermoves. The bulk of research on bargaining focuses upon the analysis of information processes and communication tactics, at the expense of the analysis of dependence relationships and the interaction of dependence and information processing. Remarkably enough against the background of the increasing internal ("disaggregative") complexity of organizations and the blurring of organizational boundaries, interest in the impact of *internal* information and bargaining processes on external information and bargaining practices has been declining. The classics on bargaining – from civil rights to labor relations and inter-state negotiations – pay as much attention to internal as to external information and communication practices and principles. As noted earlier Walton and McKersie (1965) for instance devote a substantial part of their analysis to the internal processes of consensus formation and activities which bring the expectation of "principals" into alignment with the negotiating "agents" that bargain on the former's fiat or mandate. Explicit attention for these intra-organizational constraints seems all the more justified since opposing negotiators, because of their role as "boundary spanners" or "gatekeepers", often find themselves more in agreement with their *counterparts* than with their own principals or constituencies. Even a substantial part of bargaining sophistication and brinkmanship may consist of tacit understandings between the opposing negotiators for assisting *each other* in the bargains with their own principals and constituencies. For learning more about this we have to turn to areas of research and analysis which formally lie outside the field of bargaining theory, such as transaction and contract-theory analysis. For instance, principal-agent theorizing (Akerlof, 1970; Jensen and Meckling, 1976; Fama and Jensen, 1983; Scharpf, 1990; Noorderhaven, 1990) tells us about the consequences of information asymmetries among contracting parties (employers versus employees; producers versus subcontractors; voters versus politicians; firms versus governments; or patients versus doctors) and indicates why, for reasons of efficiency, market and spot contracting tend to be superseded by hierarchical or relational control recipes wherever principals seek to reduce for themselves the (residual) risks of information inequality and "moral hazard". By reducing the problems of fairness and loyalty in two-party transactions to problems of *monitoring*, principal-agent approaches stay spiritually in the family of bounded rationality cum opportunism assumptions. A dependence view differs from an informational and moral imperfections view by relating the limits of rationality to the organizational and institutional "embeddedness" of human action (following the "where you stand, and how you behave, depends on where you sit"-maxim). In that spirit it would make more sense to speak of *bound* rationality in two respects: first, *between* the deviations of organizations from perfect rationality which originate in historical lock-ins and/or holdups, and from anticipated concerns about the eventuality of competitive imitation and/or insufficient environmental sponsorship for new ventures; second, *within* the deviations of organizations from perfect rationality which stem from "reverse" decision-making routines, observing that organizations discover preferences – by acting, *ex post*, rather than by carrying out actions on the base of their *ex ante* preferences (Cohen et al., 1972: 11–12). Analogous to the bounds of rationality stemming from external dependences and reciprocations, the logic of discovery internally follows the path of internal dependences and "provoked" reciprocities. In Allison's renowned formulation:

> In policy-making, then, the issue looking *down* is options: how to preserve my leeway until time clarifies uncertainties. The issue looking *sideways* is commitment: how to get others committed to my coalition. The issue looking *upwards* is confidence: how to give the boss confidence in doing what must be done. (Allison, 1969: 711)

Considered from an internal bargaining perspective and the analysis of intra-organizational coalition-formation processes, agency theory can be seen as an informational supplement to (or game-theoretical formalization of) the transaction-costs approach. A comparable assessment applies for the growing literature on "relational contracting" (after MacNeil, 1978). Though more explicitly attentive for questions of trust, dependence-based solidarity and norm-led behavior, "relational contracting" shares with "principal-agent" analysis the reductionist tendency to interpret the quest for reciprocity under conditions of imperfect legal enforceability and contractual holdups essentially, again, as a problem of imperfect *monitoring*. As a consequence, neither of the two can be called in as a cogent corrective for the flawless "efficient-hierarchy" illusion of the transactionalists. The diplomacy paradigm, instead, starts from an "elective-partnership" illusion for explaining the formation and dissemination of strategies – which indeed is no less an *illusion* while always being constrained by the spatial and temporal "nestedness" of rational choice. At variance with the preoccupation with monitoring problems currently in favor in rational-choice theory and its applications in institutional industrial economics, the *diplomatic* actor model conceives of the limits of rationality primarily as a *rationalization* of past holdups and future lock-ins which organizations are bound to learn to live with once their fates are interconnected.

The diplomacy paradigm argues that information asymmetry is only part of the story. Informational properties should be seen as a non-sufficient, maybe even a non-necessary, condition for deciding about the net distribution of power between the players: solving a monitoring problem ("asymmetry of information") is not synonymous with solving the competitive and collaborative dilemmas originating from other sources – for instance the "asymmetry of asset-specific investments" (the issue of so-called "holdups"). The phenomena of "adverse selection" and "coercive deficiency" in which principals are made hostage to defecting agents (as, for example, in the case of depressed industries successfully pressing for protracted state support and protection) cannot be explained by informational asymmetries solely. Rational choice – the epistemological canon on which agency and relational-contracting theorizing rests – abstracts from inter-actor contrasts in strategic dispositions (or equates dispositions, at best, with differences in the *timing* of the clearing of information, as in the case of early versus late movers). By leaving out real (positional) or perceived (reputational) differences in dispositions – for instance of investment banks vis-à-vis client firms, or producers compared to suppliers, or new entrants versus incumbent players, or firms negotiating with states – no informed guesses can be made about the net credibility of resulting commitments. Informational and moral hazards aside, contrasts in dispositions stem from (perceived or real) contrasts in *maneuverability*. The latter makes clear why it is imperative to distinguish between the *need* for monitoring and the *room* for sanctioning. What a diplomatic actor model aspires to correct for is the neglect of the latter in the agency and relational contracting offspring of rational-choice theory: differences in maneuverability lie at the heart of asymmetries in sanctioning potential between principals and agents or any other sort of contracting relationships. Leaving other things out, differences in bargaining power, and thus in commitments and disciplinary arrangements, are based upon them.

In short, rational choice and consorts do not constitute a negotiation theory. By forgetting to treat monitoring and sanctioning as analytically distinct phenomena, rational choice and associates are not in a position to foretell what will happen when information *symmetry* coincides with sanctioning *asymmetry*. By substituting the notion of "negotiated discipline" for the elusive notion of "monitoring by hierarchy", our diplomatic-actor perspective opens the possibility to discuss a wider range of arrangements for handling informational and moral hazards. The latter appears better suited to explain the miracle of order *without hierarchy* (as well as, incidentally, the incidence of hierarchy *without order*) than approaches that lump discipline and hierarchy together as interchangeable labels for a single phenomenon.

A digression on sanctioning

Arrangements for orchestrating firm-to-firm and government-to-business relationships are arrangements for the "domestication" (in various guises: segmentation, pooling, nesting or rotation, see Figure 8.3) of dependence relationships. As noted at the start of this chapter, dependences change due to shifts in the patterns of territorial, functional and sectoral mobility, followed by the blurring of (functional, territorial, etc.) boundaries between firms, states and interest groups. Focusing on mobility sensitizes for the paradox of the *convertibility* of dependence in neither purely authoritative nor purely competitive settings. Under conditions of mutual dependence agents may turn into principals; customers and producers may coincide and share common interests, as in the case of the steel industry in its early days needing railways both as a customer *and* as an efficient supplier of coal transport (a catalogue of telling examples of the "interchangeability" of competitors, suppliers and customers is listed in Brandenburger and Nalebuff, 1996). "Normal" science focuses on power in terms of coercive proficiency, assuming power and the negotiated order to be a function of an actor's eventual survival *surplus* of cash, competence and connections. Approaching the quest for power and order from the perspective of reversibility – the essence of "strategic dependence" – sensitizes for the possibility that the threat of coercive *deficiency* may be as decisive in the enactment of concerted action and negotiated orders as proficiency.

Box 8.15 The conversion of power

Weak but flexible players may be more powerful than strong but path-dependent adversaries. An "undisciplined" *node* in a chain of strong mutual dependences may derive disproportionate power from its "contagious" potential to disrupt the integrity of the chain as a whole. It is not the dramatic losses and pending bankruptcy of a mighty international investment bank or national producer, but rather its dependent suppliers and customers, that may be decisive in the mass protest against a government's (or private bank's) refusal to rescue an ailing colleague or client.

In the example of the massive opposition against the *Vredeling* directive (aiming at an EU-wide harmonization of workers councils' rights for the subsidiaries of European multinational firms) it was the loosely organized EU confederation of employers' associations (UNICE, the Union of industrial and employers' Confederations of Europe) that mobilized the more tightly organized national federations to pressure COREPER (the Permanent Committee of top civil service member states' representatives in Brussels) to oppose the directive; meanwhile the member state governments deflected hostility of the national trade unions and public opinion (all of them largely in favor of the Vredeling directive) by referring to the "undivided" opposition of UNICE (Middlemas, 1995: 492). In all these instances it remains unclear who claims or disclaims the role of principal or agent. As a rule, the powerful are those who know when to pose as powerless, switching from high to low profile, and when it pays to pose as intractable.

Most of these instances are skillfully exploited, if not consciously cultivated, variations on a classical asset: the nuisance or *obstruction* value of an actor. Approaching questions of power and order from the capacity of actors to upset the negotiated order implies a conceptualization of power that does not suffer from the methodological and operationalization pitfalls that we come across in the more familiar definitions of power. Contrary to notions such as "A's capacity to reduce B's alternative options" or "A's pressure inducing B to behave otherwise than B would have done in the absence of A's pressure" or, alternatively, "A's ability to organize away certain interests or issues from the bargaining table" – I propose, instead, to define power as an actor's capacity to maintain or improve his or her *maneuverability* in a situation of strategic dependence, so as effectively to manipulate the "scope of controversy". An attractive methodological difference with the notions of "coercion", "pressure" and "non-decision making" listed above is that the definition proposed here absolves us from the impossible mission to probe (*ex post*) or prove (*ex ante*) the degree of *intentionality* of the agents of power. In a negotiated order (alias nested-games) perspective, the freedom of maneuvering of one or more players may – intentionally or unintentionally – result in a loss of maneuverability for others. Negotiating power, then, is a function of the costs to actor A of imposing – *with or without intent* – a loss of maneuverability upon others. It is not the intentionality but the *probability* of the outcome that counts.

Box 8.16   A note on "as if" economics

My stance on matters of "intentionality" – thus, by implication, "rationality" – subscribes to Max Weber's insistence on the *subjective* nature of purposeful economic action:

> *Die Definition des Wirtschaftens…hat zum Ausdruck zu bringen, dass alle "wirtschaftlichen" Vorgänge und Objekte ihr Gepräge als solche gänzlich durch den **Sinn** erhalten, welche menschliches Handeln ihnen – als Zweck, Mittel, Hemmung, Nebenerfolg – gibt…Denn auf die **Glauben** an die Notwendigkeit der Vorsorge, nicht auf die objektive Notwendigkeit, kommt es an.* (Economic behavior is what people define as "making sense" in serving material needs and providing necessities – as a "goal, mean, constraint or side-effect"…What matters is what is *believed* to be necessary, not the objective necessity.) (Weber, 1964 [1922]: 44, bold added)

Or, alternatively:

> *Von Wirtschaft wollen…wir…nur reden, wo einen Bedürfnis…ein …, nach der Schätzung des Handelnden, knapper Vorrat von Mitteln und möglichen Handlungen zu seiner Deckung gegenüber steht…Entscheidend ist dabei für zweckrationales Handeln selbstverständlich: das diese Knappheit **subjektiv** vorausgesetzt und das Handeln daran orientiert ist.* (Decisive for goal-rational conduct is self-evidently that the scarcity of means and possible actions for need fulfillment is **subjectively** presupposed and that acting is oriented at that predisposition.) (Ibid.: 257)

"Modern" economic science solves the thorny problem of subjective attributions by *negating* it: economists counter the reproach of perfect rationality by asserting that their models of economic man are based on the assumption that ("as if") actors choose in a rational-calculative manner. This heuristic immunization, obviously, does not solve the core of the puzzle of strategic choice, that is the assessment of the nature and extent of the bounds of rationality and the identification of the scenarios that actors use to minimize the odds (or maximize the benefits) of the limits of rationality.

My stance, in short, is that actors have a subjective notion of the tentative impact on others of their own choices and will act accordingly. It is an *empirical* task to find out how and *why* actors differ in their grip on reality, both concerning the maneuverability that follows from their own past and future choices and the maneuverability that follows from the bonds of their opposites.

The costs to oneself of imposing a loss of maneuverability upon others, varies. It is *this* variation that determines an actor's "net" bargaining power in situations of interdependent choice and unforeseen resource spillovers. As set out before, the bases of bargaining power are:

1. *Horizontal* mobility: an actor's freedom, compared to others, to form, alter or substitute coalitions *around* parallel interests at a *specific* level of interest accommodation and conflict containment (e.g. firms, trade unions or state agencies considered *sui generis*).
2. *Vertical* mobility: an actor's room, relative to others, for forming, altering or substituting alliances *across* the confines of parallel interests at *different* levels of interest accommodation and conflict containment (e.g. producer-to-supplier, employers-to-workers or business-to-government links, in varying combinations).
3. *Temporal* mobility: the long-versus short-term bonds, compared to others, of an actor's (in)vested interests in coalitions and alliances, that is, the timing and duration of each actor's horizontal and vertical commitments.

By granting *time* the status it deserves in an analysis of vertical and horizontal entry and exit opportunities, we get a more realistic idea of the basically non-static and, eventually, non-symmetric nature of the rents of (inter)organizational commitments. Commitments vary from fixed and specialized ("dedicated") to flexible and generalized ("revocable/multi-purpose") investments in alliances and coalitions. In the preceding chapters we have seen how the variable and the non-symmetric nature of these investments determines the credibility of interorganizational threats and promises; and how the credibility of threats and promises determines the *sustainability* of disciplinary arrangements amongst firms, interest formations, industry and government at large. The above-suggested three-dimensional framework may at least be helpful in redressing some of the shortcomings of rational choice and game theoretical orthodoxy, such as the inability to bridge the gap between meso- (the "logic of parallel action") and macro-analysis (the "negotiated order") or between macro-regime transformations (the "renegotiated order") as these feed back into micro-sociological conduct ("strategies and tactics of organizations in response to changing environmental conditions"). Furthermore, the substitution of a *recursive*, multilevel perspective for a mono-level, *single loop* analysis may help to rectify the omission of two real-life essentials in many an area of strategic management thinking:

1. The fact that the effects of an actor's decisions depend on what other actors decide to do or undo: as argued before, omitting this *interactive*

logic of *effectiveness* – the core of realist game theory – lends a ring of autism to the provenance and proceeds of managerial thinking in this area.

2. The fact that micro-motives lead to meso-movements and the momentum of macro-order, that, over time, reverberate on micro-choice: omitting this second-order or *cumulative* logic of *effectuation* – the essence of structuration theory – fails to treat separately the status of "the logic of the actors" and "the logic of the game". Clearly, the two are interrelated, yet have to be handled as methodologically distinct phenomena.

Both omissions lead to distorted views of reality and must have far-reaching consequences for the way we look at the issues of organizational efficiency and performance on the one hand, and the phenomenon of institutional evolution and political-economic (dis)order on the other. Concerning the first point: a multilevel perspective corrects for a crucial flaw of "flat" game theory – what may be inefficient choice at the micro-level (e.g. the negative or, at best, indifferent results from mergers and acquisitions according to neo-classical performance criteria) may be an effective choice from other perspectives and levels of analysis (e.g. the *re*distribution of power in an industry or the competitive edge of the economy at large). A nested-games model, by relating the persistence of lower level inefficiencies to higher level effectiveness, provides a parsimonious explanation of the persistence of "irrational" micro-practices (because of their higher level rationale) and of the periodicity of "waves" of merger and acquisition movements (because of the time it takes before a new negotiated order gets crystallized and settled).

Concerning the second point – the evolution of institutional and political-economic order – we may refer to our earlier criticisms on the fallacy of composition in the expression of "institutional competition" (see Chapter 3, pp. 59–68). Apart from its misleading, evolutionist-functionalist connotations – suggesting that competition "selects" the most efficient "solutions" for "problems" that institutions are supposed to "solve"; *voilà* the explanation of the evolution and survival of particular institutional arrangements – the whole phraseology does not make sense: institutional arrangements do not compete; *actors* do, by exploiting selectively the options offered by the duality of institutional constraints and facilities. Moreover, actors may *combine*, in a more or less intelligent manner, elements from alternative institutional arrangements – whether imported or home-made. Over time these selective and combinatory uses of nestedness may lead, as a cumulative process, and thus virtually out of the direct control or purposeful direction of the *users*, to the rise and fall of specific institutional modes and modalities. It is solely in this metaphorical sense of the word that we may speak of the "evolution" of institutions, arising from the hybrid (or contrary) *uses* of institutional settings. As argued extensively in the chapters above, some are better positioned externally and better equipped internally than others to make the best – for themselves – of the mix of institutional alternatives open to them. Some may be in a position to trigger, or even to take the lead in, processes of redefining the mix of constraints and facilities, that is to change the rules of the institutional order itself.

What should bother researchers interested in the subtleties of the relation between micro-motives, meso-movements and macro-motion are the questions of *how* actors select options ("competence cum boundary choice"), *why* some have more degrees of freedom in the selection trajectory ("maneuverability" vis-à-vis others, horizontally and vertically, both in the past, present and future), *why* some exploit their freedom more intelligently and coherently ("mobilization") and *how* trajectories and choices result in a specific balance of change–inertia–disorder of the negotiated order at large. The sequence suggests three provisional conclusions on the matters of power and sanctioning.

First, concerning the relationship between power and *order*: power is the cement of the negotiated order, because power enables strategy and strategy creates order; but once created it is the negotiated order that recreates strategy and power.

Second, on the relationship between power and *practice*: discussions about lengths and levels of analysis are an academic pastime, since the main distinctive criterion in the analysis of power and strategy is the span of control *across* the respective lengths and levels of aggregation. Practice shows that some happen to dispose of a larger freedom to travel down, up and sidewards, as well as in time; others are locked up in their spatial-temporal theatre.

Third, on the relationship between power and *prediction*: dispositions alone, informing us about maneuverability and the conditions of monitoring and sanctioning, do not provide sufficient backing for predicting the direction and proportionality of strategic *maneuvers* and its hypothetical implications for the dynamics of the negotiated order. Summing up: for a more credible claim to generality of the links between power, strategy and order, we need a sharper and more *dynamic* specification of the "gross" association between mobility and mobilization.

Recapitulation

As argued above, approaching from this angle the generative processes
and the structuration of industrial strategies draws its inspiration from
a variety of social sciences, from economics to political science and
organization theory. The recombination of these disciplines advances
a political-economic account that envisages the structure and process
of corporate and state–market interactions as an – to some extent path
dependent and non-foreseeable – interactive outcome of intendedly
rational strategies and tactical maneuvers of firms, states and interest
formations. Not the *cognitive* bounds to rationality, which still prominently figure in the established literature, but rather the positional,
relational and temporal limits of *intelligence* and *accountability* occupy
the centre stage in our reconstruction of the political-economic order.
The underlying model remains, in spite of its multidisciplinary antecedents, relatively simple. The bare bones are shown in Figure 8.4.

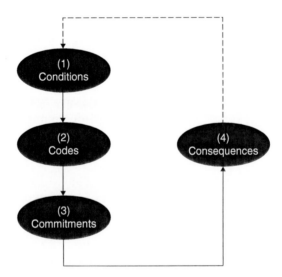

Figure 8.4   The parameters of diplomacy and discipline

Note: *conditions* are the patterns of mobility amongst and mobilization within firms, associations and state agencies; *codes* are the modes of coping with the forces underlying mobility
and mobilization, that is, resource and partner dependences and reputations; *commitments*
are the modalities of concerted action and discipline, resulting from these conditions and
codes; and *consequences* are the consolidation or change of the "negotiated" orchestration
of organizational games as a result of the continuity or change in conditions, codes and
commitments.

Summing up: competitive and complementary dependences *condition* the room for monitoring and sanctioning; the latter explain the emergence of specific *codes* (varieties of diplomacy: rules of exclusion and inclusion, recipes for conflict handling and reputation management, etc.); conditions and codes explain intra- and inter-organizational *commitments* (varieties of discipline); commitments lead to specific strategic *consequences*: intended or not-intended, that is the question. What remains to be clarified is how similar strategic conditions, bringing with them identical monitoring and sanctioning dispositions, nevertheless may lead to *non*-identical strategic responses. Dispositions identify the objective need and room to respond to the ineluctable dilemmas of capitalist coordination; *pre*dispositions catch the capacity – a subjective "state of readiness" – to *exploit* these dispositions in a more or less intelligent way. Predispositions tell us about the mobilization of bias in the responses to mobility conditions.

Our earlier exposition of *four* types of ordering (Figure 8.3) – rehearsing in more detail the ideal-typical contrasts between the old versus the new discipline – shows how predispositions vis-à-vis the dilemmas of competence choice and competition "necessarily" follow changes in the conditions of monitoring and sanctioning. But it is equally evident that sooner or later changes in predispositions *trigger*, in a serial way, changes in monitoring and sanctioning conditions. Allowing for this, essentially (see Kapp, 1976) *recursive* causation of dispositions and predispositions may lay the foundation of a necessary and sufficiently adequate explanation of the phenomenon of organizational *responsiveness*. It is precisely this – the last link in the evolutionary chain – that seeks to explain the *drift* of diplomacy and discipline in the train from conditions to commitments and its ultimate consequence: *ordering*. To this we turn now. In the final chapter I sketch the contours of a synthesis that draws the earlier strands together. It is, both in its paradigmatic and normative implications, a reconsideration of the essence of capitalist discipline and diplomacy as a *cyclical* phenomenon.

9
Consequences: On the Drift of Discipline

Enters Faust

I opened this study with the recollection of the former chief of Goldman Sachs, Henry Paulson Jr., who remembers in his memoir *On the Brink* that he, after the revolving door had made him US Treasury Secretary, attended a dinner with some of Wall Street's most powerful bankers, and how during the course of the dinner one of the bankers asked him: "Isn't there something *you* can do to order us not to take all these risks?"

How to fathom the *animation* of the drift of capitalist discipline without resorting to the metaphysics of "animal spirits" or, more down to earth, the physics of "greed"? It may be helpful to imagine a collector who has just run into a fake Vermeer or Picasso in her private collection. What should she do? Most likely she will try to get rid of the fake as quickly and discreetly as possible. That's the reason why fakes travel faster than solid matter. The swings of capitalist discipline have much to do with this: the willing suspension of disbelief, followed by the willing *remittance* of self-disbelieved beliefs. This may be, in a nutshell, the "spell" of capitalist discipline: not false class consciousness but (class-indifferent) false *consonance*.

At the end of the expedition we must come up with the answers to the questions formulated at the beginning. The leitmotiv of our journey has been the quest for a micro-foundation of the "discipline of undisciplined interests". Capitalist discipline is the explanandum. Capitalist discipline stands for the variable capacity of social order to produce and reproduce credible internal and external commitments (the term "reproduction" is meant to be free of static connotations: order may be preserved by creating *new* combinations of resources and partnerships; and the preservation of order may be the upbeat to *dis*order, triggering a new round in the quest for social order). Strategic moves and counter-moves, based on the logic of actors, constitute the micro-foundation. The logic of games (meso-level movements) and the logic of social order (macro-level regimes) are the cumulative result of the logic of actors (micro-level). On the other hand, once "constructed", disciplinary regimes (macro) and similar arrangements (meso) feedback on strategies and stratagems (micro).

My study commenced with the conjecture that the (re)constitution of the negotiated order of modern capitalism rests on a mix of Schellingian and Schumpeterian intelligence ("skill, strength or luck") in the creation of new combinations of partners and resources. The viability and variability of these combinations rest on the credibility of commitments. The latter rests on two essentials: the representativeness of the players – assumed to be based upon their internal mobilization potential and cohesion – and reciprocity – argued to be based upon the players' external mobility potential and indispensability. Both are considered essential for the (re)construction of political-economic order in so far as mobilization and mobility *differentials* "decide" about the balance of "creative" destruction versus obstruction powers in the political economy. In my argument it is the relative *distribution* of creative destruction and obstruction powers that figures as the single most important predictor of the way rival firms and rival states handle the quest for discipline.

I propose to label the perspective adopted in this study a political-economic game theory. *Political* because the anatomy of power and authority constitutes the basis. *Economic* because the circulation of resources – financial, intellectual and relational assets – plays a critical role in the explanation of the transformation of disciplinary arrangements. And a theory of *games* because strategic choice by organizations is assumed to be based on what others are expected to do or refrain from doing. What has to follow now is a resumption in dynamic terms of the problem we began this expedition with, namely that micro-rationality – the logic of the players – does not perforce lead to meso- (or macro-) rationality. For a dynamic rehearsal of that key note I propose to reconceive the logic of the respective *sub*games – from conversion and co-optation to containment and consolidation – by reconsidering them as the subsequent *stages of a cycle*. As the argument goes, each stage conveys distinct characteristics in terms of arena, agenda and timing, resulting in different sorts of disciplinary arrangements with their own specific diplomatic requisites. As a consequence, the systemic level of analysis – call it the logic of the *supra*-game – will be reconceived of as the *re*cycling of the respective subgames. The preceding chapters detailed the specifics of the subgames. The main question that remains to be answered is: what are the forces that push the transition from subgame to subgame? It is here that we arrive at the heart of the expedition: what drives the *carousel* of capitalist order and disorder?

In a schematic fashion my leitmotiv is cut up into three logical steps: explaining the *supra*-game by exposing the logic of the subgames; explaining the *sub*games by exposing the logic of the actors; and explaining the logic of the *actors* by exposing the need, room and capacity for *self*-discipline. By explicitly granting equal explanatory status to these three "productions" of social reality, my methodological position subscribes to an *interactionist* point of view, as opposed to a methodological *individualist* ("agent"-driven) or *institutionalist* ("agency"-driven) perspective. The reasoning, again in schematic fashion, runs as follows. The carousel of discipline takes off with the usual suspects, introduced in Chapter 1: the propensity for overgrazing and/or underinvestment due to pre-emptive instincts. Hence the adage we started with: *caveat preemptor* (beware of pre-emptive moves). Next, the cycle collects its self-propelling momentum from its twisting motion, namely the propensity to hedge the risks and regrets around contractual hazards. The latter constitute the core of our *thrift* axiom, that is the propensity to economize-on-commitments: at the roll-out of the cycle downstream (from producers to customers) and in subsequent stages respectively, upstream (from producers to suppliers) and sideways (from producers to producers and from state to state). The carousel is driven by a couple of constants: in the beginning figures the collective temptation of "sharing the spoils" (see for some protypes of this sort of false consonance the "Icelandic scenario" or the "Paulson-cycle" described in Chapter 1). The temptation, however, is bound to be accompanied by tacit concerns about eventual holdups, inherent to the incompleteness of contracts. As long as reasonable doubts about the final outcomes of the carousel are spontaneously *suspended* then the collective illusion holds on. Contractual incompleteness is endemic – for reasons to be elucidated below – but the *hazards* that go with it are asymmetrically distributed: in each phase of the cycle figure stage-specific captive versus non-captive combinations of resources-and-partners, generating an uneven partitioning of the divides between value creation versus value appropriation. Hence a second, more compelling adage: *caveat captor* (beware of potential capture).

One wonders whether there are countervailing powers for breaking the Faustian spell in this theatre of tacit understandings. Against the backdrop of the foregoing I suggest that for the *rendering* of counter-vailing powers we must look at other levels of conflict articulation and interest intermediation than the Platonic level Galbraith was thinking of when he introduced the idea in his *New Industrial State*. The preceding chapters suggest that it is inadvisable to invest too much confidence in the prudential or corrective powers of the "newer" industrial *state*. States appear, analogously, if not in a complementing fashion, to be equally susceptible to contractual hazard as semi-public agencies and their private counterparts. The charms of the Faustian spell apply for government as well: electoral sensitivities of democratic states tend to corroborate rather than counter the trained myopia in which adjacent links rather than the complete chain of interdependences are taken as a point of reference. Top-down attempts at tightening "codes of conduct" fail to deliver what they promise if they do not address the bottom-up working of the logic-of-cohabitation among rival states and rival firms, that is at the ground where the conditions of interdependence dictate the games organizations play. It is there that we have to look for the origin, and thus for the room for remediating, the carousel of capitalist discipline.

For an adequate understanding of the derailments of economic order we do not have to choose between the doctrines of "market" versus "state" failure. The real spell appears to be a co-product of the logic of interaction of the two: rival *firms* exploit the margins of discretion stemming from the rivalry among states (and among regulating agencies within each of them); on the other hand, rival *states* (and their agencies) benefit from the competition among firms who appear not to be equals in terms of their exposure to relational and reputational holdups. Otherwise stated: what has to be broken is the *short-cyclical consonance and contamination of public and private interests.*

The epitome of the consonance/contamination thesis are the abortive attempts to arrive at effective supranational monitoring and sanctioning standards for cross-border banking operations, aptly summarized in the dictum (reportedly voiced by Axel Weber, then president of the German Bundesbank, quoting a colleague in the *Financial Times*, 23 April 2009): "Banks are international in life but national in death."

The only, somewhat paradoxical, way out of the spell lies in changing the conditions that *obstruct the migration from subgame to subgame*, that is in *accelerating* rather than arresting the cyclical waves of consonance and contamination. The name I propose for this is *"meta-competition"*: breaking the spell by promoting the "competition" between the respective subgames by easing the transition among them – what in fact boils down to permitting more symmetric and more *timely* exit opportunities for those who find themselves hostages in a specific stage of the cycle. (Needless to repeat that it is not *games* that are competing but actors, differing in their freedom to enter or leave the games.) Attempts to change the subgames *themselves* are costly, and probably counterproductive in a political-economic order otherwise based upon the self-acclaimed preservation of the "freedom to contract": as demonstrated earlier, *over*grazing (the competition trap) as well as *under*grazing (the competence trap) remain self-inflicted events. The countervailing role, for what I further on propose to call a "Devil's advocate", is to take sides with those who regret their self-made entrapment in specific stages of the supra-cycle and seek to escape from it. The crux of a countervailing platform is to sharpen society's capacity for *anticipating potential capture* and exploring the room for more balanced power relationships among captors and captives by facilitating the latter's *chances of moving* from subgame to subgame.

The novelty of this study lies in singling out some affinities between Schumpeter and Schelling, with Galbraith as a talented soul mate – notably regarding the taste they share for the dialectics of countervailing powers in the "taming" of capitalist instincts. The upshot of their imaginary conversation is remarkably fit for an update of our understanding of the cyclical logic of cohabitation among antagonists that continue to need one another for the materialization of their own ambitions. This mutual *indispensability* of a kind is the breeding soil for what inspired Schelling to his seminal ideas on the precariousness of partnerships among "incomplete antagonists". For a better comprehension of what may come from the "incompleteness of contracts" I therefore propose to start from Schelling's idea of the "incompleteness of antagonisms". (Note, from what was said about the cyclical *convertability* of competitors and complementors, that it might be more accurate to speak of "*prot*agonists" than of – complete or incomplete – "antagonists".)

The political economy of cohabitation presented in the preceding chapters indicates the voids of the two main gestalts in the academic literature on strategic behavior and institutional forms, successively labeled the Habitus and Habitat schools of thinking. What strikes us is what both leave untouched, in spite of what they declare to aim at in their respective research agendas: the explanation of the rationality of strategic choice and the selection from alternate forms of institutional coordination. What remains untouched is the puzzling interplay between micro-organizational choices and macro-institutional consequences, that is an exploration of the mechanisms that expose the *pulse* and *pacing* of economic organization and disorganization. The main reason for this "forgotten chapter", so I surmise, is a lack of sensitivity for the crucial role of cyclical asymmetries in the *mobility* of resources and/or partners in the explanation of the orchestration (rather than "organization") of capitalist discipline and disorganization. As extensively argued in the foregoing, my framework of the nested political economy of cohabitation aims at a dynamic relinking of what became separated by those who study the macro-"institutions" of capitalism and those who look primarily at the micro-"organization" of economic life (without spelling out its macro-consequences). Take once more the following story of the two gestalts.

Habitus models overlook modern manifestations of an old topic: the separation of ownership and control (for the original canon see Berle and Means, 1932). In modern representations the divide is presented in terms of conflicts-of-interest between "principals" (shareholders) and "agents" (executives) (for the "modernization" of the 1932-canon see Jensen and Mecklin, 1976). Apart from what has been said before on the separation issue, three essentials remain uncovered in the literature on corporate governance and associated (residual) appropriation concerns. First, by assuming a monolithic and static definition of *the* interests of *the* principals, principal-agent analysts seem to be apprehensive of the need for monitoring and constraining the discretionary margins of *agents*, whilst there is ample and cumulative evidence (for some 30 years now: see North, 1981; Levi, 1988) to be concerned about the need for constraining principals as well. Second, and not unconnected to the foregoing: how *distinct* is the distinction between principals and agents? From "barbarians at the gate" (see the narrative by two Wall Street journalists, Burrough and Hellyar, 1990, concerning the whereabouts of activist shareholders, hedge funds and private equity) – principals have seen themselves systematically promoted to barbarians "*inside* the gates" – to the practical effect of wiping out the distinction between principals and agents (see the blossoming documentation on this secular travesty of corporate control and its spoils in Cohan, 2008; Tett, 2009; and more recently Akerlof and Shiller, 2009). As a result, the eye of the *real* battle for corporate command-and-control remains virtually absent in academic premises.

By eliding over the "battle of the principals" the corporate-governance literature, including transaction-costs economics, overlook another problem. With the blurring of the "gates" of organizations enters a new legal fiction: Who are the real "inmates" of the firm, and who the "outsiders"? The result is the birth of the "virtual" or "phantom" firm, that is an entity that – though posing as someone with authoritative command over its "own" resources – has lost its capacity to act as a sovereign actor. (As argued earlier, the adage "economizing on transactions" loses for this reason much of its directivity as an explanatory compass, and should therefore be replaced by the axiom of "economizing on commitments", which practically means *hedging* transaction costs by shifting them to complementors and competitors, for instance in exchange for yield-sharing and other market-splitting arrangements – the more so when the *transpiring* of the "costs-of-transacting" can be shifted to the future.)

What adds to the corrosion of corporate character is a *third* contingency that this "inside-out" perspective overlooks: the ownership and control of *what*? Principal-agent studies are primarily focused at the (formal) ownership and control of *financial* assets only, thus leaving unaddressed the ownership and control of two other sorts of "intangible" assets, that are vital to the survival of the modern firm, to wit: intellectual and network capital. Owning or controlling a firm's *cash* nexus does not imply ownership or control of its *brains* and/or *relational* nexuses. As far as not only "footloose" financial capital but also intellectual and/or network assets are observed to migrate across the boundaries of organizations – eventually without the consent of *both* principals and agents – these *spillovers* (brain drain) and *crossovers* (relational drain) must affect a firm's self-"command" as a representative licensee (an unintended effect ignored by the literature on spillover hazards, see Hamel, 1991; for an early, but rare, exception to this neglect of spillover hazards in interfirm (e.g. R&D) agreements, see Jacquemin and Spinoit, 1986). The phenomenon is particularly salient in knowledge-intensive sectors – like biotechnology (pharma), financial firms (orchestrating mergers and acquisitions in the real economy) and engineering "boutiques" (nano and medical technology) – all of them examples of (cross-)sector hybrids of brains-and-connections that are increasingly migration prone and decreasingly location specific. Summing up: for tracing the *locus* of Schumpeterian competences – the capacity to cope with spillovers originating from new combinations of resources – we must look at other places than *inside* the gates of the "sovereign" firm.

Habitus models identify, from an inside-out perspective, the sources of the "imperfection" of contracts as the consequence of the uncertain status of *organizational* boundaries. Habitat models – the outside-in perspective – struggle with, or just deny, the problem of delineating the boundaries of the relevant *domain* (a broader concept than the proverbial "relevant market" in which organizations operate). At the highest level of aggregation, the Habitat debate gets stuck between two counterpoints: supply versus demand-side economics. The trouble with the (neo-liberal) *supply*-side perspective is that it largely ignores what its founding father Adam Smith in his *Theory of Moral Sentiments* told us about the need for compensation and regulation of what the "free" market leaves undone (on this "forgotten chapter" cf. Amartya Sen, 2009: "Smith rejects interventions that *exclude* the market – but not interventions that include the market while aiming to do those important things that the market may leave *undone*"). The trouble with the (neo-Keynesian) *demand*-side perspective, on the other hand, is that it largely ignores what its founding father J.M. Keynes had to say about the need for constraining the leeway of unfettered financial speculation (cf. Minsky, 1992, a "financial Keynesian", on Ponzi schemes, and also Skidelsky, 2009). What *both* sides in the battle-of-economists seem to forget is the role of *nestedness* in their respective explanations of the organization of economic order *and* disorder (cf. Colander et al., 2009: 14: "the network structure of the economy has not been incorporated into macro-economic analysis").

Even at less aggregate levels of analysis, as for instance in industrial-organization and behavioral economics focusing on firm-to-firm interactions and market structures, the mainstream does not address the consequences of ententes among competitors (incumbents versus new entrants), complementors (suppliers and customers), sponsors (credit raters, law firms, investment bankers) and the impact of the malleable permissiveness of regulatory institutions – thus leaving to others the proper demarcation of the inner and outer confines of the relevant *circuits* in which firms operate. As a consequence we learn, again, next to nothing about the main issue at hand: how disciplinary arrangements handle the problem of "incomplete-contracts-among-incomplete-antagonists", and how that problem might affect the sustainability of economic order.

Box 9.1 Clusters: an antidote to contractual hazards?

Notable exceptions to the neglect of clusters and interfirm loyalties and learning from co-specialization are Van Tulder and Junne (1988), Best (1990), Kester (1992), Porter (1998) and Nooteboom (1999). Yet, mainly because of a predominant focus upon the competitive advantages of *geographical* proximity, allegedly fostering a higher sense of inter-actor commitments (see for instance Saxenian, 1994, and the growing empirical documentation on so-called "industrial districts", such as the knitwear industry around Modena and the automotive industry around Baden-Württenberg, in Grabherr, 1993: 204–51) – *none* of these studies addresses the challenges for the sustainability of interfirm loyalties and contractual stability that go with the increasing "flexibility" of organizational and domain boundaries in an international-izing economy. Interest in this sort of ambiguity is only just beginning (for an assessment of the immaturity of the *multi*-level analysis of clusters and spillovers, see Ebers, 1997: 8–12).

Apart from the question of *resource* spillovers, the foregoing has hinted briefly at a *second* potential source of contractual incompleteness and appropriation hazard: *crossover* hazard. Crossovers refer to the room for switching *partners*, inside or across the boundaries of existing domains. Crossovers challenge another sort of academic fiction, that is, the accreditation of a "community-of-interests" that upon closer inspection may turn out to be a perfect fake. A "fake" community is an institutional setting that – while still posing as a disciplinary arrangement – fails to define its *span of enforcement*, therewith losing its capacity to gen-erate and replicate long-term reciprocal commitments. For tracing the *focus* of this Schellingian competence – which means the capacity to cope with crossover hazards originating from *new combinations of partners* – we may have to look at other places than inside the gates of "fixed" domains.

Both sources of the imperfection of contracts – a fortiori when operat-ing in tandem – bring about a phenomenon that is known as "holdups", that is, organization- and/or domain-specific commitments that are not equally binding for all. Holdups arise from "gestation" lock-ins, that is, physical, knowledge and relation-specific investments that stand to lose their initial value-creating potential once they are cut off from their intended deployment – thereby opening the possibility of exploitation and misappropriation of the held-up by their less or non-specifically committed counterparts.

Summarizing: it is the persisting separation among a range of dis-ciplines that otherwise have serious things to say about the impact of contractual hazards on matters of corporate governance and indus-trial change that may explain why they have too little to say about the *impact of (im)mobility* on the mobilization and maintenance of new combinations of resources and partners. The Habitus corpus ignores the Schellingian paradoxes of corporate *diplomacy* – stipulating that cooperation is "disciplined" by the threat of potential competition (just as competition may become "disciplined" by the potential benefits of cooperation) – while the Habitat corpus ignores the Schumpeterian par-adoxes of corporate *governance* – asserting that competitive advantage may rest on the capacity to create new combinations of resources, critical parts of which appear to be controlled by one's (present or future) *opponents*. My *co-habitation* framework aims to address both paradoxes and thereby sharpen the focus of what has to be explained: the logic of negotiated political-economic order by specifying the links between the need, the room and the capacity for capitalist discipline under changing conditions. By "conditions" I mean variations in symbiotic as well as competitive interdependence: the specific *mix* differs from sector to sector, and covaries with the particulars of the *cyclicality* of sector- and inter-sectoral discipline. With interdependence enter the possibilities of spillover and crossover hazards: both pose challenges to the quality of Schumpeterian-annex-Schellingian skills. The room for spillovers affects a player's *license-to-operate* (a proxy for an organization's "command and control" over its critical resources) and the room for crossovers affects its *capacity-to-reciprocate* (a proxy for an organization's "command and control" over its critical partners). Both play a crucial role in a final, more decisive, problem that I address now: the *passing-on* of contractual hazards and its consequences for the capacity of the negotiated order of capitalism to reproduce itself as a sustainable mold. For that we must look at the *supra*-cycle that reconnects the respective subgames.

The plot: the recycling of discipline

Before showing the complete scenario, I will briefly line up the key terms and the main propositions on the phenomenon we are about to clarify in this section: the *carousel* of discipline (see Box 9.2).

Box 9.2 Key terms

Contractual hazards and *appropriation concerns* refer to the incompleteness respectively imperfections of contracts due to inequalities in the search and switching costs of resources and/or partners. Imperfection and incompleteness arise from spillover and/or crossover hazards. The latter affect the credibility of commitments and therefore the stability of the negotiated order based upon them.

- *Moral hazards* refer to systemic incentives for individual short-term anticipatory respectively pre-emptive behaviors that, over the longer term, may undermine in a cumulative fashion the viability and sustainability of the system.
- *Moral blame* is invoked when contractual/moral hazard is the result of intent (though proving malice turns out to be another enterprise, as we will see in a while).

- *Holdup* refers to the eventual captiveness or "lock-in" of resources and/ or partners in organization/domain-specific combinations; the lock-in makes these combinations liable to the exploitation by others, that is resource(s) and/or partner(s) that, for whatever reasons, benefit from lower switching costs when leaking/migrating across organizational/ domain boundaries.
- *Representativeness* is a proxy for an organization's command-and-control over its "critical" resources: it defines an organization's *license-to-operate*.
- *Reciprocity* is a proxy for the stability of an organization's command-and-control over its "critical" partners: it defines its *capacity-to-reciprocate*.
- *Discipline* is a proxy for credible commitments as a function of representativeness and reciprocity: it is the essence of order.
- *Diplomacy* refers to varying mixes of cooperation and competition: it stands for the continuation of rivalry by other means.

The lexicon above results in the formulation of two key propositions (see Box 9.3).

Box 9.3   Key propositions

Proposition I. *Discipline follows diplomacy*

- Diplomacy varies with the representativeness and reciprocity of organizations.
- Representativeness and reciprocity explain the symmetry or asymmetry in the distribution of contractual hazards.

Proposition II. *Changes in diplomacy and discipline follow mutations in the switch-and-recombination costs of critical resources and/or partners*

- Asymmetric *lock-ups* entail spillover hazards, which affect the representativeness of the players: the higher the spillovers, the lower representativeness.
- Asymmetric *lock-ins* entail crossover hazards, which affect the reciprocity of the players: the higher the crossovers, the lower reciprocity.

The cyclicality of "criticality"

Resources and/or partners are said to be *critical* if they are (1) non-substitutable, (2) non-imitable and (3) serve as a catalyst for new resource/partner combinations (past and future). Criticality is neither a universal nor a constant. The criticality of resources and/or partners differs from sector to sector and changes from stage to stage in the life cycle of firms and sectors. Being a critical resource and/or partner means serving as a *catalyst* for an organization's value *chain* and/or its value *domain*. The crux in this make-up, and thereby for our insight into the *circulation* of the resulting subgames, are the lower shifting and/or switching costs of critical resources and/or partners relative to their "locked-up/locked-in" collaterals. Asymmetries in shift and switching costs are the drivers of the recycling of discipline.

The thrust of the reasoning becomes clear when we translate my typology of subgames in terms of changes in the salience of spillovers and crossovers, because it shows how changes in the bases of bargaining power are directly related to changes in the distribution of contractual hazards. *Conversion* and *co-optation* games constitute respectively the "start" and the "roll-out" of the cycle. As shown in Figure 8.3 a *conversion* game – stage I: incumbent producers face new entrants – is characterized by closed organizations and variable arenas. As a consequence, not spillover but crossover hazards are a matter of primary concern in this phase. The basis of power in a *conversion* game – stage I – is the capacity to *obstruct* new entrants. In a *co-optation* game – stage II – both organizational *and* arena boundaries are open and variable. As a consequence spillover as well as crossover hazards are a matter of concern. The power base in this phase is the capacity to *bind* customers and other sorts of vertical (e.g. R&D) complementors. *Containment* and *consolidation* games constitute respectively the "roll-back" and the "closure" of the cycle. In a *containment* game – stage III: producers look for a *nested* hierarchy of suppliers and other (e.g. infrastructural) complementors – organizational boundaries are open but arena boundaries tend to become more and more fixed. As a consequence not crossovers but spillover hazards constitute the primary concern. The power base in this phase is the capacity to *contain* suppliers and secondary complementors. In the final stage – IV, the *consolidation* game: incumbents are primarily busy with horizontal takeover fights – *both* organizations and arenas become more and more closed and invariable. Spillover and crossover hazards are not a matter of primary concern. The base of power shifts to the capacity to *pre-empt* rival bidders.

In terms of the "recycling" of discipline we can summarize the foregoing as follows. The higher the salience of *spillover* hazards – the locus of mobilization resides increasingly outside the bounds of precisely defined *organizations* – and the higher the salience of *crossover* hazards – the focus of mobility lies increasingly outside the bounds of precisely defined *domains* – the less stable the resulting negotiated order.

Disorder refers to the loss of representativeness and/or reciprocity among rival interest formations that nevertheless continue to need one another for the reproduction of their own welfare – be it for each of them under different time pressures and in different gradations. Disorder is the yield

of the *incompleteness of contracting,* itself the result of the less than perfect individual and collective "command-and-control" over new combinations of critical resources and/or partners. Command-and-control over
specific resource/partner combinations (R/P) follow a cyclical pattern: each
subgame qualifies alternate R/P combinations as the leveraging catalyst.
Mutations in disciplinary arrangements follow mutations in the criticality
of R/P combinations, entailing changes in the bases of bargaining power.

Leaving further specifications out, the essence of the quest for capitalist discipline can therefore be recapitulated as follows. Discipline follows
the *migration and recombination costs* of critical R/P combinations. Power
accrues to those R/P combinations that – in each of the stages of the
cycle – serve as a catalyst for other R/P combinations, whatever the best
alternate combinations in which the latter may figure. Appropriation hazards are based upon mobility and mobilization differentials: asymmetries
in migration and recombination costs define the room for extracting and
appropriating *private* benefits from the dynamics of *collective* value creation. *Captives* are those players with the highest migration and recombination costs due to their domain and organization-specific investments.
Catalysts are those players that initiate and orchestrate the transition
from subgame to subgame due to their lower or non-existent exposure
to organization and/or domain-specific investments. Captives are bound
to follow catalysts. The former's submissiveness is a function of the latter's "creative" bases of power: obstruction, inducement, containment
or pre-emption. I think that a reconstruction in these terms places us in
a better position to explain the *encirclement* and *circulation* of capitalist
discipline – better than either of the two currently prevailing models of
"organized capitalism", namely those who specialize on the comparative
analysis of the "macro" institutions of capitalism and those who study the
"micro" organization of economic life, without spelling out the (intended
vs non-intended) systemic consequences of individual choice.

The twist: on the calculus of complicity

A decade or so before Galbraith (1968) announced "the ultra-stability"
of the new industrial state, girded by what he perceived as the virtual
absence of any "limits to the growth of big business" (see Chapter 2),
Penrose asserted, echoing Schumpeter's thesis on the *endogenous* nature
of the decline of the hegemony of "organized capitalism":

> If the case for ... big-business competition is a strong one, its strength
> rests on conditions that are not self-perpetuating, but may themselves

be destroyed by collusion, by the extension of financial control, and by the struggle to resolve the contradictions in a system where competition is at once the god and the devil, where the growth of firms may be efficient but where their consequent size, though not in itself inefficient, may create an industrial structure which impedes its own continued growth. (Penrose, 1959: 265)

Which one of the two vistas one prefers depends, apart from the benefits of hindsight, on one's appreciation of a multilevel perspective in which intendedly rational moves eventually end in non-intended, irrational consequences; and in which some suffer less than others from these irrationalities, or may even benefit from them. Penrose's apocalypse reiterates the tragedy of the commons and the waste lands: when individual rationality pre-emptively leads to overgrazing and/or underinvestment in industrial renewal, productivity losses and stagnation or greater mischief may be the return on local, as opposed to systemic, rationality.

The search for "bigness" is the rationalization of the elusive belief that "god and the devil" can be reconciled by annexation and centralization. Part of the failure by regulators, financial institutions and the academic establishment to understand the clash of micro- versus macro-rationality can be traced back to "the untenable belief that all risk is measurable (and therefore controllable), ignoring [the] crucial distinction between 'risk' and 'uncertainty'" (Skidelsky, *The Guardian*, July 27, 2009). When uncertainty obtains for everyone, investors will focus on risk – *not* because risk is easier to control but because it can be shared with or passed on to others, for some time. The only proviso is the availability of routines and rationalizations that facilitate, if not encourage, the transfer of risk and the redistribution of regrets.

The appetite for risk and regret is neither a psychological nor a folkloristic attribute. What counts are not the *nerves* of the gamblers (however breathtaking their track records; see for instance Lewis, 1989; and the cliffhangers in Cohan, 2008). What matters, instead, is the intelligence of the nervous *system* that elicits the rules and rewards for the gambling. The room for the offshoring of risk, instead of its "control", and the need for regret minimization over its adverse outcomes, instead of belief in its "inevitability", vary with one's structural position in the iron triangle of upstream, downstream and (col)lateral interdependences. The longer and the more branched off the political-economic transmission belts, the longer it takes to arrest or return the pumping around of risk and regret. The *space* for the displacement of risk and regret defines the *pace* of the return to the origin: the "appetite" for risk and regret is not a psychological but a positional affair.

Box 9.4 Share and shift

Risk-sharing versus shifting differ in direction, not necessarily in nature, because "sharing" is *shifting-in-commission*. For instance, when the Federal Deposit Insurance Corporation (FDIC, the US institution that reinsures private deposits) imposes stricter balance requirements on private equity that wants to take over banks-in-trouble but prohibits their resale within a period of three years, it suffices for private equity holders to bypass the imposed "lock-up" by *sharing* the risks of the takeover with regular investment banks (that are permitted to operate under less restrictive conditions). Another instance is the situation when a firm, fearing to become a prospective takeover target, starts with the hope of benefiting from playing off the competing bidders, only to discover after a while that the competing "black knights" managed to stage a *shared* offer that the target can't refuse. Even if the target (e.g. ABN-AMRO) expresses publicly its own strong preference to be taken over by a self-casted candidate (e.g. Barclays) it may find out after a while that it has been outbidden by an occasional consort of three, non-casted rivals that succeed *together* in tearing apart the targeted bank. In another illuminating case we meet a Dutch aircraft manufacturer (Fokker) negotiating a takeover by a German competitor (DASA, a subsidiary of Daimler Benz): for a proper understanding of the – for Fokker – dramatic outcome it is useful to keep in mind that Fokker's *core* suppliers (fuselage, wings, engines) were also supplying to – if not owned by – Fokker's *rivals*. That the "shift-by-sharing" formula is by no means an exceptional scenario can be demonstrated by numerous other examples. Take for instance the 55 percent takeover of Opel by Magna. Opel is the German subsidiary of the (then near-bankrupt) US auto-maker General Motors, and Magna is the Canadian first-tier supplier of components and Modules, not only to GM/Opel but also to Opel's Germany-based rivals, Volkswagen and BMW. During Magna's rescue annex takeover negotiations with GM/Opel, VW and BMW kept silent (around that time, the automotive industry in its entirety was crisis-stricken and in need of some form of "collective" state help). Promptly after the settlement of Magna's takeover of Opel, VW and BMW announced to swap Magna for another main supplier. Magna may not have been suprised.

Two conclusions can be drawn. First, sharing is shifting-hazards-in-disguise. Second, what at first sight resembles a *bilateral* game – for instance ABN-AMRO trying to shake-off advances by the Royal Bank of Scotland (RBS) by selling part of itself (Lasalle) to a rival of RBS, or Fokker versus DASA, or GM/Opel versus Magna, or private equity versus Federal rules on "lock-ups" – appears upon closer inspection to be *trilateral* games: the shadow of a *tertium gaudens* (the laughing third) decides how the bilateral burdens of risk and regret will be shifted to others who, of course, will try to shift *their* burdens further onwards.

What keeps the carousel turning? Several dispositions can be identified – each of them retraceable to the earlier mentioned rationales for antagonistic cooperation and the underlying division of bargaining powers. Crucial for the turnaround is the capacity of players to *reframe* bilateral transactions into three-party games. The reframing is based neither on assumptions of "trust" nor "loyalty": what suffices is orchestrating the *containment of distrust*. Neither are assumptions of fraudulent intent or bad faith needed: controlling for *disloyalty* will do, as soon as "loyalty" proves to be another word for solidarity, and solidarity a survival constraint. It is the *foreboding that others prematurely may opt out and thereby arrest the carousel* that explains why (in Pareto's adage, 1966: 142):

> Spoliation … seldom meets with a really effective resistance from the despoiled. What sometimes stops it is the destruction of wealth consequent upon it, which may entail the ruin of the country. History shows us that more than once spoliation has finished by killing the goose that lays the golden eggs.

Compare Pareto's conjecture with a recent review of instances of corporate fraud and corruption: "fluctuations in predatory activity [are] related to changes in opportunities for such activity" (Akerlof and Shiller, 2009: 38). The authors opt for a cultural "norms and values" explanation of the spread of corporate corruption by calling upon:

> varieties through time in the perceived penalties for such behavior. [When] everyone else is doing it … and no one seems to be getting punished … lowering one's adherence to principles is [to some extent] a perfectly rational thing to do … Such a process may be part of the confidence multiplier, as corruption feeds back into more corruption. [Cultural] changes unrelated to fear of punishment or to changes in technology … are clearly within the realm of pure animal spirits. Culture changes over time to facilitate or to hinder aggressively competitive and predatory activities. (Ibid.: 38–9)

Akerlof and Shiller's "confidence multiplier" and their "realm of pure animal spirits" remind us of Lowi's leanings to an "oversocialized" (Wrong, 1961) conception of economic man in his explanation of the mysterious coexistence of "conformism-in spite of-coercion" (see Chapter 4, p.111). The crucial question rests on what causes "culture", or more pertinently, what engenders "varieties through time [in the] fear of punishment" and fosters the reanimation of the "realm of pure animal spirits"? Akerlof and Shiller fail to provide an answer, except for the mass-psychological, tautological notion of "corruption-breeds-corruption" *epidemics*. There must be another, more structural and less "over-socialized" way to look at "opportunity"-driven behavior – that is, an envisioning where another sort of "confidence multiplier" appears to be acting. Capitalism, by nature *and* nurture, is a speculative affair: the *calculus* of speculation aims at getting others engaged in collective ventures on the base of convergent illusions, otherwise the Faustian spell won't work. At the end of Chapter 4 we came across one possible reason for the conspiracy of speculative beliefs (or "false consonance", as I prefer to call it): part of the puzzle lies, as we saw there, in the logic of the unforeseen escalation of coercive commitments – that is in the transition from the (intendedly *transitory*) politics-of-accommodation to the (unintendedly *non*-transitory) politics of complicity-and-containment (cf. Offe and Wiesenthal, 1980). The other half of the puzzle of "consonance" lies in the supporting narratives that *moralize and rationalize* the complicity – largely the ("Schattschneiderian") task of sponsors-and-spinners – like premier league investment banks, credit rating agencies, accountancy and law firms, and permissive regulatory authorities.

The *countdown* of the Faustian spell normally starts with an insider's hunch of a "promising project", igniting a grapevine of converging speculations. The follow-up is the activation of a pro-cyclical *complicity* multiplier: a self-propelling *proliferation* of shifts (up and downstream) and *hedgings* (sideways) of risks and regrets. The complicity multiplier works as long as the bad risks and regrets remain sufficiently *dispersed*, no matter how visibly the gains are concentrated (cf. Pareto on "spoliation" in the excerpts from his *Cours d'Economie Politique* (1896) and *Manuel d'Economie Politique* (1909) in Pareto, 1966: 114–17; 137–8). The twist rolls out in tiers – up to the momentum of a *hype* (cf. Kindleberger, 2000) – until over-exploitation breaks the spell.

Over-exploitation is the drying up of the lateral and vertical flow of risks and regrets – the "desertification" of the soil of the real economy. It announces the turning point in the cycles of "creative destruction". Recast in terms of the cycle of our four subgames: the value-*creating* part takes off in stage I, the *conversion* game (the incubation phase); it rolls out in stage II, the *co-optation* game (the expansion phase), that is when new combinations of intellectual, relational and venture capital succeed in neutralizing or breaking the obstructive power of the dominant mold of formerly firmly entrenched combinations of resources and partners. The value-*destroying* part obtains at the roll-back in stage III, the *containment* game (the recentralization phase), and ends in stage IV, the *consolidation* game (the shake-out/out-bidding phase) when a structural mismatch surfaces between long-term *over*crediting and short-sighted *under*investment in improved productivity and real innovations. The cyclical overstretch becomes manifest when the carousel is about to lose its momentum, followed by a serial withdrawal of "trust" in the self-disbelieved beliefs of *others*. Once the "desertification" sets in, a negative multiplier of shake-outs sets off in a massive *sauve qui peut*, accelerated by the aggressively discounted resale of the lucrative pieces of affected firms – all the way up to the origin of the Faustian fake.

The "moral" disclaimer for the fake does not rest upon the methodological *individualist* axiom of "bounded rationality" nor on the *institutionalist* veil of "pluralistic ignorance". It depends, instead, on the "veil" of *known unknowns*: each sequel in the roll-out of the cycle is virtually free to join or not to join, dependent on the perceived room for *passing on the risks and regrets* – thus remaining perfectly free to waive any sort of accountability for the carousel as a whole. Clearly, this is not a specimen of herd behavior or "animal spirits" (*pace* Keynes and Akerlof et al.). What, on the contrary, explains the "bandwagon" of complicity and the false consonance that goes with it, is a collective stake in the unimpaired *prolongation* of the momentum of the train of risk and regret – the term *"animating* spirits" may come closer to what we see actually happening – thus creating, not on purpose but de facto, a tacitly shared conspiracy-of-*ignoring*. Once underway it proves virtually impossible (or *unprofitable*) to back out – lest the pull of the slipstream is arrested. Numerous instances of firms that "overstretched" themselves over past decades bear witness to the practices of "creative" bookkeeping, widely handled as an internally known-but-silenced secret by the inner circles of stakeholders *and* stockholders, who by no means want to see the unmasking of their overrated shares before having been able to sell them *as noiselessly as possible*: exactly the pure Catch-22 situation that accelerates rather than attenuates, let alone arrests, the exchange of known unknowns, for as long as the inmates have informed reasons to expect – and the means to see to it – that others will hand on the "perfect fake" (cf. the false Vermeers and Picassos we started with).

At least two supplementary conditions must be met lest the preservation of the transfer of self-disbelieved beliefs will be arrested. A first candidate, *inside* large (public and private) bureaucratic oligarchies, is the widely documented practice of "functional" ignorance that holds that "the left hand was kept in the dark about the right hand's whereabouts" (see the Samsung, and Siemens examples of corporate corruption in Box 9.7 below). What happens, in fact, is that "agency costs" are *incorporated*: the top echelons do not know and, since it is the result that counts, do not *want* to know which creative risks their own "specialists", down the ranks, are taking. On closer inspection these practices are hardly instances of "cultural" predispositions, but a matter of "structural" *dis*position of the "where you stand depends on where you sit" category. A second, equally lasting, source of the persistence of the practice of ignoring is the difficulty of proving insider knowledge *cum* malicious intent from the *outside*. The test case in Box 9.5 illustrates the point.

Box 9.5   Known unknowns

At the end of 2009 the only Wall Street bankers who faced criminal charges relating to the subprime mortgage mess were two Bear Stearns hedgefund managers reported to have exchanged, privately, emails stating that they were "concerned about the health of the funds" they were trading, while publicly one of them continued to tell investors that Bear Stearns "felt comfortable" with the funds. Jurors and judge, though, decided there was "no proof of bad faith". The verdict put an end to the short-lived jurisprudential heritage of a former New York attorney general, Eliot Spitzer, who successfully prosecuted a Merrill Lynch analyst who told investors to buy stocks about which he privately wrote in emails to colleagues were "horrible", a "disaster" and a "piece of shit". Unfortunately the lesson of the Bear Stearns case came too late for Arthur Andersen, the accounting firm that earlier was indicted for its role in Enron's financial fraud, in part because of an email that instructed its employees to eliminate any "unnecessary paperwork": apparently not the *content* of the mails constitute a criminal affront but the *shredding* of them. The obstruction of procedures is easier to corner than the *substantive* obstruction of social order. Imaginably, then, a credit-rating agent wrote in mid-2008 to a colleague, "Let's hope we're all wealthy and retired by the time this house of cards falters" (*The Financial Times*, November 12, 2009). As said before: regret is a positional matter, and position is a reputational, not a personal, matter.

Risk, regret and "loyalty"

The appetite for risk and the attitude of regret enjoy a prominent status in behavioral economics. A general, at first sight plausible, assumption is that (most) people are risk averse and do not like to regret (publicly) ill-conceived decisions. Schenk and Schenk (2006) resume the risk and regret *avoidance* axiom for explaining the paradox of the resurgence of waves of mergers and acquisitions (M&A) *despite* ample proof of its (mostly) disappointing outcomes. More often than not M&A perform badly: they appear to be economically inefficient, destroy rather than create value and choke the slack needed for innovative investments. Worse, when M&A do not generate wealth, economies as a whole will suffer. Yet the phenomenon persists. How can we explain this sort of anomaly?

The prevailing explanations are variations on the premise of imitation in small-number games. The game starts with the assumption of discretionary margins for *economically* irrational behavior (as for instance is stipulated in agency theory). When agents' income, perks and status rise with the size of a firm, boosting size rather than profits will be the likely result: agents are consuming funds that should accrue to the principals. Furthermore, self-confidence based on prior overpayment and, by the way, an industry-wide lack of solid understanding of the objective causes of corporate success and failure, may strengthen the propensity to mimic what others are doing, that is embarking on M&A even when proven to be unprofitable.

Reputational effects – sharing the blame with peers that apparently misread the signals in a similar way – and economizing on the costs of independently gathering information on the "real" threats and opportunities respectively "real" strengths and weaknesses of the others that consider M&A – all these specimens of "adverse selection" will but reinforce the mimetic drive. Schenk, though subscribing to these "herding-and-cascade" theories of the diffusion of irrationality in economic life, criticizes the "static" nature of the interpretation since none of them is able to clarify why M&A occur in *waves*. To rectify that shortcoming Schenk proposes his "minimax-regret" theorem – following the experimental tenets of "prospect theory" (launched by Kahneman and Tversky, 1979, establishing the new orthodoxy in *behavioral* economics) – holding that "the displeasure associated with losing a sum of money is greater than the pleasure associated with gaining the same amount". According to "minimax-regret" routines decision-makers will always follow the merger initiative of their peers: imitating a successful M&A is a joy for the imitators while imitating a failing M&A is a fault of all who failed to read the odds correctly. However, failing to follow a *successful* M&A is a regret forever. So far, so good: "minimax-regret and defensive routines lead to bursts of merger activity".

But, then, what will turn the tide? Schenk (2006: 170) states that: "the merger boom levels off as a result of lacking and/or lagging productivity/profitability gains, and price rises for targets... Reconstitution management sets in (selloffs, divestitures, demergers, lay-offs)". Would this hypothesis of the "petering out" of the M&A bubble not suffice for satisfying also the previous, more familiar, imitation routines listed above? Occam's razor would rather say so.

As argued extensively in this study, the "tolerance" for the *dis*pleasures of risk and regret can be looked at from a positional as opposed to a psychological angle. At variance with the mimetic, bilateral, move-elicits-countermove cascades of the psychological schools of regret reduction, the positional antagonistic cooperation framework stresses the basically *nested* and *trilateral* nature of the carousel of the rationalization and passing on (rather than "reduction") of risk and regret. (In passing, a fallacy-of-composition problem with behaviorists' studies of risk attitudes should be noted: they are based on face-to-face or double-bind laboratory experiments, invariably "pinned up" in eventually mixed (i.e. competitive/cooperative but always, that is closed, settings), that is *without allowing for the possibility of maneuvering risk (and regrets) out of the walls of the laboratory*: what an experimenter locks up in the confines of his computer tournaments is bound to re-emerge in his findings.)

Apart from the matrix of upstream, downstream and lateral dependences – the three-dimensional space that defines the room for two-against-one switches – the *triadic* stamp highlights the primordial role of the risk and regret *prompters*, that is those (other than "principals" and "agents") who are in a key position to advise on the room and the timing of the *displacement* of risk and regret. The latter – the *traders* in credibility, including investment bankers, lawyers, accountants and credit raters – are the real *stayers* in the Schumpeterian/Schellingian small-number games of regime prolongation-and-proliferation: they orchestrate and distribute the spoils, both in the up – and downswings of the carousel. At the end of the bonfire of the vanities, after an apposite mourning intermezzo on behalf of their clients in the real economy, they are ready to *check in again* for recombining cash, competence and connections for a fresh turnaround of the supragame. In order to pin-point the contrast with the "behavioral" (as opposed to our "positional") approach the foregoing may be called a "minimax *distrust*" theorem. Much that seems to be irrational or barely understandable from an economist's "prospect", "expected utility", "cognitive imperfections" or "minimax regret" theory becomes perfectly *logical* and conceivable from a "minimax distrust" theorem. The simple reason is that the latter starts from the premise that intelligent players know how to operate in the context of a *nested* game whereas the former start from the basically *atomist* (as opposed to contextual) assumption of discrete tit-for-tats. Apparently Doktor Faustus doesn't need the "framing" of the behaviorists to keep afloat in the suction of the vortex of captors, captives and prompters.

Analogous to theories of decision versus non-decision-making (Lukes, 1974), wishing versus unwishing-to-know – or at least making sure that others cannot surmise what *you* know and that the "known unknowns" *remain* unknown – are deliberate acts.

Box 9.6 The *calculus* of ignoring

During the 16 years that Bernard ("too good to be true") Madoff managed to embezzle $65 billion of his investors' deposits, the US Securities and Exchange Commission (SEC) received, as the SEC itself confessed in a recently published report, *at least six times* convincing clues that there was something seriously rotten in the state of Madoff's pyramid. When asked by the SEC why he (Madoff) eventually suspended his options trade and refrained from extracting his hedge funded profits for a while, he was reported to have answered: "I am not greedy". The SEC decided to settle for that (*Financial Times*, March 9, 2009). Another, more discomforting proof of the *calculus* of ignoring is provided by the US Congress, which at the end of 2009 was ready to vote (see Chapter 1) to repeal a crucial part of the Sarbanes–Oxley Act – a law that was passed in 2002 and required public companies to make sure that their internal controls against fraud were not full of holes. The (successful) pressure on Congress for the repeal is reported to have originated from the American Bankers Association, arguing that it had to be made "easier for banks to ignore the market values of the toxic securities they owned" and therefore "to give...the Federal Reserve or some panel of regulators...the power to override accounting standards". In the view of the bankers "the financial crisis did not stem from the fact the banks made lots of bad loans and invested in dubious securities; *it was caused by accounting rules that required disclosure when the losses began to mount*" (Floyd Norris, *The International Herald Tribune*, November 6, 2009: 19; my italics).

As argued above, fear of a self-propelling spiral of distrust-by-*disclosure* – the so-called "whistleblower's curse" – seems a likely candidate for understanding the *persistence* of the veils of ignoring – incidentally assisted by a self-serving "forbearance" on the side of the rating and regulatory agencies (when reappraising their prudential and corrective powers). Where you stand in this pyramid of checks and balances does not simply depend on "where you *sit*" (Allison, 1971), but more pertinently on where you come from and where you are preparing to move on to. Let's therefore amend Allison's dictum to: where you *stand* in a nested game-of-cohabitation depends on your freedom of *movement* within and across the cyclical "encirclements" of the game – a freedom that appears not to be symmetrically distributed for each of the inmates. This Allison amendment rehearses what we said earlier on the contrast between first-mover/market sharing vs footloose-mover/market *reframing* games. First-mover/market *sharing* games hold: whenever there is a split between individual and collective rationality, and you can't beat your rivals, join them. Footloose-mover/market *reframing* games assert: when joining is too costly, risky or otherwise prohibited, then bind your rivals by interfering in their freedom of movement. *Both* belong to the repertory of capitalist discipline, but they differ in the mix of underlying principles, namely: assure (1) entry barriers for outsiders, (2) exit barriers for insiders, and (3) flexibility in the entry and exit options for oneself.

The foregoing sheds a different light on the "exit, voice and loyalty" grammar that Hirschman (1970) once proposed to analyze and remediate the laws of "organizational decline". By substituting *cross*-loyalty for loyalty, Hirschman's seminal study on organizational decline-and-recovery can be converted into a study of the laws of organizational cum interorganizational *discipline*. Incidentally, Hirschman's (near-tautological) use of the concepts of voice-and-loyalty is replaced by something that is morally less exacting, yet practically more compelling: not loyalty but "reciprocation" – the capacity for exchanging credible threats and promises – is a disciplining force free of normative connotations and provisos. By dissecting exit-voice-and-loyalty we refocus the analysis on the constituents of bargaining power and the negotiated order, namely entry and exit conditions and their distribution across actors over time and place. The example in Box 9.7 illustrates our, more skeptical, view on the sources and "blessings" of loyalty.

Box 9.7   Loyalty, a reappraisal

Towards the end of 2007, Samsung, a Korean electronics manufacturing giant relying on thousands of parts suppliers, was battered by allegations of corruption. Prosecutors ransacked Samsung's offices to find traces of a slush fund allegedly topping $217 million. The head of one of the numerous component suppliers of Samsung (quoted in the *International Herald Tribune* (December 4, 2007) stated: "Everyone is watching what's going to happen to Samsung. If Samsung takes a punch, we feel the shock too. If Samsung shrinks because of the investigation and cuts its investments, smaller companies like us will shut down in droves".

The *International Herald Tribune* went on to comment that striking these behemoths too harshly might well hurt the economic wellbeing of the rest of the economy and by the time the scandal had run its course executives accused of bribery would walk away with light punishment: usually a suspended prison term accompanied by an admonition from the judge that "they would have been punished more sternly were it not for their 'contribution to the economy'...*Being the spine of the economy, if it shakes, the economy shakes.*"

Not too big but too *connected* to fail is the name of the verdict. The *International Herald Tribune* quoted an electronic components supplier, owing 70 percent of his yearly turnover to Samsung: "No matter what problems it might have, Samsung is still the cleanest...company we can depend on in this time of economic uncertainty...*If we hurt Samsung too much, we will make the mistake of burning down our house to kill bedbugs.*"

Nested games inspire to another sort of "loyalty" than the one Hirschman envisaged. It is not strong versus weak ties (Granovetter, 1985) but asymmetries in the length and time horizon of the ties with suppliers, customers and the rest of the pyramid that appear to be decisive. Each subgame selects its own sort of compliance-by-complicity. The resulting discipline is not reducible to the cliché of clashing interests between stock and stakeholders: both tend to suffer from the eventual collapse of (in this case) Samsung. Disclosure hurts all in the extended family of entangled interests. It is the *horizon* and the *timing* of the encircle-ment that disciplines – not the stasis of the ties. Even Samsung's *rivals* (like Siemens, shortly after Samsung's exposure it became involved in a similar slush affair) suffer rather than benefit from full disclosure: in terms of competitive matching it is tempting to follow Samsung's benchmark – in bad as well as best practices. Hence the spontaneity of the conspiracy-of-ignoring. Ignoring is a *survival* constraint.

It is worth noting that this sort of "solidarity" is by no means restricted to situations of complementary (e.g. producer-supplier) interdependence. It obtains equally in situations of *competitive* interdependence as, for instance, the so-called principle of "burden sharing" asserts. According to the rulings of the US Federal Deposit Insurance Corporation (FDIC), as in the European Union, individual banks are collectively held account-able for compensating (to some limit) the troubled deposits of the clients of a "colleague" in trouble. In that situation the *individual* benefits of disclosure – offering a windfall opportunity for welcoming a flood of freshly migrating clients – has to be weighed against the *collective* dis-comfort of having to pay for a reckless rival. Capitalist discipline is a matter of selfish altruism. What behaviorists tend to see as a specimen of "cognitive dissonance" (in search of its relief), others, more conver-sant with the logic of incomplete antagonisms, will see as a specimen of "consonance" (in search of its *preservation*).

As introduced in the foregoing, the ultimate sarcasm lies in the "return" of risk and regret once the carousel has come to a (periodic) stand-still: the pivotal linkers that triggered the roll-out of material and moral hazards, happen to be the same that will be asked to take the lead in the roll-*back*. The reason is obvious: when it comes to collateral ravage-and-reputation control they are the gate keepers – the Barbarians *inside* – with the highest (short-term) obstruction and (long-term) "crea-tive" destruction potential for the economy as a whole. They are the *proto*-agonists for the orchestration of the "creative" reanimation of cash, competence and connections ("proto" because they *reset* the stage for the "real" protagonists). Apparently Penrose's god *and* the devil need one another for the bail-out of the powers that be. (The only assistance the recycling needs is the *rewinding* by the gate keepers: lawyers, accountants, credit raters and rival states (agencies), *all of them* reluctant to give up the alleged competitive advantages of "sovereignty" in matters of regulatory arbitrage.)

Box 9.8 On the calculus of complicity: the tale about a fox watching the geese

One of the gate keepers, Lloyd Blankfein, chairman and CEO of Goldman Sachs, is reported to have understood his bounden calling: "The financial system led us into the financial crisis and it will lead us out ... As the guardians of the interests of the shareholders and, by the way, for the purposes of society, I'd like them [my fellow Goldmanites] to continue to do what they are doing ... [I am] just a banker 'doing God's work'" (*The Sunday Times*, November, 2009)

The *Wall Street Journal*, on May 5, 2009, describes how Goldman Sachs – the "Wizard of Wall Street" – guards the gates between Wall Street, the New York branch of the Central Bank and the Washington administration, by exporting its alumni to crucial positions in the public sector and vice versa. The head of the New York Fed has a seat in the Board of non-executive directors of the Bank while its alumni work at the Treasury. The Fed and the Treasury decide on life-or-death matters of Goldman Sachs's *rivals*. The top officials of the US administration – Henry Paulson Jr., Timothy Geithner, Ed Liddy – who are reported to have had a decisive say in the yes-or-no rescue of Goldman Sachs's rival Lehman Brothers (a "no") and American International Group (a "yes"), were former colleagues (or disciples-of-colleagues) from Goldman Sachs. (For an overview and update of the connections, including the overseas extensions, see "Sachs in the City", *The Sunday Times*, November 8, 2009).

The *New York Times*, on August 9, 2009, reports how Lloyd Blankfein's predecessor, Goldman Sachs's former chief Henry Paulson Jr., explicitly promised, upon leaving the bank in 2006 to enter the government as the minister of the Treasury, to "avoid any substantive interaction with executives [of Goldman Sachs] for his entire term unless he first obtained an ethics waiver from the government". The *New York Times* counted, before the waiver was granted, more than two dozen occasions when there were contacts between Paulson and his former employer, beginning with the launch of a (for Goldman Sachs $13 billion worth) bailout of the mega-insurer American International Group (AIG), which received a government loan of $85 billion to be "*used ... to pay off Goldman and other big banks that were financially threatened by AIG's potential collapse*". As Neil M. Barofsky stated – in his role as special inspector general for the Troubled Asset Relief Program (TARP), in his office's report on the US Government's $182 billion "rescue" of AIG – part of which was "funneled inexorably and directly" as a "backdoor bailout" to AIG's counterparts, including Goldman Sachs: "by providing AIG with the capital to make these payments, Federal Reserve officials provided AIG's counterparties with tens of billions of dollars that they likely would have not otherwise received had AIG gone into bankruptcy" (*The International Herald Tribune*, November 23, 2009, qualifying Barofsky as "one of the few truth-tellers in Washington"; cf. also Barofsky (2012)).

Does this specimen of *patronage* offer an illustration of the alleged contrasts between Anglo/American versus Continental versus Asian regimes of corporate governance, as we are invited to believe in comparative surveys on "regional" or "national" business systems (Schmitter, 1977; Schmitter and Lehmbruch, 1979; Streeck and Schmitter, 1985; Whitley, 1992)? Some, commenting on the "blood brotherhood" between the Treasury, the Fed and Goldman Sachs, make the explicit comparison with the French elite schools Ecole Nationale d'Administration and Ecole Polytechnique, showing a similar traffic of their alumni amongst the upper tiers of the industrial-financial establishment and the *sommets de l'État* (*Le Monde*, September 24/25, 2009), counting more than ten successful crossings, either directly or in a hop, step and jump via the Fed, between the commanding heights of Goldman Sachs and the US Administration.

Or, alternatively, does this specimen of *pantouflage* (the "revolving door") announce a new chapter in the evolution of capitalist discipline? Apart from reminiscences of similar positions of the "Rothschilds" in Europe in the Twentieth Century ("quelque chose de similaire à ce que furent longtemps les Rothschild en Europe" (*Le Monde, September 24–5, 2009*) the scenery is not a far cry from Pareto's "circulation" – in our grammar, the "recycling" of elites. His treatise (Pareto [1935] vol. III, paras 2170–8, reprinted in Pareto, 1963) is still helpful for unraveling the conditions of elite eligibility-and-recruitment and, especially, for clarifying the miraculous *persistence* of the basic principles of the exchange-of-hostages in the preambles of public–private power. The intrigue, in short, is this: how to comprehend that, in spite of the vertigo of international high finance that spoiled the cohesion of the real economy worldwide, *including* the banking system itself, it is again – borrowing Pareto's metaphor for the treasurers of the "residue of combinatory and speculative instincts" in the political economy, relying on "intelligence and cunning" (ibid.: para. 2275) – the *Fox* who is charged to watch the Geese – in Pareto's grammar the *Lion*, standing for the guardians of the "residue of group-persistence and social order", relying on "physical force and on religious or other similar sentiments" (ibid.: para. 2274).

Two preliminary conclusions can be inferred from this excursion. First, the corrosion of character in the financial league of honor does not perceptibly spoil its import, not necessarily because of its treasuring of extraordinary talents or its critical mass but because of its nodal position in the iron triangle of rival financial institutions, firms and states, in addition to the acumen of the most *prepared* in exploiting their nodality in a (self-serving) disciplined fashion. (For a notorious example of this ruthless, as some say "Darwinian" discipline in the specific case of Goldman Sachs, see Cohan, 2011.)

Second, when looking at the foregoing from our rival states', rival financial institutions' and rival firms' perspective, and from the paradox of the perennial search for discipline-cum-permissiveness (cf. Chapter 7, on "Ulysses" versus "Houdini"), it is not the academic construct of the comparative contrasts between governance regimes and business systems that matters (cf. Chapter 5, on system–level studies). What counts, instead, are asymmetries in the room and capacity for game *switches* (arena and agenda substitution) that enable some to press others – even against the latter's interests, public and private – for matching or preferably *outpacing* the permissiveness of alternate disciplinary regimes. Summing up, what essentially matters is not the static *distribution* of bargaining power; decisive is the Paretian *circulation* of semi-sovereign powers. With that we arrive at the key question: what about the animation that prompts the transition of encirclements from subgame to subgame? A better understanding of the logic of the Faustian *anima* pushes our journey to its final track: the *recapture* of capitalist discipline.

Conclusion: the conquest of discipline

In the section above (The twist: on the calculus-of-complicity) I illustrated the potential gains from a perspective that seeks to restore the cyclical links that are separated by the academic canons of the Habitus and Habitat mode. What, from a *co*-habitation perspective, begins as *agent*-driven disciplinary arrangements in the respective subgames, "drifts away" into *agency*-driven regime transformations in the supragame. Reiterated in terms of the discussion on (new) institutional theory at the end of Chapter 3: *agent*-focused approaches in the Habitus mode neglect the macro-regime consequences of micro-motives and meso-movements. As Aoki (2001, chs 1, 7, and 2003: 17–18) argues: "[in a] Williamsonian frame, institutional environment is incorporated as the (exogenous) rules of the game", whereas in reality "[institutions] are endogenously created but regarded as exogenous constraints by individual players", because they are " *reflected in self-sustaining shared beliefs (common expectations) of the players about ways how the game is repeatedly being played"*.

On the other hand, as we saw earlier, *agency*-focused approaches in the Habitat mode tend to neglect the role of specific agents – i.e. the prompting hand – in the enactment of regime changes from subgame to subgame.

I have summarized the *inter*links between the micro-, meso- and macro-levels of analysis – from organizational competences to interorganizational commitments and institutional consequences – in Figure 9.1. The figure shows how, from an interactionist perspective, the disjointed fields of the Habitus and Habitat mode might be brought together into a mutually

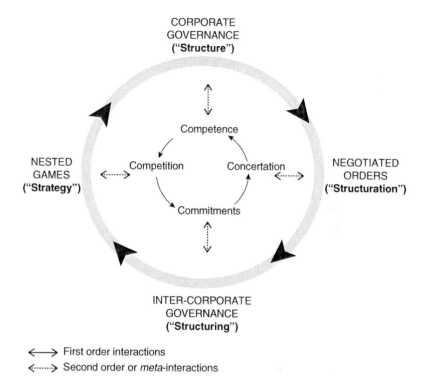

CORPORATE
GOVERNANCE
("**Structure**")

Competence

NESTED
GAMES
("**Strategy**")

Competition   Concertation

NEGOTIATED
ORDERS
("**Structuration**")

Commitments

INTER-CORPORATE
GOVERNANCE
("**Structuring**")

⟵⟶ First order interactions
⟵·····> Second order or *meta*-interactions

Figure 9.1 Agents versus agency: on the "implication" of strategy, structuring and negotiated order

Notes: The *inner* circle (actor level) represents "*agents*": the Habitus-perspective; the *outer* circle (regime level) represents "*agency*": the Habitat-perspective; the dotted *arrows*, linking the inner and outer circle, represent the "implication" (recursive *inter*action) of actors and regimes.

inspiring, more dynamic whole. The inner and outer circle describe the mutual implication ("reflexivity") of micro-practices, meso-arrangements and macro-order. The *inner* circle recapitulates what has been said about the interrelationships between core competence, core competition and core cooperation. The *outer* circle resumes the institutional forces that enable and constrain what happens in the inner-circle dynamics. The inner circle asserts that what organizations consider their distinctive skills and capabilities will affect their perception of what they consider their most exemplary competitors. The selection of core competitors ("bench markers") affects the search and selection of core complementors and sponsors, that is, will generate specific forms of concerted action. Learning over time from experience with specific forms of concertation feeds back on reappraisals of the initial definition of the core competence of organizations.

The core competence of an organization is inspired by its structure of governance. The governance structure "mobilizes" specific strategies and stratagems, that is the search and selection of core competitors and complementors, and from there the selection of specific forms of *inter*-organizational governance. Interorganizational arrangements are the result of boundary and level-spanning choices. Structures of interorganizational governance lead to varieties in the "negotiated order" of disciplinary regimes. And inversely: mutations in regime discipline feedback on inter-organizational arrangements that feedback, in turn, on the initial structures of organizational governance, triggering a "new round" in the inner circle from core competence to competition and cooperation – and so on. In the hypothesis of the "concentric" *implication* of inner and outer circle dynamics resounds the sociological notion of the "duality" of social structure, arguing that "strategies" of the actors *draw* on the structural rules and resources that constitute social systems while, by acting, they *reconstitute* the structure of social systems ("structuration"). In Giddens's grammar (1984, more specifically, 1979: 69): "the structural properties of social systems are both the medium and outcome of the practices that constitute those systems". In *our* grammar (see pp. 259 ff., Box 8.10 "The Argument"), "strategies constitute order; and order constrains and enables strategies that reconstitute order".

Unraveling the "dark matter" of the *animation* of order and disorder requires a nearer specification of the ontological status of such expressions as the "conspiracy of ignoring" and its *multiplier*: the "calculus of complicity". Essential for that specification, from a methodological interactionist perspective, is the distinction between motives and mechanisms. *Motives* refer to "intent/reason/volition", whereas *mechanisms* relate to the "generative principles" of the cyclical reproduction of order and disorder. Intents belong to an *agents* perspective, that is "Weberian" *reasons* for economic action. Examples belonging to this *subjective* domain range from "defining the scope of controversy" to "the creative use of darkness/the judicious use of light":

> The definition of alternatives is the supreme instrument of power … He who determines what politics is about runs the country because the definition of alternatives is the choice of conflicts, and the choice of conflict allocates power. (Schattschneider, 1957: 937)

Or more pertinently:

> If policy analysis is the science of rational choice among alternatives, it is dependent on another more imaginative activity – the invention

of alternatives worth considering...Selecting the alternatives to be compared, and selecting the emphasis to be placed on the criteria for evaluation may be what matters, and the creative use of darkness may be as much needed as the judicious use of light. (Schelling, 1985: 27–8)

Causation or the "generative principles" of the dynamics of the organization of economic life, on the other hand, belong to the *objective* domain, that is an *agency* perspective in the "Elsterian" sense of the *mechanisms* of, for instance, the "prolongation/proliferation" of self-disbelieved beliefs generating "waves" of mergers and acquisitions, and the cyclical "drift" of capitalist order and disorder. The explanation of the latter phenomena – "waves", "drift" and the like – satisfies even the stricter criteria of a "full" functionalist explanation of the collective or systemic consequences of individual rationales, as stipulated by Elster (1984: 28), namely the systemic consequences must be *unintended* by the actors partaking in the intended "sharing of the spoils" while, in addition, the consequences (or at least the *causal* relationship between a behavioral pattern and its consequences) are *unrecognized* by the actors. In that sense the "coordination and compliance" of the actors do not require formal or explicit communication (see the tacitly shared sequence of *sous-entendues* in, for instance, the "Paulson cycle" or the "Icelandic scenario" in Chapter 1). The latter echoes the "spontaneity" of the Galbraithian imperatives of size-and-technostructure that "supersede" the market as a coordination mechanism (cf. Chapter 2). Succinctly stated: *causation overrules motivation* when it comes to the explanation of the swings of discipline in the orchestration of undisciplined interests.

The notions of consonance and complicity, like its dynamic correlate *animation*, cover both meanings: from an *agent*-driven perspective the term has, knowingly, strong volitional leanings – we speak of the "*willing* suspension of disbeliefs". On the other hand, from an *agency* perspective, there are equally strong connotations of a self-fulfilling, that is agent-*insensitive* multiplier, that is contamination and proliferation of the "remittance of self-disbelieved beliefs" – necessary for understanding the "generation" of capitalist order and disorder as a cyclical phenomenon. It is exactly the notion of contamination and proliferation that provides the moral disclaimer for the "Faustian fake" we noticed earlier: contamination and proliferation effectively absolve the "calculus" of complicity from the pejorative connotations of malicious *intent*. In that sense it might be more accurate to speak of a "calculus of *implicit* complicity". Both interpretations – the mutual *implication* of motives and mechanisms – are involved in the "empowerment" of the prompt-ing hand, that is in the rationalization and legitimation of coercive mechanisms without a cause. (The foregoing is a perfect illustration of the potential merits of a methodological interactionist perspec-tive: what "takes-off" in the inner circle of Figure 9.1 as agent-driven motives and movements re-emerges as "structurated" in the outer circle as agent-insensitive coercive practices. As we will see below both *agents* and *agency* are invoked when we come to speculate about the role of the prompting hand in the "shuttle" from inner-to outer-circle interactions, and about eventual venues for breaking the Faustian spell that drives the recycling of capitalist discipline.)

As it is beyond my scope to cover the entire implications of this study in a conclusive sense, I propose to single out two related issues that in my opinion deserve priority in further research, both for scientific and practical reasons: the issue of organizational *self*-discipline – the "capacity to bind oneself" – and, as a normative windfall, the room for restoring the "respectability" of corporate diplomacy and capi-talist discipline. I will proceed as follows. For exploring the possi-ble venues for countervailing the "Faustian spell", and delineating the hypothetical role for a "Devil's advocate" in that venture – we must, first, open the black box of the *prompting hand*. At the closure of Chapter 3 we conjectured that the "backstage whips" that figure as the prompting hand play a decisive role in the (re)constitution of capitalist discipline along three axes: (1) the accommodation of risk assessments and regret, (2) the containment of distrust arising from the divides between value creation and value appropriation, and (3) the manipulation of reputations.

However, insight into the diplomatic and disciplinary "definition of the scope of controversies" and the "creative uses of light and dark-ness" by the *prompters* presupposes insight into the (*ex ante* versus *ex post*) *promptness* of the responses of rival firms and states to the risks of contractual hazards and other dilemmas in the coordination of inter-ests in situations of strategic interdependence. The state of the art on these questions is rudimentary and a far cry from rigorous theorizing and firm empirical results. As long as we know next to nothing about the responsiveness of states and firms, speculations about the modes of operation of the prompting hand – and therefore about the counter-vailing role of a Devil's advocate – are bound to remain at best artists' impressions. Yet a study that announces as its leitmotiv the exploration of a "micro-foundation for the explanation of the drift of capitalist dis-cipline" must, however tentatively, face the issue.

The preceding chapters contain some scattered clues on the two main dimensions of responsiveness, namely the promptness and pro-portionality of responding. Conceivably, from an *agents'* perspective a suitable first source of inspiration would be game theory. The prin-cipal contribution of game theory lies in its radical correction of the naïve-functionalist illusion that interdependence teaches perforce self-restraint and mutual deference, that is *self-discipline* in the choice of timely and proportional responses in the exchange of threats and promises. (Even Axelrod, 1984, seemed to be too optimistic about the self-disciplining effect of parties knowing they would "meet again", instead of the more pertinent question whether parties expect to meet again at the *end* of a chain of transactions.) Chapter 5 reviewed the advantageous versus adverse consequences of a deliberate *lack* or *loss* of self-discipline in different game settings. The "benefits" range from showing an adversary that further escalation may push everyone over the brink, thus forcing others to accommodate, to the demonstration that over-perception may induce unnecessary surrender. Much depends on brinkmanship, that is the capacity to steer a "proportionate" mid-dle course between over-and under-responding. Game theory, in short, sensitizes for the sort of Schellingian and Schumpeterian paradoxes of cooperation and conflict we came across earlier. However, given its logical-experimental predispositions, game theory does not have the reputation of being very helpful when it comes to clarifying the *causes* of self-discipline, that is identifying the empirical (as opposed to exper-imental) conditions that explain variations or changes in the prompt-ness and proportionality of organizational responses to the moves and signals of others in situations of strategic interdependence.

At first sight Smith et al. (1992) break fresh ground for paving the way from experimental impressionism to empirical structuralism. Theirs is an admirably complete, though extremely complex, "stimulus-response" model of the interactive dynamics of competitive and col-laborative moves and countermoves. As we saw in Chapter 8 all the relevant ingredients for a *structural* analysis are present, such as inter-nal characteristics of the actors and responders, external characteristics of the industrial and competitive environment, the ease and speed of imitation by rivals, the role of reputation and risk attitudes, as well as the possible interactions between these variables. However instructive and stimulating for the analysis of *tactical* moves and countermoves (such as pricing and advertising campaigns), the model remains unfit for the analysis of strategic movements (such as waves of investments and divestments in mergers and alliances) and the politics of capitalist coordination at higher levels of analysis. For that purpose we need both an extension *and* simplification of the analytical framework that integrates (see Figure 9.1) the inner and outer circles of, respectively, the "structuring" of strategy and the "structuration" of economic order.

The *simplification* starts by going back to the "orthodoxies" of game theory and transaction-costs economics. Parkhe (1993), for instance, offers a blend of structural and behavioral arguments for explaining the institutional response of organizations to the problems of cheating and opportunism in interfirm strategic alliances. The author mentions the "shadows of the past and future", that is (fear of) path dependences ("lock-ins") as a consequence of "non-recoverable investments", leading to potential "holdups", and the role of cooperative "reputation", that is the perception of opportunism versus trust based on (learning from) the history of cooperative ventures. Both trust and mutual dependence are shown to explain the robustness and longevity of alliances, the reduction of coordination and compliance costs, and the declining dependence on non-recoverable investments and contractual safeguards as a deterrent against opportunism and the hazards of interorganizational cooperation. Others, among them Inkpen and Beamish (1997), come to less optimist conclusions on the "robustness" and "performance" of collaborative agreements, mainly because they take into account, more than Parkhe, shifts in *bargaining power* due to – eventually unplanned and unforeseen – *spillover* hazards in cooperative ventures, to the effect of making "knowledge and skills sharing" obsolete bargains.

As argued in Chapter 8 (pp. 273 ff.), the analysis of (over- versus under-) responding to the dilemmas of cooperation and conflict in situations of interdependent choice will benefit from an approach that more explicitly centers on the question as to how *culture* affects the perception and *valuation* of structural dependence conditions. In my framework "culture" refers to the codes of rationalization and legitimation of the disciplinary arrangements that emanate from structural dependences. As elaborated in the foregoing the response to structural dependences is related to the "ease" of monitoring and sanctioning. The ease of monitoring and sanctioning was said to be related to the size and stability of intra-actor coalitions and interorganizational alliances. In Chapter 7 I linked the "trade-offs" between the "marginal utilities" of coalitions and alliances to path dependences following from an actor's choice of his or her strategic "core" on the one hand and the concentration and centralization of the arena on the other. *How* organizations perceive and evaluate the trade-off is *filtered* by cultural dispositions. A non-psychological proxy for "culture" may be borrowed from the comparative literature on corporate governance regimes, asserting, for instance, that the Rhineland type of governance fosters "slow but stable and more proportionate responses", whereas the Anglo-Saxon type induces "quick but unstable responses" to the stakeholder versus stockholder dilemmas of discipline in situations of mixed competitive and complementary dependences.

Box 9.9 Culture's cause

Speaking of "culture"-driven responses by organizations to threats and opportunities is only meaningful when accompanied by an indication of the "structural" forces – such as the ease and pertinence of monitoring and sanctioning associated with contrasting governance regimes. Without making explicit the question *why* and *how* the costs of monitoring and compliance co-vary with different sorts of corporate governance, "cultural" referrals are bound to end in circular reasoning, of the sort "some respond differently because they are differently *predisposed* by culture". The missing link in these cases is time, and again, *position precedes disposition.* Position derives from, for instance, path-dependent choices in the past (e.g. organization- and/or domain-specific investments) that entail switch and recombination costs – inevitably leading to contrasting perceptions, and *valuations*, of "possible" future worlds of markets, rivals and allies. By granting "structure" the weight it deserves we come closer to a refutable assessment of the discriminatory weight of "culture" indeed.

The issue of culture versus structure reiterates the question as to what comes first in the explanation of (changes in) the promptness and proportionality of responsiveness: agents or agency? The foregoing suggests the following solution.

Strategic choices constitute order and order enables strategic choices. "Choices" cover the range from competence and competition to cooperation and commitments (see the inner circle in Figure 9.1). *How* the *mobilization* of distinct mixes of rivalry and cooperation lead to distinct forms of concerted action and further to structural shifts in regime discipline (a movement from the inner to the outer circle in Figure 9.1) depends on (a)symmetries in the entry and exit options of the respective actors, that is on their differences in *mobility.* Mobility differentials refer to the (non-)equivalence of the switch and recombination costs of the actors – determining, ultimately, their *power* equivalences.

Our analysis of the dynamic of order is enhanced by finding out about the *intervening* variables that govern the mutual conditioning of mobilization and mobility. Figure 9.2 recapitulates the argument: mobility affects – through the "ease of monitoring and sanctioning" – the *promptness* of the responses to the competitive and collaborative moves of others;

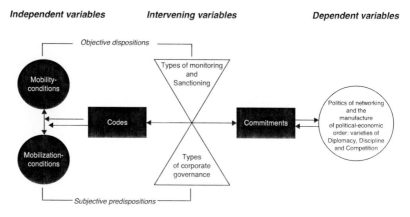

Figure 9.2 Cohabitation and the production of politico-economic order

and the *perception* and *valuation* of mobility affect – via the prevailing type of "corporate governance" – the *proportionality* of the responses.

By including the variables intervening in the "crossing" of mobility and mobilization conditions, and granting similar status to the "agent" versus "agency" characteristics of strategic choice and economic order, we avoid the polarization of both voluntarist *and* determinist reductionism. This, I think, will help to pave the way for upgrading (in Elster's terms) a "mechanistic" into a "genuine" *causal* explanation. For that purpose we have to upgrade the nested game perspective – games-*within*-games – towards a meta-game theoretical perspective, that is a theory of games-*changing-games*.

What does the foregoing imply for the role of the *backstage whips* that are said to prompt the mobilization of bias in the rationalization and legitimation of disciplinary arrangements? Insight into the responsiveness of states and firms provides insight into the effective reach of the prompting hand. In Chapter 3 I proposed to make a distinction between regime formalization ("endorsement") and regime formation ("enforcement"). It is in the *enforcement* that we situate the activism of the prompting hand in three respects: the accommodation of risk and regret appreciations, the manipulation of reputations, and the containment of distrust caused by the divides between value creation and value appropriation.

A privileged way to learn about the activism of the prompting hand is to start from its aversion to visibility. At the closure of Chapter 1 I described the world of the backstage whips as a non-conspicuous, essentially "non-recorded", negotiated order. Indeed, for *recording* that order a useful start is Schelling's mix of "the creative use of darkness (and) the judicious use of light". A hilarious example of the "uses of darkness" can be recognized in the shared conviction among bankers that not *banks* circulating bad loans and dubious securities caused the financial crisis but "accounting rules that required disclosure when the losses began to mount" (cf. a comparable consensus among politicians that WikiLeaks disclosures are not the consequence but the *cause* of the fragility of diplomatic practices). The most appropriate time and place to learn more about the backstage whips is not to be found *within* the encirclement of the games but at the time of *switching* between them, that is whenever the promptness and proportionality of the responses of firms and states, from *conversion* to *consolidation*, are put to the test. Game switches constitute a "natural" disruption of the dominant mold of sector and stage-specific conditions, codes and commitments. For that reason they are the "ideal" time and place for examining the realism of our propositions on the "politics of cohabitation" and assessing the pertinence of the "thrift–shuttle–drift" multiplier for the explanation of the *re*cycling of discipline.

As stipulated above we do not know enough about the determinants of the responsiveness of states and firms. That inevitably complicates the concretization of the countervailing role of the Devil's/Dissenters' advocate. An additional complication is the *time lag* between the inner versus outer clockwork in Figure 9.1: the *agent*-driven inner clockwork, representing actor-specific interactions, typically "revolves" in a shorter time frame than the *agency*-driven mechanic, representing the outer regime-level interactions. At first sight the *practical* implication is therefore: should corrective measures be primarily agent or agency oriented? Our earlier excursus on the distinction between "motives" and "mechanisms" suggests another implication. Motives, such as *thrift* ("economizing on commitments"), are situated in the inner circle. Mechanisms, such as *drift* ("swings in capitalist discipline"), are situated in the outer circle. As far as the diplomatic role of the prompting hand lies essentially in the *timing* of the interaction between inner- and outer-circle dynamics, the role of an effective Devil's/Dissenters' advocate must *not* be "either" agent "or" agency oriented but should focus, instead, on the *manipulation of the inter-temporalities* between the two "productions" of social order.

Calls for the (re)codification of corporate conducts are bound to fail as long as they remain "footloose", that is as long as they do not reflect the underlying conditions of interdependence in the "iron triangle" of states, firms and the shadow of the "third agent": the intermediary complex of the traders-in-credibility. Remedial interventions should aim at controlling for the "spontaneity" of contamination and complicity, whose control requires the decentralization and insulation of the respective parts of the "iron triangle". Crucial for control is the *timing*: successful interventions are bound to be situated at the moments that it still makes sense to *anticipate* game switches and prevent game *capture*, that is when knowledgeable insiders foresee changes in the locus and focus of critical resource/partner dependences and, thus, rearrangements in the balance of bargaining powers between catalysts and captives.

Call this the principle of remedial intervention. As regards the *pragmatics* some additional caveats should be kept in mind. We have argued that corrective measures cannot be organized top down (economies typically consist of sectors in different stages of the life cycle), let alone firm specific (preferential treatment corrupts). Countervailing powers, instead, ask for a bottom-up mobilization of skepticism, that is the organization of a platform for "organized *dissonance*". The primary task of the platform is to challenge the *anonymous* hegemony of the backstage whips that drive the *momentum* of the cycle, namely law firms, accountants, consultants and rating agencies that feed the prolongation and proliferation of the transfer of risk and regrets. The only way to break the semi-sovereignty of this "reputational complex" is to challenge its *implicitness*. Undoing the invisibility of the prompters by promoting the explicitness of their *mandate* (by certification or accreditation) is bound to alter the agenda: from short-term credibility ratings to long-term *respectability* assessments (resulting, ultimately, in more consequential proofs of corporate and regulatory compliance to sound governance principles). Yet, as argued extensively in the foregoing, changing the *agenda* of corporate games requires changing the *arena*, that is intervening in the *conditions* that determine the politics of cohabitation and the Production of political-economic order.

Changing the arena means installing a "whistle blowers" platform that takes as its point of reference the *cumulative* nature of asymmetries in vertical (upstream and downstream) dependences between captives and captors – as opposed to the focus on horizontal collusion and market domination that prevails in the *statics* of competition control. Such a countervailing platform of *informed dissenters* may help to arrest the encroachments on regulatory intransigence and the creeping corrosion of corporate character by the "reputational complex".

The league of dissenters that qualifies for this Devil's advocate role recruits its talents from various sources: investigative journalists; former (career-free) insiders turned knowledgeable informants respectively chroniclers of (Wall) Street corner society; platforms of critical academic researchers; certified analysts and credit raters; and the "backstage" know-how of (former) accountants and contract lawyers. Essential for the effective *impact* of such a league is, first, its *tuning* as an authoritative – but independent – *insider* as opposed to the free-floating "educational estate" that figures in Galbraith's notion of "countervailing powers" (see Box 9.10 below); and, second, it depends on the league's superior feeling for the appropriate *timing* of the moment of jumping on the tides of dissent, namely when the mold of "dominant designs" for the orchestration of the stage-specific subgames is on the brink of being broken by *the discontents themselves* (that is when they are about to discover they have made the wrong calculations in their calculus-of-complicity). Otherwise stated: the Devil's hand must rival the skills and wits of the Prompting hand but with an opposite mission: the orchestration of skepticism.

Box 9.10   The orchestration of skepticism

Galbraith (1968) was somewhat ambivalent on the countervailing capabilities of the "scientific estate". Much of his backhanded pessimism on the role of academia seems related, in hindsight, to the historicity of his diagnosis of the "new" industrial state – including his time-honored prognostics on the convergence of "capitalist" and "communist" versions of the "new industrial state" due to the ineluctable and omnipresent "compulsions" of the "techno structure" and the "mature corporation": *"given the decision to have modern industry, much of what happens is inevitable and the same"* (ibid.: 403).

According to Galbraith it is the combination of (1) the corrosion of self-confidence of the academic establishment and (2) the latter's surrender to the requirements of "the planning system" that conspires to the compulsory adaptation of the "scientific estate" to the "vocational needs of the industrial system" (ibid.: 389). The "economic" branch of academia is said to be susceptible to a fatal symbiosis with the industrial estate "for reasons of sunk costs and convenience" (ibid.: 390). The only "liberalization" Galbraith could conceive of – inspired by the former century's idea of *Zivilcourage* – is the renaissance of the soft power of "aesthetic goals" by which the scientific establishment might emancipate itself from the conformist diktats of the "industrial system", to the effect of restoring scholarly respect for "the larger purposes of the society" (ibid.: 406).

The minor key of Galbraith's assessment has to do with the time of his writing. Those were the days of the old discipline: a virtually perfect fit between oligarchic cum oligopolist rule. In the new discipline radically different mobility and mobilization conditions obtain for rival firms, rival states and the intermediary legal-financial-reputational complex. Clearly, as suggested above, when the Visible hand of a nation state's "technostructure" is replaced by the Prompting hand of an internationally shifting "reputational complex", the locus and focus of countervailing forces have to be relocated and refocused as well.

Apart from the specific competences – in terms of timing and tuning – of the earlier mentioned candidates for the league of "organized dissenters", the mobilization of another score of potential "insiders" presents itself, namely firms in the real economy who suffer from the adverse consequences of the unfettered and increasingly asymmetric mobility options that benefit the financial-industrial complex. When the Prompting hand, in spite of its internal rivalries, manages to organize itself "spontaneously" (that is without explicit communication) there are no compelling reasons to see why the mobilization of a *Dissenting* hand should prove to be an impossible mission. It just amounts to the intelligent mobilization of competing loyalties. The corrective powers of the dissenting hand reside in the *diversity* of its financial, intellectual and relational sources and, more particularly, its feeling for the *timing* of game switches.

Epilogue

The mission of scientific inquiry is not to establish definitive "truths" but to tighten the net around puzzles still waiting for an answer. Among the latter, as one of the most outstanding "known unknowns", is the composition and complexion of the *prompting hand* and a precise description of its modes of encirclement in and through the respective subgames. So, as announced at the outset, this conceivably is not the end of our story. Ours is, Ulysses-wise, a first step on a longer journey towards the construction of a realist and robust framework for the analysis of the "politics of cohabitation" among rival firms and rival states. At the end of Chapter 1 I confessed to subscribe to the epistemological position that asserts that models are useful only in the instrumental sense of screening, instead of representing, social reality. Well-founded ones – *si no è vero* – are models that dissolve as soon as they have done their work, lifting the veils of the *appearance* of reality. Considering our work from this angle may resemble the way the British painter Francis Bacon told viewers to look at the "subjects" that posed as models for his paintings: "the subject is the bait, but the bait shrivels; what remains is the reality of the subject and the bait, the subject, fades away. The reality is the remains of the subject" (Francis Bacon, interviewed by the Dutch literary magazine *Raster*, no. 35, 1985; my translation).

Considering the fiascos of capitalist self-discipline, the "modern" industrial state must learn to rival the *political* skills of the market players, lest the recapture of capitalist discipline remains an impossible mission. Market players, due to their larger maneuverability and internal resolve, appear to be better versed, more than "the" modern state, at playing the play of nested games. For matching these skills we must know more about the *market* skills of rival states, that is about the determinants of the intelligence and responsiveness of political institutions.

To the extent that states appear to be susceptible to the same logic of thrift – and drift as markets, the countervailing mission of the third player – the Dissenters' advocate – comes to lie in-between the two, that is in its capacity to affect the *shuttle* diplomacy between market and state. For effectively accomplishing this mission – the mobilization of "organized skepticism" – the Dissenters' advocate has to be an insider in both domains but at the same time independent of them, professionally as well as materially. Being an *insider* it must equal the feel for timing of the market players; being *independent* it must equal the tuning of the public players. Learning more about the politics of cohabitation in this *trias economica* (triple political economy) constitutes an appealing research agenda. From a pragmatist standpoint the mobilization of skepticism serves a dual purpose: the more pertinent the works of the Dissenting hand the more likely it provokes a response from the Prompting hand; the latter's response, in return, provides indispensable material for probing the pertinence – and repairing the flaws – of the propositions presented in my reconstruction of the orchestration of corporate games and the logic of capitalist discipline.

References

Agnelli, U. (1992) Excerpts from a transcript of a speech given at the *Collège d'Europe*, Bruges, January 16.

Ahdieh, R.B. (2003) Making Markets: Network Effects and the Role of Law in the Creation of Strong Securities Markets, *Southern California Law Review*, 76, 277–350.

Ahdieh, R.B. (2004) Law's Signal: A Cueing Theory of Law in Market Transition, *Southern California Law Review*, 77, 219–306.

Ahdieh, R.B. (2009) The Visible Hand: Coordination Functions of the Regulatory State (December 9). Emory Public Law Research Paper 09–86; Emory Law and Economics Research Paper 09–50.

Akerlof, G.A. (1970) The Market for "Lemons": Qualitative Uncertainty and the Market Mechanism, *Quarterly Journal of Economics*, 84, 488–500.

Akerlof, G.A. and R.J. Shiller (2009) *Animal Spirits: How Human Psychology Drives the Economy, and Why it Matters for Global Capitalism*, Princeton University Press, Princeton.

Allison, G.T. (1969) Conceptual Models and the Cuban Missile Crisis, *The American Political Science Review*, 63(3), 689–718.

Allison, G.T. (1971) *Essence of Decision: Explaining the Cuban Missile Crisis*, Scott, Foresman and Company, Glenview, Ill.

Aoki, M. (2001) *Toward a Comparative Institutional Analysis*, MIT Press, Cambridge, Mass.

Aoki, M. (2003) An Organizational Architecture of T-form: Silicon Valley Clustering and its Institutional Coherence, *RIETI Discussion Paper Series* 04-E-003.

Aoki, M., B. Gustafsson and O.E. Williamson (eds) (1990), *The Firm as a Nexus of Treaties*, Sage Publications, London.

Arthur, W.B. (1988) Self-reinforcing Mechanisms in Economics, in P.W. Anderson, K.J. Arrow and D. Pines (eds), *The Economy as an Evolving Complex System*, Addison-Wesley, Reading, 9–31.

Arthur, W.B. (1989) Competing Technologies, Increasing Returns, and Lock-in by Historical Events, *The Economic Journal*, 99.

Arthur, W.B., Y.N. Ermolier and M. Kaniovski (1987) Path-dependent Processes and the Emergence of Macro-Structure, *European Journal of Operational Research*, 30.

Atkinson, M.C. and W.D. Coleman (1985) Corporatism and Industrial Policy, in *Organized Interests and the State, Studies in Meso-corporatism*, Sage Series in Neo-Corporatism, Sage Publications, London.

Atkinson, M.C. and W.D. Coleman (1989) Strong States and Weak States, *British Journal of Political Science*, 19(1), 46–67.

Audretsch, D.B. (1989) *The Market and the State: Government Policy towards Business in Europe, Japan and the United States*, Harvester Wheatsheaf, New York.

Axelrod, R. (1984) *The Evolution of Co-operation*, Basic Books, New York.

Bachrach, P. and M. Baratz (1962) Two Faces of Power, *American Political Science Review*, 56, 947–52.

Bachrach, P. and M. Baratz (1963) Decisions and Non-decisions, *American Political Science Review*, 57, 641–52.

Bailey, D. and K. Cowling (2006) Industrial Policy and Vulnerable Capitalism, *International Review of Applied Economics*, 20(5), 537–53.

Balakrishnan, S. and M.P. Koza (1993) Information Asymmetry, Adverse Selection and Joint Ventures: Theory and Evidence. *Journal of Economic Behavior and Organization*, 6(1), 99–117.

Barney, J.B. (1997) *Gaining and Sustaining Competitive Advantage*, Addison-Wesley Publishing Company, Reading, Mass.

Barofsky, N. (2012) *Bailout. An Inside Account of How Washington Abandoned Main Street while Rescuing Wall Street*, Free Press, New York.

Benn, T. (1980) Manifestos and Mandarins: *Policy and Practice: the Experience of Government*, 57–8.

Berle, A. and G.C. Means (1932) *Modern Corporation and Private Property*. Hancourt, Brace, Jovanovich, New York.

Best, M.H. (1989) *The New Competition and Industrial Policy*, Polity Press, Oxford, Cambridge.

Best, M.H. (1990) *The New Competition: Institutions of Industrial Restructuring*, Polity Press, Cambridge.

Bhide, A. (1986) Hustle as Strategy, *Harvard Business Review*, September–October, 59–65.

Biles, B.A. (1983) Harmonizing the Regulation of New Chemicals in the United States and in the European Economic Community, *American Chemical Society Symposium Series*, 213, 39–65.

Blankart, C.B. and G. Knieps (1991) Path Dependence, Network Externalities and Standardization, *Research Memorandum*, 439, University of Groningen.

Borys, B. and D.B. Jennison (1989) Hybrid Arrangements as Strategic Alliances: Theoretical Issues in Organizational Combinations, *Academy of Management Review*, 14(2), 234–49.

Bowersox, D.J. (1990) The Strategic Benefits of Logistics Alliances, *Harvard Business Review*, July–August, 36–45.

Bowman, J.R. (1989) *Capitalist Collective Action*, Cambridge University Press, Cambridge.

Bradach, J.L. and R.G. Eccles (1989) Markets versus Hierarchies: From Idealtypes to Plural Forms, *Annual Review of Sociology*, 97–118.

Brandenburger, A.M. and B.J. Nalebuff (1996) *Co-opetition: A Revolutionary Mindset that Combines Competition and Co-Operation: The Game Theory Strategy that's Changing the Game of Business*, Broadway Books, New York.

Breton, A. and R. Wintrobe (1982) *The Logic of Bureaucratic Conduct: An Economic Analysis of Competition, Exchange, and Efficiency in Private and Public Organizations*, Cambridge University Press, Cambridge.

Buck Consultants International (1995), Internal working paper, March 23.

Burrough, B. and J. Hellyar (1990) *Barbarians at the Gate: The Fall of RJR Nabisco*, Harper and Row, New York.

Butler, R.J. (1983) Control through Markets, Hierarchies and Communes: A Transactional Approach to Organisational Analysis, *Administration & Society* November 15(3), 323–62.

Campbell, J.R. Hollingsworth and L.L. Lindberg (eds) (1991) *Governance of the American Economy,* Cambridge University Press, Cambridge UK.

Campbell, J.L. and L.N. Lindberg (1991) The Evolution of Governance Regimes, in J.L. Campbell J.R. Hollingsworth and L.L. Lindberg (eds), *Governance of the American Economy,* Cambridge University Press, Cambridge UK, 319–355.

Cawson, A. (ed.) (1985) *Organized Interests and the State, Studies in Meso-corporatism,* Sage Series in Neo-Corporatism, Sage Publications, London.

Cawson, A. (1986) *Corporatism and Political Theory,* Wiley & Sons, New York.

Cawson, A., L. Hadden and I. Miles (1990) *Hostile Brothers: Competition and Closure in the European Electronics Industry,* Clarendon Press, Oxford.

Cecchini, P. (1988) *The European Challenge 1992: The Benefits of a Single Market,* Wildwood House, Aldershot.

Central Planning Bureau (1992) *The Netherlands in Triplicate,* SDU Uitgeverij, The Hague.

Chamberlain, N. (1962) *The Firm: Micro-economic Planning and Action,* McGraw-Hill, New York.

Chandler, A.D. (1977) *The Visible Hand,* Harvard University Press, Cambridge Mass.

Chandler, A.D. (1984) The Emergence of Managerial Capitalism, *Business History Review,* 58(4), 473–503.

Choate, P. (1991) *Agents of Influence,* Simon & Schuster, New York.

Coase, R.H. (1988) The Nature of the Firm: Influence, *Journal of Law, Economics and Organisation,* 4, 33–47.

Coffee, J.C., Jr. (2005) *A Theory of Corporate Scandals: Why the U.S. and Europe Differ,* The Center for Law and Economic Studies, New York, Working Paper 274, March.

Cohan, W.D. (2008) *House of Cards: How Wall Street's Gamblers Broke Capitalism,* Allen Lane/Penguin, London.

Cohan, W.D. (2011) *Money and Power: How Goldman Sachs Came to Rule the World,* Allen Lane, New York.

Cohen E. (1989) *L'Etat brancardier: Politiques du déclin industrial (1974–1984),* Calmann-Lévy, Paris.

Cohen, M.D., J. March and J.P. Olsen (1972) A Garbage Can Model of Organizational Choice, *Administrative Science Quarterly,* March.

Colander, D., H. Follmer, A. Haas, M.D. Goldberg, K. Juselius, A. Kirman, T. Lux and B. Sloth (2009) *The Financial Crisis and the Systemic Failure of Academic Economics,* Kiel Institute for the World Economy, Working Paper 1489, February.

Coleman, W.D. and W.P. Grant (1988) The Organizational Cohesion and Political Access of Business: a Study of Comprehensive Associations, *European Journal of Political Research,* 16, 467–87.

Coleman, W.D. and W.P. Grant (1989) Regional Differentiation of Business Interest Associations: A Comparison of Canada and the United Kingdom, in W.D. Coleman and H.J. Jacek (eds), *Regionalism, Business Interests and Public Policy,* Sage Publications, London 35–58

Coleman, W.D. and H.J. Jacek, (eds) (1989) *Regionalism, Business Interests and Public Policy,* Sage Series in Neo-Corporatism, Sage Publications, London.

Cowart, A., T. Hansen and K.E. Brofoss (1975) Budgetary Strategies and Success at Multiple Decision Levels in the Norwegian Urban Setting, *American Political Science Review,* 69, 543–58.

Cowling, K. (1990) A New Industrial Strategy: Preparing Europe for the Turn of the Century, *International Journal of Industrial Organization*, 8(2), 165–83.

Cowling, K. and R. Sugden (1999) The Wealth of Localities, Regions and Nations: Developing Multinational Economies, *New Political Economy*, 4(3), 361–78.

Crossman, R.H. (1976) *Diaries of a Cabinet Minister*, 3 vols, (1964–1970), Hamish Hamilton and Jonathan Cape, London.

Crouch, C. and Marquard, D. (eds) (1990) *The Politics of 1992: Beyond the Single European Market*, Basil Blackwell, London.

Crozier, M. (1963) *Le phénomène bureaucratique*, Editions Du Seuil, Paris.

Cyert, R. and J.G. March (1963) *A Behavioural Theory of the Firm*, Prentice-Hall, Englewood Cliffs.

D'Aveni, R.A. (with R. Gunther) (1994) *Hypercompetition: Managing the Dynamics of Strategic Maneuvering*, The Free Press, New York.

Daems, H. (1983) The Determinants of the Hierarchical Organization of Industry, in A. Francis, J. Turk, P. Willman (eds), *Power, Efficiency & Institutions*, Heinemann, London, 35–54.

Dahl, R.A. (ed.) (1966) *Political Opposition in Western Democracy*, Yale University Press, New Haven.

David, P.A. (1985) Clio and the Economics of QWERTY, *American Economic Review*, 75.

David, P.A. (1988) *Path-dependence: Putting the Past into the Future of Economics*, Institute for Mathematical Studies in the Social Sciences, Technical Report 533, Stanford University, Stanford.

David, P.A. (1993) Path-dependence and Predictability in Dynamic Systems with Local Network Externalities: A Paradigm for Historical Economies, in D. Foray and C. Freeman (eds), *Technology and the Wealth of Nations*, Francis Pinter, London.

David, P.A. (1994) Why are Institutions the "Carriers of History"? Path Dependence and the Evolution of Conventions, Organizations and Institutions, in *Structural Change and Economic Dynamics*, Oxford University Press, Oxford, 205–20.

De Hen, P.E. (1980) *Actieve en reactieve industriepolitiek in Nederland*, De Arbeiderspers, Amsterdam.

De Jong, H.W. (1972) Multinational Enterprise in the Low Countries, in *La croissance de la grande firme multinationale*, Colloques Internationaux, CNRS, 549, Rennes, 291–310.

De Jong, H.W. (1985) Industrial Policy, An Empty Box, *Economisch Statistische Berichten*, 27 February 142–98.

De Jong, H.W. (1987) Industrial Organization and Industry Policy, in H. Schenk (ed.), *Industry and Technology Policy*, Wolters-Noordhoff, Groningen, 13–28.

De Jong, H.W. (1992) Combination movement in Banking, *ORDO, Jahrbuch für die Ordnung von Wirtschaft und Gesellschaft*, Band 43, 475–99.

Dixit, A.K. and B.J. Nalebuff (1991) *Thinking Strategically: The Competitive Edge in Business, Politics and Everyday Life*, W.W. Norton & Company, New York, London.

Dornbusch, R. (1989) Europe-1992: Macroeconomic Implications, *Brookings Papers on Economic Activity*, (20), 341–62.

Dubbink, W. and M. van Vliet (1996) Market Regulation versus Co-management: Two Perspectives on Regulating Fisheries Compared, *Marine Policy*, 20(6), 499–516.

Duchene, F. and G. Shepherd (eds) (1987) *Managing Industrial Change in Western Europe*, Francis Pinter, London.

Dunning, J.H. (1993) The Governance of Japanese and US Manufacturing Affiliates in the U.K.: Some Country-specific Differences, in B. Kogut (ed.), *Country Competitiveness: Technology and the Organizing of Work*, Oxford University Press, New York/Oxford, 203–25.

Dyson, K. and S. Wilks (eds) (1985) *A Comparative Study of the State and Industry*, Basil Blackwell, Oxford.

Ebers, M. (ed.) (1997) *The Formation of Interorganizational Networks*, Oxford University Press, Oxford, New York.

Eco, U. (1983) *The Name of the Rose*, Harcourt and Secker, Warburg.

Elias, N. (1969) *Die höfische Gesellschaft*. Luchterhand, Neuwied and Berlin.

Elster J. (1978) *Logic and Society*, Wiley & Sons, New York.

Elster, J. (1982) Marxism, Functionalism and Game Theory, *Theory and Society*, 11, 453–82.

Elster, J. (1984) *Ulysses and the Sirens*, Cambridge University Press, Cambridge (rev. edn).

Elster, J. (1986) Further Thoughts on Marxism, Functionalism, and Game Theory, in J. Roemer (ed.), *Analytical Marxism*, Cambridge University Press, Cambridge, 202–20.

Elster, J. (1989a) *The Cement of Society: A Study of Social Order*, Cambridge University Press, Cambridge.

Elster, J. (1989b) *Nuts and Bolts for the Social Sciences*, Cambridge University Press, Cambridge.

Emerson, M. (1988) The Economics of 1992, *European Economy* (35), Brussels, March.

Emerson, M. (1989) The Emergence of the New European Economy of Europe-1992, *Business Economics*, 24(4): 5–9.

ERI (European Roundtable of Industrialists) (1993) *Europe's industrial future – Beating the Crisis*, ERI, Brussels, December.

Etzioni, A. (1961) *A Comparative Analysis of Complex Organizations*, Free Press, New York.

Evans, P. (1995) *Embedded Autonomy: States and Industrial Transformation*, Princeton University Press, Princeton.

Fama, E.F. and M.C. Jensen (1983) Separation of Ownership and Control, *Journal of Law and Economics*, 26, June, 301–25.

Farrell, J. and G. Saloner (1985) Standardization, Compatibility and Innovations, *Rand Journal of Economics*, 16(1), 70–83.

Feagin, J.R. and M.P. Smith (1987) Cities and the New International Division of Labour: An Overview, in M.P. Smith and J.R. Feagin (eds), *The Capitalist City: Global Restructuring and Community Politics*, Basil Blackwell, Oxford, 3–34.

Fligstein, N. and J. Choo (2005) Law and Corporate Governance, *Annual Review of Law and Social Science*, 61–84.

Fox, A. (1974) *Beyond Contract: Work, Power and Trust Relations*, Faber & Faber, London.

Galbraith, J.K. (1952) *American Capitalism: The Concepts of Countervailing Power*, Houghton Mifflin, Boston, Mass.

Galbraith, J.K. (1968) *The New Industrial State*, Signet Books, New American Library, New York.

Galbraith, J.K. (1974) *Economics and the Public Purpose*, Houghton Mifflin, Boston.

Geelhoed, L.A. (1991) Het subsidiariteitsbeginsel: een communautair principe?, *Sociaal-economische Wetgeving*, 7(8).

Gerlach, M.L. (1992) *Alliance Capitalism: The Social Organization of Japanese Business*, University of California Press, Berkeley.

Geroski, P.A. (1989) European Industrial Policy and Industrial Policy in Europe, *Oxford Review of Economic Policy*, 5(2), 20–36.

Giddens, A. (1979) *Central Problems in Social Theory*, Macmillan, London.

Giddens, A. (1984) *The Constitution of Society*, Polity Press, Cambridge.

Gilsing, V. and B. Nooteboom (2005) Density and Strength of Ties in Innovation Networks, *European Management Review*, 2, 179–97.

Goodin, R.E. (1975) The Logic of Bureaucratic Back-scratching, *Public Choice*, 21, 53–67.

Gouldner, A.W. (1960) The Norm or Reciprocity: A Preliminary Statement, *American Sociological Review*, 25(2), 161–78.

Gourevitch, P. (1986) *Politics in Hard Times: Comparative Responses to International Economic Crises*, Cornell University Press, Ithaca and London.

Gourevitch, P. and J.P. Shinn (2007) *Political Power and Corporate Control: The New Global Politics of Corporate Governance*, Princeton University Press, Princeton.

Grabherr, G. (ed.) (1993) *The Embedded Firm: On the Socioeconomics of Industrial Networks*, Routledge, London.

Granovetter, M. (1973) The Strength of Weak Ties, *American Journal of Sociology*, 78(6), 1360–80.

Granovetter, M. (1985) Economic Action and Social Structure: The Problem of Embeddedness, *American Journal of Sociology*, 91(3), 481–510.

Granovetter, M. (1992) Problems of Explanation in Economic Sociology, in N. Nohria and R.G. Eccles (eds), Networks and organization: Structure, form and action, HBS Press, Boston, 25–56.

Grant, W.P., W. Paterson and C. Whitston (1988) *Government and the Chemical Industry*, Clarendon Press, Oxford.

Grant, W., W. Paterson and C. Whitston (1989) Government-industry Relations in the Chemical Industry: An Anglo-German comparison, in S. Wilks and M. Wright (eds), *Comparative Government-Industry Relations, Western Europe, the United States, and Japan*. Clarendon Press, Oxford, 35–61.

Groenewegen, J. (ed.) (1996) *TCE and Beyond*, Kluwer Academic Publishers, Dordrecht/Boston.

Groenewegen, J. and J.J. Vromen (1996) A Case for Theoretical Pluralism, in J. Groenewegen (ed.), *TCE and Beyond*, Kluwer Academic Publishers, Dordrecht/Boston, 365–80.

Guéhenno, J.M. (1993) *La fin de la democratie*, Flammarion, Paris.

Gulati, R. (1995) Does Familiarity Breed Trust? The Implications of Repeated Ties for Contractual Choice in Alliances, *The Academy of Management Journal*, 38(1), 85–112.

Gulati, R. and Singh, H. (1998) The Architecture of Cooperation: Managing Coordination Costs and Appropriation Concerns in Strategic Alliances, *Administrative Science Quarterly*. 43, 781–814.

Hagedoorn, J. (1993) Understanding the Rationale of Strategic Technology Partnering: Interorganizational Modes of Cooperation and Sectoral Differences, *Strategic Management Journal*, 14, 371–85.

Hagedoorn, J. and J. Schakenraad (1990) Strategic Partnering and Technological Co-operation, in B. Dankbaar, J. Groenewegen, and H. Schenk (eds), *Perspectives in industrial organization*, Springer, Heidelberg, 171–91.

Hagedoorn, J. and J. Schakenraad (1993) A comparison of private and subsidized inter-firm linkages in the European IT industry, *Journal of Common Market Studies*, 14(3), 373–90.

Hall, P. and D. Soskice (2001) *The Varieties of Capitalism: The Institutional Foundations of Comparative Advantage*, Oxford University Press, Oxford.

Halperin, M.H. (1974) *Bureaucratic Politics & Foreign Policy*. Brookings Institution, Washington.

Hamel, G. (1991) Competition for Competence and Interpartner Learning within International Strategic Alliances. *Strategic Management Journal*, 12, 83–103.

Hamel, G. and C.K. Prahalad (1994) *Competing for the Future: Breakthrough Strategies for Seizing Control of your Industry and Creating the Markets of Tomorrow*, Harvard Business School Press, Boston, Mass.

Hamel, G., Y.L. Doz and C.K. Prahalad (1989) Collaborate with your Competitors: And Win, *Harvard Business Review*, January–February, 133–9.

Hancher, L. (1990) *Regulating for Competition: Government, Law and the Pharmaceutical Industry in the United Kingdom and France*, Clarendon Press, Oxford.

Hancher, L. and M. Moran (eds) (1989) *Capitalism, Culture and Regulation*, Clarendon Press, Oxford.

Hardin, G. (1968) The Tragedy of the Commons, *Science*, 162, 1243–48.

Hardin, R. (1982) *Collective Action*, Johns Hopkins University Press, Baltimore Md.

Harrigan, K.R. (1985) An Application of Clustering for Strategic Group Analysis, *Strategic Management Journal*, 7, 535–55.

Harrigan, K.R. (1988) Joint Ventures and Competitive Strategy, *Strategic Management Journal*, 9, 141–58.

Harrigan, K.R. and W.H. Newman (1990) Bases of Interorganization Cooperation: Propensity, Power, Persistence, *Journal of Management Studies*, 27(4), 417–34.

Hartigan, J.A. (1975) *Clustering Algorithms*, Wiley & Sons, New York.

Hatten, K.J., D.E. Schendel and A.C. Cooper (1978) A Strategic Model of the U.S. Brewing Industry: (1952–1971), *Academy of Management Journal*, 21, 592–610.

Hickson, D.J., C.R. Hinings, C.A. Lee, R.E. Schneck and J.M. Pennings (1971) A Strategic Contingencies' Theory of Intra-organizational Power, *Administrative Science Quarterly*, 6, 216–29.

Hirschman, A.O. (1970) *Exit, Voice and Loyalty: Responses to Decline in Firms, Organizations and States*, Harvard University Press, Cambridge, Mass.

Hirschman, A.O. (1982) Rival Interpretations of Market Society: Civilizing, Destructive, or Feeble, *Journal of Economic Literature*, 20, 1463–84.

Hirschman, A.O. (1991) *The Rhetoric of Reaction: Perversity, Futility, Jeopardy*, Belknap Press/Harvard University Press, Cambridge, Mass.

Hodgson G. (1988) *Economics and Institutions*, Polity Press, Cambridge.

Hodgson, G. (1996) Corporate Culture and the Nature of the Firm, in John Groenewegen (ed.), *Transaction Cost Economics and Beyond*, Kluwer, Boston, pp. 249–69.

Hodgson G. M. (1998) Evolutionary and competence-based theories of the firm, *Journal of Economic Studies*, 25(1), 25–6.

Hodgson, G.M. (2006) What Are Institutions?, *Journal of Economic Issues*, 40, 1, 1–25.

Hogwood, B.W. (1979) *Government and Shipbuilding: The Politics of Industrial Change*, Saxon House, Westmead.

Howes, C. (1993) Are Japanese Transplants Restoring U.S. Competitiveness or Dumping their Social Problems in the U.S. Market? unpublished mimeo.

Imai, K. and H. Itami (1984) Interpenetration of Organization and Market, Japan's Firm and Market in Comparison with the U.S., *International Journal of Industrial Organization*, 2, 285–310.

Inkpen, A.C. and P.W. Beamish (1997) Knowledge, Bargaining power, and the Instability of International Joint Ventures, *Academy of Management Journal*, 22(1), 177–202.

Jacquemin, A. (1977) Concentratie en overleg: de verhoudingen tussen overheid en privé-sector, *Sociaal-economische Wetgeving*, 4(5), 333–45.

Jacquemin, A.P. and H.W. de Jong (eds) (1976) *Markets, Corporate Behavior and the State*, Martinus Nijhoff, The Hague.

Jacquemin, A. and B. Spinoit (1986) Economic and Legal Aspects of Cooperative Research: A European view, *The Annual Proceedings of Fordham Corporate Law Institute*, Matthew Bender & Co., New York, 487–519.

Jarillo, J.G. (1988) On Strategic Networks, *Strategic Management Journal*, 9, 31–41.

Jensen, M.C. and W.H. Meckling (1976) The Theory of the Firm: Managerial Behavior, Agency Costs and Ownership Structure, *Journal of Financial Economics*, 3, 305–60.

Johnson, C. (1984) Introduction: The Idea of Industrial Policy, in C. Johnson (ed.), *The Industrial Policy Debate*, Institute for Contemporary Studies, San Francisco, Calif., 3–26.

Jorde, T.M. and D.J. Teece (1989) Competition and Cooperation: Striking the Right Balance, *California Management Review*, 31(3), 25–37.

Junne, G. (1972) *Game Theory in International Relations: Bounded Rationality in Strategy Thinking*, Bertelsmann Universitätsverlag, Dusseldorf.

Kahneman D. and A. Tversky (1979) Prospect Theory: An Analysis of Decision under Risk, *Econometrica*, 47(2), 263–91.

Kapp, K.W. (1976) The Nature and Significance of Institutional Economies, *Kyklos*, 29, 209–32.

Katzenstein, P.J. (ed.) (1978) *Between Power and Plenty: Foreign Economic Policies of Advanced Industrial States*, The University of Wisconsin Press, Madison, London.

Kenis, P. and V. Schneider (1987) The EC as an International Corporate Actor: Two Case Studies in Economic Diplomacy, *European Journal of Political Research*, 15, 437–57.

Kenis, P. and V. Schneider (1991) Policy Networks and Policy Analysis: Scrutinizing a New Analytical Toolbox, in B. Marin and R. Mayntz, *Policy Networks*, Campus Verlag/Westview Press, Frankfurt am Main/Boulder, Colorado, 25–59.

Kenney, M. and R. Florida (1993) *Beyond Mass Production: The Japanese System and its Transfer to the U.S.*, Oxford University Press, New York, Oxford.

Kester, W.C. (1992) Industrial Groups as Systems of Contractual Governance, *Oxford Review of Economic Policy*, 8(3), 24–44.

Keynes, J.M. (1936) *The General Theory of Employment, Interest and Money*, Macmillan Cambridge University Press, Cambridge.

Kindleberger, C. P. (2000) *Manias, Panics and Crashes: A History of Financial Crises*, Palgrave Macmillan, Basingstoke.

Kissinger, H. (1979) *The White House Years*, Weidenfeld & Nicolson, London.

Kissinger, H. (1982) *Years of Upheaval*, Little, Brown & Company, Boston, Toronto.

Kissinger, H. (1994) *Diplomacy*, Simon & Schuster, New York.

Kogut, B. (1988) Joint Ventures: Theoretical and Empirical Perspectives, *Strategic Management Journal*, 9 , 319–32.

Kreiken, E.J. (1986) De Coalitiestrategie: creatieve coöperatieve competitie (Het voorbeeld van Airbus Industries), in J. Bilderbeek, J.M.L. Janssen, G.W.R. Vijge and J. Kreiken, Ondernemingsstrategie: *Theorie & Praktijk*, Stenfert Kroese, Leiden, 285–94.

Krepps, D.M., (How) Can Game Theory Lead to a Unified Theory of Organization?, Unpublished manuscript.

Kuhn, T. (1962) *The Structure of Scientific Revolutions*, University of Chicago Press, Chicago.

La Palombara, J. (1964) *Interest Groups in the Italian System*, Princeton University Press, Princeton, NJ.

Lehmbruch, G. and P.C. Schmitter (eds) (1982) *Patterns of Corporatist Policymaking*, Sage Publications, Beverly Hills.

Leonard-Barton, D. (1992) Core Capabilities and Core Rigidities: A Paradox in Managing New Products, *Strategic Management Journal*, 13, 111–25.

Levi, M. (1988) *Of Rule and Revenue*, The University of California Press, Berkeley.

Levi, M. (1990) A Logic of Institutional Change, in K.S. Cook and M. Levi (eds), *The Limits of Rationality*, The University of Chicago Press, Chicago & London, 402–18.

Levitt, B. and J.G. March (1988) Organizational Learning, *Annual Review of Sociology*, 14.

Lewis, M. (1989) *Liars' Poker*, Coronet, London.

Lieberman, M.B. and D.B. Montgomery (1988) First-mover Advantages, *Strategic Management Journal*, 9, 41–58.

Lijphart, A. (1975) *The Politics of Accommodation*, California University Press, Berkeley.

Long, N.E. (1958) The Local Community as an Ecology of Games, *American Journal of Sociology*, 64(3), 251–62.

Lowi, T.A. (1964) American Business, Public Policy, Case Studies and Political Theory, *World Politics*, 16, 677–715.

Lowi, T.A. (1969) *The End of Liberalism*, Norton, New York.

Lowi, T.A. (1970) Decision Making versus Public Policy: Toward an Antidote for Technocracy, *Public Administration Review*, 30, 314–25.

Lowi, Th.J. (1979) *The End of Liberalism: The Second Republic of the United States*, Norton & Company, New York, London.

Lukes, S. (1974) *Power: A Radical View*, Macmillan, London.

MacNeil, I.R. (1978) Contracts: Adjustments of Long-term Economic Relations under Classical, Neoclassical, and Relational Contract Law, *Northwestern University Law Review*, 72, 854–905.

March, J.G. (1988) *Decisions and Organizations*, Basic Blackwell, Oxford.

March, J.G. (1991) Exploration and Exploitation in Organizational Learning, *Organization Science*, 2(1), 71–87.

March, J.G. and H.A. Simon (1958) *Organizations*, John Wiley, New York.

Marin, B. and R. Mayntz (eds) (1991) *Policy Networks: Empirical Evidence and Theoretical Considerations*, Campus Verlag/Westview Press, Frankfurt am Main, Boulder, Colo.

Marks, G., F.W. Scharpf and P.C. Schmitter (1996) *Governance in the European Union*, Sage Publications, London.

Marshall, A. (1961 [1920]) *Principles of Economics*, Macmillan, London.

Martinelli, A. (ed.) (1991) *International Markets and Global Firms: A Comparative Study of Organized Business in the Chemical Industry*, Sage Publications, London.

Mascarenhas, B. and D.A. Aaker (1989) Mobility Barriers and Strategic Groups, *Strategic Management Journal*, 10, 475–85.

Mayntz, R. (1991) *Modernization and the Logic of Interorganisational Networks*, MPIFG Discussion Paper 91/8, Max Planck-Institut für Gesellschaftsforschung, Köln.

Mayntz, R. and F.W. Scharpf (1975) *Policy-making in the German Federal Bureaucracy*, Elsevier, Amsterdam.

McGee, J. and H. Thomas (1986) Strategic Groups: Theory, Research and Taxonomy, *Strategic Management Journal*, 7, 141–60.

Merlini, C. (ed.) (1984) *Economic Summits and Western Decision Making*, Croom Helm, London.

Michels, R. (1968) *Political Parties: A Sociological Study of the Oligarchical Tendencies of Modern Democracy*, Free Press, New York.

Middlemas, K. (1995) *Orchestrating Europe: The Informal Politics of European Union (1973–1995)*, Fontana Press, London.

Miles, S. (2001) *How to Hack a Party Line: The Democrats and Silicon Valley*, Farrar, Straus and Giroux, New York.

Minsky, H. P. (1992) *The Financial Instability Hypothesis*, Working Paper No.74, Jerome Levy Economics Institute of Bard College, May 1992.

Morris, D. and M. Hergert (1987) Trends in International Collaborative Agreements, *Columbia Journal of World Business*, (Summer) 15–21.

Moss Kantor, R. (1990) *When Giants Learn to Dance*, Unwin Paperbacks, London.

Murphy, R. (1988) *Social Closure: The Theory of Monopolization and Exclusion*, Clarendon Press, Oxford.

Mytelka, L.K., (ed.) (1991) *Strategic Partnerships: States, Firms and International Competition*, Pinter Publishers, London.

Mytelka, L.K. and M. Delapierre (1987) The Alliance Strategies of European Firms in the Information Technology Industry and the Role of Esprit, *Journal of Common Market Studies*, 26(2), 231–53.

Nelson, R.R. (1995) Co-evolution of Industry Structure, Technology and Supporting Institutions, and the Making of Comparative Advantage, *International Journal of the Economics of Business*, 2(2), 171–84.

Nelson, R. and S. Winter (1982) *An Evolutionary Theory of Economic Change*, Harvard University Press, Cambridge, Mass.

Neustadt, R.E. (1966) White House and Whitehall, *Public Interest*, 2, 55–69.

Niskanen, W.A. (1971) *Bureaucracy and Representative Government*, Aldine Atherton, Chicago.

Niskanen, W.A. (1973) *Bureaucracy: Servant or Master, Lessons from America*, Institute of Economic Affairs, London.

Niskanen, W.A. (1979) Competition among Government Bureaux, in C.H. Weiss and A.H. Barton (eds), *Making Bureaucracy Work*, Sage, Beverly Hills, 167–74.

Noorderhaven, N.G. (1990) *Private Competence and Public Responsibility: Anatomy of a Government–Firm Relationship*, Groningen University Press, Groningen.

Nooteboom (1999) B. *Inter-firm Alliances: Analysis and Design*, Routledge, London and New York.

North, D. (1981) *Structure and Change in Economic History*, W.W. Norton, New York.

Offe, C. and H. Wiesenthal (1980) Two Logics of Collective Action: Theoretical Notes on Social Class and Organizational Form, in M. Zeitlin (ed.), *Political Power and Social Theory*, Vol. I, JAI Press, Greenwich.

Ohmae, K. (1985) *Triad Power: The Coming Shape of Global Competition*, The Free Press, New York.

Ohmae, K. (1989) The Global Logic of Strategic Alliances, *Harvard Business Review*, March–April, 143–54.

Olsen, J.P. (1981) Integrated Organizational Participation in Government, in P.C. Nystrom and W.H. Starbuck (eds) *Handbook of Organizational Design, Vol. 2., Remodeling Organizations and Their Environments*, Oxford University Press, Oxford, 492–516.

Olsen, J., P. Roness and H. Spetren (1982) Norway: Still Peaceful Coexistence and Revolution in Slow Motion, in J. Richardson (ed.), *Policy Styles in Western Europe*, George Allen and Unwin, London, 47–79.

Olson, M. (1975) *The Logic of Collective Action, Public Goods and the Theory of Groups*, Harvard University Press, Cambridge, Mass.

Olson, M. (1986) Supply-side Economics, Industrial Policy and Rational Ignorance, in C.E. Bargield and W.A. Schambra (eds), *The Politics of Industrial Policy*, American Enterprise Institute for Public Policy Research, Washington, DC, 245–69.

Ostrom, E. (1990) *Governing the Commons: The Evolution of Institutions for Collective Action*, Cambridge University Press, Cambridge.

Ozaki, R.S. (1984) How Japanese industrial policy works, in C. Johnson, *The Industrial Policy Debate*. Institute for Contemporary Studies, San Francisco, CA, 47–70.

Pareto, V. (1963) *The Mind and Society: A Treatise on General Sociology*. Dover Publications, New York.

Pareto, V. (1966) *Sociological Writings*, Pall Mall Press, London.

Parkhe, A. (1993) Strategic Alliance Structuring: A Game Theoretic and Transaction Cost Examination of Interfirm Cooperation, *Academy of Management Journal*, 36(4), 795–829.

Parkin, F. (1979) *Marxism and Class Theory: A Bourgeois Critique*, Tavistock, London.

Peck, M.J. (1989) Industrial Organization and the Gains from Europe-1992, *Brookings Papers on Economic Activity*, 20, 277–99.

Pelkmans, J. (1988) The Economic Gains from Europe-1992, *Economisch Statistische Berichten*, 73, 447–52.

Penrose, E. (1959) *The Theory of the Growth of the Firm*, Oxford University Press, Oxford.

Perruci, R. (1994) *Japanese Auto-transplants in the Heartland: Corporatism and Community*, Aldine de Gruyter, New York.

Peterson, J. (1991) Technology Policy in Europe: Explaining the Framework Programme and Eureka in Theory and Practice, *Journal of Common Market Studies*, 29(3), 269–90.

Piettre, A. (1955) *Les trois ages de l'économie*, Fayard, Paris.

Piore, M. and C.F. Sabel (1984) *The second industrial divide*, Basic Books, New York.

Pitelis, Ch. (1991) *Market and Non-market Hierarchies: Theory of Institutional Failure*, Blackwell, Oxford.

Porter, M.E. (1980) *Competitive Strategy: Techniques for Analyzing Industries and Competitors*, Free Press, New York.

Porter, M.E. (ed.) (1986) *Competition in Global Industries*, Harvard Business School Press, Boston.

Porter, M.E. (1998) Clusters and the New Economics of Competition, *Harvard Business Review*, November/December.

Porter, R.B. (1984) *The U.S.–U.S.S.R. Grain Agreements*, Cambridge University Press, Cambridge.

Prahalad, C.K. and G. Hamel (1994) The Core Competence of the Corporation, *Harvard Business Review*, May/June.

Raiffa, H.S. (1982) *The Art and Science of Negotiation*, Harvard University Press, Cambridge, Mass.

Raiffa, H., Richardson, J. and Matcalfe, D. (2002) *Negotiation Analysis*, Harvard University Press, Cambridge, Mass.

Reve, T. (1990) The Firm as a Nexus of Internal and External Contracts, in M. Aoki, B. Gustafsson and O.E. Williamson (eds), *The Firm as a Nexus of Treaties*, Sage Publications, London, 133–61.

Rhodes, R.A.W. (1986) *The National World of Local Government*, Allen & Unwin, London.

Rhodes, R.A.W. (1990) Policy Networks: A British Perspective, *Journal of Theoretical Politics*, 2(3), 293–317.

Richardson, K. (1960) *Information and Investment: A Study in the Working of the Competitive Economy*, Oxford University Press, Oxford.

Roijakkers, N. and J. Hagedoorn (2006) Inter-firm R&D Partnering in Pharmaceutical Biotechnology since (1975): Trends, Patterns, and Networks, *Research Policy*, 35(3), 431–46.

Roscam Abbing, M. and J. Schakenraad (1991) The European Case of Joint R & D Activities in Core Technologies, in A.M. Rugman and A. Verbeke (eds), *Global Strategic Management*, Vol. 2, Jai-Press Inc., Greenwich, London, 203–41.

Rosecrance, R. (1996) The Rise of the Virtual State, *Foreign Affairs*, 75(4), 45–61.

Ruigrok, W. A. Pettigrew, S. Peck and R. Whittington (1999) Corporate Restructuring and New Forms of Organizing: Evidence from Europe, *Management International Review*, 39(2), 41–46.

Sabel, C.F. (1989) The Reemergence of Regional Economies, Discussion Paper I, 89–3, Wissenschaftszentrum Berlin für Sozialforschung, Berlin.

Sabel, C.F. (1993) Constitutional Ordering in Historical Context, in F.W. Scharpf (ed.), *Games in Hierarchies and Networks*, Campus Verlag/Westview Press, Frankfurt/Boulder, 65–124.

Sachwald, F. (ed.) (1993) *L'Europe et la globalisation: Acquisitions et accords dans l'industrie*, Masson, Paris.

Sadler, P. (1992) The Politics of the Corporate Jungle, *Director*, 45(10), 29.

Santer, J. (1993) Some Reflections on the Principle of Subsidiarity, in J. Delors, *Subsidiarity: The Challenge of Change*, EIPA, Maastricht.

Saxenian, A. (1994) *Regional Advantage: Culture and Competition in Silicon Valley and Route 128*, Harvard University Press, Cambridge, Mass.

Scharpf, F.W. (1972) Complexity as Bounds to Political Planning, *Politische Vierteljahresschrift*, 13(4), 168–92.

Scharpf, F.W. (1985) The Joint-Decision Trap: Lessons from German Federalism and European Integration, Discussion paper IIM/LMP 85–1, International Institute of Management, Berlin, May.

Scharpf, F.W. (1989) Decision Rules, Decision Styles, and Policy Choices, *Journal of Theoretical Politics*, 1, 149–76.

Scharpf, F.W. (1990) Games Real Actors Could Play: The Problem of Mutual Predictability, *Rationality and Society*, 2, 471–94.

Scharpf, F.W. (1991) Games Real Actors Could Play: The Challenge of Complexity, *Theoretical Politics*, 3, 277–304.

Scharpf, F.W. (ed.) (1993) *Games in Hierarchies and Networks: Analytical and Empirical Approaches to the Study of Governance Institutions*, Campus Verlag/ Westview Press, Frankfurt/Boulder.

Scharpf, F.W. (1994) Games Real Actors Could Play: Positive and Negative Coordination in Embedded Negotiations, *Journal of Theoretical Politics*, 6, 27–53.

Schattschneider, E.E. (1957) Power: Intensity, Visibility, Direction and Scope, *American Political Science Review*, 51, December.

Schattschneider, E.E. (1960) *The Semisovereign People: A Realist's View of Democracy in America*. Holt, Rinehart & Winston, New York.

Scheiberg, M. and J.R. Hollingsworth (1990) Can Transaction Cost Economics Explain Trade Associations?, in M. Aoki, B. Gustafsson and O.E. Williamson (eds), *The Firm as a Nexus of Treaties*, Sage Publications, London, 320–46.

Schelling, Th.C. (1956) An Essay on Bargaining, *American Economic Review*, 46, 281–306.

Schelling, Th.C. (1969) *Strategy of Conflict*, Harvard University Press, New York.

Schelling, Th.C. (1973) *Arms and Influence*, Yale University Press, London.

Schelling, Th.C. (1985) Policy Analysis as a Science of Choice, in R.S. Ganapathy, S.R. Ganesh, R.M. Maru, S. Paul and R.M. Rao (eds), *Public Policy and Policy Analysis in India*, Sage, New Delhi.

Schelling, Th.C. (ed.) (1993) *Incentives for Environmental Protection*, MIT, Cambridge, Mass.

Schenk, H. (1992) Some Comments on the Competitive Strategy Aspects of Industrial Policy, in K. Cowling and R. Sugden (eds), *Current Issues in Industrial Economic Strategy*, Manchester University Press, Manchester.

Schenk, H. (1997) Mergers, Efficient Choice, and International Competitiveness: Bandwagon Behaviour and Industrial Policy Implications, mimeo (doct. diss.), Tilburg/Rotterdam.

Schenk, H. (2005) Organisational Economics in an Age of Restructuring, in P. De Gijsel and H. Schenk, (eds), *Multidisciplinary Economics*, Springer, Dordrecht.

Schenk, H. and Schenk, E.J.J (2006). Concentration and Mergers. In P. Bianchi and S. Labory (eds), *International Handbook on Industrial Policy* Cheltenham: Edward Elgar.

Schenk, H., Warmenhoven, J.P. and Velzen, M. van (1997) Démasqué of Diversification, Corporate Split-offs Explained and Assessed, *Economisch Statistische Berichten*, October (in Dutch).

Scherer, F.M. and D. Ross (1990) *Industrial Market Structure and Economic Performance*, Houghton Mifflin, Boston.

Schmitter, P.C. (1974) Still the Century of Corporatism?, *Review of Politics*, 36(1), 85–131.

Schmitter, P.C. (1977) Modes of Interest Intermediation and Models of Societal Change in Western Europe, *Comparative Political Studies*, 10(1), 7–38.

Schmitter, P.C. and L. Lanzalaco (1989) Regions and the Organization of Business Interests, in W.D. Coleman and H.J. Jacek (eds), *Regionalism, Business Interests and Public Policy*, Sage Publications, London, 201–30.

Schmitter, P.C. and G. Lehmbruch (eds) (1979) *Trends toward Corporatist Intermediation*, Sage Publications, Beverly Hills.

Scholten, I. (1980) Does Consociationalism exist? A Critique of the Dutch experience, in R. Rose (ed.), *Electoral Participation: A Comparative Analysis*, Sage Publishers, London.

Schumpeter, J.A. (1970 [1943]) *Capitalism, Socialism and Democracy*, Unwin University Books, Allen & Unwin, London.

Scientific Council on Government Policy (Wetenschapplijke Raad voor net Regeringsbeleid) (1980) *PFI '80 Plaats en Toekomst van de Nederlands Industrie*, Staatsuitgeverij, The Hague.

Sen, A. (2009) Capitalism beyond the Crisis, *The New York Review of Books*, March 26.

Sharp, M. (1990) The Market and European Policies for Advanced Technologies, in C. Crouch and D. Marquand (eds), *The Policies of 1992: Beyond the Single European Market*, Basil Blackwell, London, 100–20.

Shepherd, W.G. (1970) *Market Power and Economic Welfare*, Random House, New York.

Shonfield, A. (1969) *Modern Capitalism: The Changing Balance of Public and Private Power*, Oxford University Press, Oxford.

Shubik, M. (1967) The Uses of Game Theory, in J.C. Charlesworth (ed.), *Contemporary Political Analysis*, Free Press, New York, 239–72.

Simon, H.A. (1965) The Architecture of Complexity, *General Systems Yearbook*, 10.

Skidelsky, R. (2009) *Keynes: The Return of the Master*, Allen Lane/Penguin Books, London.

Smith, K.G., C.M. Grimm and M.J. Gannon (1992) *Dynamics of Competitive Strategy*, Sage Publications, London.

Smith, K.G., Ferrier, W.J. and Ndofor, H. (2001) Competitive Dynamics Research: Critique and Future Directions, in M. Hitt, Freeman, R. and Harrison, J., *Handbook of Strategic Management*, Blackwell Publishers, London.

Snyder, G.H. (1971) "Prisoner's Dilemma" and "Chicken" Models in International Politics, *International Studies Quarterly*, 15, 66–103.

Sorge, A. and M. Maurice (1993) The Societal Effect in the Strategies of French and West German Machine-Tool Manufacturers, in B. Kogut (ed.), *Country Competitiveness: Technology and the Organizing of Work*, Oxford University Press, New York/Oxford, 75–95.

Sorkin, A. R. (2010) *Too Big to Fail: The Inside Story of How Wall Street and Washington Fought to Save the Financial System from Crisis: And Themselves*. Viking, New York.

Stopford, J. and S. Strange (1991) *Rival States, Rival Firms: Competition for World Market Shares*, Cambridge University Press, Cambridge UK.

Strange, S. (1992) States, Firm and Diplomacy, *International Affairs*, 68(1), 1–15.

Streeck, W. (1989) The Territorial Organization of Interests and the Logics of Associative Action, in W.D. Coleman and H.J. Jacek (eds), *Regionalism, Business Interests and Public Policy*, Sage Publications, London 59–94.

Streeck, W. (1996) Neo-Voluntarism: A New European Social Policy Regime?, in G. Marks, F. W. Scharpf, P. C. Schmitter, and W. Streeck, *Governance in the European Union*, Sage Publications, London, 64–94.

Streeck, W. and Ph.C. Schmitter (eds) (1985) *Private Interest Government: Beyond market and State*, Sage Series in Neo-Corporatism, Sage Publications, London.

Teece, D.J. (1986) Profiting from Technological Innovations: Implications for Integration, Collaboration, Licensing and Public Policy, *Research Policy*, 15, 285–305.

Teece, D.J. (1990) Contributions and Impediments of Economic Analysis to the Study of Strategic Management, in Frederickson, J.W. (ed.), *Perspectives on Strategic Management*, Harper Business Press, New York, 39–80.

Tett, G. (2009) *Fool's Gold: How the Bold Dream of a Small Tribe at J.P. Morgan Was Corrupted by Wall Street Greed and Unleashed a Catastrophe*. Free Press, New York.

Thompson, J.D. (1967) *Organizations in Action*, McGraw-Hill Book Company, New York.

Thorelli, H.B. (1986) Networks: Between Markets and Hierarchies, *Strategic Management Journal*, 7, 37–51.

Tullock, G. (1965) *The Politics of Bureaucracy*, Public Affairs, Washington, DC.

Tullock, G. (1970) *Public Wants, Private Means*, Basic Books, New York.

UNCTAD (United Nations Conference on Trade and Development) (1996) *World Investment Report (1996): Investment Trade and International Policy Arrangements*, New York/Geneva.

Usunier, J.C. (1991) The European Consumer: Globalizer or Globalized?, in A.M. Rugman and A. Verbeke (eds), *Global Strategic Management*, Vol. 2, Jai-Press, Greenwich, London, 57–81.

Van de Vall, M. (1970) *Labor Organisations*, Cambridge University Press, Cambridge.

Van der Geest, L. (1989) Concurrentie en samenwerking, in *Economisch Statistische Berichten*, 29 November, 1173.

Van der Zwan, A. (1989) Strategische samenwerking, in *Economische Statistische Berichten*, 29 November 1.

Van Doorn, J.A.A. (1984) Introduction: The Anatomy of the Interventionist State, in J.W. de Beus and J.A.A. van Doorn (eds), *The Interventionist State*, Boom, Amsterdam/Meppel, 9–25.

Van Tulder, R. and G. Junne (1988) *European Multinationals in Core Technologies*, Wiley, Geneva.

Vernon, R. (1991) Adapting to the European Single Market: An Overview, in L.-G. Mattson and B. Stymne (eds), *Adapting to the European Single Market: An Overview*, North Holland, Haarlem, 1–7.

Vos, P.J. (1982) Labour policy and Supply-side economics, *Pre-advies voor de Vereniging van Staathuishoudkunde*, Stenfert Kroese, Leiden [in Dutch].

Walter, A. (1994) Corporate Identity and European Technology Policy: The Political Economy of Access, unpublished mimeo, St Antony's College, Oxford, April.

Walton, R.E. and R.B. McKersie (1965) *A Behavioral Theory of Labor Negotiations: An Analysis of a Social Interaction System*, McGraw-Hill, New York.

Ward, B. (1972) *What's Wrong with Economics?*, Macmillan, Basic Books, London.

Wassenberg, A.F.P. (1978) De "georiënteerde" markteconomie: een aanvulling op de smalle marges van de economische orde?, in A.W.M. Teulings (ed.), *Herstructurering van de Industrie, Praktijk, beleid en perspectief*, Samson Uitgeverij, Alphen aan den Rijn, 271–95.

Wassenberg, A.F.P. (1980a) Neo-corporatisme: de carrière en de schutkleuren van een begrip, in H.J.G. Verhallen, R. Fernhout and P.E. Visser (eds), *Corporatisme* in *Nederland, Belangengroepen en democratie*, Samson Uitgeverij, Alphen aan den Rijn, 337–70.

Wassenberg, A.F.P. (1980b) *Networks: Their Organization and Strategy*, Boom, Meppel–Amsterdam.

Wassenberg, A.F.P. (1982a) Industrial Policy: On Prisoners, Chickens and other Animal Spirits in the Low Countries, XIIth World Congress IPSA, Rio de Janeiro, August 9–14.

Wassenberg, A.F.P. (1982b) Neo-Corporatism and the Quest for Control: the Cuckoo-game, in G. Lehmbruch and P.C. Schmitter (eds), *Patterns of Corporatist Policy-making*, Sage, Beverly Hills.

Wassenberg, A.F.P. (1983) *Dossier RSV: Schijnbewegingen van de industriepolitiek*, Stenfert Kroese, Leiden.

Wassenberg, A.F.P. (1985) Organizational Instinct: On the Political Economy of Bargaining, in A.H.G. Rinnooy Kan (ed.), *New Challenges for Management Research*, North Holland, Amsterdam.

Wassenberg, A.F.P. (1987) Bij het scheiden van de overheid leert men de markt kennen, in H. Schenk (ed.), *Industrie- en technologiebeleid*, Wolters-Noordhoff, Groningen, 29–63.

Wassenberg, A.F.P. (1988) *Strategy and Policy: Bargaining Behavior in Interorganizational Networks*, Uitgeverij Scriptum, Nederlands Studiecentrum, Schiedam/Vlaardingen.

Wassenberg, A.F.P. (1990) Strategic Alliances: mixed motives, mixed blessings, *International Marketing Magazine*, June 5–10.

Wassenberg, A.F.P. (1991) Strategic Alliances and Public Policy in the EC: The Case of Information Technology, in A.M. Rugman and A. Verbeke (eds), *Global Strategic Management*, Vol. 2, Jai-Press, Greenwich, London, 151–203.

Wassenberg, A.F.P. (1992a) Corporate Strategies, Industrial Policies and Entrepreneurial Hybrids: A European Ménage à Trois, in J.J.J. van Dijck and A.A.L.G. Wentink (eds), *Transnational Business in Europe*, Tilburg University Press, Tilburg, 309–23.

Wassenberg, A.F.P. (1992b) Industriebeleid in Europa: van pacificatiepolitiek naar industriële guerilla, *Tijdschrift voor Sociologie*, 13(3/4), 409–446.

Weber, M. (1978) [1922] *Economy and Society: An Outline of Interpretive Sociology*, University of California Press, Berkeley.

Weber, M. (1964) [1922] *The. Sociology of Religion*, Boston: Beacon.

Weissing, F., and E. Ostrom (1993) Irrigation Institutions and the Games Irrigators Play: Rule Enforcement on Government- and Farmer-managed Systems, in F.W. Scharpf (ed.), *Games in Hierarchies and Networks: Analytical and Empirical Approaches to the Study of Governance Institutions*, Campus Verlag/Westview Press, Frankfurt/Boulder, 387–428.

Wernerfelt, B. (1984) A Resource-based View of the Firm, *Strategic Management Journal*, 5.

Wernerfelt, B. and A. Karnani (1987) Competitive Strategy under Uncertainty, *Strategic Management Journal*, 8, 187–94.

Whitley, R. (ed.) (1992) *European Business Systems: Firms and Markets in their National Contexts*, Sage Publications, London.

Wildasky, W.A. (1964) *The Politics of the Budgetary Process*, Scott, Foresman & Co., Glenview.

Wilks, S. (1989) Government-industry Relations: Progress and Findings of the ESRC Research Initiative, *Public Administration*, 67, Autumn, 329–39.

Wilks, S. and M. Wright (eds) (1987) *Comparative Government-industry Relations: West Europe, the United States and Japan*, Clarendon Press, Oxford.

Wilks, S. and M. Wright (eds) (1989) *Comparative Government-Industry Relations, Western Europe, the United States, and Japan*, Clarendon Press, Oxford.

Williamson, O.E. (1964) *The Economics of Discretionary Behavior: Managerial Objectives in a Theory of the Firm*, Prentice-Hall, London.

Williamson, O.E. (1975) *Markets and Hierarchies: Analysis and Antitrust Implications*, The Free Press, New York.

Williamson, O.E. (1979) Transaction Cost Economics: The Governance of Contractual Relations, *Journal of Law and Economics*, 22, 233–61.

Williamson, O.E. (1983) Credible Commitments: Using Hostages to Support Exchange, *American Economic Review*, 73, 519–40.

Williamson, O.E. (1985) *The Economic Institutions of Capitalism: Firms, Markets and Relational Contracting*, The Free Press, New York.

Williamson, O.E. (1993) Comparative Economic Organization, in S. Lindenberg and H. Schreuder (eds), *Interdisciplinary Perspectives on Organization Studies*, Pergamon, Oxford.

Williamson, O.E. (1996) *The Mechanisms of Governance*, Oxford University Press, New York.

Williamson, O.E. and W.G. Ouchi (1983) The Markets and Hierarchies Programme of Research: Origins, Implications, Prospects, in A. Francis, J. Turk, and P. Willman (eds), *Power, Efficiency and Institutions*, Heinemann, London.

Wilson, G. (1985) *Business and Politics: A Comparative Introduction*, Macmillan, London.

Windmuller, J.P. (1969) *Labor Relations in the Netherlands*, Cornell University Press, Ithaca.

Winter, S.G. (1988) On Coase, Competence, and the Corporation, *Journal of Law, Economics, and Organizations*, 4(1), 163–80.

Wright, M. (1988) Policy Community, Policy Network and Comparative Industrial Policies, *Political Studies*, 36, 593–612.

Wrong, D. (1961) The Oversocialized Conception of Man in Modern Sociology, *American Sociological Review*, 26, 184–93.

Index